Mainstreaming Cryptocurrency and the Future of Digital Finance

Hamed Taherdoost
University Canada West, Canada

A volume in the Advances
in Finance, Accounting, and
Economics (AFAE) Book Series

Published in the United States of America by
    IGI Global
    Business Science Reference (an imprint of IGI Global)
    701 E. Chocolate Avenue
    Hershey PA, USA 17033
    Tel: 717-533-8845
    Fax: 717-533-8661
    E-mail: cust@igi-global.com
    Web site: http://www.igi-global.com

Library of Congress Cataloging-in-Publication Data

Names: Taherdoost, Hamed, 1983- editor.
Title: Mainstreaming cryptocurrency and the future of digital finance /
  edited by Hamed Taherdoost.
Description: Hershey, PA : Business Science Reference, [2023] | Includes
  bibliographical references and index. | Summary: "This book is expected
  to add a valuable source to the existing knowledge and research in the
  field of cryptocurrency digital finance; This book is expected to
  provide the advantages and disadvantages of current cryptocurrency-based
  payment methods aiming to leverage technology to create better financial
  services in different businesses; The reader is expected to gain an
  understanding of trends in cryptocurrency, concepts, technologies,
  trading methods, wallets, analytical tools and platforms; The reader is
  expected to realize technological trends that are happening to shape the
  future of financial technologies; The reader is expected to gain an
  understanding of existing opportunities and challenges of cryptocurrency
  and financial technologies; The reader is expected to gain insight into
  trending technologies that add value to cryptocurrency and financial
  technologies; The reader is expected to identify the role of each
  technology in cryptocurrency and financial technologies"-- Provided by
  publisher.
Identifiers: LCCN 2023008226 (print) | LCCN 2023008227 (ebook) | ISBN
  9781668483688 (hardcover) | ISBN 9781668483695 (paperback) | ISBN
  9781668483701 (ebook)
Subjects: LCSH: Cryptocurrencies. | Finance--Technological innovations.
Classification: LCC HG1710.3 .M26 2023 (print) | LCC HG1710.3 (ebook) |
  DDC 332.4--dc23/eng/20230316
LC record available at https://lccn.loc.gov/2023008226
LC ebook record available at https://lccn.loc.gov/2023008227

This book is published in the IGI Global book series Advances in Finance, Accounting, and Economics (AFAE) (ISSN: 2327-5677; eISSN: 2327-5685)

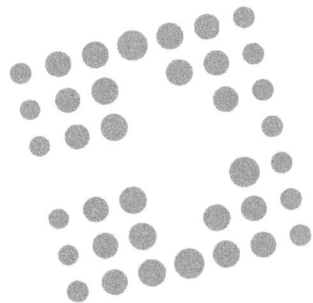

Advances in Finance, Accounting, and Economics (AFAE) Book Series

ISSN:2327-5677
EISSN:2327-5685

Editor-in-Chief: Ahmed Driouchi, Al Akhawayn University, Morocco

MISSION

In our changing economic and business environment, it is important to consider the financial changes occurring internationally as well as within individual organizations and business environments. Understanding these changes as well as the factors that influence them is crucial in preparing for our financial future and ensuring economic sustainability and growth.

The **Advances in Finance, Accounting, and Economics (AFAE)** book series aims to publish comprehensive and informative titles in all areas of economics and economic theory, finance, and accounting to assist in advancing the available knowledge and providing for further research development in these dynamic fields.

COVERAGE

- Economic Downturn
- Labor Economics
- Managerial Accounting
- Economic Policy
- Accounting information systems
- Banking
- International Trade
- Evidence-Based Studies
- Behavioral Economics
- Accounting Standards

IGI Global is currently accepting manuscripts for publication within this series. To submit a proposal for a volume in this series, please contact our Acquisition Editors at Acquisitions@igi-global.com or visit: http://www.igi-global.com/publish/.

Titles in this Series

For a list of additional titles in this series, please visit:
http://www.igi-global.com/book-series/advances-finance-accounting-economics/73685

Handbook of Research on Designing Sustainable Supply Chains to Achieve a Circular Economy
Yanamandra Ramakrishna (Skyline University College, UAE) and Siti Norida Wahab (Universiti Teknologi MARA, Malaysia)
Business Science Reference • © 2023 • 697pp • H/C (ISBN: 9781668476642) • US $295.00

Emerging Insights on the Relationship Between Cryptocurrencies and Decentralized Economic Models
Dhanapal Kesavan (SRM Institute of Science and Technology, India) and N. Mari Anand (Department of Business Studies, University of Technology and Applied Sciences, Salalah, Oman)
Business Science Reference • © 2023 • 256pp • H/C (ISBN: 9781668456910) • US $250.00

Exploring Business Ecosystems and Innovation Capacity Building in Global Economics
Mihir Joshi (Banasthali Vidyapith University, India) Mohsen Brahmi (University of Sfax, Tunisia) Luigi Aldieri (University of Salerno, Italy) and Concetto Paolo Vinci (University of Salerno, Italy)
Business Science Reference • © 2023 • 393pp • H/C (ISBN: 9781668467664) • US $250.00

Accounting and Financial Reporting Challenges for Government, Non-Profits, and the Private Sector
Fábio Albuquerque (Instituto Politécnico de Lisboa, Portugal) and Paula Gomes dos Santos (Instituto Politécnico de Lisboa, Portugal)
Business Science Reference • © 2023 • 320pp • H/C (ISBN: 9781668472934) • US $240.00

Handbook of Research on Changing World Economic Order in the Post-Pandemic Period
Sushanta Kumar Mahapatra (IBS Hyderabad, The ICFAI Foundation for Higher Education, India) and Vishal Sarin (Lovely Professional University, India)
Business Science Reference • © 2023 • 470pp • H/C (ISBN: 9781799868965) • US $325.00

For an entire list of titles in this series, please visit:
http://www.igi-global.com/book-series/advances-finance-accounting-economics/73685

701 East Chocolate Avenue, Hershey, PA 17033, USA
Tel: 717-533-8845 x100 • Fax: 717-533-8661
E-Mail: cust@igi-global.com • www.igi-global.com

*To my daughter and son, who are the stars in my sky, the beat in my heart, and
the reason for my existence.*
This book is dedicated to you, Hamta and Kiasha, with all my love and gratitude.

Table of Contents

Detailed Table of Contents

*Hamed Taherdoost, University Canada West, Canada & Hamta Group–
Hamta Business Corporation, Canada*

The advancement of technology has reshaped financial services and payment systems. The trends in financial technologies indicate that FinTech is still growing and there are even more growth opportunities in the future. Several key factors, from improved customer expectations to compliance regulations, are fueling FinTech's growth. New features provided through technological advancements equip FinTech providers with the opportunity to offer more delightful experiences to their users. This study aims to concentrate on drivers that are leading to the growth of financial technologies and provides guides through finding the opportunities FinTech's growth offers.

Mitra Madanchian, Hamta Group–Hamta Business Corporation, Canada

Cryptocurrency has transformed the global economic system. It offers a novel and creative form of trade that has rapidly transformed the financial markets and the world of cash. A person's best allocation is determined by combining their priorities for risk reduction and upside opportunity with bitcoin's predicted diversity and return qualities. However, people have a poor tolerance for blockchain-based cryptocurrencies, owing to the rise of online fraud and the lack of a legal framework. In addition, there is a widespread misperception about its use on various platforms, which has left a void in the literature addressing this topic. This chapter will discuss the role and views of cryptocurrency users.

In recent years, the effectiveness of FinTech has become very important, but new technologies are created and implemented without considering their risks, only focusing on their advantages. Previous research found that the unmet needs for basic banking have been solved through financial technologies while, at the same time, bringing benefits to both people and businesses. Using a deductive approach to the mixed data found previously made it more manageable to understand FinTech's background and intercorrelation with e-business. Contrary to what many people assume about the risks of FinTech, findings have shown that 88% of data breaches come from human mistakes leading us to validate that the problem with FinTech is not the technology itself but the improper use of it and the ignorance around them—concluding that these challenges can be minimized and regulated with the right strategies. The overall effectiveness of FinTech is deemed positive, with the advantages outweighing the challenges.

The emergence of cryptocurrencies has posed challenges to governments in managing the money supply. For years, governments have exercised monetary policy by controlling the supply of national currencies. However, cryptocurrencies are decentralized, meaning governments have little or no power to control them. This chapter provides a literature review on the impact of cryptocurrencies on (1) the national monetary policy, (2) the international monetary system, and (3) the role of cryptocurrency within the banking system. Research reveals that governments could consider developing their own cryptocurrency to maintain power and influence the money supply. Alternatively, they can use the legal framework to enable or disable cryptocurrency as legal tender within their jurisdictions. Due to its global nature, cryptocurrency can be used as an international payment method and become an integrated part of the FOREX market. Lastly, as cryptocurrency continues to gain popularity worldwide, regulations on crypto exchanges and issuers will be needed to avoid price bubbles.

The world of finance has been transforming alongside the rapid growth of technology significantly. FinTech companies have emerged as a consequence of technological developments in the financial sector. Despite the upward trends in the growth of FinTech, they definitely need a business model to survive and grow in the competitive market. A FinTech business model includes operating strategy, revenue sources, and intended customer base. FinTech organizations need to adopt approaches to ensure their services and products are available to their customers across different platforms and are not necessarily reliant on a convoluted sign-up process. This chapter reviews the main considerations in FinTech business models, and the success factors of a business model, and provides a guide to having a business model that wins in the market.

Some of the constraints that cryptocurrencies now face, such as the fact that one's digital wealth might be lost in the event of a computer breakdown, may in the future be solved by technical advancements. Organizational structure, power distribution, and decision-making capacity are susceptible to disruption as a result of technological development. Consequently, culture will become fragile if executives do not take the essential steps to go ahead. Given that disruption will alter the present world, the time has come to comprehend blockchain and its consequences for corporate culture. This chapter discusses the future of cryptocurrencies and their impact on corporate culture and structure.

FinTech refers to the integration of information technology and financial services. Over the years, digital transformation went from being perceived as an option to becoming a competitive advantage and a necessity for any organization to survive in such a hyper-competitive business market. A successful digital transformation goes beyond complying exclusively with the technical requirement and thrives on delivering sustainable outcomes. Change management's core motive is to sustain change by guiding and supporting individuals through change and adaptation to further contribute to the organization's success and outcomes. Many authors have contributed by proposing management models, starting with Kurt Lewin in 1947.

This chapter aims to analyze nine change management models to identify necessities and challenges faced by individuals, organizations, and industries, such as FinTech, when embarking on a digital transformation journey.

As cryptocurrency (crypto) has become more and more popular, so has crypto-related crime. There has been a lack of academic research on crypto-related crime, but it is becoming more prevalent in the last couple of years. Crypto-related crime became especially significant in the impact it had on victims and the awareness of these crimes in the media and the government in late 2019 and early 2020 as various criminal organizations and criminal opportunities opened up as cryptocurrency became mainstream. The common crimes related to cryptocurrency include fraud, theft, and money laundering. In 2021 estimates of crypto-related crime were estimated to be as high as $14 billion, which is a small fraction of a percent of the cryptocurrency transactions that were around $15.8 trillion in 2021. The purpose of the chapter is to provide a detailed account of the common crypto-related crimes and scams that have occurred and to evaluate the effectiveness of enforcement of these crimes.

This chapter examines how familiarity influences the adoption and how education may increase cryptocurrency users. This project will use a systematic approach highlighting the growth of acceptance of cryptocurrency from 2017 to 2023 using a mixed methods approach since there has been little research on how individuals have embraced and accepted cryptocurrencies. Due to a lack of study, this study examines cryptocurrency adoption, its drivers, and its hazards. This study's outcomes will be a form of Literature Review for future research, increase knowledge of cryptocurrency acceptance, and help in cryptocurrency adoption.

This chapter examines the marketing trends and strategies used in the cryptocurrency industry. A qualitative research design was used, with case studies of five cryptocurrency firms as the primary data source. Secondary data sources such as websites, social media accounts, articles, and blogs were also analyzed. The study found that content marketing, social media marketing, and influencer marketing are the industry's most commonly used marketing strategies. Community building and brand reputation were also found to be essential for the success of companies operating in the cryptocurrency industry. However, the study's limitations including the limited sample size, reliance on secondary data, the potential for researcher bias, and lack of triangulation should be considered when interpreting the findings. The insights gained from this study can inform the development of marketing strategies in the cryptocurrency industry and guide future research in this area.

Cryptocurrencies that are virtual and dematerialized are online and entirely digital currencies. Cryptocurrency has been the subject of many studies from different aspects; however, it is still a new area of investment for businesses as there are positive trends in the crypto space. Trending technologies, on the other hand, are making significant changes in all industries, and the cryptocurrency market is no exception. The employment of trending technologies can facilitate the crypto market with pattern recognition and secure transactions. This chapter aims to analyze the application of trending technologies in the crypto market and the benefits they can add to traders and brokers.

Foreword

Digital finance and cryptocurrency have become two of the most intriguing topics in the financial world. The advent of technology has revolutionized the way we do business, and the financial sector is no exception. FinTech has disrupted traditional banking systems, and cryptocurrencies have provided an alternative to fiat currencies. The growing popularity of digital finance and cryptocurrency has led to many opportunities and challenges, and this book provides an in-depth analysis of both.

As we enter into a new era of digital transformation, the intersection of finance and technology has given rise to a new industry known as FinTech. This rapidly growing field has the potential to disrupt traditional financial systems and reshape the way we do business. Cryptocurrency, in particular, has gained significant attention and investment in recent years, with its potential to transform the way we store, transfer, and manage value.

In this book, the authors provide a comprehensive overview of the latest developments in digital finance, focusing on the rise of cryptocurrency and its impact on the financial industry. They delve deep into the core concepts and technologies behind cryptocurrency, while also examining its potential for mass adoption and the challenges it faces.

What sets this book apart from others in the field is its emphasis on real-world applications, making it a valuable resource for both practitioners and researchers. The authors have done an excellent job of providing a balanced and nuanced perspective on the topic, highlighting the potential benefits of cryptocurrency while also addressing the risks and challenges that must be overcome. Written in an accessible and engaging style that makes it accessible to readers of all backgrounds, its insights and analysis provide valuable guidance for businesses, investors, and policymakers alike.

This book is a must-read for anyone interested in the latest trends and future of finance and technology. Whether you are an entrepreneur looking to launch a new cryptocurrency venture, a financial advisor seeking to stay ahead of the curve, or simply someone who wants to better understand this fascinating and rapidly evolving technology, this book will inspire and educate.

George Drazenovic
University Canada West, Canada

Preface

In recent years, financial technology or FinTech has rapidly evolved, becoming a vital element of the global financial system. FinTech has made financial services accessible, affordable, and more efficient, enabling people to conduct transactions more conveniently than ever before. It has also opened up new opportunities for businesses and investors. Cryptocurrency, one of the FinTech innovations, has emerged as a new form of currency that has gained popularity among investors and traders.

As we continue to advance in the digital age, the integration of financial services and technology is becoming more and more essential for businesses to thrive. The successful implementation of digital transformation is necessary for organizations to remain competitive and achieve sustainable outcomes. The growth and development of cryptocurrencies has added to the digital finance landscape, bringing about new challenges and opportunities.

This book provides a comprehensive overview of the current state of the art in cryptocurrency and its potential to shape the future of finance. It brings together insights from leading experts in the field to explore key topics such as the history and evolution of cryptocurrency, the role of blockchain technology, the regulatory landscape, and the challenges and opportunities facing the industry.

One of the key themes of this book is the potential of cryptocurrency to democratize finance and empower individuals and businesses around the world. Cryptocurrency has the potential to provide access to financial services for the unbanked and underbanked populations, reduce transaction costs, and enable fast and secure cross-border payments. It is also an exciting area for innovation, with new and innovative applications emerging every day.

However, cryptocurrency also presents significant challenges and risks, including the potential for fraud, theft, and money laundering. Regulators around the world are struggling to keep up with the pace of innovation, and the regulatory landscape is complex and rapidly evolving. This book provides an in-depth analysis of the regulatory challenges facing the industry and offers insights into how businesses and investors can navigate this complex landscape.

The book also explores the key technological innovations that are driving the evolution of cryptocurrency. Blockchain technology, which underpins most cryptocurrencies, has the potential to revolutionize the way we think about security, trust, and transparency in financial transactions. However, it is also a complex and rapidly evolving technology that presents significant challenges for developers, businesses, and regulators. This book provides a detailed analysis of the role of blockchain technology in cryptocurrency and its potential to shape the future of finance.

Finally, this book provides an analysis of the key trends and challenges facing the cryptocurrency industry today, as well as insights into the future of the industry. It examines the potential of emerging technologies such as artificial intelligence and machine learning to drive innovation in the industry, as well as the potential for new and innovative applications of blockchain technology.

This book presents a collection of 11 chapters that explore various aspects of digital finance and cryptocurrency. The chapters cover a broad range of topics, from digital transformation in the financial industry to the challenges and opportunities of cryptocurrency. The book aims to provide insights into the latest developments in FinTech and cryptocurrency, their challenges, and their future prospects.

Overall, this book provides a comprehensive overview of the current state of the art in cryptocurrency and its potential to shape the future of finance. It brings together insights from leading experts in the field to explore key topics such as the history and evolution of cryptocurrency, the role of blockchain technology, the regulatory landscape, and the challenges and opportunities facing the industry. Whether you are a business leader, investor, regulator, or simply someone interested in the future of finance, this book is an essential resource for understanding the potential of cryptocurrency and its role in shaping the future of finance.

This book may compete in popular topics in FinTech and cryptocurrency such as "Blockchain Basics: A Non-Technical Introduction in 25 Steps" by Daniel Drescher, "Cryptoassets: The Innovative Investor's Guide to Bitcoin and Beyond" by Chris Burniske and Jack Tatar, and "The Age of Cryptocurrency: How Bitcoin and Digital Money Are Challenging the Global Economic Order" by Paul Vigna and Michael Casey.

This book stands out from its competitors in several ways. Firstly, it provides a comprehensive overview of the latest trends and practices in the cryptocurrency and digital finance industry, including both technical and non-technical aspects. The book covers not only the underlying technology of cryptocurrencies, but also their economic, legal, social, and ethical implications.

Secondly, the book offers insights and perspectives from a diverse group of authors with different backgrounds and expertise. This ensures that readers can gain a broad and balanced understanding of the cryptocurrency landscape, and can appreciate the various perspectives and debates surrounding this emerging field.

Thirdly, the book is written in a clear and accessible style, making it suitable for both academic researchers and industry practitioners. The authors avoid technical jargon and instead provide clear explanations and examples to illustrate key concepts and ideas.

Overall, this book is a valuable resource for anyone seeking to understand the rapidly evolving world of cryptocurrency, and its potential impact on finance, economics, and society as a whole and is an excellent resource for digital finance leaders, researchers, and professionals to be an addition to their libraries since it offers leaders what they need to know about employing digital finance for the advancement of their businesses.

ORGANIZATION OF THE BOOK

The book is organized into 11 chapters. A brief description of each of the chapters follows:

Chapter 1 explores the growth of financial technology (FinTech) and the opportunities it presents for the future, driven by factors such as improved customer expectations and compliance regulations. Technological advancements equip FinTech providers with the ability to offer more delightful user experiences, and this study aims to focus on the drivers leading to FinTech growth and provide guidance for finding opportunities in this field.

Chapter 2 delves into the transformation of the global economic system by cryptocurrency, which offers a novel and creative form of trade that has rapidly impacted financial markets and cash. To determine a person's best allocation, combining priorities for risk reduction and upside opportunity with bitcoin's predicted diversity and return qualities is crucial. However, widespread misperceptions and poor tolerance for blockchain-based cryptocurrencies exist due to online fraud and lack of legal framework. The chapter focuses on the role and views of cryptocurrency users.

Chapter 3 discusses the importance of considering risks when implementing new financial technologies and highlights the benefits of FinTech in solving unmet needs for basic banking. Using a deductive approach to mixed data, the chapter explores FinTech's background and intercorrelation with e-business. Contrary to common assumptions, findings suggest that the problem with FinTech is not the technology itself but rather improper use and ignorance around it. Strategies to minimize challenges and regulate FinTech are crucial, and the overall effectiveness of FinTech is positive, with advantages outweighing challenges.

Chapter 4 reviews the impact of cryptocurrencies on national monetary policy, the international monetary system, and the role of cryptocurrency within the banking system. As cryptocurrencies are decentralized, governments struggle to manage their money supply. Governments can either develop their own cryptocurrency or use the legal framework to enable or disable cryptocurrencies as legal tender. Cryptocurrency has the potential to be used as an international payment method and integrated into the FOREX market. Regulations on crypto exchanges and issuers will be necessary to prevent price bubbles.

Chapter 5 discusses the importance of having a business model for FinTech companies to survive and thrive in a competitive market. The chapter reviews different business models that entrepreneurs and investors can adopt, based on their business goals, audience, processes, and partners. It highlights the need for FinTech organizations to ensure their services and products are easily accessible to their customers across various platforms, without a complicated sign-up process. The chapter also provides a guide on the success factors of a business model to create a sustainable and profitable FinTech business.

Chapter 6 discusses the potential future of cryptocurrencies and their impact on corporate culture and structure. Technical advancements may help solve current constraints faced by cryptocurrencies, such as the possibility of losing digital wealth due to computer breakdowns. However, disruptive technological developments may also impact organizational structure, power distribution, and decision-making capacity. The chapter emphasizes the importance of understanding blockchain and its potential consequences for corporate culture, as disruption could significantly alter the current world.

Chapter 7 discusses the importance of digital transformation in the financial industry and the need for effective change management to support it. The chapter reviews nine change management models to identify the challenges and requirements that individuals, organizations, and industries face when undertaking digital transformation initiatives, specifically in FinTech. The aim is to provide insight into effective change management strategies that promote sustainable outcomes and contribute to the success of the organization.

Chapter 8 discusses the increase in crypto-related crimes as cryptocurrency becomes more popular, with fraud, theft, and money laundering being the most common crimes. The chapter provides an overview of these crimes and evaluates the effectiveness of enforcement. In 2021, crypto-related crimes were estimated to be as high as $14 billion, a small fraction of cryptocurrency transactions.

Chapter 9 discusses how familiarity with cryptocurrencies affects their adoption and how education can increase the number of cryptocurrency users. Using a mixed methods approach, the chapter examines the growth of cryptocurrency acceptance from 2017 to 2023 and highlights the drivers and risks associated with cryptocurrency adoption. The chapter aims to provide a literature review of cryptocurrency adoption and increase knowledge in this area to promote further research and support the adoption of cryptocurrencies.

Chapter 10 explores marketing strategies in the cryptocurrency industry through qualitative case studies and analysis of secondary data. Content marketing, social media marketing, and influencer marketing are identified as primary approaches, with community building and brand reputation crucial for success. While limited sample size and reliance on secondary data are limitations, the chapter offers valuable insights for industry professionals and researchers.

Chapter 11 discusses the application of trending technologies in the cryptocurrency market, which can facilitate secure transactions and pattern recognition for traders and brokers. As cryptocurrencies continue to gain popularity, the use of trending technologies can help to improve their functionality and add value for investors. The chapter examines the benefits of these technologies in crypto space and their potential impact on the industry.

Hamed Taherdoost
University Canada West, Canada & Hamta Group–Hamta Business Corporation, Canada

Acknowledgment

I would like to express my deepest gratitude and appreciation to all the individuals who have contributed to the creation and publication of this book. Without their unwavering support, dedication, and expertise, this book would not have been possible.

First and foremost, I extend my sincere thanks to each one of the authors for their valuable contributions to this book. Their time, knowledge, and efforts have been instrumental in shaping the contents and enhancing the overall quality of this book. I am deeply grateful to the chapter's authors who generously shared their expertise, insights, and research findings.

Secondly, I would like to acknowledge and thank the reviewers who have provided their constructive feedback and recommendations on the quality, coherence, and presentation of the book's contents. Their critical evaluation and comments have significantly contributed to the book's improvement and made it more informative and engaging. I would also like to thank the authors who took on the additional responsibility of serving as referees, and I highly appreciate their dedication and commitment to ensuring the book's high standards.

Thirdly, I would like to express my appreciation to my colleagues at Hamta Group | Hamta Business Corporation and University Canada West for their support and valuable contributions to this book. Their encouragement, advice, and assistance throughout the publishing process have been invaluable, and I am grateful for their unwavering support.

Lastly, I would like to thank my family and friends who have been a constant source of motivation and encouragement throughout the book's creation and publication process. Their love and support have been my driving force, and I am forever grateful for their unwavering support.

Once again, I extend my sincere appreciation and thanks to all those who have played a part in the making of this book. Your contributions have made it a valuable resource for readers, and it is a source of pride for us all.

Chapter 1
Drivers of Financial Technologies

Hamed Taherdoost

https://orcid.org/0000-0002-6503-6739

University Canada West, Canada & Hamta Group–Hamta Business Corporation, Canada

ABSTRACT

The advancement of technology has reshaped financial services and payment systems. The trends in financial technologies indicate that FinTech is still growing and there are even more growth opportunities in the future. Several key factors, from improved customer expectations to compliance regulations, are fueling FinTech's growth. New features provided through technological advancements equip FinTech providers with the opportunity to offer more delightful experiences to their users. This study aims to concentrate on drivers that are leading to the growth of financial technologies and provides guides through finding the opportunities FinTech's growth offers.

INTRODUCTION

The digital revolution and technical improvements imply a paradigm shift in the financial sector. New business models that place cutting-edge technology at the service of the customer are the foundation of this transition (Breidbach, Keating, & Lim, 2020). Another crucial element of the value proposition of financial technology is the ability to focus on the customer with more flexible financial services than those offered by the previous model (FinTech). The early competition between banking and FinTech has been replaced by cooperation (Basole & Patel, 2018; O'Halloran & Nowaczyk, 2019).

DOI: 10.4018/978-1-6684-8368-8.ch001

The digitization and connectivity of technology have led to an increase in the number of banking websites and companies that specialize in electronic transfers, online brokers, online loans, crowdsourcing, and digital payments. This has led to the growth of the global financial system. From this vantage point, the word "FinTech" refers to new technologies that have revolutionized and reshaped the financial industry (Song, 2015). This is because the terms "finance" and "technology" are related to each other. FinTech is the use of technological advancements in financial operations, products, and services. (Tian, Han, Wang, Lu, & Zhan, 2015). In this regard, FinTech is being utilized to draw in conventional banking customers, optimize business transactions, enhance credit giving and marketing, and increase the efficiency of banking operations (Li, Liu, & Xie, 2019; Wonglimpiyarat, 2019). The outdated systems are being replaced by ones that allow for the automation of financial services thanks to the use of biometric identification, cryptocurrencies, artificial intelligence, machine learning, blockchain, and big data, among other technologies (H.-y. Chang, Liang, & Wang, 2019; Hendrikse, 2019; Yacoub, 2017).

The rise of FinTech has altered consumer behavior, ecosystems, the role of technology, and industrial and regulatory structures (Gozman, Liebenau, & Mangan, 2018; Wonglimpiyarat, 2017). FinTech's growth has led to "financial service disintermediation" and the need for a new kind of investor and consumer protection (Giudici, 2018; Guo & Liang, 2016). FinTech start-ups can sidestep the minimum capital requirements and intermediation fees often associated with conventional banking services (Iman, 2018). Big data analytics and data science have altered how data are collected, processed, and analyzed, which has drastically decreased search costs (Giudici, 2018). Owing to the COVID-19 pandemic's limitations and subsequent quarantine, methods like contactless payments, lower costs, and more mobility have become popular. Indeed, convenience and security are the main e-commerce trends right now (Gu, Ślusarczyk, Hajizada, Kovalyova, & Sakhbieva, 2021). Financial institutions have only lately incorporated FinTech advances into their services and products, even though the majority of the technology on which they are built is not brand-new (Schindler, 2017).

Financial institutions, regulators, and FinTech businesses are just a few of the elements that make up the FinTech ecosystem. Running a successful FinTech service may benefit from the integration of procedures and rules in these three components (Taherdoost, 2023). This chapter focuses on the factors influencing the development of FinTech and gives tips for identifying the possibilities that development in the field presents.

BACKGROUND

The Great Financial Crisis, shifting regulations, low profitability, and diminishing public trust were just a few of the many issues that financial institutions have had to deal with during the past 10 years. This has caused technical development in the finance industry to advance. If anything, the ongoing COVID-19 issue, which has increased demand for digital services, is causing this tendency to accelerate more quickly. Large technological companies and inventive start-ups are posing a threat to incumbents (Boot, Hoffmann, Laeven, & Ratnovski, 2021).

FinTech is the application of technology in the delivery of various financial services (Mehrotra, 2019). Innovative financial intermediaries known as FinTech firms use new technology to support innovative business models, changes to operational processes, and the delivery of improved products and services (Zhang, Ashta, & Barton, 2021). The emergence of FinTech coincided with the internet revolution in the early 1990s. One of the key determinants of the development of the FinTech sector has been the Internet (Haddad & Hornuf, 2019). FinTech is thought to present an opportunity to increase financial transparency, consumer friendliness, and cost efficiency. Additionally, by competing with traditional banks, insurance companies, and investment businesses, it is predicted to radically disrupt the financial landscape. Because it has different regulatory criteria than the present financial service providers, FinTech is expanding not just as a result of technical improvement but also because it allows enterprises to operate more freely within the regulatory sandbox to create new products (Buchak, Matvos, Piskorski, & Seru, 2018).

FinTech is the integration of technology, including mobile apps, software, and other types of technology, with money, to provide better financial services to organizations and customers (Pant, 2020). A FinTech firm is any business that offers financial services using technological means, such as mobile apps and software (M. R. Lee, Yen, & Hurlburt, 2018). The primary goals of FinTech businesses are to simplify, automate, and alter financial services. FinTech services include things like mobile banking, cryptocurrency wallets, and trading platforms. The creation of distinctive services provided by several different FinTech firms has completely transformed how people and businesses transact every day, deposit checks, purchase stocks, and engage in other financial activities (Lu, Wu, & Ye, 2020).

Early in the 1950s, credit cards were first made available to do away with the need to carry cash with you for everyday transactions. This is when the foundation of FinTech was first presented. In 1998, PayPal was founded as one of the first FinTech businesses to operate online. As long as substantial developments were made in the creation of mobile apps and social media, PayPal was then completely transformed (Allayarov & Ravshanova, 2021). FinTech was primarily known for its usage in financial institutions, but it was rapidly applied to many other fields and businesses, including education, retail banking, investment management, and many more (M. R. Lee et al., 2018). Since they adhere to relevant banking standards, the majority of consumers of financial services depend on financial instruments created by FinTech businesses. Additionally, since customers value the advantages offered by FinTech businesses so highly, they could overlook potential concerns (Cai, Marrone, & Linnenluecke, 2022).

The Evolution Trend of FinTech

The financial and banking sectors have seen a development in FinTech (Prawirasasra, 2018; Thakor, 2020). (Figure 1):

2.1.1. FinTech 1.0

During this stage, the infrastructure that will enable global financial services is being constructed. The first transatlantic cable (1866) and Fedwire (1918) in the US made it feasible for the first electronic money transfer system, which used telegraph and Morse code technology. Even if it was straightforward by today's standards, the ability to transact business over a wider area was revolutionary at a time when transportation and infrastructure were developing.

2.1.2. FinTech 2.0

This era, which is defined by the conversion of money from analog to digital, officially began with the launch of the first ATM by Barclays in 1967. The Society for Worldwide Interbank Financial Telecommunications (SWIFT), a method for financial institutions to communicate with one another that permitted the large volume of international transactions, and NASDAQ, the first computerized stock exchange in the world, were both established in the 1970s. This era survived the 1980s because of the emergence of bank mainframe computers and a "Gordon Gecko" sense of Wall Street style. Moreover, when internet banking grew in popularity throughout the 1980s, people's business habits altered, which hurt their perception of financial institutions. When connected consumers started managing their money in different ways in the 1990s, the first steps toward digital banking were made. The launch of PayPal in 1998 served as a precursor to the new payment technologies that would emerge as society's reliance on the internet increased. The economy looked to be going well, prompting Gordon Brown, the UK's then-chancellor, to declare the "end of boom and bust." The global financial crisis of 2008, however, was the bust that ended this period of FinTech and sparked the innovation that would mark the one that followed.

2.1.3. FinTech 3.0

Following the financial crisis of 2008, various regulatory modifications were implemented, which resulted in higher costs of compliance and a reduction in profitability. A significant number of workers were laid off, and many of them decided to launch FinTech firms that provide novel financial solutions. These new businesses were not banks in the traditional sense, but they did provide financial services. The twenty-first century saw the birth of several innovative financial concepts, including crowdfunding, mobile payments, cryptocurrencies, initial coin offerings, many new types of peer-to-peer financing, and data-driven finance.

Figure 1. FinTech different eras

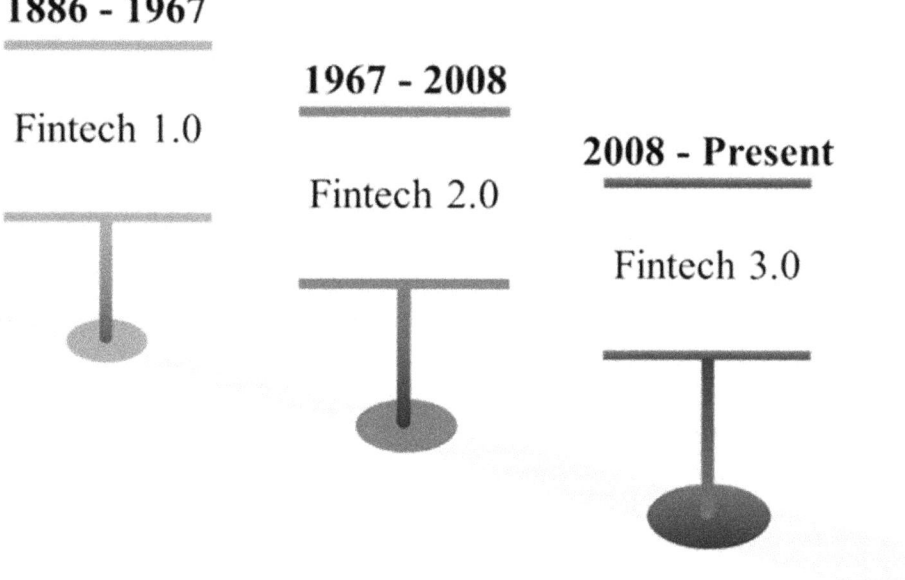

1886 - 1967

Fintech 1.0

1967 - 2008

Fintech 2.0

2008 - Present

Fintech 3.0

In many nations, FinTech has had an impact on overall economic development. The new generation of retail trading companies and investment banking have successfully combined the strength of the internet with the usability of smartphones. Banking applications have slashed banking processes and given users the ability to conduct digital technology transactions, making banks more reachable online than via conventional ways (S. Wang, 2021). More disruptive and digitally transformative technologies, including artificial intelligence, extended reality, the Internet of Things (IoT), etc., are transforming our way of life in the new environment brought about by the fourth industrial revolution (Schulte & Liu, 2017). The financial industry has also been impacted by this transition, leading to the emergence of FinTech, which is largely defined by the introduction of technological advancements that promote the development of original, fruitful business models involving financial services (Stern, Makinen, & Qian, 2017). Wonglimpiyarat (Wonglimpiyarat, 2017) defines FinTech as financial services that are technologically enabled and make use of integrated IT to improve critical performance. FinTech stabilizes the financial system by transforming the financial industry more swiftly than traditional financial services, providing high-quality services at cheaper prices, and generating quick profits. (Shin & Choi, 2019). Process optimization, forecasting, and technology integration in diverse finance operations are examples of how the financial service business quickly adapted from the inquiry stage to the application stage (Kou, 2019).

As a result of this abrupt transformation, it is difficult to examine the emergence of new business models, as well as the entrance of new rivals and applications in the financial services industry. Due to variables including shifting customer expectations, the regulatory environment, macroeconomic change, and the quick development of technology, this revolution has occurred in services like active wealth management, digital payments, and insurance (Arslanian, Fischer, Arslanian, & Fischer, 2019). Several components with different business models and services make up the FinTech ecosystem (Baber, 2019). The government, consumers, conventional or current financial institutions, technology developers, and FinTech start-ups make up the FinTech ecosystem. The FinTech business model may further encompass insurance business methods, capital market, peer-to-peer (P2P) lending, crowdfunding, wealth management, and payment (I. Lee & Shin, 2018).

2.2. Elements of FinTech

FinTech businesses use innovative technology to assist financial services, making it impossible to ignore this sector of the finance industry. The possibility of innovation and development in this sector has inspired several new start-ups to be established. Digital lending, e-commerce, digital marketing, investment, the insurance sector, business processes, information security, human resources, payments, data solutions, and capital management divisions are all being significantly impacted by FinTech (Lu et al., 2020). FinTech businesses, the government or regulators, and Financial institutions make up the three main participants in the FinTech ecosystem. By exchanging data and working with FinTech firms, financial institutions provide the primary operating foundation for FinTech businesses. To safeguard the environment in which FinTech businesses operate, the government should develop relevant laws and regulations. As a result, it encourages appropriate cooperation between financial institutions and FinTech firms, in line with that, creates a competitive environment for such firms (Pant, 2020). Innovative FinTech businesses provide cutting-edge solutions to the financial services sector and make money in the sector by introducing new financial services and products to the market. A flourishing FinTech requires innovation, flexible rules, demand from the market, and money for early investment (Sjamsudin, 2019).

2.3. FinTech Adoption

Growing profitability, new financial innovations, and better risk management are all outcomes of the increased use of FinTech. In addition, FinTech has the potential to enhance the traditional business model by lowering bank operating costs, increasing service efficiency, bolstering risk control capabilities, and developing improved customer-oriented business models for customers, which will ultimately result in an improvement in comprehensive competitiveness (Panchal & Krishnamoorthy, 2019). Therefore, the incorporation of FinTech innovations into corporate strategy is an essential component of the financial and banking sector. When financial institutions fully utilize the adoption process strategically, the innovations brought forth by FinTech have a favorable influence on those institutions. This results in greater performance and increased competitiveness in the present market (Ahn & Kim, 2019). FinTech developments made possible with the assistance of artificial intelligence, mobile technology, and blockchain are the primary reason for the increase in competitiveness brought about by enhanced client services (Momaya, Pandey, Vallaturu, Sonar, & Bodduri, 2020).

The effectiveness of the organization is increased when managers take on an active part in the promotion of the desired technical advancements in various industries, therefore producing a change in cultural norms. This results in the company's ability to better serve its customers. Businesses have a significant amount of room for efficiency growth if they adopt and put into practice sound strategic management strategies (Bai, Jin, McElheran, & Williams, 2018).

3. DRIVERS OF THE GROWTH

Human behavior and the choice to accept innovation are influenced by both inner and external influences. The sociocultural milieu in which people live influences a lot of their motivation and behavior (Deci & Ryan, 2008). Environmental variables were shown to be one of the most important indicators of consumer acceptance of mobile payments (Sahu & Singh, 2018). Infrastructure, compatibility, governmental policy, and cultural considerations were all put to the test. Environmental factors such as lifestyle compatibility, enabling circumstances, payment culture, and added value have an impact on people's choices to use mobile payment systems (Putri, Handayani, & Shihab, 2020).

3.1. Safety and Trust Perception

The danger of loss from fraud or hack that undermines FinTech transactions is known as the safety risk (Ryu, 2018). Consumers of FinTech are growing concerned about the security risk associated with e-services, which is tied to the possibility of privacy invasion (Lwin, Wirtz, & Williams, 2007). Consumers' opinions of the system's ability to safely trade are reflected in their perceptions of safety (E.-Y. Lee, Lee, & Jeon, 2017; Morosan, 2012). Indeed, adoption will benefit from safety perceptions in the transaction system via a FinTech service (Ryu, 2018). The adoption of the technology, however, is adversely affected by perceived danger (Lam & Shankar, 2014). Given identity theft, financial fraud, and cybersecurity issue for organizations, biometric security alternatives are expanding significantly, which will impact the user experience in the future (Xu, 2022). FinTech businesses can achieve their objectives for sustainable development by having a thorough understanding of how trust and risk affect the ongoing use of the technology.

3.2. COVID-19

Due to the epidemic, internet purchasing expanded and quickly replaced offline buying, leading many physical stores to eventually develop an online presence (Hasan, Ashfaq, & Shao, 2021). The pandemic problem puts a burden on governments, markets, companies, and people. All nations are suffering from the sharp rise in the expenses of the economy, people, and money, but emerging market developing nations are more vulnerable. Digital wallets and other non-contact transactions have also become highly practical substitutes as a result of the present climate when physical touch has been avoided to stop the spread of COVID-19 (Arner et al., 2020). Government efforts to control transportation and encourage safe physical contact during the COVID-19 epidemic led to a significant uptake of FinTech (Fu & Mishra, 2020). There are adequate arguments to show that user behavioral adjustments have also fueled FinTech development during the epidemic, without discounting the influence of laws and regulations in influencing behavior (Ahorsu et al., 2020).

3.3. Risk Control

FinTech can disrupt the financial industry and alter it, making it more transparent, safe, and affordable, according to experts. (Kabulova & Stankevičienė, 2020) (p. 1). In addition, FinTech offers financial services that are frequently only offered by traditional banking institutions. The variety of goods and service providers offered by FinTech is substantial. The rapid feedback provided by the user's client also allows for improved risk management (Moro-Visconti, Cruz Rambaud, & López Pascual, 2020). In terms of risk management, FinTech innovation may leverage cutting-edge technology, like speech recognition and biometrics, to lower labor, capital, and time expenses to increase data accuracy, which can minimize systemic risk as well as internal fraud risk (Fuster, Plosser, Schnabl, & Vickery, 2019). Additionally, FinTech innovation may work in tandem with banks' loan services to lessen information asymmetry between borrowers and banks, making institutions more secure and adaptable while lowering the likelihood of default by borrowers (Gomber, Koch, & Siering, 2017).

3.4. Governmental Assistance

The government is crucial in promoting the use of innovative technology, such as FinTech services. The government may use its credibility to promote cutting-edge financial applications while also supporting FinTech. To build a strong technological infrastructure, it might also spend in building a reliable communication network. Additionally, by passing appropriate rules and regulations, it may persuade users to use FinTech services. Research that has already been done has shown the importance of government backing in getting people to embrace and utilize FinTech services. Government support had a substantial effect on consumers' acceptance of FinTech, both indirectly and directly through affecting bank customers' faith in the services offered, which in turn had a beneficial impact on their adoption of FinTech (Hu, Ding, Li, Chen, & Yang, 2019). The majority of governments embrace FinTech as a way to accomplish the four main objectives shown in Figure 2.

Figure 2. Key objectives of government assistance for FinTech

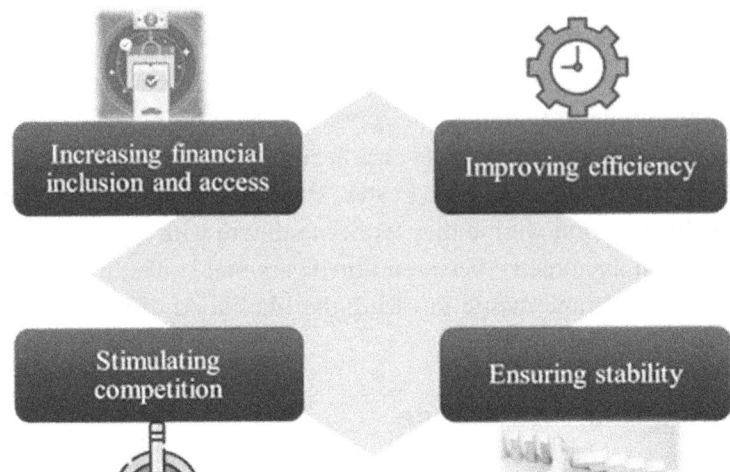

3.5. Competence in Technology

Technology is mostly to blame for the rise of FinTech. It has completely changed how financial services work, making them nearly unrecognizable from a decade ago since it functions almost solely in the virtual world. FinTech is superior to conventional financial institutions in several ways because of technology, which has enabled us to automate tasks that were previously done by people:

- **Cheaper:** FinTech was able to recruit fewer people while maintaining a very high level of productivity because of technology, which also enabled them to avoid paying for physical offices. FinTech solutions may appeal to a wide audience by offering lower service prices due to personnel and local branch cost savings.
- **Productive:** Automation speeds up mundane processes, but it also gives staff members more time to work on complex projects like strategy and innovation. Productivity has grown as a consequence.
- **Accessible:** FinTech eliminated middlemen like brokers and bank managers by providing a wide variety of financial services online and via applications, allowing everyone immediate access to services and information.

Consumer perception of the resources and assistance required to perform behaviors, such as the availability of necessary technical facilities and infrastructure as well as the assistance needed to make the process of utilizing a service quick and simple, is referred to as technological readiness (Venkatesh, Thong, & Xu, 2012). Literature has shown that the technical context of a country affects how quickly individuals accept innovations (Frimpong, Shuridah, Wilson, & Sarpong, 2020). Studies in the past have shown that technical factors influence the adoption of new technology beneficially (Gerlach & Lutz, 2019; Oliveira & Martins, 2010). It seems to sense that having access to necessary infrastructure, like an internet connection, would inspire people to experiment with cutting-edge technologies.

3.6. Social Impact

The extent to which a person's social circle, including their family, friends, and coworkers, influences their choice to use a particular technology is known as social impact. The influence of the social circle is more pronounced when it comes to disruptive new technologies since people tend to give higher weight to others' opinions when they lack personal experience with a technology or innovation. Since it is expected that people will consult their social circles when learning about new technology and may be influenced by the information they provide, social norms have a considerably greater impact on disruptive breakthroughs. When lacking firsthand experience, individuals tend to give other people's opinions and impressions of the technical elements more weight. Furthermore, because the service is new, cultural norms affect how people see technology (Singh, Sahni, & Kovid, 2020).

3.7. Reduced Ecological Impact

Even in the financial industry, environmental hazards and climate change are presently receiving a lot of attention. Institutional investors' need for more sustainable investments has significantly increased as a result of worries about things like reputational consequences. A key method of cooperation between FinTechs and sustainable finance is crowdfunding. In this scenario, businesses get many little payments from other users through an internet platform. In practice, these green crowdfunding platforms may aid in the financing of eco-friendly firms and the raising of more affordable, accessible, and quick capital. These also provide investors the chance to put their money toward more environmentally friendly projects. Additionally, the COVID-19 pandemic illustrated the connection between finance, technology, and sustainability since it compelled all nations to reconsider their conventional business structures and depend more heavily on sustainability and technology (Macchiavello & Siri, 2020).

3.8. Market Organization

FinTech is essential for maintaining market and market structure stability. Although financial innovations provide many advantages for both companies and consumers, there are also possible hazards associated with their widespread use to take into account since consumer tastes and choices are continually evolving. Three key factors— composition, concentration, and contestability —define market structure (Barry & Street, 2020). The term "contestability" describes a scenario where there is intense rivalry in the market as a consequence of new entries, yet there are few opportunities to set prices differently. Concentration is the ability of a small number of powerful companies to affect the market (Vučinić, 2020). Limiting concentration increases competition, which creates more options for innovation and cheaper pricing. The capacity of service providers to work together and deliver a portfolio of services that is more useful for the client is referred to as composition. FinTech businesses may provide financial services that are distinct from those provided by conventional banks based on the composition characteristic (Vučinić, 2020).

4. OPPORTUNITIES FOR FINTECH

The opportunities and benefits of FinTech for the financial industry are discussed in various studies and specialized reports from various angles. This section aims to get a deeper and more useful knowledge of the potential provided by FinTech developments after recognizing the essential components of the present FinTech ecosystem.

Without a question, the most distressing and significant element now affecting the sector is the growth of the FinTech ecosystem (Laidroo, Koroleva, Kliber, Rupeika-Apoga, & Grigaliuniene, 2021). FinTech, or emerging technologies, provide inventive ways to deliver financial services that are not available through traditional channels (Rupeika-Apoga & Thalassinos, 2020). An innovation known as new technology fundamentally alters how consumers, businesses, and entire economic sectors function. Due to their measurable advantages over existing processes or systems, new technologies can be used to replace them. Emerging technology may be defined as a new technology that significantly alters the way a market or sector currently operates. Because they have the potential to upend the status quo, emerging technologies sometimes encounter early resistance from established enterprises (Barroso & Laborda, 2022). However, they have the potential to fundamentally alter how a sector runs over time. New technologies include things like internet shopping, Wi-Fi 6 and 5G, and ad blockers. However, the potential of new technologies might occasionally be overstated (Bilan et al., 2019).

Emerging technology should have the capacity to completely change a particular market or industry, even if it is neither innovative nor revolutionary. This kind of technology is used in many industries, from agriculture to education (Chonsawat & Sopadang, 2020). New technologies are often not immediately embraced by the general public. This is due to the widespread belief that it is overly dangerous or unproven. But as technology develops, it may eventually be utilized broadly. Numerous advantages might result from this, including increased competition, higher quality, and reduced pricing (Anshari, Almunawar, & Masri, 2020).

The handling and transmission of money by individuals are impacted by new technologies, which also change consumer expectations (Truby, Brown, & Dahdal, 2020). E-commerce, virtual/augmented reality, IoT, AI, cloud computing, cryptocurrencies, and blockchain are just a few examples of emerging technologies used in the banking industry.

FinTech development has focused on using cutting-edge technology like big data, cloud computing, artificial intelligence (AI), the IoT, and blockchain. These innovations have fundamentally altered how financial organizations handle the storage, transmission, and security of customer digital cash. FinTech businesses use AI to evaluate customer behavior in financial transactions and give insightful information for decision-making. So, AI will also help with wise investing decisions. Big data analytics may be used to forecast market changes and create new strategies. Additionally, blockchain technology's decentralized transactions with encrypted data allow more secure transactions (Lu et al., 2020). One of the most well-known uses of blockchain, the smart contract, has also been used in the financial sector. One use for the IoT is the verification and evaluation of accidents, followed by the ultimate payment of compensation (Suryono, Budi, & Purwandari, 2020). Applications for learning created by FinTech firms depend on cutting-edge technology to learn about users' spending patterns and involve them in realizing their subconscious judgments around saving and spending. Another technology tool that FinTech businesses use to assist their clients in carrying out protected transactions is intelligent chatbots (Kavuri & Milne, 2019).

4.1. AI

Banks employ AI and machine learning in a variety of applications. Although chatbots are what the general public is most familiar with, AI also has an impact on back-office operations, product delivery, risk management, marketing, and security. Major banks save hundreds of thousands of staff hours yearly by using machines to do tasks like data input, risk analysis, and loan form processing (Schulte & Liu, 2017). However, AI is a young technology that raises questions. Systems for making decisions that are poorly designed are more prone to produce mistakes that lead to legal issues and raise costs (Truby et al., 2020). AI and machine learning provide significant benefits for automation and robots. New technologies in the financial services industry, such as chatbots and automation, reduce labor costs, improve client relationships, and increase profitability (Bilan et al., 2019). Robo-advisors have several advantages over conventional human advisors, including more timely and universal access to financial services, a significant reduction in management fees, and a wider selection of investment options based on systematic and quantitative studies free from conflicts of interest (Park, Ryu, & Shin, 2016).

4.2. Financial Inclusion and Social Accountability

The attention investors and entrepreneurs have paid to bring about constructive change for society, especially for impoverished groups of people, is a positive aspect of the present FinTech revolution. To do this, technology can significantly assist in addressing challenges related to financial inclusion and ensuring equitable access to financial services (Demir, Pesqué-Cela, Altunbas, & Murinde, 2022). Owing to unsustainable business models and weak business incentives, the incumbent financial institutions are not paying much attention to this issue. Hence, FinTech companies have joined the lending and payment industry in several developing nations to close the gap in the availability of fundamental banking services (Varga, 2017).

4.3. Agility

Digital technology may help firms swiftly adjust to changes in their environment, as has been well-documented in academic research (Fitzgerald, 2016). For competitive firms, flexibility and agility are essential qualities, particularly when a market is through a considerable transition. Future banks should be "digitally ambidextrous"—a term used to describe how an organization should be at the nexus of innovation and change—to meet the aforementioned requirements (Gupta, Mejia, Gianchandani, & Kajikawa, 2021). The financial sector's quick rise has accelerated the pace of business model innovation. Any business that makes use of FinTech should be able to change with the times to satisfy clients and stay competitive.

4.4. Controlling the Information Economy

To evaluate financial risks, banks have proven successful in analyzing credit history data. They will learn how to use new kinds of data sources in a similar way to open new business opportunities. In this situation, analytical tools will assist them in achieving outcomes since they will be able to anticipate clients' wants earlier and more accurately (Navaretti, Calzolari, Mansilla-Fernandez, & Pozzolo, 2018). Many banks are embarking on a path of digital transformation that will prepare them to address their legacy difficulties (both around organizational and technological systems) and take advantage of possibilities in the data economy when they arise. The right use of data may significantly improve a variety of corporate processes and duties, including fraud detection, anti-money laundering, cybersecurity, operational efficiency, successful marketing, and the sale of individualized services (Liberti & Petersen, 2019).

4.5. Blockchain

Due to the decentralized nature of blockchain, there are no governing authorities, which might replace institutional actors' control mechanisms with a more dynamically dispersed environment (Velasco, 2017). Transactions on the Internet are regulated and given legitimacy thanks to blockchain systems with auditable ledgers (X. Wang et al., 2018). Therefore, researchers looked at how blockchain technology may be used in the financial sector to improve credit judgments, enhance regulatory oversight, and implement open banking (Srivastava & Dashottar, 2020). A large shift in financial services from conventional banks to neo-banks is referred to as a FinTech disruption. Several technical developments in the FinTech sector have a direct influence on the delivery of goods and services for retail banking (Truby et al., 2020). These adjustments should be seen as crucial planning tools as consumer and commercial banking habits shift. FinTech is anticipated to enhance customer welfare while also benefiting the sector in terms of oversight and regulation (Musabegovic, Özer, Djukovic, & Jovanovic, 2019). While avoiding the moral pitfalls associated with negative interest rates and quantitative easing, FinTech may provide decentralized instruments for improving system-wide resilience. This is significant given the current state of the world economy and the tendency of conventional banks to take unwarranted risks (Hayes, 2016).

4.6. Innovative Business Strategies for Digital Ecosystems

The basis of banking as well as the organizations that function in this context—the banks—are on the verge of changing significantly. The most crucial aspect of this change is that banks should deal with competition from several stakeholders who have not previously been a part of their conventional rivalry to stay competitive. In various aspects of the financial services architecture, businesses from the high-tech industry (providing hardware or software), as well as players from retail, telecommunications, and other industries, as well as FinTech and new digital banks, are all vying for market share (Dapp, Slomka, AG, & Hoffmann, 2014).

Open banking, however, extends well beyond the restrictive confines of finance and "FinTegration." Financial institutions will be capable of communicating with companies, apps, and platforms outside of banking as API types and standards expand, opening up new opportunities for them to offer their services and the services of their partners by using access to cutting-edge data (M Zachariadis, Ozcan, & Dinckol, 2018). Existing literature extensively covers platform economics and outlines the tactics banks could use to promote ecosystem development and open innovation inside their walls (Markos Zachariadis & Ozcan, 2017; M Zachariadis et al., 2018). For instance, the primary duty of retail banking is to provide financial services to the general population (Demirgüç-Kunt, Klapper, Singer, Ansar, & Hess, 2020). FinTech is anticipated to significantly improve the banking sector via several channels, including automated client segmentation procedures, reduced payment transaction costs, quality-controlled customer service, optimized accounting, and an increased customer base (Melnychenko, Volosovych, & Baraniuk, 2020). The supply of financial services to underserved communities with limited access to conventional finance channels might be considered a kind of financial inclusion (Grima, Özen, & Boz, 2020).

5. FUTURE APPLICATIONS

FinTech may benefit regulators in other ways as well. Many are more in tune with the banking community and its demands since they are concentrating on creating more consumer-centric methods. Sharing information with FinTech businesses may help regulators become more aware of customer preferences, behaviors, and habits. This knowledge may then be used to assist create regulatory frameworks that support increasing consumer confidence in FinTech platforms. On the other hand, by including a behavioral insights approach in FinTech developments, innovation managers may assist regulators in achieving their objectives by optimizing their capacity to bring about desirable behavioral changes (Lockton, Harrison, & Stanton, 2010).

Additionally, the combination of blockchain and FinTech offers safe venues for improved data exchange where users may trust more reliable systems. Each transaction may be tracked and illegal alterations can be avoided by using Distributed Ledger Technology. Digital assets and non-fungible tokens (NFT) are all examples of FinTech tools; their success is dependent on developments in areas like as smart contracts, distributed data storage, and exchange (Aysan & Ünal, 2021). Because of its difficulties in application in reality, blockchain technology has not yet been embraced by many FinTech organizations; yet, due to the safe platforms that it may give, it is a potential component for the future of FinTech firms. Cloud computing is anticipated to significantly alter the financial markets when maintenance and data storage expenses are taken into account. Utilizing cloud services may drastically lower infrastructure expenses and application downtime (Chaikovskyi & Kovalchuk, 2020). The next phase of core banking and FinTech is thus anticipated to be dependent on cloud services as a result of the recognition of the potential of the cloud in FinTech. Since it may be used for digital payments, property finance, and risk management via the observation of financial activities, the IoT is also playing a significant role in the financial industry. Additionally, IoT may be used in the insurance industry to accurately assess risk and streamline processes. It's also necessary to adopt and adhere to relevant laws and regulations in light of emerging FinTech trends (Cai et al., 2022).

Since 2019, new study lines have emerged as a result of the continued advancement of research on a global scale. In addition, several phrases can be connected to the many potential thematic axes that relate to the various facets of FinTech (Table 1).

Table 1. Applications of FinTech in different sectors

Sectors	Applications
Technologies	Internet Big Data Bitcoin (Nodes, Network, Mining Pool, Merchants) Blockchain (Regulation, Agent, Consortium Blockchain) Computational (Methods, Constraints, Electronic Payment Infrastructure, Computing Power, Computer Architecture) Digital Era (Cryptoassets, Conglomerates, Digital Economy Era, Payments, Identity, Farming, Wealth Management) Others (Disruptive Innovations, Visual Analytics Systems, Visual Reasoning, P2P/Marketplace Lending, Mobile Cloud Computing, Fog Computing, Smart Technologies, Internet Technology and Supporting Technology Individual Recommendation, Internet Search Behavior, Creative Computing, FinTech Features, and Payment Services Directive 2)
Sustainability	Ecological Concerns, Sustainable Business Models, and Sustainable Management and Investment
Banking	Personalized Recommendations, Defined Contribution Pension Plan, Customer Records, Payment Services Directive 2, Peer To Peer Lending, Conventional Commercial Banks, Corporate Banking, Banking Sector, Banking Industry, Consumer Loans, Operating Effectiveness, Savings, P2P/Marketplace Lending, Credit Provision, and Bank Misconduct
Management	Relationship Management, Organizational Management, Decision-Making, Human Resource Management, Financial Management, Asset Management Firms, Trust Management, Automated Investment Management
Commercial	Marketing Strategy, Understanding The Client Life Cycle Market Stability, Public Relations, and Pricing
Economic and business	Entrepreneur, Small and Medium Businesses, Labor Transfer, Policy Risk, Poverty Reduction, Social Change, Service Sector, Business Cycle, Economic Welfare, Future Of Real Estate, Development History, Economic Cycle, Development Process, Capital Bubble, Industrial Economics, Capitalism, Industry Revolution 4.0, Migration, Social Restrictions, Inequality, Small And Medium Businesses, Small Business Finance, Social Restrictions
Financial	The efficiency of The Supply Chain, Finances, and Financing, Financial well-being, Start-Up Funding, FinTech, Financial Fragility, Financial Frontier Technology FinTech Businesses, Events, Education, Opportunities, Threats, Corporate Finance, Inclusive Finance, Household Finance, Digital Financial Services, Electronic Payment Infrastructure Sentiment Analysis, Early Financial Risk Detection, Interest Rate Liberalization, And Financial Access
Legal	Model Driven Regulation and Regulatory Body, Institutional Reform, General Data Protection Regulation, Controversy, Inclusive Development, Privacy and Security Issues, Government Role, Digital Regulatory Reporting, Institutional Change, Robo-Advisors, Payment Services Directive 2, Institutionalization, Labour Transfer, Ontology, Consumer and Legal Protection

6. MAIN CHALLENGES

FinTech has various difficulties despite having revolutionized financial services and given customers a distinctive customer experience. Instead of utilizing conventional banking services, customers may easily make personal investments, trade, and utilize insurance and credit services by depending on algorithms, processes, software, applications, and new business models. Some clients continue to utilize conventional banking due to a lack of confidence in FinTech firms (Suryono et al., 2020). Customers assert that since there is little transparency and risk of security breaches, they prefer to conduct their financial transactions via conventional banking services. Since FinTech organizations are among the most appealing targets for hackers, privacy and security concerns are the major challenges in FinTech development. Businesses and people with important financial data are dealt with by FinTech firms. For businesses and people that rely heavily on online transactions and digital currency, the loss of this data poses serious challenges. Because hackers are always refining their methods of cyberattack, even the most respectable financial businesses find it difficult to safeguard data effectively. To assure data security, including data encryption, biometric authentication, and multifactor authentication, high-level security infrastructure should be established (Suryono et al., 2020). The need to stay up with technical advances may provide another challenge for FinTech businesses. Innovation is the driving force behind FinTech, which might soon face threats from rivals as new FinTech develops. Outdated software and application architecture prevent alignment with contemporary digital financial services. As a result, adopting cutting-edge technologies that are useful in providing financial services is becoming more important for the survival of financial firms (Suryono et al., 2020). The ability to give clients better, safer services are made possible by the use of current, suitable technology, and customer satisfaction goes up dramatically as a result. Although businesses should make early expenditures to implement cutting-edge technology, happy clients are more likely to extend their use of FinTech and depend on digital currency assets, which will enhance the institution's income. On the other side, over-reliance on technology makes FinTech organizations susceptible to issues with the general functionality of the software, defects in working systems, the speed of operations, and the quality of apps. Due to the dependency of FinTech on user experience, a single element about the functioning of the online systems may either help the firm outperform its rivals or lead it to lose the faith of its clients (Kavuri & Milne, 2019). Other elements, like the industry and governmental rules, might provide challenges for the FinTech sector. Companies in the FinTech industry should adhere to the same compliance rules as banks and other financial institutions. The need to comply with rules might hinder the operations of FinTech businesses and cause their processes to become less agile (Kavuri & Milne, 2019).

Machine learning, AI, and big data utilization cannot be isolated from new technological advances in the growth of FinTech (Brownsword, 2019). The use of data has complex and wide-ranging effects, which drives this sector to pay particular attention to security (Anugerah & Indriani, 2018). In this regard, security encompasses both technology and data (Gai, Qiu, & Sun, 2018). FinTech should protect consumers from data breaches, access restrictions, and data privacy issues. As a result, strict rules controlling the protection of personal data are required (Abubakar & Handayani, 2018). Consumers should also get digital literacy training. Digital literacy requires intelligent technology users (Hatammimi & Krisnawati, 2018). While utilizing technological integration to stop fraud, the FinTech industry should also maintain the caliber of its software (H. Wang, Wang, Zhang, & Zhou, 2019).

Among the many financial services kinds influenced by FinTech are loans, digital insurance, wealth management, and payments (Leong, Tan, Xiao, Tan, & Sun, 2017). FinTech practices that depend on user trust, have led to the emergence of several unlawful FinTech loans (Pantielieieva, Krynytsia, Khutorna, & Potapenko, 2018). Regulators need to use a "regulatory sandbox" strategy for this reason. The sandbox enables regulators to collaborate with business stakeholders to grow this sector (Azarenkova, Shkodina, Samorodov, & Babenko, 2018). Operators in the FinTech sector are required to be legally registered and a member of government-approved organizations. A direct inspection system should be put in place by the regulator, who should monitor the application channels and website. Additionally, it is suggested that the government establish a complaint channel for unlawful FinTech. Utilizing social media comments data to investigate public opinion is a more intriguing proposal (Niu, Ren, Zhao, & Li, 2020).

The creation of a workable and organized framework for FinTech is the future's challenge (Abdullah, Rahman, & Rahim, 2018; Eickhoff, Muntermann, & Weinrich, 2017). Several research projects are attempting to develop sustainable adoption models by figuring out what characteristics motivate people to utilize FinTech services (Y. Chang, Wong, Lee, & Jeong, 2016). How customers will utilize these services moving forward is still up in the air. Additionally, identifying these elements is not the only technique to examine adoption rates. The operation of the FinTech sector may be aided by stakeholder support and public awareness of financial literacy. The cooperation of all stakeholders depends on this function (Fermay, Santosa, Kertopati, & Eprianto, 2018). FinTech should not be seen as a disruptive industry anymore. FinTech and regulators should have excellent connections for their practices to continue (Suryono, Marlina, Purwaningsih, Sensuse, & Sutoyo, 2019), and this is also true of other financial service companies like banks (Huang, 2018). FinTech should be able to aid in the change in the economy. The government should recognize that the FinTech sector is a driving force behind this transformation, for example, by recognizing the use of digital wallets and electronic money and permitting their acceptance as payment options. These procedures undoubtedly make it simpler for users to use their devices to make cash payments. FinTech used to be the enemy of banking, but today banks can work together, and the government is not just a regulator but also an active participant in building a better digital payment environment.

7. CONCLUSION

The development of new technologies has led to significant changes in the structure of financial services and payment systems. When developments in FinTech are taken into consideration, it can be seen that FinTech is still expanding, and there will be even more prospects for expansion in the future. The growth of the FinTech sector is being fueled by several significant factors, including stricter compliance regulations and higher client expectations. FinTech companies now have the ability, thanks to the introduction of new features made possible by technological progress, to give their customers more satisfying and enjoyable experiences. The purpose of this research was to focus on the factors that are contributing to the expansion of the FinTech industry and to suggest directions for locating the possibilities that the expansion of the industry presents. This chapter discussed some of the factors that are driving this rise, such as the sense of safety and trust, COVID-19, risk management, governmental aid, technological expertise, social effect, and decreased environmental impact. Opportunities for FinTech such as AI, financial inclusion and social responsibility, agility, regulating the information economy, blockchain, and creative business methods for digital ecosystems are described. The challenges, which included protection, teamwork, and supervision, were presented in the end.

REFERENCES

Abdullah, E. M. E., Rahman, A. A., & Rahim, R. A. (2018). Adoption of financial technology (FinTech) in mutual fund/unit trust investment among Malaysians: Unified Theory of Acceptance and Use of Technology (UTAUT). *Int. J. Eng. Technol, 7*(2), 110.

Abubakar, L., & Handayani, T. (2018). *Financial technology: Legal challenges for Indonesia financial sector.* Paper presented at the IOP Conference Series: Earth and Environmental Science. 10.1088/1755-1315/175/1/012204

Ahn, S., & Kim, J. (2019). The effect of managerial characteristics on the performance of technology-based start-ups in Korea. *International Journal of Global Business and Competitiveness, 14*(1), 11–23. doi:10.100742943-019-00001-4

Ahorsu, D. K., Lin, C.-Y., Imani, V., Saffari, M., Griffiths, M. D., & Pakpour, A. H. (2020). The fear of COVID-19 scale: Development and initial validation. *International Journal of Mental Health and Addiction*, 1–9. PMID:32226353

Allayarov, S. A., & Ravshanova, M. (2021). Financial technology: Development of innovative FinTech start-ups and its application in banking system of Uzbekistan. *International Journal of Multicultural and Multireligious Understanding*, 8(9), 214–219. doi:10.18415/ijmmu.v8i9.3017

Anshari, M., Almunawar, M. N., & Masri, M. (2020). Financial technology and disruptive innovation in business: Concept and application. *International Journal of Asian Business and Information Management*, 11(4), 29–43. doi:10.4018/IJABIM.2020100103

Anugerah, D. P., & Indriani, M. (2018). *Data Protection in financial technology services: Indonesian legal perspective.* Paper presented at the IOP Conference Series: Earth and Environmental Science.

Arner, D. W., Barberis, J. N., Walker, J., Buckley, R. P., Dahdal, A. M., & Zetzsche, D. A. (2020). *Digital finance & the COVID-19 crisis.* University of Hong Kong Faculty of Law Research Paper (2020/017).

Arslanian, H., Fischer, F., Arslanian, H., & Fischer, F. (2019). The rise of FinTech. The Future of Finance: The Impact of FinTech, AI, and Crypto on Financial Services, 25-56.

Aysan, A. F., & Ünal, İ. M. (2021). FinTech and blockchain in islamic finance: A bibliometric analysis. *Efil Journal*, 4(3), 21–37.

Azarenkova, G., Shkodina, I., Samorodov, B., Babenko, M., & Onishchenko, I. (2018). The influence of financial technologies on the global financial system stability. *Investment Management & Financial Innovations*, 15(4), 229–238. doi:10.21511/imfi.15(4).2018.19

Baber, H. (2019). Relevance of e-SERVQUAL for determining the quality of FinTech services. *International Journal of Electronic Finance*, 9(4), 257–267. doi:10.1504/IJEF.2019.104070

Bai, J. J., Jin, W., McElheran, K., & Williams, R. (2018). *The effects of technology adoption on firms, supply chains, and rivals.* Academic Press.

Barroso, M., & Laborda, J. (2022). Digital transformation and the emergence of the FinTech sector: Systematic literature review. *Digital Business*, 100028.

Barry, J. J., & Street, O. L. (2020). *Re: Addressing the Regulatory*. Supervisory and Oversight Challenges Raised by Global Stablecoin Arrangements.

Basole, R. C., & Patel, S. S. (2018). Transformation through unbundling: Visualizing the global FinTech ecosystem. *Service Science, 10*(4), 379–396. doi:10.1287erv.2018.0210

Bilan, A., Degryse, H., O'Flynn, K., Ongena, S., Bilan, A., Degryse, H., . . . Ongena, S. (2019). FinTech and the Future of Banking. *Banking and Financial Markets: How Banks and Financial Technology Are Reshaping Financial Markets*, 179-199.

Boot, A., Hoffmann, P., Laeven, L., & Ratnovski, L. (2021). FinTech: What's old, what's new? *Journal of Financial Stability, 53*, 100836. doi:10.1016/j.jfs.2020.100836

Breidbach, C. F., Keating, B. W., & Lim, C. (2020). FinTech: Research directions to explore the digital transformation of financial service systems. *Journal of Service Theory and Practice, 30*(1), 79–102. doi:10.1108/JSTP-08-2018-0185

Brownsword, R. (2019). Regulatory fitness: FinTech, funny money, and smart contracts. *European Business Organization Law Review, 20*(1), 5–27. doi:10.100740804-019-00134-2

Buchak, G., Matvos, G., Piskorski, T., & Seru, A. (2018). FinTech, regulatory arbitrage, and the rise of shadow banks. *Journal of Financial Economics, 130*(3), 453–483. doi:10.1016/j.jfineco.2018.03.011

Cai, C., Marrone, M., & Linnenluecke, M. (2022). Trends in FinTech research and practice: Examining the intersection with the information systems field. *Communications of the Association for Information Systems, 50*(1), 40. doi:10.17705/1CAIS.05036

Chaikovskyi, Y., & Kovalchuk, Y. (2020). Modern FinTech directions in the banking sector. *Zeszyty Naukowe ZPSB Firma i Rynek*, (1 (57)), 71–79.

Chang, H.-y., Liang, W., & Wang, Y. (2019). Do institutional investors still encourage patent-based innovation after the tech bubble period? *Journal of Empirical Finance, 51*, 149–164. doi:10.1016/j.jempfin.2019.02.003

Chang, Y., Wong, S. F., Lee, H., & Jeong, S. P. (2016). What motivates chinese consumers to adopt FinTech services: a regulatory focus theory. *Proceedings of the 18th annual international conference on electronic commerce: e-commerce in smart connected world*. 10.1145/2971603.2971643

Chonsawat, N., & Sopadang, A. (2020). Defining SMEs' 4.0 readiness indicators. *Applied Sciences (Basel, Switzerland), 10*(24), 8998. doi:10.3390/app10248998

Dapp, T., & Slomka, L., AG, D. B., & Hoffmann, R. (2014). FinTech–The digital (r) evolution in the financial sector. *Deutsche Bank Research*, *11*, 1–39.

Demir, A., Pesqué-Cela, V., Altunbas, Y., & Murinde, V. (2022). FinTech, financial inclusion and income inequality: A quantile regression approach. *European Journal of Finance*, *28*(1), 86–107. doi:10.1080/1351847X.2020.1772335

Demirgüç-Kunt, A., Klapper, L., Singer, D., Ansar, S., & Hess, J. (2020). The Global Findex Database 2017: Measuring financial inclusion and opportunities to expand access to and use of financial services. *The World Bank Economic Review*, *34*(Supplement_1), S2–S8. doi:10.1093/wber/lhz013

Eickhoff, M., Muntermann, J., & Weinrich, T. (2017). *What do FinTechs actually do? A Taxonomy of FinTech Business Models.* Paper presented at the ICIS.

Fermay, A. H., Santosa, B., Kertopati, A. Y., & Eprianto, I. M. (2018). The development of collaborative model between FinTech and bank in Indonesia. *Proceedings of the 2nd International Conference on E-commerce, E-Business and E-Government.* 10.1145/3234781.3234783

Fitzgerald, M. (2016). General Motors relies on IoT to anticipate customers' needs. *MIT Sloan Management Review*, *57*(4).

Frimpong, K., Shuridah, O., Wilson, A., & Sarpong, F. (2020). A cross-national investigation of trait antecedents of mobile-banking adoption. *Thunderbird International Business Review*, *62*(4), 411–424. doi:10.1002/tie.22132

Fu, J., & Mishra, M. (2020). *The global impact of COVID-19 on FinTech adoption.* Swiss Finance Institute Research Paper (20-38).

Fuster, A., Plosser, M., Schnabl, P., & Vickery, J. (2019). The role of technology in mortgage lending. *Review of Financial Studies*, *32*(5), 1854–1899. doi:10.1093/rfs/hhz018

Gai, K., Qiu, M., & Sun, X. (2018). A survey on FinTech. *Journal of Network and Computer Applications*, *103*, 262–273. doi:10.1016/j.jnca.2017.10.011

Gerlach, J. M., & Lutz, J. K. (2019). Evidence on usage behavior and future adoption intention of FinTechs and digital finance solutions. *The International Journal of Business and Finance Research*, *13*(2), 83–105.

Giudici, P. (2018). Financial data science. *Statistics & Probability Letters*, *136*, 160–164. doi:10.1016/j.spl.2018.02.024

Gomber, P., Koch, J.-A., & Siering, M. (2017). Digital Finance and FinTech: Current research and future research directions. *Journal of Business Economics*, *87*(5), 537–580. doi:10.100711573-017-0852-x

Gozman, D., Liebenau, J., & Mangan, J. (2018). The innovation mechanisms of FinTech start-ups: Insights from SWIFT's innotribe competition. *Journal of Management Information Systems*, *35*(1), 145–179. doi:10.1080/07421222.2018 .1440768

Grima, S., Özen, E., & Boz, H. (2020). *Contemporary Issues in Business, Economics and Finance* (Vol. 104). Emerald Publishing Bingley. doi:10.1108/9781839096051

Gu, S., Ślusarczyk, B., Hajizada, S., Kovalyova, I., & Sakhbieva, A. (2021). Impact of the covid-19 pandemic on online consumer purchasing behavior. *Journal of Theoretical and Applied Electronic Commerce Research*, *16*(6), 2263–2281. doi:10.3390/jtaer16060125

Guo, Y., & Liang, C. (2016). Blockchain application and outlook in the banking industry. *Financial Innovation, 2*, 1-12.

Gupta, R., Mejia, C., Gianchandani, Y. B., & Kajikawa, Y. (2021). Ambidextrous firm strategy insights from internet of things linked interfirm deals. *IEEE Transactions on Engineering Management*, *70*(1), 112–127. doi:10.1109/TEM.2020.3041250

Haddad, C., & Hornuf, L. (2019). The emergence of the global FinTech market: Economic and technological determinants. *Small Business Economics*, *53*(1), 81–105. doi:10.100711187-018-9991-x

Hasan, R., Ashfaq, M., & Shao, L. (2021). Evaluating drivers of FinTech adoption in the Netherlands. *Global Business Review*. doi:10.1177/09721509211027402

Hatammimi, J., & Krisnawati, A. (2018). Financial literacy for entrepreneur in the industry 4.0 era: A conceptual framework in Indonesia. *Proceedings of the 2018 10th International Conference on Information Management and Engineering*. 10.1145/3285957.3285985

Hayes, A. (2016). *Decentralized banking: Monetary technocracy in the digital age.* Springer.

Hendrikse, R. (2019). Can selfies spark the identity (r) evolution in financial services? *Biometric Technology Today*, *2019*(4), 5–7. doi:10.1016/S0969-4765(19)30053-0

Hu, Z., Ding, S., Li, S., Chen, L., & Yang, S. (2019). Adoption intention of FinTech services for bank users: An empirical examination with an extended technology acceptance model. *Symmetry*, *11*(3), 340. doi:10.3390ym11030340

Huang, R. H. (2018). Online P2P lending and regulatory responses in China: Opportunities and challenges. *European Business Organization Law Review*, *19*(1), 63–92. doi:10.100740804-018-0100-z

Iman, N. (2018). Assessing the dynamics of FinTech in Indonesia. *Investment Management and Financial Innovations*, *15*(4), 296–303. doi:10.21511/imfi.15(4).2018.24

Kabulova, J., & Stankevičienė, J. (2020). Valuation of FinTech innovation based on patent applications. *Sustainability*, *12*(23), 10158. doi:10.3390u122310158

Kavuri, A. S., & Milne, A. (2019). *FinTech and the future of financial services: What are the research gaps?* Academic Press.

Kou, G. (2019). Introduction to the special issue on FinTech. *Financial Innovation, 5*(1), 45.

Laidroo, L., Koroleva, E., Kliber, A., Rupeika-Apoga, R., & Grigaliuniene, Z. (2021). Business models of FinTechs–Difference in similarity? *Electronic Commerce Research and Applications*, *46*, 101034. doi:10.1016/j.elerap.2021.101034

Lam, S. Y., & Shankar, V. (2014). Asymmetries in the effects of drivers of brand loyalty between early and late adopters and across technology generations. *Journal of Interactive Marketing*, *28*(1), 26–42. doi:10.1016/j.intmar.2013.06.004

Lee, E.-Y., Lee, S.-B., & Jeon, Y. J. J. (2017). Factors influencing the behavioral intention to use food delivery apps. *Social Behavior and Personality*, *45*(9), 1461–1473. doi:10.2224bp.6185

Lee, I., & Shin, Y. J. (2018). FinTech: Ecosystem, business models, investment decisions, and challenges. *Business Horizons*, *61*(1), 35–46. doi:10.1016/j.bushor.2017.09.003

Lee, M. R., Yen, D. C., & Hurlburt, G. F. (2018). Financial technologies and applications. *IT Professional*, *20*(2), 27–33. doi:10.1109/MITP.2018.021921648

Leong, C., Tan, B., Xiao, X., Tan, F. T. C., & Sun, Y. (2017). Nurturing a FinTech ecosystem: The case of a youth microloan startup in China. *International Journal of Information Management*, *37*(2), 92–97. doi:10.1016/j.ijinfomgt.2016.11.006

Li, Y., Liu, Y., & Xie, F. (2019). Technology directors and firm innovation. *Journal of Multinational Financial Management*, *50*, 76–88. doi:10.1016/j.mulfin.2019.04.001

Liberti, J. M., & Petersen, M. A. (2019). Information: Hard and soft. *Review of Corporate Finance Studies*, *8*(1), 1–41. doi:10.1093/rcfs/cfy009

Lockton, D., Harrison, D., & Stanton, N. A. (2010). The Design with Intent Method: A design tool for influencing user behaviour. *Applied Ergonomics*, *41*(3), 382–392. doi:10.1016/j.apergo.2009.09.001 PMID:19822311

Lu, H., Wu, Q., & Ye, J. (2020). *FinTech and the future of financial service: A literature review and research agenda*. Academic Press.

Lwin, M., Wirtz, J., & Williams, J. D. (2007). Consumer online privacy concerns and responses: A power–responsibility equilibrium perspective. *Journal of the Academy of Marketing Science*, *35*(4), 572–585. doi:10.100711747-006-0003-3

Macchiavello, E., & Siri, M. (2020). Sustainable finance and FinTech: Can technology contribute to achieving environmental goals. A Preliminary Assessment of 'Green FinTech'. SSRN *Electron. J*. doi:10.2139/ssrn.3672989

Mehrotra, A. (2019). *Financial inclusion through FinTech–a case of lost focus*. Paper presented at the 2019 International conference on automation, computational and technology management (ICACTM). 10.1109/ICACTM.2019.8776857

Melnychenko, S., Volosovych, S., & Baraniuk, Y. (2020). Dominant ideas of financial technologies in digital banking. *Baltic Journal of Economic Studies, 6*(1), 92-99.

Momaya, K., Pandey, P., Vallaturu, V., Sonar, R., & Bodduri, A. (2020). FinTech platforms, and competitiveness: Exploring role of MoT as a differentiator for firms of Indian origin (FIOs). *Proceedings of the 29th International Conference on Management of Technology*.

Moro-Visconti, R., Cruz Rambaud, S., & López Pascual, J. (2020). Sustainability in FinTechs: An explanation through business model scalability and market valuation. *Sustainability*, *12*(24), 10316. doi:10.3390u122410316

Morosan, C. (2012). Theoretical and empirical considerations of guests' perceptions of biometric systems in hotels: Extending the technology acceptance model. *Journal of Hospitality & Tourism Research (Washington, D.C.)*, *36*(1), 52–84. doi:10.1177/1096348010380601

Musabegovic, I., Özer, M., Djukovic, S., & Jovanovic, S. (2019). Influence of financial technology (FinTech) on financial industry. *Ekonomika Poljoprivrede*, *66*(4), 1003–1021. doi:10.5937/ekoPolj1904003M

Navaretti, G. B., Calzolari, G., Mansilla-Fernandez, J. M., & Pozzolo, A. F. (2018). *FinTech and banking. Friends or foes?* Friends or Foes. doi:10.2139srn.3099337

Niu, B., Ren, J., Zhao, A., & Li, X. (2020). Lender trust on the P2P lending: Analysis based on sentiment analysis of comment text. *Sustainability*, *12*(8), 3293. doi:10.3390u12083293

O'Halloran, S., & Nowaczyk, N. (2019). An artificial intelligence approach to regulating systemic risk. *Frontiers in Artificial Intelligence*, *2*, 7. doi:10.3389/ frai.2019.00007 PMID:33733096

Oliveira, T., & Martins, M. F. (2010). Understanding e-business adoption across industries in European countries. *Industrial Management & Data Systems*, *110*(9), 1337–1354. doi:10.1108/02635571011087428

Panchal, D., & Krishnamoorthy, B. (2019). Developing an instrument for business model dimensions: Exploring linkages with firm competitiveness. *International Journal of Global Business and Competitiveness*, *14*(1), 24–41. doi:10.100742943-019-00004-1

Pant, S. K. (2020). FinTech: Emerging Trends. *Telecom Business Review, 13*(1).

Pantielieieva, N., Krynytsia, S., Khutorna, M., & Potapenko, L. (2018). *FinTech, transformation of financial intermediation and financial stability.* Paper presented at the 2018 International Scientific-Practical Conference Problems of Infocommunications. Science and Technology (PIC S&T). 10.1109/ INFOCOMMST.2018.8632068

Park, J. Y., Ryu, J. P., & Shin, H. J. (2016). Robo advisors for portfolio management. *Advanced Science and Technology Letters*, *141*(1), 104–108. doi:10.14257/ astl.2016.141.21

Prawirasasra, K. P. (2018). Financial technology in Indonesia: Disruptive or collaborative. *Reports on Economics and Finance*, *4*(2), 83–90. doi:10.12988/ ref.2018.818

Rupeika-Apoga, R., & Thalassinos, E. I. (2020). *Ideas for a regulatory definition of FinTech.* Academic Press.

Ryu, H.-S. (2018). What makes users willing or hesitant to use FinTech?: The moderating effect of user type. *Industrial Management & Data Systems*, *118*(3), 541–569. doi:10.1108/IMDS-07-2017-0325

Schindler, J. W. (2017). *FinTech and financial innovation: Drivers and depth.* Academic Press.

Schulte, P., & Liu, G. (2017). FinTech is merging with iot and AI to challenge banks: How entrenched interests can prepare. *Journal of Alternative Investments*, *20*(3), 41–57. doi:10.3905/jai.2018.20.3.041

Shin, Y. J., & Choi, Y. (2019). Feasibility of the FinTech industry as an innovation platform for sustainable economic growth in Korea. *Sustainability*, *11*(19), 5351. doi:10.3390u11195351

Singh, S., Sahni, M. M., & Kovid, R. K. (2020). What drives FinTech adoption? A multi-method evaluation using an adapted technology acceptance model. *Management Decision*, *58*(8), 1675–1697. doi:10.1108/MD-09-2019-1318

Sjamsudin, S. H. (2019). The impact of the development of FinTech on the existing financial services in Indonesia. *International Journal of Advanced Research in Technology and Innovation*, *1*(1), 14–23.

Song, K. (2015). Investigation of Business Model on FinTech Payment System. *The E-Business Studies, 16*(6), 65-94.

Srivastava, V., & Dashottar, S. (2020). Default probability assessment for project finance bank loans and Basel regulations: Searching for a new paradigm. *The Journal of Structured Finance*, *25*(4), 41–53. doi:10.3905/jsf.2019.1.088

Stern, C., Makinen, M., & Qian, Z. (2017). FinTechs in China–with a special focus on peer to peer lending. *Journal of Chinese Economic and Foreign Trade Studies*.

Suryono, R. R., Budi, I., & Purwandari, B. (2020). Challenges and trends of financial technology (FinTech): A systematic literature review. *Information (Basel)*, *11*(12), 590. doi:10.3390/info11120590

Suryono, R. R., Marlina, E., Purwaningsih, M., Sensuse, D. I., & Sutoyo, M. A. H. (2019). *Challenges in P2P lending development: Collaboration with tourism commerce.* Paper presented at the 2019 International Conference on Computer Science, Information Technology, and Electrical Engineering (ICOMITEE).

Taherdoost, H. (2023). FinTech: Emerging Trends and the Future of Finance. *Financial Technologies and DeFi: A Revisit to the Digital Finance Revolution*, 29-39.

Thakor, A. V. (2020). FinTech and banking: What do we know? *Journal of Financial Intermediation*, *41*, 100833. doi:10.1016/j.jfi.2019.100833

Tian, X., Han, R., Wang, L., Lu, G., & Zhan, J. (2015). Latency critical big data computing in finance. *The Journal of Finance and Data Science*, *1*(1), 33–41. doi:10.1016/j.jfds.2015.07.002

Truby, J., Brown, R., & Dahdal, A. (2020). Banking on AI: Mandating a proactive approach to AI regulation in the financial sector. *Law and Financial Markets Review*, *14*(2), 110–120. doi:10.1080/17521440.2020.1760454

Varga, D. (2017). FinTech, the new era of financial services. *Vezetéstudomány-Budapest Management Review*, *48*(11), 22–32. doi:10.14267/VEZTUD.2017.11.03

Velasco, P. R. (2017). Computing ledgers and the political ontology of the blockchain. *Metaphilosophy*, *48*(5), 712–726. doi:10.1111/meta.12274

Venkatesh, V., Thong, J. Y., & Xu, X. (2012). Consumer acceptance and use of information technology: Extending the unified theory of acceptance and use of technology. *Management Information Systems Quarterly*, *36*(1), 157–178. doi:10.2307/41410412

Vučinić, M. (2020). FinTech and financial stability potential influence of FinTech on financial stability, risks and benefits. *Journal of Central Banking Theory and Practice*, *9*(2), 43–66. doi:10.2478/jcbtp-2020-0013

Wang, H., Wang, Z., Zhang, B., & Zhou, J. (2019). *Information collection for fraud detection in P2P financial market*. arXiv preprint arXiv:1910.02009.10.2991/aebmr.k.210319.097

Wang, S. (2021). *Opportunities of Financial Technology Under the Impact of COVID-19*. Paper presented at the 6th international conference on financial innovation and economic development (ICFIED 2021). 10.2991/aebmr.k.210319.097

Wang, X., Xu, X., Feagan, L., Huang, S., Jiao, L., & Zhao, W. (2018). *Inter-bank payment system on enterprise blockchain platform*. Paper presented at the 2018 IEEE 11th international conference on cloud computing (CLOUD). 10.1109/CLOUD.2018.00085

Wonglimpiyarat, J. (2017). FinTech banking industry: a systemic approach. *Foresight*, *19*(6), 590-603.

Wonglimpiyarat, J. (2019). What is it about strategic implications of using financial models in the process of technology management? *The Journal of High Technology Management Research*, *30*(1), 82–90. doi:10.1016/j.hitech.2018.12.001

Xu, J. (2022). Biometrics in FinTech: A Technological Review. *Future And FinTech, The: Abcdi and Beyond*, 361.

Yacoub, G. (2017). Collaborative Innovation and Appropriability in Start-ups: Evidence from the FinTech Sector. *Academy of Management Proceedings*. 10.5465/AMBPP.2017.13674abstract

Zachariadis, M., & Ozcan, P. (2017). *The API economy and digital transformation in financial services: The case of open banking*. Academic Press.

Zachariadis, M., Ozcan, P., & Dinckol, D. (2018). The economics and strategy of platforms: Competing in the era of open banking. *The book on open banking: A series of essays on the next evolution of money*, 59-70.

Zhang, B. Z., Ashta, A., & Barton, M. E. (2021). Do FinTech and financial incumbents have different experiences and perspectives on the adoption of artificial intelligence? *Strategic Change, 30*(3), 223–234. doi:10.1002/jsc.2405

Chapter 2
People in Cryptocurrency:
Role and Beliefs

Mitra Madanchian
Hamta Group–Hamta Business Corporation, Canada

ABSTRACT

Cryptocurrency has transformed the global economic system. It offers a novel and creative form of trade that has rapidly transformed the financial markets and the world of cash. A person's best allocation is determined by combining their priorities for risk reduction and upside opportunity with bitcoin's predicted diversity and return qualities. However, people have a poor tolerance for blockchain-based cryptocurrencies, owing to the rise of online fraud and the lack of a legal framework. In addition, there is a widespread misperception about its use on various platforms, which has left a void in the literature addressing this topic. This chapter will discuss the role and views of cryptocurrency users.

INTRODUCTION

Worldwide, the digital economy is growing swiftly, forcing profound changes in all market actors' business models (Nasir et al., 2020). As technology evolves, consumer demand for quick, inexpensive, easy, and flexible transactions continues to fuel the expansion of payment systems (DeVries, 2016). The development of decentralized digital currencies known as cryptocurrencies and their online payment systems based on a peer-to-peer network referred to as blockchain are two of the most recent and exciting innovations in the financial scene (Sas & Khairuddin, 2017).

Due to advancements in blockchain-based technology, international businesses are switching to bitcoin for financial transactions (Han, Lee, Radic, Ngah, & Kim,

DOI: 10.4018/978-1-6684-8368-8.ch002

2021; Hooper & Holtbrügge, 2020). E-commerce is one of today's rising sectors, but it often deals with issues including exploitation of personal data, restricted buyer-seller communications, commission fees, and fraud (Frik & Mittone, 2019). However, using cryptocurrency for smart contracts and payments to increase security and transparency resolves these problems (Ismanto, Ar, Fajar, & Bachtiar, 2019). They are becoming more and more popular since they handle the current payment systems by offering a novel view of money and carrying out online transactions without the need of a middleman (Johar, Ahmad, Asher, Cruickshank, & Durrani, 2021). It is a crucial investment vehicle that cannot be disregarded in the modern digital era (Uematsu & Tanaka, 2019). However, the way in which investors utilize it and the way financial institutions regulate it will influence how it evolves in the future (Berentsen & Schär, 2018). In the past, researchers hypothesized that individuals could be more willing to accept new innovations if they are aware of technology (Irfan, Ali, & Sabir, 2022). Government regulations, as well as other factors like a lack of knowledge about digital handling, are also impeding its deployment (Putri, Wijayanti, & Ariani, 2021). A user's choice to use bitcoin is significantly influenced by perceived factors such as experience, ease of use, trust, and usefulness as well as legislation and backing from the government. (Wu & Tran, 2018). Studies on cryptocurrencies have shown that one of the most important criteria in determining whether to use it for electronic payments are perceived behavioral aspects (Schaupp & Festa, 2018).

People are more likely to utilize cryptocurrencies if they think they are easy to use. According to Shahzad et al. (Shahzad, Xiu, Wang, & Shahbaz, 2018), perceived variables have a significant influence on people's intentions to use cryptocurrencies. The gap between the outcomes and the extent to which innovation is applied determines the perceived risk (San Martín & Camarero, 2009). There are several reasons why people are reluctant to adopt new technologies, but the main one is the degree of uncertainty (Mizanur & Sloan, 2017). Perceived risk is also a key element in the use and adoption of technology. From the perspective of the user, legislation and legality are the main considerations when implementing this technical breakthrough in the monetary system (Albayati, Kim, & Rho, 2020). However, due to the surge in online fraud and the absence of a regulatory environment, consumers have a low tolerance for blockchain-based cryptocurrencies. Furthermore, there is a gap in the literature on this subject due to the widespread misconception regarding its utilization across numerous platforms. The chapter will address the role that bitcoin users play as well as their perspectives.

BACKGROUND OF CRYPTOCURRENCY

According to the World Bank, a digital or paperless economy is a framework for cultural, economic, or social relations that is centered on the use of communication technologies and digital information. It is the most crucial component of the system, and it continues to make a significant contribution to the creation, gathering, processing, and transmission of information. Additionally, some experts think that the paperless economy is a stage in the development of the current economic system's efficiency as it moves closer to the sixth or fourth technology revolution (Solovykh, Koroleva, Stompeleva, Terskaya, & Aliev, 2019). Cryptocurrency, which has been instrumental in the development of the digital economy model, is a major component of the digital financial market. The history of cryptocurrencies is really impressive.

Although the concept of digital currency has existed since the 1980s, it was not until 2009 that cryptocurrency began to be widely utilized with the launch of Bitcoin, a decentralized cryptocurrency that uses Blockchain technology (Nakamoto, 2008). Blockchain was developed with the goal of developing a decentralized environment free from outside interference with data and transaction processing. Blockchain is a kind of distributed database that keeps an ever-growing list of data entries that are verified by mining nodes. The information is maintained in a public ledger that includes information on every transaction that has been made (Yli-Huumo, Ko, Choi, Park, & Smolander, 2016). Blockchain is a decentralized system that operates without external interference. Due to blockchain, every node has access to every data pertaining to every transaction that has ever been made (Niranjanamurthy, Nithya, & Jagannatha, 2019). This characteristic makes blockchain transactions more transparent and open than typical centralized transactions via a third party. As an additional degree of security for nodes to verify the transaction, all notes on the blockchain are anonymous (Evans, Aré, Forth, Harlé, & Portincaso, 2016). Each node finishes the whole mining process each time a block is verified, and they are compensated for their labor. Since a sizable user base is eager to examine and confirm recent Bitcoin transaction data, anybody may start mining (Fung & Halaburda, 2014).

Cryptocurrency technology moved the banking industry one step closer to the future by decentralizing the money and releasing it from hierarchical power systems. Instead, peer-to-peer networks are used by consumers and companies to conduct digital transactions (DeVries, 2016). With the usage of bitcoin, consumers may transact value electronically on their own without the assistance of third parties or intermediaries (Treiblmaier & Sillaber, 2021). The concept behind an encryption technique is often solved in the course of a bitcoin transaction to provide a set of unique, finite hash values (DeVries, 2016). By leveraging a network of computer nodes to certify transactions, consumers may exchange and trade hushes similarly to regular fiat money (Vaz & Brown, 2020).

As the usage of cryptocurrencies developed, many businesses found the new platform to be enticing due to its lack of processing fees, higher security, and improved functionality. Processing costs are an additional important consideration since each transaction is billed to the company (Halaburda, 2018). Theoretically, adopting the new system would provide a rapid, safe, automated method of transferring goods or services for cash, free of fee to banks or other types of brokers (Dumitrescu, 2017). How satisfied a cryptocurrency user is with the value of that bitcoin product may be determined by the customer satisfaction statistic. This information is useful when a business wishes to enhance or modify its offerings to better cater to bitcoin users (Chen et al., 2022). It is essential to comprehend what is meant by rapid in terms of transaction processing.

FACTORS

Bitcoin and other cryptocurrencies have been hailed as innovative and possibly disruptive financial technologies. Without the aid of a central clearinghouse or other reliable third party, the "double spending problem" inherent to digital currencies could be resolved in a novel way thanks to Bitcoin's blockchain (Böhme, Christin, Edelman, & Moore, 2015). Therefore, it is possible to see how active support for Bitcoin is fundamentally connected to the opportunities made possible by these distinctive technologies, making it an alluring alternative to conventional money for certain user groups (Ermakova, Fabian, Baumann, Izmailov, & Krasnova, 2017). Bitcoin's ability to do away with the need for a reliable third party or disintermediation, as well as its cryptographic technology, which enables pseudonymity in online transactions, both result in opportunities (Cohen, 2017). This section examines the elements that affect the choice to adopt.

Income Equality

Given the adoption cost and auxiliary considerations like human capital, technology adoption in developing nations has lagged behind that of industrialized ones (De Gregorio, 2018). Technology has the potential to increase social and economic disparities by eroding certain occupations while creating others for technical workers. Analyzing the opposite causality from that considered in the present study, technology advancement may also lessen income disparity (Adrián Risso & Sánchez Carrera, 2019). The adoption of blockchain technology and cryptocurrencies may both be influenced by income inequality (Sai, Buckley, & Le Gear, 2021).

Inflation

Due to its position as a worldwide currency that is unconnected to any particular economy, bitcoin has the potential to serve as a hedging option against country-specific risk. Particularly, investing in bitcoins offers a fresh opportunity to hedge against (very) high inflation, just as gold and other assets have been known to do in the past (Arnold & Auer, 2015). As indicated by the large numbers of Bolivians and Peruvians who moved to US dollars during similar national crises in the 1980s because they felt safer, Luther (Luther, 2016) asserts that currency shifts typically occur during times of hyperinflation. As a result, people who are negatively affected by exceptionally high inflation could be more keen to promote, use, and own bitcoin as a rival financial system. Cryptocurrencies have undoubtedly received plaudits from their supporters as a means of constructing a financial system that is less vulnerable to crises (Maurer, Nelms, & Swartz, 2013) and as a means of balancing (hyper)inflation (Kapsis, 2020). According to other studies, interest in bitcoins has increased in nations with high levels of inflation. This is evident in the case of Venezuela, where inflation shot through the roof, confidence in the currency and monetary policies of the country fell, and interest in bitcoins rose as indicated by the widespread use of bitcoin mining (Kliber, Marszałek, Musiałkowska, & Świerczyńska, 2019).

Cost of Transactions

According to studies, Bitcoin transactions, for instance, are less frequent than those on the retail foreign exchange market. The bid-ask margins for Bitcoin are 2% less than those of retail foreign currency markets (Kim, 2017). When high transaction costs of typical transactions either make a transaction unprofitable or reduce its advantages, Bitcoin provides a welcome alternative (Dierksmeier & Seele, 2018). Cryptocurrencies' ease of exchange may provide much-needed liquidity to beneficiaries of micropayments or loans in emerging and undeveloped nations, providing the world's "unbanked" millions with an unheard-of level of comfort and security (Vigna & Casey, 2016). Such people are forced to save cash because they lack access to or the necessary papers to utilize a banking institution, putting themselves in risk and restricting their ability to conduct business with anybody except those near them (Dierksmeier & Seele, 2018).

High Control Level

The user has complete control over their own money thanks to cryptocurrency systems. It is regarded as one of the most alluring and alluring benefits offered to customers by cryptocurrencies. With the use of cryptocurrencies, users may send and receive any amount of money to anybody, anywhere in the world. The users have complete control over the data about their finances. More financial control is possible with the removal of middlemen. Users of this potent instrument should be capable of managing and controlling their finances (Folkinshteyn & Lennon, 2016). The possibility of human mistakes is one danger. Additionally, the individual should ensure the safety and security of the infrastructure used to hold money. Even if many users prefer to have complete control over their finances, there are also drawbacks like the possibility of losing coins for a variety of causes. The fact that users are responsible for the coins' security is one concern. According to one research, hardware failure accounted for 26.5% of the sample's reported Bitcoin losses, software failure accounted for 24.4%, and security breaches accounted for 18% (Krombholz, Judmayer, Gusenbauer, & Weippl, 2017).

Banking Market Development and Alternative

Cryptocurrency may be used to store money or to replace existing banking systems since it is often unattached to a government or other central authority. It may be utilized as a store of assets or wealth as well as money. A study of the experiences of Bitcoin users revealed that some of them use cryptocurrency as both an insurance policy for their savings and a store of value for their investments (Sas & Khairuddin, 2017).

The insufficient availability of traditional banking services may be replaced by financial technology, as shown, for instance, by the use of mobile money accounts for money transfers in Sub-Saharan Africa (Demirguc-Kunt, Klapper, Singer, & Ansar, 2018). Digital currencies have been hailed as an effective tool for connecting with businesses and people in remote and disadvantaged areas (Kshetri, 2021). Most modern payment systems, including credit and debit cards, rely on the existence of middlemen with bank accounts. Digital currencies might end up becoming the unbanked's preferred means of payment (i.e., those without bank accounts). According to a detailed examination of the Bitcoin community, helping the unbanked is one of the currency's key asserted promises (Vigna & Casey, 2016).

Level of Democracy

Democracy is thought to lower the digital gap by encouraging innovation and quick adoption of new technologies (Gao, Zang, Roth, & Wang, 2017). By decreasing information asymmetries via e-democracy procedures, e-governance, identity management, and decentralized voting, blockchain-based solutions provide people with greater power. According to Aysan et al. (Aysan, Demir, Gozgor, & Lau, 2019), geopolitical concerns have a positive and negative relationship with Bitcoin's price volatility and returns. They contend that using Bitcoin as a hedge against geopolitical risks is a good idea. Cryptocurrencies are also the ideal answer to the issues of decentralization and bad governance in many democracies since they cannot be counterfeited. Decentralized local spending, according to Boret et al. (Boret, Gawande, & Kobb, 2021), may aid in reducing poverty. Decentralization, however, requires either confidence in the local administration or a strong mechanism that prevents theft. Cryptocurrencies provide solutions to these issues, making them more likely to be accepted by democratic nations and strengthening them overall.

BELIEFS

Cryptocurrencies are used by people for several reasons, such as quick payments, avoiding transaction fees levied by traditional banks, or because they provide some degree of anonymity. Some individuals make investments in cryptocurrencies with the expectation that they would rise in value. Researchers are starting to be interested in user adoption in addition to studies on the technical features of bitcoin, such as the validation of transactions as mentioned in (Decker & Wattenhofer, 2013). Darlington (Darlington III, 2014) proposes the argument that since bitcoin addresses the issues of inaccessibility, counterfeiting, exchange, and hyperinflation, it offers a specific benefit to people living in suffering and undeveloped economies. The article also suggests three barriers to bitcoin adoption in these failing economies: apprehension about the future, possible issues with the bitcoin network itself, and a lack of infrastructure. Lack of faith in the financial system (about 10% of the sample), freedom (about 16% of the sample), and anonymity (about 8% of the sample) were determined to be the primary motivating factors, according to Bohr and Bashir's (Bohr & Bashir, 2014) study. The varied perspectives of people—both good and negative—are attempted to be presented in this part.

Social Behavior

A prerequisite for economic commerce, trust is positively correlated with financial investments and growth (Zak & Knack, 2001). According to Cohen (Cohen, 2017), the 99% movement, which was sparked by the Occupy Wall Street rallies, and discontent with banks that had grown to be too large to fail were the driving forces behind the emergence of bitcoin. The creation of the Bitcoin system was motivated by idealistic ideas of fostering an alternative monetary and financial system that would allow for more autonomy, privacy, and anonymity (Dodd, 2018). The blockchain that underpins cryptocurrencies enables inexpensive and automated verification on distributed ledgers, allowing for the replacement of trust in an intermediary with trust in the developed code and rules that specify how the network reaches consensus (Goldfarb & Tucker, 2019). A decrease in confidence in banks and other financial institutions, according to Saiedi et al. (Saiedi, Mohammadi, Broström, & Shafi, 2022), boosts the involvement of borrowers and lenders, respectively, in online peer-to-peer (P2P) lending marketplaces. Also developing are theoretical works that simulate intermediary and Fintech firm replacements motivated by trust (Thakor & Merton, 2018).

Possibility of Facilitating Illegal Activity

Bitcoin's unique pseudonymity technology makes it appealing to those involved in criminal activity, including the trafficking of guns, drugs, and prescription drugs (Foley, Karlsen, & Putniņš, 2019). According to Bohannon (Bohannon, 2016), criminals were attracted to bitcoin because of its alleged anonymity. According to Böhme et al. (Böhme et al., 2015), the primary motivations for early users of bitcoin were increased anonymity and a lack of restrictions on what could be bought with the money. Dark-net marketplaces, or markets on encrypted websites that do not show via standard Internet surfing, are the source of almost all bitcoins used for illegal activities and cleaned up through exchange services (Fanusie & Robinson, 2018). In theory, limiting the use of bitcoin for illegal purposes may be possible with more efficient law enforcement. However, recent evidence indicates that modern law enforcement is unable to significantly reduce Internet-related crime (Holt, Smirnova, Chua, & Copes, 2015). Most nations do not specifically investigate drug trafficking through the Internet (Lavorgna, 2014). Compared to other methods, drug purchasers and dealers on the dark web believe their chances of being arrested are substantially reduced (Aldridge & Decary-Hétu, 2016).

Anonymity

The idea of virtual currency is a new, somewhat unanticipated development in the contemporary financial landscape. The first profitable virtual currency was Bitcoin, which was thereafter adopted by several other systems. Similar to physical currencies, it is clear that consumers' acceptance of virtual currencies is influenced by two key factors: privacy and anonymity (Amarasinghe, Boyen, & McKague, 2019). An important element of the financial sector is anonymity, and bitcoin has offered a greater degree of it than the conventional banking system. On the other side, people could see this functionality as a facilitator for crime, which might constitute an adoption obstacle.

Subjective Norms

The adoption's outcome is significantly influenced by the impact of family and friends. A "person's judgment that most people who are significant to him believe he should or should not conduct the action in issue" is described as having subjective norms (Douglass, 1977). The Unified Theory of Acceptance and Use of Technology (UTAUT) (Venkatesh, Morris, Davis, & Davis, 2003) and the Technology Acceptance Model 2 (TAM2) (Venkatesh & Davis, 2000) are two models and theories that have looked at the adoption and acceptance of technology. To capture social impact as a predictor of the desire to adopt technology, the subjective norms construct was developed. The degree to which a person believes that significant individuals think they should accept and utilize cryptocurrencies is known as social influence. Families and friends are influencing one another's purchases of alternative currencies since cryptocurrency is popular. The subjective norm construct was a common addition to the models used in several research that looked at the adoption and usage of cryptocurrencies. Subjective norm was identified as a crucial component for the future acceptance of cryptocurrencies in interview-based research looking at the perspectives of bitcoin users (Baur, Bühler, Bick, & Bonorden, 2015). To investigate user behavior around Bitcoin and comprehend its uptake, Silinskyte (Silinskyte, 2014) utilized the UTAUT. The goal of the research was to discover key elements, such as subjective norms, that predict individuals' intentions to embrace Bitcoin. According to Baur et al. (Baur et al., 2015), the nature of Bitcoin encourages peer influence. If their peers accept cryptocurrencies, users are prepared to do the same. Another subjective norm aspect that may encourage adoption is word of mouth.

Technological Curiosity

Many individuals invest in cryptocurrencies only to research this cutting-edge technology. For all technology, there are innovators and early adopters who are motivated by their curiosity about cutting-edge new solutions. The first two stages of the technology adoption lifecycle are the inventors and early adopters. The popularity of cryptocurrencies is influenced by people's curiosity about this novel idea of money (Bohannon, 2016). Technology curiosity is a key driver of Bitcoin adoption, according to a study by Presthus and O'Malley (Presthus & O'Malley, 2017) on the user incentives for doing so. According to Dokic et al. (Đokić, Radman-Funarić, & Potnik Galić, 2015), financial, political, and intellectual curiosity are the main drivers of Bitcoin adoption. The market for new technologies is being examined with enthusiasm and interest by younger generations.

Perceived Risk

One should take into account both a risk's defining qualities and the likelihood of undesirable results and effects to evaluate risk. Perceived risk has been included in consumer decision-making models as an explanatory factor (Srinivasan & Ratchford, 1991). Perceived risk has a significant impact on consumer decision-making (Conchar, Zinkhan, Peters, & Olavarrieta, 2004). According to Taylor's (Taylor, 1974) theory, it is simple to predict how individuals will act about a danger once the amount of perceived risk has been established. Thus, if their perception of risk is established, investors' goals and motives may be better comprehended.

Assessments of products and services, as well as the adoption of new technology and services, have all been researched about risk perceptions. Studies have demonstrated that views or evaluations of the dangers related to specific conduct, known as risk perceptions, may influence how individuals behave and think. The likelihood that a customer would choose an alternate product is decreased by risk perceptions associated with making a bad or improper selection (Vijayasarathy & Jones, 2000). Investment items have a potentially greater level of risk for consumers than other products since the financial value is typically bigger and there are no assurances or ways to return a purchase and get a complete refund. Arias-Oliva et al. (Arias-Oliva, Pelegrín-Borondo, & Matías-Clavero, 2019) discovered that danger was not a significant factor in affecting the adoption of cryptocurrencies in Spain and suggested that this may be because the majority of respondents believed that there was no risk involved with cryptocurrencies. According to Faqih (Faqih, 2016), perceived risk in behavioral research refers to how uncertain customers believe utilizing or buying a product would be, as well as any potential negative repercussions. The findings of recent research examining how perceived risk influences people's willingness to utilize financial technology have been conflicting. For instance, Mendoza-Tello et al. (Mendoza-Tello, Mora, Pujol-López, & Lytras, 2018) found no relationship between perceived risk and the choice to use cryptocurrencies for electronic payments. Perceived risk is taken into account in the current research to comprehend how retail investors perceive risk while making bitcoin investments. The following hypothesis was thus put out based on the idea that cryptocurrencies are a novel financial technology with potential dangers.

Perceived Value

The anticipated benefit or loss from utilizing a certain item or service is known as perceived value (Zeithaml, 1988). The two domains of perceived utility and pleasure of a person being investigated as two aspects of the exceedingly complicated component known as perceived value (Hsu & Lin, 2015). Usefulness is cited as a driving force behind people's desire to utilize a particular technology in studies on technology adoption. Numerous studies define the benefits a person may get from a particular technology and its relative worth to the person as the assessment of the desire to apply a new technology (Pham & Ho, 2015). People's opinions of the usage and pleasure of blockchain technology are thus anticipated to affect their intentions to adopt it (Yang, Yu, Zo, & Choi, 2016). According to many types of research, behavioral intention is influenced by utility and pleasure (Baabdullah, 2018). The research has also discussed the effects of perceived value as an independent variable and behavioral intention as a dependent variable (Abramova & Böhme, 2016). If the perceived value is seen as a multidimensional component, people may have stronger behavioral intentions to utilize blockchain if they anticipate it to deliver higher perceived value. Even though cryptocurrencies have no inherent value, investors' attitudes toward large returns are significantly more important for identifying greater times of return predictability (Cheah & Fry, 2015).

Exchange rate swings between cryptocurrencies and fiat currencies enable trading and speculation on exchange markets. Many buyers of cryptocurrencies want to take advantage of the significant price volatility and hold onto their investments until exchange rates rise rather than utilize them to pay for products or services (Böhme et al., 2015). This fact relates to the continuing discussion regarding whether cryptocurrencies should be seen as a form of money or just an investing tool in academics and practice (Glaser, Zimmermann, Haferkorn, Weber, & Siering, 2014). According to Mendoza-Tello et al. (Mendoza-Tello et al., 2018), people's intentions to use cryptocurrencies for electronic payments are most strongly influenced by their perception of their utility. They also discovered that people are more likely to utilize cryptocurrencies if they think they are simple to use.

According to a study by Polasik et al. (Polasik, Piotrowska, Wisniewski, Kotkowski, & Lightfoot, 2015), the level of transactions and media attention they get, as well as the acceptance of cryptocurrencies like Bitcoin, all have an impact on how lucrative and successful they are. Investors are drawn to cryptocurrencies as an investment option due to their perceived attractive qualities, accessibility even on the weekends, high average return, extremely high market volatility, and low correlation with traditional assets, all of which are features that have significant diversification benefits (Briere, Oosterlinck, & Szafarz, 2015).

Since the launch of Bitcoin in 2009, the cryptocurrency market has undergone significant upheaval, and it is only now beginning to penetrate significant global financial institutions. A key factor influencing the growth and proliferation of cryptocurrencies is the public's growing acceptance and knowledge of them. As a consequence, cryptocurrencies are now a favored mode of payment and pose a threat to important global commodity currencies. This suggests that cryptocurrencies' evolution, adoption, and use as a method of the cross-border payment will be influenced by how people perceive them in the future (Gorbunov, 2021).

ROLES AND EFFECTS

In addition to its many benefits, such as fast, simple, traceable, and secure transactions, cryptocurrencies also have certain drawbacks, including financial and technical complexity, inherent risk, and a murky social concept of ownership. Due to the intricacy and implications of these developments, it is crucial to explore the consequences and challenges of the cryptocurrency and blockchain revolution from an interdisciplinary perspective. Utilizing technology acceptance models, it specifically looks at how perceived risk, performance expectation, enabling factors, effort expectancy, social influence, and financial literacy affect users' intentions to use bitcoins. If the main factors influencing consumer acceptance of cryptocurrencies were to be determined, current and future market players may focus on the most important qualities a cryptocurrency should have. The role of people in cryptocurrencies is covered in this section.

Risk and Trust

Customers believe that the danger associated with blockchain technology is what worries them the most. Technology has to have enough confidence to advance in the fiercely competitive market (Wunsche, 2016) to prevent this. The feedback findings demonstrate how crucial consumer adoption of new technology is. Little feedback on technological viability is given to inventors, who then proceed to enhance their company's innovation. Additionally, greater information and projections might raise the likelihood of acceptance (Tornatzky, Fleischer, & Chakrabarti, 1990). By gauging client behavior intentions, attitude may forecast the actual usage of a given technology (Salloum, Alhamad, Al-Emran, Monem, & Shaalan, 2019). Blockchain technology has recently gained popularity across many new platforms, particularly for use in financial applications. However, the degree of client utilization was lower than anticipated (Wunsche, 2016). This worry prompts researchers to look into why users do not adopt blockchain-based cryptocurrencies, preferring instead to continue using conventional banking systems that are expensive, time-consuming, and provide them little privacy or control (Martins, Oliveira, & Popovič, 2014).

Several recent studies have looked at the effect of perceived risk on the willingness to use financial technology, with mixed results. Internet banking supports perceived security as a strong predictor of behavioral intentions, according to Khan et al. (Khan, Hameed, & Khan, 2017) According to Kishore and Sequeira's (Kishore & Sequeira,

2016) study, the adoption of mobile banking in rural regions is somewhat moderately explained by perceived risk. According to the study by Shaikh et al. (Shaikh, Glavee-Geo, & Karjaluoto, 2021), while perceived risk has a usually minimal direct impact on the intention to use mobile banking, it has a significant pre-adoption impact by affecting other factors that subsequently have a direct impact on the intention to use. Moon and Hwang find no evidence that the motivation to use crowdfunding is negatively impacted by the sense of risk (Moon & Hwang, 2018).

Demand

The price that people are prepared to pay for Bitcoins is socially-agreed upon the amount that is also dependent on supply and demand, just like any asset or object of worth. Some individuals find it difficult to understand that Bitcoins are scarce and that they have a cost of creation since they are virtual and only exist inside computer networks. They continue to believe that Bitcoins are worthless because they are hesitant to believe that digital traces may have value in this manner. Others who are familiar with the Bitcoin system concur that it has value.

Cryptocurrency demand is influenced by a variety of elements, including how useful the coins are and whether or not companies accept them. The following are some more elements that affect how much a cryptocurrency is worth.

- **Availability:** The value of a cryptocurrency may increase if it is more easily accessible on multiple exchanges.
- **Regulation:** When it comes to value, there are both good and bad effects of the absence of regulation. While some investors like the independence that comes with no rules, others are concerned about security and control. Regulations may be advantageous since they would make investors feel more confident about investing in cryptocurrencies. Requirements, however, may potentially have a detrimental impact on the value of cryptocurrencies by reducing demand and altering investing regulations.
- **Increasing Usefulness:** When companies embrace cryptocurrencies and if there is an investment potential, utility rises. Its value may also be impacted by its use in decentralized financial protocols or decentralized applications.
- **Fame in the Media:** When a cryptocurrency is covered in the media, prices often change; this also applies to social media advertising.

Role of Media

When examining the interplay of social factors affecting the bitcoin market, it is essential to consider the effect of media on public perception. Newspapers, radio, television, and now online and mobile phone technologies all fall under the category of mass media communication and are used to disseminate information to the general public. The power of the media to instruct the public on what to think about, how to think about, and maybe even what to do about, important topics is the subject of agenda-setting and framing theories in mass communication. Information and trust are important elements influencing market capitalization and user confidence in these exchanges, according to research by Tsvetkova et al. (Tsvetkova et al., 2017) on human-machine interactions in prediction markets.

Financial Literacy

To benefit from financial breakthroughs, one should be financially literate and sophisticated (Campbell, 2006). Gazel and Schwienbacher (Gazel & Schwienbacher, 2021), for instance, discover that areas with more bank headquarters and financial competitiveness attract more Fintech clusters. Externalities from such a development might include increased knowledge of financial technology and, as a result, interest in cryptocurrencies like bitcoin. Additionally, it's feasible that in a more dynamic banking environment where competition spurs bank to innovate, customers may be less hesitant to test out novel electronic services. According to research by Grohmann et al. (Grohmann, Klühs, & Menkhoff, 2018), financial inclusion and financial literacy go hand in hand, and it follows that using sophisticated financial innovations like bitcoins would likely need a high degree of both.

Investment Opportunity

Rather than the desire to utilize them as money, investing in cryptocurrencies may be driven more by the financial prospects they may provide. Users are more interested in cryptocurrencies as investment possibilities than as payment options or as a medium of exchange (Glaser et al., 2014). Due to the market's high volatility and uncertain exchange rate, choosing to invest in cryptocurrencies demands careful consideration (Vo & Xu, 2017).

Personal Growth

Data on per capita income, level of education, and life expectancy are all combined to create the human development index. The use of information, communication, and technology for human development in sub-Saharan Africa is shown by Asongu and Le Roux (Asongu & Le Roux, 2017). With enhanced data accessibility, the capacity to conduct analytical operations, enhancing the effectiveness of the Internet of Healthy Things, protecting of internet-connected medical equipment, and battling fake medicine, it can transform the drug research and development process (Clauson, Breeden, Davidson, & Mackey, 2018). Significantly lowering the use of fake drugs may be accomplished with the use of blockchain-enabled auditability, traceability, and secure databases for storing and retrieving data from drug trials (Rehman, Javed, Qureshi, Margaria, & Jeon, 2022). The right to share a patient's data stored on a blockchain network may facilitate speedier information exchange, assist prevent data corruption, and prevent the unlawful sale of data (Hughes, Park, Kietzmann, & Archer-Brown, 2019). Certain advantages related to human development may result from identification using blockchain technology. Smith and Floro (Smith & Floro, 2021) draw attention to the importance of remittance and migrant movements in alleviating food insecurity, particularly in low- and middle-income countries. These advantages may be multiplied in such economies utilizing blockchain. Blockchain-based solutions, including cryptocurrencies, have the potential to reduce bureaucracy and encourage collaboration among donors to guarantee the optimal use of resources in addition to enabling traceability, transparency, and cost reduction via the removal of middlemen (Galen et al., 2018).

Management of the System

The presence of the central authority is significant. The user network is trusted because cryptocurrencies are decentralized (Arli, van Esch, Bakpayev, & Laurence, 2021). With a system like this, there is no need for a centralized authority, consumers may participate in the free market, and the system is based on blockchain technology. Decentralized cryptocurrencies provide a higher level of transparency since all transactions are recorded in the public ledger and available to all users of the network (Chuen, Guo, & Wang, 2017). The network's miners validate the transactions. People utilize the network since only the users have control over it (Krombholz et al., 2017). Because the financial systems that rely on a trustworthy central authority have lost their trust, users are lured to this new system (Vo & Xu, 2017).

KEY DIFFERENTIATORS OF CRYPTOCURRENCY VIEW

Numerous individuals possess cryptocurrencies like Bitcoin. There are several influencing aspects to take into account, however. One of the main barriers to cryptocurrencies' mainstream acceptance is their largely unregulated status. This means that there are no laws governing their usage, which can deter some people from investing in them. Additionally, it is considerably more challenging for exchanges to defend their users from fraud and financial crime. Governments should control the cryptocurrency industry to protect investors from potential fraud and crime. Regulation, nevertheless, should not be too limiting and should allow for unrestricted creativity.

Scalability

Because cryptocurrencies have scalability issues, they may not be able to handle large numbers of transactions at once. As a result, it could be challenging to use them for normal transactions since they might take too long to process and finish. Additionally, due to the growing competition for block space, scalability issues may eventually result in increased transaction prices. For cryptocurrencies, developers are constantly creating new scaling methods and protocols to solve this issue. In the end, these developments should make it easier to use cryptocurrency for everyday transactions.

Utilitarian Benefit

Since Bitcoin has not yet gained widespread acceptance, many people still think of it as just an investment tool, despite the fact that this is not the case. Some of the most common uses of Bitcoin include payments, money transfers, and wealth preservation. Not everyone has, however, taken notice of these real-use cases. Moreover, utilizing digital wallets to keep bitcoin assets has significant dangers such as theft and hacking. Investors are encouraged to establish several levels of security, including the use of two-factor authentication and strong passwords, to safeguard their digital assets. To safeguard the safety of the funds belonging to its consumers, cryptocurrency exchanges should also have strong security protocols and carry out regular audits. Finally, investors should choose trustworthy secure wallets to protect their assets. As time goes on and the bitcoin market develops, it is anticipated that these security worries will decrease in frequency.

Regulatory and Legal Issues

Bitcoin has the potential to reach unbanked and underbanked populations due to its distinctive features, enabling them to take part in transactions they were previously excluded from. However, due to localized legal and regulatory issues, this objective is still being hindered in some areas. Even though bitcoin is decentralized, countries and their central banks still have the power to decide whether or not it is legal; some people remain dubious to this day. On the other hand, many nations that support Bitcoin have welcomed it with open arms.

Education

One of the biggest barriers to widespread cryptocurrency adoption is a general lack of understanding of what cryptocurrencies are and how they work. Greater awareness of the topic is required so that individuals can understand the risks associated with investing in digital money. Given that Bitcoin has just reached record highs, it is reasonable to argue that more people than ever are aware of it. With all the headlines, media references, social media postings, and more in only the last two years, it has established a mainstream presence. The next stage would be to educate people about how Bitcoin operates for it to have a real influence on the globe. For many people, the blockchain technology that underpins many of the most well-known cryptocurrencies today is complicated and challenging to comprehend. It is crucial to provide precise and succinct explanations of how cryptocurrencies work, their advantages over conventional financial systems, and their cutting-edge uses. Access to resources like online lessons and courses will raise awareness and motivate more individuals to engage in cryptocurrency.

Technological Aspect

The first of its kind, Bitcoin is a true digital money that uses cutting-edge technology to function. Bitcoin mining, the process of obtaining it, the need for digital storage space, a dependable internet connection, and powerful hardware. An internet-connected smartphone or desktop computer is necessary for purchasing, storing, and using Bitcoin. Even if the majority of people now have access to the necessary digital gadgets, having a reliable connection is still a problem. Due to high prices and unstable connectivity, not all regions of the globe have dependable internet access.

CONCLUSION

The worldwide economy has changed as a result of cryptocurrencies. The financial markets and the world of cash have quickly changed as a result of its unique and inventive style of exchange. Combining a person's goals for risk mitigation and upside possibility with bitcoin's anticipated variety and return characteristics yields the appropriate allocation for that individual. People's tolerance for blockchain-based cryptocurrencies is low, nevertheless, as a result of the surge in online fraud and the absence of a regulatory environment. Additionally, there is a gap in the literature on this subject due to the widespread misconception regarding its utilization across numerous platforms. The role and perspectives of bitcoin users were covered in this chapter. The results of this study aid in a better understanding of people's intentions regarding cryptocurrency adoption and their role of them. The market for cryptocurrencies and blockchain technology is growing despite the risks. The much-needed financial infrastructure is being built, and institutional-grade custodial services are becoming more readily available to investors. Both professional and retail investors are increasingly getting access to the tools needed to manage and safeguard their bitcoin assets. Before cryptocurrencies are broadly accepted by the general public, several issues should be resolved. These obstacles, which range from a lack of knowledge to regulatory ambiguity and security concerns, should be removed before consumers would use cryptocurrencies.

REFERENCES

Abramova, S., & Böhme, R. (2016). *Perceived benefit and risk as multidimensional determinants of bitcoin use: A quantitative exploratory study*. Academic Press.

Adrián Risso, W., & Sánchez Carrera, E. J. (2019). On the impact of innovation and inequality in economic growth. *Economics of Innovation and New Technology*, *28*(1), 64–81. doi:10.1080/10438599.2018.1429534

Albayati, H., Kim, S. K., & Rho, J. J. (2020). Accepting financial transactions using blockchain technology and cryptocurrency: A customer perspective approach. *Technology in Society*, *62*, 101320. doi:10.1016/j.techsoc.2020.101320

Aldridge, J., & Decary-Hétu, D. (2016). Cryptomarkets and the future of illicit drug markets. *The Internet and Drug Markets*, 23-32.

Amarasinghe, N., Boyen, X., & McKague, M. (2019). A survey of anonymity of cryptocurrencies. *Proceedings of the Australasian Computer Science Week Multiconference*. 10.1145/3290688.3290693

Arias-Oliva, M., Pelegrín-Borondo, J., & Matías-Clavero, G. (2019). Variables influencing cryptocurrency use: A technology acceptance model in Spain. *Frontiers in Psychology*, *10*, 475. doi:10.3389/fpsyg.2019.00475 PMID:30949085

Arli, D., van Esch, P., Bakpayev, M., & Laurence, A. (2021). Do consumers really trust cryptocurrencies? *Marketing Intelligence & Planning*, *39*(1), 74–90. doi:10.1108/MIP-01-2020-0036

Arnold, S., & Auer, B. R. (2015). What do scientists know about inflation hedging? *The North American Journal of Economics and Finance*, *34*, 187–214. doi:10.1016/j.najef.2015.08.005

Asongu, S. A., & Le Roux, S. (2017). Enhancing ICT for inclusive human development in Sub-Saharan Africa. *Technological Forecasting and Social Change*, *118*, 44–54. doi:10.1016/j.techfore.2017.01.026

Aysan, A. F., Demir, E., Gozgor, G., & Lau, C. K. M. (2019). Effects of the geopolitical risks on Bitcoin returns and volatility. *Research in International Business and Finance*, *47*, 511–518. doi:10.1016/j.ribaf.2018.09.011

Baabdullah, A. M. (2018). Consumer adoption of Mobile Social Network Games (M-SNGs) in Saudi Arabia: The role of social influence, hedonic motivation and trust. *Technology in Society*, *53*, 91–102. doi:10.1016/j.techsoc.2018.01.004

Baur, A. W., Bühler, J., Bick, M., & Bonorden, C. S. (2015). Cryptocurrencies as a disruption? empirical findings on user adoption and future potential of bitcoin and co. *Open and Big Data Management and Innovation: 14th IFIP WG 6.11 Conference on e-Business, e-Services, and e-Society, I3E 2015, Delft, The Netherlands, October 13-15, 2015, Proceedings, 14*. 10.1007/978-3-319-25013-7_6

Berentsen, A., & Schär, F. (2018). A short introduction to the world of cryptocurrencies. *FRB of St. Louis Working Review*.

Bohannon, J. (2016). *The bitcoin busts*. American Association for the Advancement of Science. doi:10.1126cience.351.6278.1144

Böhme, R., Christin, N., Edelman, B., & Moore, T. (2015). Bitcoin: Economics, technology, and governance. *The Journal of Economic Perspectives*, *29*(2), 213–238. doi:10.1257/jep.29.2.213

Bohr, J., & Bashir, M. (2014). *Who uses bitcoin? an exploration of the bitcoin community.* Paper presented at the 2014 Twelfth Annual International Conference on Privacy, Security and Trust. 10.1109/PST.2014.6890928

Boret, N., Gawande, K., & Kobb, D. P. (2021). Can decentralization lower poverty? Cambodia's Commune and Sangkat Fund. *World Development*, *146*, 105548. doi:10.1016/j.worlddev.2021.105548

Briere, M., Oosterlinck, K., & Szafarz, A. (2015). Virtual currency, tangible return: Portfolio diversification with bitcoin. *Journal of Asset Management*, *16*(6), 365–373. doi:10.1057/jam.2015.5

Campbell, J. Y. (2006). Household finance. *The Journal of Finance*, *61*(4), 1553–1604. doi:10.1111/j.1540-6261.2006.00883.x

Cheah, E.-T., & Fry, J. (2015). Speculative bubbles in Bitcoin markets? An empirical investigation into the fundamental value of Bitcoin. *Economics Letters*, *130*, 32–36. doi:10.1016/j.econlet.2015.02.029

Chen, X., Miraz, M. H., Gazi, M. A. I., Rahaman, M. A., Habib, M. M., & Hossain, A. I. (2022). Factors affecting cryptocurrency adoption in digital business transactions: The mediating role of customer satisfaction. *Technology in Society*, *70*, 102059. doi:10.1016/j.techsoc.2022.102059

Chuen, D. L. K., Guo, L., & Wang, Y. (2017). Cryptocurrency: A new investment opportunity? *Journal of Alternative Investments*, *20*(3), 16–40. doi:10.3905/jai.2018.20.3.016

Clauson, K. A., Breeden, E. A., Davidson, C., & Mackey, T. K. (2018). Leveraging Blockchain Technology to Enhance Supply Chain Management in Healthcare: An exploration of challenges and opportunities in the health supply chain. *Blockchain in Healthcare Today*.

Cohen, B. (2017). The rise of alternative currencies in post-capitalism. *Journal of Management Studies*, *54*(5), 739–746. doi:10.1111/joms.12245

Conchar, M. P., Zinkhan, G. M., Peters, C., & Olavarrieta, S. (2004). An integrated framework for the conceptualization of consumers' perceived-risk processing. *Journal of the Academy of Marketing Science*, *32*(4), 418–436. doi:10.1177/0092070304267551

Darlington III, J. K. (2014). *The future of Bitcoin: mapping the global adoption of world's largest cryptocurrency through benefit analysis*. Academic Press.

De Gregorio, J. (2018). *Productivity in Emerging-Market Economies: Slowdown or Stagnation?* Peterson Institute for International Economics Working Paper (18-12).

Decker, C., & Wattenhofer, R. (2013). Information propagation in the bitcoin network. *IEEE P2P 2013 Proceedings*. 10.1109/P2P.2013.6688704

Demirguc-Kunt, A., Klapper, L., Singer, D., & Ansar, S. (2018). *The Global Findex Database 2017: Measuring financial inclusion and the fintech revolution*. World Bank Publications. doi:10.1596/978-1-4648-1259-0

DeVries, P. D. (2016). An analysis of cryptocurrency, bitcoin, and the future. *International Journal of Business Management and Commerce*, *1*(2), 1–9.

Dierksmeier, C., & Seele, P. (2018). Cryptocurrencies and business ethics. *Journal of Business Ethics*, *152*(1), 1–14. doi:10.100710551-016-3298-0

Dodd, N. (2018). The social life of Bitcoin. *Theory, Culture & Society*, *35*(3), 35–56. doi:10.1177/0263276417746464

Đokić, K., Radman-Funarić, M., & Potnik Galić, K. (2015). The Relationship between the Cryptocurrency Value (Bitcoin) and Interest for it in the Region. *ENTRENOVA-ENTerprise REsearch InNOVAtion*, *1*(1), 419–426. doi:10.2139srn.3281915

Douglass, R. B. (1977). *Belief, attitude, intention, and behavior: An introduction to theory and research*. JSTOR.

Dumitrescu, G. C. (2017). Bitcoin–a brief analysis of the advantages and disadvantages. *Global Economic Observer*, *5*(2), 63–71.

ErmakovaT.FabianB.BaumannA.IzmailovM.KrasnovaH. (2017). Bitcoin: drivers and impediments. *Available at* SSRN 3017190.

Evans, P., Aré, L., Forth, P., Harlé, N., & Portincaso, M. (2016). *A Strategic Perspective on Blockchain and Digital Tokens*. Boston Consulting Group. Available at: https://www. bcg. com/en-gb/publications/2016/blockchain-thi nking-outside-the-blocks.aspx

Fanusie, Y., & Robinson, T. (2018). *Bitcoin laundering: An analysis of illicit flows into digital currency services*. Center on Sanctions and Illicit Finance Memorandum.

Faqih, K. M. (2016). An empirical analysis of factors predicting the behavioral intention to adopt Internet shopping technology among non-shoppers in a developing country context: Does gender matter? *Journal of Retailing and Consumer Services*, *30*, 140–164. doi:10.1016/j.jretconser.2016.01.016

Foley, S., Karlsen, J. R., & Putniņš, T. J. (2019). Sex, drugs, and bitcoin: How much illegal activity is financed through cryptocurrencies? *Review of Financial Studies*, *32*(5), 1798–1853. doi:10.1093/rfs/hhz015

Folkinshteyn, D., & Lennon, M. (2016). Braving Bitcoin: A technology acceptance model (TAM) analysis. *Journal of Information Technology Case and Application Research*, *18*(4), 220–249. doi:10.1080/15228053.2016.1275242

Frik, A., & Mittone, L. (2019). Factors influencing the perception of website privacy trustworthiness and users' purchasing intentions: The behavioral economics perspective. *Journal of Theoretical and Applied Electronic Commerce Research*, *14*(3), 89–125. doi:10.4067/S0718-18762019000300107

Fung, B., & Halaburda, H. (2014). Understanding platform-based digital currencies. *Bank of Canada Review*, *2014*(Spring), 12–20.

Galen, D., Brand, N., Boucherle, L., Davis, R., Do, N., El-Baz, B., . . . Lee, J. (2018). *Blockchain for social impact: Moving beyond the hype.* Center for Social Innovation, RippleWorks.

Gao, Y., Zang, L., Roth, A., & Wang, P. (2017). Does democracy cause innovation? An empirical test of the popper hypothesis. *Research Policy, 46*(7), 1272–1283. doi:10.1016/j.respol.2017.05.014

Gazel, M., & Schwienbacher, A. (2021). Entrepreneurial fintech clusters. *Small Business Economics, 57*(2), 883–903. doi:10.100711187-020-00331-1

Glaser, F., Zimmermann, K., Haferkorn, M., Weber, M. C., & Siering, M. (2014). *Bitcoin-asset or currency? revealing users' hidden intentions. In Revealing Users' Hidden Intentions.* ECIS.

Goldfarb, A., & Tucker, C. (2019). Digital economics. *Journal of Economic Literature, 57*(1), 3–43. doi:10.1257/jel.20171452

Gorbunov, E. (2021). *Changing Cryptocurrency Perceptions: An Experimental Study.* Academic Press.

Grohmann, A., Klühs, T., & Menkhoff, L. (2018). Does financial literacy improve financial inclusion? Cross country evidence. *World Development, 111*, 84–96. doi:10.1016/j.worlddev.2018.06.020

Halaburda, H. (2018). Blockchain revolution without the blockchain? *Communications of the ACM, 61*(7), 27–29. doi:10.1145/3225619

Han, H., Lee, K.-S., Radic, A., Ngah, A. H., & Kim, J. J. (2021). The extended self-identify-based electric product adoption model and airline business strategy: A new theoretical framework for green technology products. *Journal of Travel & Tourism Marketing, 38*(3), 247–262. doi:10.1080/10548408.2021.1906386

Holt, T. J., Smirnova, O., Chua, Y. T., & Copes, H. (2015). Examining the risk reduction strategies of actors in online criminal markets. *Global Crime, 16*(2), 81–103. doi:10.1080/17440572.2015.1013211

Hooper, A., & Holtbrügge, D. (2020). Blockchain technology in international business: Changing the agenda for global governance. *Review of International Business and Strategy, 30*(2), 183–200. doi:10.1108/RIBS-06-2019-0078

Hsu, C.-L., & Lin, J. C.-C. (2015). What drives purchase intention for paid mobile apps?–An expectation confirmation model with perceived value. *Electronic Commerce Research and Applications, 14*(1), 46–57. doi:10.1016/j.elerap.2014.11.003

Hughes, A., Park, A., Kietzmann, J., & Archer-Brown, C. (2019). Beyond Bitcoin: What blockchain and distributed ledger technologies mean for firms. *Business Horizons, 62*(3), 273–281. doi:10.1016/j.bushor.2019.01.002

Irfan, E., Ali, Y., & Sabir, M. (2022). Analysing role of businesses' investment in digital literacy: A case of Pakistan. *Technological Forecasting and Social Change, 176*, 121484. doi:10.1016/j.techfore.2022.121484

Ismanto, L., Ar, H. S., Fajar, A., & Bachtiar, S. (2019). *Blockchain as E-commerce platform in Indonesia.* Paper presented at the Journal of Physics: Conference Series.

Johar, S., Ahmad, N., Asher, W., Cruickshank, H., & Durrani, A. (2021). Research and applied perspective to blockchain technology: A comprehensive survey. *Applied Sciences (Basel, Switzerland), 11*(14), 6252. doi:10.3390/app11146252

Kapsis, I. (2020). Blockchain and cryptocurrencies: Essential tools in a two-tier financial system. *Capital Markets Law Journal, 15*(1), 18–47. doi:10.1093/cmlj/kmz025

Khan, I. U., Hameed, Z., & Khan, S. U. (2017). Understanding online banking adoption in a developing country: UTAUT2 with cultural moderators. *Journal of Global Information Management, 25*(1), 43–65. doi:10.4018/JGIM.2017010103

Kim, T. (2017). On the transaction cost of Bitcoin. *Finance Research Letters, 23*, 300–305. doi:10.1016/j.frl.2017.07.014

Kishore, S. K., & Sequeira, A. H. (2016). An empirical investigation on mobile banking service adoption in rural Karnataka. *SAGE Open, 6*(1). doi:10.1177/2158244016633731

Kliber, A., Marszałek, P., Musiałkowska, I., & Świerczyńska, K. (2019). Bitcoin: Safe haven, hedge or diversifier? Perception of bitcoin in the context of a country's economic situation—A stochastic volatility approach. *Physica A, 524*, 246–257. doi:10.1016/j.physa.2019.04.145

Krombholz, K., Judmayer, A., Gusenbauer, M., & Weippl, E. (2017). The other side of the coin: User experiences with bitcoin security and privacy. *Financial Cryptography and Data Security: 20th International Conference, FC 2016, Christ Church, Barbados, February 22–26, 2016, Revised Selected Papers, 20.* 10.1007/978-3-662-54970-4_33

Kshetri, N. (2021). The Economics of Central Bank Digital Currency. *Computer, 54*(6), 53–58. doi:10.1109/MC.2021.3070091

Lavorgna, A. (2014). Internet-mediated drug trafficking: Towards a better understanding of new criminal dynamics. *Trends in Organized Crime*, *17*(4), 250–270. doi:10.100712117-014-9226-8

Luther, W. J. (2016). Cryptocurrencies, network effects, and switching costs. *Contemporary Economic Policy*, *34*(3), 553–571. doi:10.1111/coep.12151

Martins, C., Oliveira, T., & Popovič, A. (2014). Understanding the Internet banking adoption: A unified theory of acceptance and use of technology and perceived risk application. *International Journal of Information Management*, *34*(1), 1–13. doi:10.1016/j.ijinfomgt.2013.06.002

Maurer, B., Nelms, T. C., & Swartz, L. (2013). "When perhaps the real problem is money itself!": The practical materiality of Bitcoin. *Social Semiotics*, *23*(2), 261–277. doi:10.1080/10350330.2013.777594

Mendoza-Tello, J. C., Mora, H., Pujol-López, F. A., & Lytras, M. D. (2018). Social commerce as a driver to enhance trust and intention to use cryptocurrencies for electronic payments. *IEEE Access : Practical Innovations, Open Solutions*, *6*, 50737–50751. doi:10.1109/ACCESS.2018.2869359

Mizanur, R. M., & Sloan, T. R. (2017). User adoption of mobile commerce in Bangladesh: Integrating perceived risk, perceived cost and personal awareness with TAM. *International Technology Management Review*, 103-124.

Moon, Y., & Hwang, J. (2018). Crowdfunding as an alternative means for funding sustainable appropriate technology: Acceptance determinants of backers. *Sustainability*, *10*(5), 1456. doi:10.3390u10051456

Nakamoto, S. (2008). Bitcoin: A peer-to-peer electronic cash system. *Decentralized Business Review*, 21260.

Nasir, A., Shaukat, K., Khan, K. I., Hameed, I. A., Alam, T. M., & Luo, S. (2020). What is core and what future holds for blockchain technologies and cryptocurrencies: A bibliometric analysis. *IEEE Access : Practical Innovations, Open Solutions*, *9*, 989–1004. doi:10.1109/ACCESS.2020.3046931

Niranjanamurthy, M., Nithya, B., & Jagannatha, S. (2019). Analysis of Blockchain technology: Pros, cons and SWOT. *Cluster Computing*, *22*(S6), 14743–14757. doi:10.100710586-018-2387-5

Pham, T.-T. T., & Ho, J. C. (2015). The effects of product-related, personal-related factors and attractiveness of alternatives on consumer adoption of NFC-based mobile payments. *Technology in Society*, *43*, 159–172. doi:10.1016/j.techsoc.2015.05.004

Polasik, M., Piotrowska, A. I., Wisniewski, T. P., Kotkowski, R., & Lightfoot, G. (2015). Price fluctuations and the use of bitcoin: An empirical inquiry. *International Journal of Electronic Commerce*, *20*(1), 9–49. doi:10.1080/10864415.2016.1061413

Presthus, W., & O'Malley, N. O. (2017). Motivations and barriers for end-user adoption of bitcoin as digital currency. *Procedia Computer Science*, *121*, 89–97. doi:10.1016/j.procs.2017.11.013

Putri, G. A., Wijayanti, A. W., & Ariani, K. R. (2021). The application of technology acceptance model to assess the role of complexity toward customer acceptance on mobile banking. *Proceedings of International Conference on Smart Computing and Cyber Security: Strategic Foresight, Security Challenges and Innovation (SMARTCYBER 2020)*. 10.1007/978-981-15-7990-5_25

Rehman, M., Javed, I. T., Qureshi, K. N., Margaria, T., & Jeon, G. (2022). A Cyber Secure Medical Management System by Using Blockchain. *IEEE Transactions on Computational Social Systems*, 1–14. doi:10.1109/TCSS.2022.3215455

Sai, A. R., Buckley, J., & Le Gear, A. (2021). Characterizing wealth inequality in cryptocurrencies. *Frontiers in Blockchain*, *4*, 730122. doi:10.3389/fbloc.2021.730122

Saiedi, E., Mohammadi, A., Broström, A., & Shafi, K. (2022). Distrust in banks and fintech participation: The case of peer-to-peer lending. *Entrepreneurship Theory and Practice*, *46*(5), 1170–1197. doi:10.1177/1042258720958020

Salloum, S. A., Alhamad, A. Q. M., Al-Emran, M., Monem, A. A., & Shaalan, K. (2019). Exploring students' acceptance of e-learning through the development of a comprehensive technology acceptance model. *IEEE Access : Practical Innovations, Open Solutions*, *7*, 128445–128462. doi:10.1109/ACCESS.2019.2939467

San Martín, S., & Camarero, C. (2009). How perceived risk affects online buying. *Online Information Review*, *33*(4), 629–654. doi:10.1108/14684520910985657

Sas, C., & Khairuddin, I. E. (2017). Design for trust: An exploration of the challenges and opportunities of bitcoin users. *Proceedings of the 2017 CHI Conference on Human Factors in Computing Systems*. 10.1145/3025453.3025886

Schaupp, L. C., & Festa, M. (2018). Cryptocurrency adoption and the road to regulation. *Proceedings of the 19th Annual International Conference on Digital Government Research: Governance in the Data Age*. 10.1145/3209281.3209336

Shahzad, F., Xiu, G., Wang, J., & Shahbaz, M. (2018). An empirical investigation on the adoption of cryptocurrencies among the people of mainland China. *Technology in Society*, *55*, 33–40. doi:10.1016/j.techsoc.2018.05.006

Shaikh, A. A., Glavee-Geo, R., & Karjaluoto, H. (2021). How relevant are risk perceptions, effort, and performance expectancy in mobile banking adoption? In *Research Anthology on Securing Mobile Technologies and Applications* (pp. 692–716). IGI Global. doi:10.4018/978-1-7998-8545-0.ch038

Silinskyte, J. (2014). *Understanding Bitcoin adoption: Unified theory of acceptance and use of technology (UTAUT) application* [Unpublished master's dissertation]. University Leiden.

Smith, M. D., & Floro, M. S. (2021). The effects of domestic and international remittances on food insecurity in low-and middle-income countries. *The Journal of Development Studies*, *57*(7), 1198–1220. doi:10.1080/00220388.2020.1849619

Solovykh, N. N., Koroleva, I. V., Stompeleva, E. S., Terskaya, G. A., & Aliev, V. M. (2019). Digital economy and socio-economic contradictions of information society. *Ubiquitous Computing and the Internet of Things: Prerequisites for the Development of ICT*, 655-662.

Srinivasan, N., & Ratchford, B. T. (1991). An empirical test of a model of external search for automobiles. *The Journal of Consumer Research*, *18*(2), 233–242. doi:10.1086/209255

Taylor, J. W. (1974). The role of risk in consumer behavior: A comprehensive and operational theory of risk taking in consumer behavior. *Journal of Marketing*, *38*(2), 54–60.

Thakor, R. T., & Merton, R. C. (2018). Trust in lending. Academic Press. doi:10.3386/w24778

Tornatzky, L. G., Fleischer, M., & Chakrabarti, A. K. (1990). Processes of technological innovation. Lexington Books. doi:10.3386/w24778

Treiblmaier, H., & Sillaber, C. (2021). The impact of blockchain on e-commerce: A framework for salient research topics. *Electronic Commerce Research and Applications*, *48*, 101054. doi:10.1016/j.elerap.2021.101054

Tsvetkova, M., Yasseri, T., Meyer, E. T., Pickering, J. B., Engen, V., Walland, P., Lüders, M., Følstad, A., & Bravos, G. (2017). Understanding human-machine networks: A cross-disciplinary survey. *ACM Computing Surveys*, *50*(1), 1–35. doi:10.1145/3039868

Uematsu, Y., & Tanaka, S. (2019). High-dimensional macroeconomic forecasting and variable selection via penalized regression. *The Econometrics Journal*, *22*(1), 34–56. doi:10.1111/ectj.12117

Vaz, J., & Brown, K. (2020). Sustainable development and cryptocurrencies as private money. *Economia e Politica Industriale*, *47*(1), 163–184. doi:10.100740812-019-00139-5

Venkatesh, V., & Davis, F. D. (2000). A theoretical extension of the technology acceptance model: Four longitudinal field studies. *Management Science*, *46*(2), 186–204. doi:10.1287/mnsc.46.2.186.11926

Venkatesh, V., Morris, M. G., Davis, G. B., & Davis, F. D. (2003). User acceptance of information technology: Toward a unified view. *Management Information Systems Quarterly*, *27*(3), 425–478. doi:10.2307/30036540

Vigna, P., & Casey, M. J. (2016). *The age of cryptocurrency: how bitcoin and the blockchain are challenging the global economic order*. Macmillan.

Vijayasarathy, L. R., & Jones, J. M. (2000). Print and Internet catalog shopping: Assessing attitudes and intentions. *Internet Research*, *10*(3), 191–202. doi:10.1108/10662240010331948

Vo, N. N., & Xu, G. (2017). *The volatility of Bitcoin returns and its correlation to financial markets*. Paper presented at the 2017 International Conference on Behavioral, Economic, Socio-cultural Computing (BESC). 10.1109/BESC.2017.8256365

Wu, J., & Tran, N. K. (2018). Application of blockchain technology in sustainable energy systems: An overview. *Sustainability*, *10*(9), 3067. doi:10.3390u10093067

Wunsche, A. (2016). *Technological disruption of capital markets and reporting? An introduction to blockchain. Chartered Professional Accountants Canada*. CPA.

Yang, H., Yu, J., Zo, H., & Choi, M. (2016). User acceptance of wearable devices: An extended perspective of perceived value. *Telematics and Informatics*, *33*(2), 256–269. doi:10.1016/j.tele.2015.08.007

Yli-Huumo, J., Ko, D., Choi, S., Park, S., & Smolander, K. (2016). Where is current research on blockchain technology? A systematic review. *PLoS One*, *11*(10), e0163477. doi:10.1371/journal.pone.0163477 PMID:27695049

Zak, P. J., & Knack, S. (2001). Trust and growth. *Economic Journal (London)*, *111*(470), 295–321. doi:10.1111/1468-0297.00609

Zeithaml, V. A. (1988). Consumer perceptions of price, quality, and value: A means-end model and synthesis of evidence. *Journal of Marketing*, *52*(3), 2–22. doi:10.1177/002224298805200302

Chapter 3
FinTech Status in the Global Market:
Challenges and the Future

Itzel Natalia Carrillo Leguizamon
University Canada West, Canada

Billy Alessandro Grimaldi Milla
University Canada West, Canada

Rodrigo Alexander Cortez Solano
University Canada West, Canada

Monica Sofia Najera Moreno
University Canada West, Canada

Daniel Esteban Ortega Pinzón
University Canada West, Canada

ABSTRACT

In recent years, the effectiveness of FinTech has become very important, but new technologies are created and implemented without considering their risks, only focusing on their advantages. Previous research found that the unmet needs for basic banking have been solved through financial technologies while, at the same time, bringing benefits to both people and businesses. Using a deductive approach to the mixed data found previously made it more manageable to understand FinTech's background and intercorrelation with e-business. Contrary to what many people assume about the risks of FinTech, findings have shown that 88% of data breaches come from human mistakes leading us to validate that the problem with FinTech is not the technology itself but the improper use of it and the ignorance around them—concluding that these challenges can be minimized and regulated with the right strategies. The overall effectiveness of FinTech is deemed positive, with the advantages outweighing the challenges.

DOI: 10.4018/978-1-6684-8368-8.ch003

INTRODUCTION

Financial technologies, commonly referred to as FinTech, have become indispensable to modern society. They offer substantial advantages that have made them a daily routine for many people. The implementation of these technologies has empowered individuals with electronic devices to carry out various functions, such as transferring funds, executing online payments, saving money, and investing their capital.

Financial technologies have been a part of the industry for several decades, and their presence has become increasingly relevant in modern society. In fact, the majority of individuals who own electronic devices have access to apps or functions that allow them to engage in financial transactions, such as moving money, making purchases, saving, or investing. For businesses of any size, failure to support or utilize financial technology may result in missing out on a substantial portion of the market, as a growing number of people rely exclusively on such software for their financial needs. As such, implementing access to financial technology has become a necessary component for businesses to remain competitive in the market.

The FinTech industry comprises a diverse range of services and products, including platforms for lending and financing, payment and transfer solutions, wealth management and investing tools, and insurance products. Emerging technologies such as automation and blockchain have accelerated the expansion of FinTech, which has disrupted established financial organizations and systems. Although FinTech has offered many benefits, such as increased efficiency and speed of transactions, there are also potential risks associated with its use. These risks range from theft of personal information to cyber-attacks and financial loss, which can lead to skepticism about implementing FinTech. Therefore, it is essential to investigate whether the benefits of FinTech outweigh the risks.

The objective of this research is to examine the advantages, risks, opportunities, disadvantages, and potential threats of FinTech to determine its effectiveness in the long run for businesses, society, and individuals. This information is necessary to facilitate better performance of financial technologies in communities and companies, build a more trustworthy relationship with people, and provide businesses with easier ways to operate. The research has a global scope, targeting companies and users worldwide, and does not consider additional variables, such as people's economic situation when acquiring this technology and their ability to invest in their security.

This chapter was written with ethical principles in mind. The methodology used in this research comprises three aspects: approach, purpose, and philosophy. A deductive approach was employed, as the growing impact and knowledge of FinTech have created a shift from traditional banking, and the exponential growth of businesses implementing FinTech is noteworthy. The central question of this research is how the advantages or challenges of FinTech affect its effectiveness.

A hypothesis was formulated, stating that FinTech is effective in businesses as its advantages outweigh the negative aspects. The hypothesis was evaluated based on a theoretical framework, findings within this research, and a conclusion.

The research purpose has two categories: exploratory and reporting. The exploratory aspect investigates issues and general qualities of a known circumstance, which aligns with the deductive approach, is low-cost, and will be useful to future researchers in understanding FinTech's effectiveness. The reporting aspect involves the use of secondary data from previous researchers for the findings and analysis. The research philosophy adopted is a mixed approach, as the data to be analyzed will be both statistical and descriptive, making it more efficient given the time limitations and nature of the financial topic.

BACKGROUND

Definition of FinTech

As mentioned above, the relationship between technology and financial companies has changed forever. Companies in the sector have seen how the Internet and the FinTech sector have been gaining more and more weight, transforming how people relate to money in their daily lives. Purchasing products, paying bills, and transferring are carried out through increasingly innovative products and services. A very clear example of this is FinTech, but what is it?

According to CFA Institute (2023), FinTech comprises companies that use technology to improve or automate financial services and processes. FinTech refers to using technology to provide customers with different financial services and products. FinTech is a rapidly growing sector geared towards consumer and business interests. According to different reports, from mobile banking to insurance companies to investment applications, this financial technology is the product of the mix between financial services and the vast development of technology (Trificana, 2022). This mixture has generated innovative solutions to traditional financial institutions' issues and inefficiencies.

FinTech is a technology that covers a broad range of services and products, including online and mobile banking, investments and wealth management, crowdfunding, payment processing, etc. FinTech is continuously growing as technology does. Therefore, the FinTech range will only continue to grow. According to the CFI Team, technologies implemented in FinTech vary considerably, taking advantage of revolutionary features and systems such as Blockchain, artificial intelligence (AI), machine learning, and robot process automation (RPA), among many others. The use of these technologies allows FinTech to create and keep evolving in order to provide more convenient, efficient, and cost-efficient products and services than those offered by traditional financial providers.

Another relevant factor to take into consideration when talking about FinTech development and adoption is the increase in adoption rates of mobile devices with access to the internet. This adoption leads consumers to shift their behavior toward digital channels. Therefore, consumers are most likely to adopt FinTech services and products. The CFI team believes the proof of the shift is that different FinTech apps as Applepay, Venmo, and Stripe, are part of everyday household use.

The Evolution of FinTech

From a periodical perspective, FinTech history and evolution can be categorized into four periodical timelines. According to Setiawan and Maulisa (2020), "FinTech 1.0 is the period when the financial sector is still widely an analog industry, FinTech 2.0 is the period when the financial sector adopted computational and digital technology to improve their activities, FinTech 3.0 and 3.5 is the on-going period when financial startups and big tech companies (TechFins) are the umbilical cord of digital innovation". Setiawan and Maulisa did not consider FinTech 4.0 a periodical timeline. However, this paper will consider FinTech 4.0 as one due to the significant changes in the current timeline of the FinTech industry.

FinTech 1.0: Analogue Technologies

FinTech 1.0 was the beginning of FinTech, and this period started almost parallel to the early financial globalization when the industry adopted analog technologies. "It was marked by the first interconnection of transatlantic cable between Europe and America in 1866 until Barclays invented the first ATM Machine in 1967" (Setiawan & Maulisa, 2020, p. 219) and it is called analog due to the now traditional but obsolete technologies such as railroads, the telegraph, printing press, steamships, and many other technologies of that period. All these are considered financial technologies due to their capacity for financial interlinkage across nations and frontiers and their fast transmission of financial information, payments, and other financial transactions, making them possible worldwide.

FinTech 2.0: FinTech Introduction to the Internet and First Online Banking Experiences

As previously mentioned, FinTech 2.0 will see the light until 1967, when the first ATM was invented, marking the beginning of the digitalization period in the financial sector. This event resulted in technological advancements in electronic payment systems. "However, the next level of this era is the inception of the first internet banking protocols via the World Wide Web (WWW) by Wells Fargo in 1995 to create the first-ever internet banking experience for financial costumers, followed with the emergence of the first branchless banks such as ING Direct and HSBC Direct launched in the UK financial market scheme in 2005" (Setiawan & Maulisa, 2020, p. 219). At this point in history is when online banks and all the services a traditional bank will start establishing their way into the internet.

FinTech 3.0 and 3.5: FinTech Startups Era

In this period of FinTech history, financial startups, telecommunication providers, and big tech companies started joining the digital financial services industry. "These startups disruptions can be traced to the creation of the first digital wallet concept by confinity in 1999, which is popularly known today as modern-day PayPal" (Plotkin, 1999, as cited in Setiawan & Maulisa, 2020, p. 219). Many others followed by launching digital wallets, developing lending platforms, and implementing more online banking services. On the other hand, FinTech startups began to emerge also in developing markets such as Africa, some regions in Asia, and South America. By this point, these startups and FinTech implementation in these markets were still undeveloped projects with high expectations and goals. "The periodical timelapse of the FinTech startups in third world countries are known as the FinTech 3.5" (Arner et al., 2015, as cited in Setiawan & Maulisa, 2020, p. 219).

FinTech 4.0: Artificial Intelligence-Based FinTech

FinTech 4.0 timeline is the present era that is happening by the time of this paper. "The emergence of FinTech 4.0 is marked by two significant events. The first was the announcement of Libra (now called Diem) by a Metaled consortium, a clear example of a BigTech seeking to build an extraordinary digital finance platform. The second was the halting of the planned initial public offering (IPO) of Ant in 2020 due to regulators' concerns about its model of platformization and related risks concentration and dominance" (Arner et al., 2022, p. 6). New technologies and big tech companies have evolved and developed a "combination of technological evolution (digitization, datafication, digitalization), conducive regulatory approaches, in the United States and China in particular (at least prior to 2019-2020), and the network effects that characterize data industries" (Arner et al., 2022, p. 3). In addition, the Covid-19 pandemic increased and reinforced the FinTech trend during 2020 and 2021, leading to a point where big tech companies and government institutions have realized the need to control and regulate the present fourth industrial revolution, where its main course is the digitalization of everything.

This is due to the rapid growth of the FinTech industry that "platform-based models of finance require regulation across multiple fields, including data protection, competition and antitrust, telecommunications, and finance in ways that do not easily allow for coherence in regulatory approach and scope, both nationally and internationally" (Arner et al., 2022, p. 6).

FinTech 4.0 also presents enormous opportunities for developing countries, converting the undeveloped projects in FinTech 3.5 into more sustainable ones through new business models with greater access and reach. However, the world and the financial sector are at the beginning of FinTech 4.0; its future remains uncertain. However, its current state has brought many questions and concerns regarding the enormous scale of this new FinTech boom, possibly even "too big to regulate."

Main Sectors in FinTech Industry

The FinTech industry has seen significant developments in the last decades. However, four FinTech areas have become particularly strong due to their rapid growth and impact on the industry. The four major sectors are digital lending, blockchain, payments, and digital wealth management.

Digital Lending

Digital lending enables borrowers (personal, financial institutions, businesses) to apply for loans from any internet-capable device. According to Bennett et al. (2016), digital lending "access to expansive data, sophisticated algorithms, and considerable computing power enabled new companies to compete with traditional banks by providing appealing new offerings to would-be borrowers." This sector of FinTech is used mainly by companies that want to facilitate funding. Digital lending has got to a point where can offer a wide range of loans as a traditional bank. Now, "offerings range from consumer and student loans to small-business loans, equipment-financing loans and lines of credit. Mortgages and auto loans are other emerging areas. Digital lending companies match borrowers and lenders, benefiting from loan relationships and processing transactions". The wide range of options, the easy application process, and the convenience of obtaining funding at any time in any location have become critical factors in its popularity and implementation. According to Grand View Research (2023), "The global digital lending platform market size was valued at USD 7.04 billion in 2022 and is expected to register a compound annual growth rate (CAGR) of 26.5% from 2023 to 2030," which ensures the continuous expansion for digital lending in the future.

Blockchain

Blockchain is another result of the innovations and development the FinTech sector has experienced. It is a platform that uses a distributed database containing the most recent information and makes it available to an entire network. The blockchain contains three major components: "a peer-to-peer network with randomized groups, or nodes; a database, digital ledger; and third parties. When a third party submits an entry or payment to the ledger, the nodes work together seamlessly to approve or reject transactions. With no central authority, this eliminates the need to trust one party such as a payment processor." (Bennett et al., 2016). This technology and how it works provide efficiency, authentication, and transparency to financial services. Blockchain is usually associated with digital currencies/ cryptocurrencies because is the reason that allows these digital currencies to operate without the need for a central authority. However, this same characteristic of having a decentralized structure increases "the risk of users dodging taxes, laundering money, and distributing illegal goods." (Bennett, J. et al., 2016). This sensitivity around blockchain calls for global regulations, but governments and institutions are still working on developing those rules.

Payments

Digital payments are the most common FinTech nowadays due to the proliferation of smartphones. This sector counts three significant areas: person-to-person (P2P) payments, in-store retail payments, and credit and debit transactions. Person-to-person (P2P) payments refer to transferring funds from one personal account to another. It is a prevalent way to move money in our society because most traditional banks have their app with these features available on electronic devices, and companies like PayPal provide the same services. Moving on, in-store retail payments refer to those apps that enable payments through apps like Apple Pay or Google Pay that use NFC, QR codes, or barcodes to complete payment. Finally, "the processing and settlement of credit and debit card transactions rely on a complex web of firms, including payment acquirers/processors, independent sales organizations (ISOs), card networks and issuing banks. This ecosystem is largely responsible for processing all transactions made with a debit or credit card, both in person and online" (Bennett et al., 2016). In this case, the significant risks are fraud and theft, and, as a consequence, there has been a significant growth in two-factor authentication as a form of prevention and protection against those risks.

Digital Wealth Management

Digital Wealth Management is basically how digital money can be managed. Typically, this is done through robo-advisors that "are retail-focused, automated wealth management services that use algorithms to evaluate risk tolerance and generally manage assets in low-cost portfolios of exchange-traded funds. Some robo-advisors offer fully automated advice, while others are a hybrid of digital and human services." (Bennett et al., 2016). Due to the automatization that robo-advisors provide to their users, there has been a shift in the industry from active to passive management and investment. However, of the four sectors of FinTech, this one in specific is the one that shows the slowest adoption, probably because of the lack of engagement and trust from the consumer when a person controls the situation.

FinTech Services

Smart Contract Investment Vehicles

According to Clements (2019), the use of blockchain technology and smart contracts has the potential to transform investing by lowering entry barriers and fees for investors and enhancing transparency of records for audit purposes. However, there are limitations to using smart contracts in investment vehicles, including verification problems and computer coding challenges. Despite not experiencing widespread adoption, smart contract investment vehicles raise important legal questions such as accountability and liability in case something goes wrong, according to the federal Department of Justice.

Robo-Advisers and Automated Personal Wealth Management Services

The growing demand for robo-advisers and algorithmic wealth management services, including successful platforms such as Nest Wealth, Justwealth, Wealthsimple, and WealthBar. However, these platforms are subject to various federal and provincial laws related to anti-money laundering, securities, consumer protection, banking standards, and fraud prevention. The regulatory framework applicable to robo-advisors requires a "hybrid model" of human advice and technology, and platforms providing "order execution only" services are prohibited from providing investment advice. Additionally, robo-advisors are subject to restrictions on conventional trading mechanisms such as margin, leverage, or short selling. This information according to Clements (2019).

Algorithmic Trading and Market Automation

According to Clements (2019), the rise of algorithmic and high-frequency trading (HFT) and market automation has transformed trading, providing benefits such as enhanced liquidity, lower trading costs, and improved price discovery. However, these developments have attracted criticism due to their impact on market stability, efficiency, and the creation of "illusory liquidity". Algorithmic and automated trading strategies can have a "procyclical" impact and "exacerbate" price swings, leading to irrational catastrophic events like "flash crashes." IIROC, the regulatory body responsible for establishing regulatory policy and industry standards for trading and market integrity, has created Universal Market Integrity Rules (UMIR) to reduce risk and maintain market stability for automated order systems. Provincial regulations and harmonized rules developed by CSA have also been active in adjusting existing regulatory frameworks to automated and algorithmic trading. Joint guidance relating to automated trading on marketplaces and alternative trading systems has also been issued for crypto-asset trading platforms.

Artificial Intelligence and Financial Contracts

Major banks have the opportunities to integrate AI innovations, or partner with AI firms to enhance customer products and services, particularly in wealth management, financial budgeting and planning, and to increase the efficiency of internal operations. For instance, the Government of Canada has launched an Advisory Council on Artificial Intelligence, created a new department called "Innovation Canada" to provide support to AI companies and committed $125 million in research and development public funds for AI with a subsequent pledge for $950 million for an "innovation supercluster initiative" with industry.

AI has many applications in financial services and FinTech, including cost savings for back-office operations, enhanced customer service, and process automation. It can also improve advisory services, provide inter-application user enhancements, portfolio allocation and management, client risk profiling, credit assessment and underwriting, research, and valuation. AI is also useful for financial institutions to reduce the cost of regulatory compliance by instituting regtech innovations to ensure that they meet regulatory standards and are up to date on regulatory changes. This information according to Clements (2019).

Advances in AI and automated contract analysis mechanisms have the potential to disruptively transform the services landscape, and several start-up companies are at the forefront of this revolution. There are many legal risks in deploying AI into financial services and processes, and some uncertainty on whether existing regulatory structures will be sufficient to manage the risks once widespread adoption takes place. Regulation in this area is one that will continually be adapted and adjusted to ensure necessary safeguards and established.

Decentralized Autonomous Organizations

According to Clements (2019), DAOs are virtual organizations that operate through self-executing computer code, eliminating the need for centralized human management and oversight. While they offer many benefits, such as increased efficiency and transparency, they also present significant legal challenges. There are concerns around assessing liability and recovering damages, establishing legal standing, applying rules of evidence, maintaining proper corporate governance, enforcing competition and consumer protection rules, and ensuring tax compliance. Additionally, since DAOs operate through servers distributed worldwide, they can be considered borderless and difficult to regulate domestically. These challenges will need to be addressed by regulators and legal experts as DAOs continue to gain popularity and influence.

Crypto Hedge Funds

Nowadays the emergence of investment funds focuses on cryptocurrencies, such as the FBC Bitcoin Trust and Rivemont Crypto Fund, which are available only to accredited investors. The British Columbia Securities Commission has granted registration to First Block Capital as an investment fund manager and exempt market dealer, while 3iQ has established the Global Cryptoasset Fund and Bitcoin Trust as a mutual fund trust. An application for the trading of a pure bitcoin ETF has been filed with securities regulators but hasn't yet received regulatory approval. These developments highlight the growing interest in cryptocurrencies as an asset class and the efforts being made to provide investment opportunities in this space. This information according to Clements (2019).

E-Business in the Modern Era

The present discourse expounds on the concept of electronic business, commonly referred to as e-business, which encompasses intricate business processes, enterprise applications, and organizational structure in an online environment. The Internet plays a critical role in engaging stakeholders such as customers and vendors, as noted by Combe (2006). The trend towards online commerce has necessitated that traditional businesses adapt to e-business methods to remain competitive. Moreover, scholarly discourse suggests that electronic businesses are no longer a choice but a requirement for success. For example, Neykova and Miltchev (2019) conducted a study that found that 97% of the seventy enterprises surveyed believed that no business activity in their company could be executed without information and communication technology (ICT). This indicates that surveyed firms must maintain existing technology while also employing sophisticated solutions to enhance their online approach.

One of the key elements of business success is a robust business model that describes the methodology and structure used to generate profit, focusing on how the company earns income. This also outlines the advantages gained from business partners and their roles within the business process, as described by Pandya, Arenyeka-Diamond, and Bhogal (2001). Among the various business models that currently predominate in both traditional and e-business settings are business-to-business (B2B), business-to-consumer (B2C), and consumer-to-consumer (C2C). These business models can be improved through the use of new technologies for higher efficiency. For example, B2B e-business technology enables direct cooperation among business partners worldwide, and in B2C, customers can review services and information about the business while saving time with online technology (Jovarauskiene & Pilinkienė, 2009). Managers are aware that to increase sales and competitiveness, they must implement an online setting in their work but are concerned about the challenges that may arise (Gloor, 2012).

FinTech Implementation

The process of selecting an appropriate FinTech solution for a business necessitates careful consideration of several factors, including the specific needs, budgetary constraints, and business model. Theaud (2022) provides insight into the process by outlining several steps that businesses can undertake to select the most suitable FinTech solution. The first step is to identify the specific financial requirements of the business, which may include tasks such as payment processing, accounting, invoicing, or risk management. Once the needs have been identified, it is crucial to research the available FinTech solutions that can help address them. In this regard, it is advisable to review feedback, ratings, and testimonials from users to assess the effectiveness of each solution.

Furthermore, as suggested by Natsir (2022), it is essential to consider the integration capabilities of the FinTech solution. The author emphasizes the importance of ensuring that the selected FinTech solution integrates seamlessly with existing systems, such as accounting software or payment processing platforms. This will help prevent data silos and streamline financial operations, leading to enhanced efficiency and productivity. In summary, the selection of the appropriate FinTech solution for a business entails a thorough evaluation of its financial requirements, available solutions, and integration capabilities to ensure optimal performance and benefits.

Implementing FinTech in e-business can bring many benefits, such as improved payment processing, increased customer convenience, and more efficient financial management. However, it also poses some challenges, including:

1. **Integration With Existing Systems:** E-businesses often have existing systems and processes, and integrating new FinTech solutions can be complex and time-consuming. It may require significant changes to the existing IT infrastructure and business processes.
2. **Cost:** Implementing FinTech solutions can be expensive, especially for smaller e-businesses that may not have the resources to invest in the latest technologies. In addition to the cost of the solution, additional costs may be associated with integrating and maintaining the new technology.
3. **Data Security:** E-businesses handle sensitive customer information, and FinTech solutions can create additional vulnerabilities. It's critical to ensure that any FinTech solution implemented is secure and complies with relevant data protection regulations.

MAIN FOCUS OF THE CHAPTER

FinTech in Businesses: Impact and Advantages

Today, the banking industry faces an inevitable transformation because of the importance of reinventing itself and society's changing habits in recent years. The emergence of new companies (such as FinTech) has meant that the more traditional companies must face new challenges to avoid disappearing. The objectives of FinTech companies, as said by Lele (2023), are to "serve the unmet financial needs of those segments of the population which are not the core target segments of traditional financial services models" and to reach that the business plan to position itself as innovative financial services, add value to existing financial services, simplify financial processes that now require too many intermediaries, achieve greater cost efficiency, making financial products more accessible and improving their transparency, offering better solutions to people through the possibilities of technology (Amsad, 2019).

Enhanced Customer Experience and Accessibility

The advent of financial technology (FinTech) has revolutionized the financial landscape, providing customers with a plethora of opportunities to conduct various financial operations in real-time, thereby enhancing their overall experience. The rapid pace of technological advancements has facilitated the integration of FinTech into various sectors such as mobile banking, online loans and credits, mobile payments, blockchain, and investments. Undoubtedly, this breakthrough in technology promises to bolster the development of finance, enabling greater security and efficiency for diverse products and services.

A growing number of countries have recognized the immense potential of FinTech and are proactively working towards its implementation. According to The World Bank Group and International Monetary Fund, nearly two-thirds of all surveyed jurisdictions acknowledge the benefits of FinTech and have either initiated or developed a national strategy aimed at improving consumer awareness, policy frameworks, and institutional capacity. This proactive approach by countries signifies a broad acceptance of FinTech and an effort towards making it accessible and safe for society.

Given the government's active involvement in promoting FinTech, an upsurge in its utilization and integration is imminent. Statista's data supports this claim by revealing that 75% of global consumers employ online money transfers and payment services, underscoring the widespread adoption of FinTech. Moreover, the insurance technology sector has grown exponentially, increasing from 8% in 2015 to almost 50% in 2019. These figures reinforce the notion that FinTech is fast becoming a ubiquitous phenomenon and is poised to become a critical component of the financial ecosystem in the foreseeable future.

An Alternative Option for Traditional Banking and Finance

FinTech, a term that refers to the use of technology to provide financial services, has experienced remarkable growth in recent years, attaining an economically significant scale. This growth has had a notable impact on traditional banking and finance by offering an alternative option that is more accessible to individuals who face limitations in accessing traditional financing and banking. Jon Frost (2020) noted that FinTech adoption is often driven by unmet demand for basic banking, means of payment, and money transfer services, and FinTech provides a solution to these unmet demands.

The evolution of FinTech in mitigating fraud risk without compromising customer experience has fostered trust, to the point where many people cannot do without them. Consequently, this industry has gained considerable ground worldwide. For instance, a 2015 survey on Financial Inclusion, conducted by the Bank for International Settlements and applied by the National Consulting Center, found that 47% of the population interviewed had savings accounts in traditional banks but used digital wallets more frequently.

FinTech's economic landscape provides several benefits and convenience to its users, as Feyen et al. (2022) assert. For example, FinTech can lower costs, increase speed, transparency, security, and availability of tailored financial services. Digitization can reduce friction in every step along the financial service lifecycle, such as opening an account, conducting customer due diligence, authenticating transactions, and automating other product-specific processes like assessing creditworthiness. The broad economic landscape, combined with its accessibility, has led many businesses to integrate FinTech into their operations.

Notably, not only conventional businesses have embraced FinTech. E-businesses have also adopted FinTech in their operations, leveraging technological advancements to offer platform-based business models in e-commerce and social media markets. These businesses exploit the connectivity of individuals and businesses, allowing them to collaborate, discover counterparties, and package and deliver a range of digital and physical goods and services. For e-businesses, FinTech is a tool that enables them to achieve customers' trust, convenience, and tailored experience, which are essential components of the industry. FinTech can serve as a replacement for traditional interfaces but also as an enhancer due to its functionalities and ability to generate valuable data. However, careful consideration of potential risks and threats is necessary. In summary, Deng et al. (2020) conclude that the integration of FinTech in e-business represents a significant opportunity for businesses to improve their operations and better serve their customers. Therefore, FinTech and e-business are intertwined and expanding daily.

Besides SMEs, major financial institutions have realized how fundamental FinTech is. FinTech started impacting how banks and organizations view the market's future and interact with customers. A survey made by Statista Research Department (2022) interviewed face-to-face senior banking executives worldwide. The purpose was to learn their perspective on how FinTech had impacted selected banking products and services offered in the market. The outcome is projected in Figure 1, showing that, since 2018, 66.7% of significant banking executives consider that FinTech has enormously impacted how their customers manage their wallets and mobile payments globally. Almost as many agreed, traditional payment methods, such as credit and debit cards, have been directly impacted by FinTech. Nowadays, it would be hard to think of a way for the regular person to leave aside FinTech resources, interact efficiently with financial institutions, and access all the products and services offered.

Figure 1. Services impacted by FinTech according banking executives
Note: *Products and services highly impacted by FinTech according banking executives worldwide on 2018. Adapted from "Impact of non-traditional financial firms on selected banking products and services according to senior banking executives worldwide in 2018" by Capgemini and EFMA, 2018, September 20, Statista. https://www-statista-com.ezproxy.myucwest.ca/statistics/946886/impact-FinTech-banking-products-services-globally/*

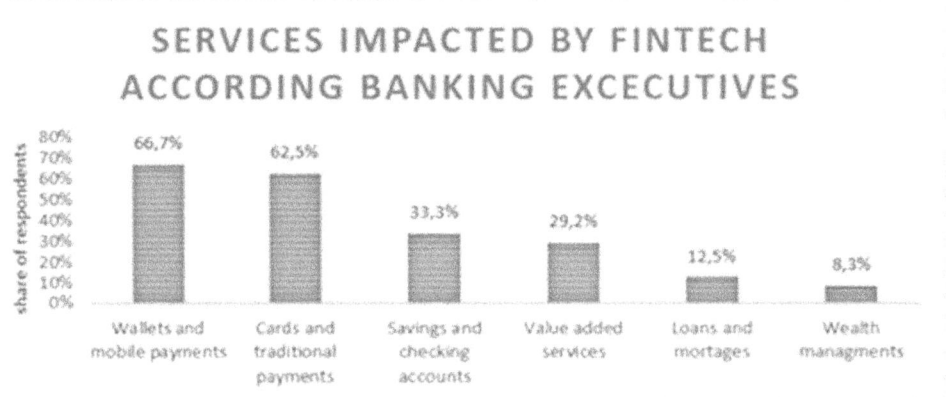

Access to Capital for Businesses

FinTech, or financial technology, can help businesses in a number of ways, including a) Streamlining financial processes: FinTech tools can help automate financial processes such as invoicing, payment processing, and bookkeeping, making them faster and more efficient. b) Providing access to capital: FinTech companies offer alternative lending options, such as peer-to-peer lending and crowdfunding, which can provide businesses with access to capital that they may not be able to obtain through traditional banks. c) Enhancing payment options: According to Douglas (2016), FinTech solutions can provide businesses with a broader range of payment options, such as mobile payments and e-wallets, which can increase customer convenience and reduce transaction fees.

When it comes to business, one of the advantages provided by FinTech is that it enhances the likelihood of small and medium-sized enterprises (SMEs) acquiring low-interest rates (Odinet & College, 2018). Abbasi (2021) agrees with the latter statement and states that FinTech simplifies the loan application procedure, allowing borrowers to acquire loans faster and enhancing SMEs' capacity to deploy funds at an adequate moment. Furthermore, FinTech provides advice in investment management to SMEs. The research conducted by Fuster, Plosser, Schnabel, and Vickery (2018) shows statistical data in support of accessible lending – FinTech lenders review loan applications around 20% quicker than conventional lenders.

Another advantage is that FinTech opens the door to many emerging businesses and e-businesses. It gives them tools to compete almost at the same level as those already established and well-positioned businesses. The same report published by The World Bank Group and International Monetary Fund (2019) stated that financial tools are expected to increase competition from payments, clearing, and settlement services to a minor intent in credit and deposit services. These expectations have been met because "there were approximately 27,000 FinTech startups around the world by 2021 contrary to the approximately 10,000 startups in 2018" (Statista, 2021), as shown in Figure 2, which is almost triple the number of startups in just a three-year difference. The assumptions made in the previous report by The World Bank Group and International Monetary Fund were accurate and will most likely continue being that way. In a business environment with higher and better competition, innovation is promoted, increases customer choice, and boosts economic growth by creating jobs, attracting investments, and increasing consumer spending. All these advantages make the integration of FinTech more appealing.

Figure 2. The number of FinTech startups per region
Note: *Number of FinTech startups per each major region. Adapted from "Number of FinTech startups worldwide from 2018 to 2021, by region" by BCG, 2021, November 8, Statista. https://www-statista-com.ezproxy.myucwest.ca/statistics/893954/number-FinTech-startups-by-region/*

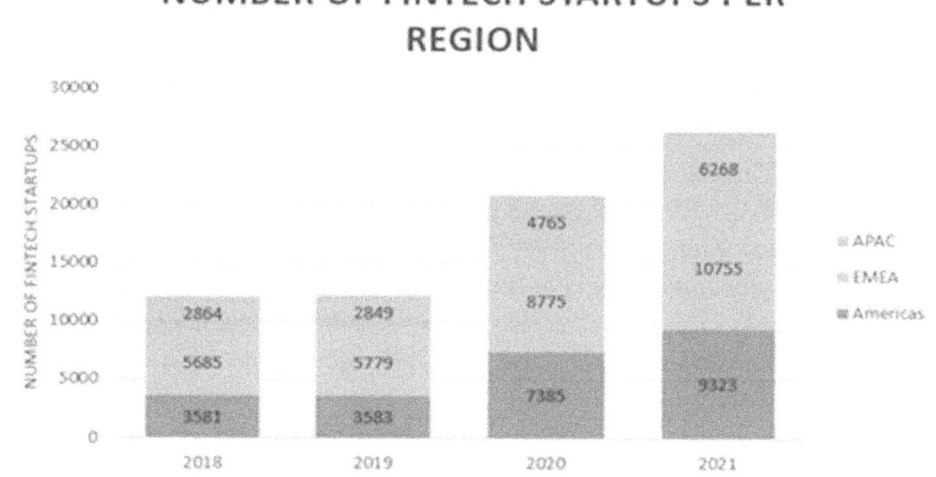

FinTech in Society: Challenges

When a new technology is introduced to society, it has to be evaluated to know if there is a potential breach or use that could harm people. FinTech is not an exception, and "experts have agreed that FinTech is a disruptive phenomenon, but the potential effect on current bank institutions and people's daily life is still unknown" (Clements, 2019). The situation being so vast and delicate makes it more challenging for regulators to aim their efforts at the most imminent threat. Therefore, regulations on FinTech are a matter of time and understanding of this phenomenon. Even if there are no formal regulations on FinTech, many use an already regulated asset, cryptocurrencies. Every FinTech that uses cryptocurrencies in any aspect must be careful in following the government's regulations.

Currently, one of the most controversial and impactful issues that media and modern technologies carry on is their power over their customers' disinformation. FinTech has a considerable responsibility in this aspect since it's based on tools that contain, carry, and use sensitive information from each user in different ways. The financial knowledge held by the FinTech providers and those who use them to provide services is way over their users. This situation "places consumers in a vulnerable position and elevates the importance of trust in the planner–client relationship" (Tharp, 2020). Having to trust important aspects and information almost blindly on a corporation that is not regulated can lead to many fraudulent actions by the providers leaving the general public heavily affected. Therefore, until regulations are set, the only thing holding users back is morals and ethics.

FinTech, like any other rapidly evolving industry, faces its own unique set of challenges. For instance, regulation; FinTech companies often operate in a complex regulatory environment and must comply with various regulations and laws that vary by jurisdiction. This can be a significant challenge for smaller FinTech startups, which may not have the resources to navigate these regulations. Another challenge is cyber security; according to Douglas (2019), FinTech companies are a prime target for cyberattacks due to the sensitive financial information they hold. Ensuring the security of their platforms and customer data is a significant challenge and requires ongoing investment and attention. Lastly, FinTech companies often face challenges in building customer trust, particularly in the face of high-profile data breaches or other security incidents. They must take proactive steps to ensure that customers feel confident in the security and reliability of their platforms.

Throughout the research, it was identified that previous researchers would list data security as one of the main challenges of FinTech. A deeper investigation was conducted, and data showed that in 2021, there were around 1,862 data breaches with an average cost of $4.24 million across seventeen different countries (IBM Security, 2021). However, research by Forbes (2021) also shows that around 88% of data breaches come from human mistakes, which can come from a lack of training from business employees. This means that less than ¼ of attacks are not from hackers and can be prevented with the right strategies.

Aside from business, when it comes to society's FinTech users, there is a significant amount of threat from mobile applications. Mobile platforms are among the most popular targets for hackers (Davis, 2019). This is alarming as a report from EY FinTech Adoption Index (2017) outlines that 64% of users prefer digital channels, such as mobile platforms, to employ FinTech – with a high demographic audience between 25-44 years old. Furthermore, 54% of FinTech users use mainly smartphones to use financial services (EY FinTech Adoption Index, 2017). These users are at risk from direct contact with cyber criminals, as a recent analysis showed a 41% increase in fraud through mobile devices from 2020 to 2021 (Murphy, 2022).

Additionally, another barrier to the effective implementation of FinTech is the lack of trust users have in this software. As statistics have previously shown, this lack of trust comes from a potential threat of data leakages on confidential information and different types of fraud. However, another factor should be considered when describing the weak, trusting relationship between users – education on preventing these threats. The latter does not seem strong in society, as research shows that 34% of FinTech users do not read the terms and conditions when registering for a new financial service. Similarly, 42% of FinTech non-users do not (EY FinTech Adoption Index, 2017). Furthermore, a surprising study from Intel Security (2015) with 19,000 survey participants from 144 different countries stated that 80% of respondents misidentify phishing emails from which cyberattacks can take place.

Another challenge of FinTech is that due to the uncertainty of FinTech's risks and the unclarity of which laws are applicable and what jurisdictions are in charge of enforcing those laws, there is no specific allocation of risk loss under the applicable law. These are related to the "treatment of operational vulnerabilities in the underlying technology, fraud, theft, erroneous transfers, and the law of mistake" (International Monetary Fund, 2019). FinTech has recently gained dominance in the market and society, and has brought with it new and unique risks that the existing law is not able to handle as well as it is required. Also, these new companies operate in a grey area where the existing law does not apply to their business model. This brings many questions on who will be responsible in certain situations and who should provide the security that is needed. As we discussed in the advantages section, many nations have implemented regulations specifically for FinTech; however, changing the existing legal framework and making it efficient while considering all the possible risks is a complex and slow process. This means that even though regulations are already in place, they are far from perfect, and it will take time to make them work efficiently. During this period of transitions and trial, companies and users of FinTech are exposed to risks and uncertainty of them.

FinTech Challenges in North America

The Future of FinTech

The potential of financial technology (FinTech) is optimistic, despite the fact that a number of individuals do not appreciate or acknowledge its benefits when implemented correctly. The rapid progress of technology brings numerous changes that individuals may struggle to adapt to. However, individuals from the technological era, such as millennials and newer generations, are accustomed to these advancements and can more readily adjust to these transformations. As noted by Frost (2020), FinTech usage is higher among the younger demographic, with 48% of individuals aged 25 to 34 utilizing these services compared to a mere 9% of individuals aged 75 and above. Moreover, countries with younger populations also exhibit higher FinTech use. With an increasing number of individuals born with an aptitude for technology, it is probable that FinTech usage will continue to grow in the future.

The benefits of FinTech are not solely restricted to larger corporations, as a survey by Javelin Research suggests that 56% of small to medium businesses (SMEs) are interested in improving their financial tools to enhance usability, affordability, and time efficiency by circumventing traditional banking processes (Moreira-Santos, Au-Yong-Oliveira, & Palma-Moreira, 2022). Additionally, up to 70% of companies that have already adopted some form of FinTech have indicated their willingness to provide sensitive banking data, assuming it will positively impact their business (Moreira-Santos, Au-Yong-Oliveira, & Palma-Moreira, 2022).

Aside from SMEs, several large enterprises have also incorporated FinTech and have realized substantial success, which has been recognized by competitors who have not yet ventured into this realm. Examples of significant firms that have integrated FinTech include Amazon, eBay, Jd.com, Shopify, Walmart, and Rakuten.

Moreover, many nations are implementing or have developed a national strategy, with the creation of regulations being a significant priority. The World Bank Group (2021) global database on FinTech-enabling regulations reveals that 197 nations have digital banking regulations, 85 nations have marketplace lending regulations, 178 nations have e-money regulations, and 25 nations have cryptocurrency regulations. This database, which encompasses approximately 200 nations, is aimed at comparing and contrasting global FinTech-related regulations. Nations worldwide are already working towards regulating these technologies, and while most have regulations in place, they are continuing to refine them to ensure their appropriate use and mitigate potential risks.

DISCUSSION

FinTech companies use various technologies, such as artificial intelligence, machine learning, blockchain, and mobile apps, to offer innovative financial products and services that are faster, more convenient, and more accessible than traditional financial services. FinTech has disrupted the traditional financial industry by introducing new business models, lowering costs, and increasing competition. FinTech companies are also making financial services more inclusive by offering products and services to underserved communities. This company is transforming the way people access and manage their finances, making it easier and more convenient than ever before. With the rise of FinTech, consumers have more choices and better control over their financial lives. However, there are also potential risks and challenges associated with FinTech, such as data privacy, cybersecurity, and regulatory compliance.

In recent years, FinTech has gained strength in the financial market, hand in hand with technology. Innovation and digital transformation have marked this new financial world, offering tools that help people have easier access to the banking system. Likewise, there is a significant lack of knowledge by the people about what FinTech is and how it has directly impacted traditional banks. Nevertheless, this essay has shown that this technology has brought immense improvements, such as easy ways people can spend, save and move money and the speed they can do it compared to the possible theft of information. As previously recognized, specific applications have revolutionized the system, such as robotic automation of processes, open banking, conversational banking, regtech, digital wallets, and social media lending. All these options provide technological solutions to help financial institutions improve regulatory compliance parameters.

Therefore, after a discussion in which several results of the applications in companies and their pros and cons were evaluated, it can be stated that every time technology enters a production sector, it transforms it and makes a difference concerning the way things are being done and how they will be done afterward. Its implementation has challenges; however, education and training can prevent and overcome these difficulties. Through FinTech, companies have been able to identify the needs of their customers and adapt to market changes at low-cost, thus responding to one of the purposes and objectives of this paper.

The increase of ventures related to this topic and their growing portfolio of clients is an example of how the benefits they can offer meet the needs of the public. In addition, using existing technologies also opens the way to business models that are only possible on digital platforms. An example of this would be crowdfunding and crowdlending. However, FinTechs face numerous challenges, one of the most prominent being cybersecurity. As many services move towards complete digitalization, they must pay particular attention to cybersecurity when offering their services to the public. An important point regarding finance and users is the personal information leaks individuals, and companies can fall victim to. To give an idea of the magnitude of cyber attacks, during the first half of 2020 alone, a total of 36 trillion records were exposed.

It is essential to mention that most data breaches are accompanied by human error. According to Harrison (2022), it is said that 88% of these leaks are caused by human error. These figures intensify the need for staff training and warnings to users on protecting their information. That is why having a cybersecurity team prepared to counteract or prevent any attack is vital in this type of company. As an investor, new technologies can be eye-catching to add to your investment portfolio, and proper advice distinguishes between success and failure.

In summary, after evaluating all the findings of this digital platform with its pros, cons, applications, and benefits, it can be said with certainty that these challenges do not originate directly from FinTech and can be amended that can be solved through education in the prevention of these and give better guidance on the system, such as knowing how to recognize the keywords in an email that is a scam.

FUTURE RESEARCH DIRECTIONS

The findings and analysis of this study are expected to become a good starting point for any policymaker, business, or individual that uses these technologies while at the same time giving more information to those who are planning to get involved in any way with these financial technologies. Furthermore, understand FinTech's issues to find solutions and ways to improve these financial technologies. Future researchers expect to find measures to help FinTech users at a personal and business level to avoid security inconveniences.

CONCLUSION

In conclusion, FinTech has transformed the financial industry by leveraging technology to provide innovative and accessible financial services. FinTech companies have disrupted traditional financial institutions by offering lower costs, increased accessibility, greater efficiency, and more customized financial products and services. However, FinTech also comes with some risks, including security vulnerabilities and a lack of regulation. As the FinTech industry continues to grow, it will be important to strike a balance between innovation and regulation to ensure the protection of consumers and the stability of the financial system. Overall, FinTech has the potential to bring significant benefits to individuals and businesses alike, and its impact on the financial industry is likely to continue to grow in the years ahead.

After profoundly analyzing the advantages, disadvantages, and risks of implementing FinTech, some decisive aspects define an answer. FinTech brings a new level of efficiency to the table of financial markets. The evolution provided in the different sectors, products, and services banks offer to customers has had a rising global engagement due to the benefits generated. In addition to the level of evolution, FinTech currently shows, the possibility of FinTech surpassing its efficiency and applications is just a matter of time due to the high amount of investments worldwide.

With every single step comes new risks that have already started to be relevant and affect many people worldwide, and there might be different risks that society is not aware of yet. Due to the evolving pace, authorities may not get to act on time to correct breaches in FinTech. However, technology's evolution and market changes have become more aggressive with the passing of the years. The number of benefits has overcome the different risks, and FinTech has become part of our daily basis. Once the regulations arrive, many current hazards will no longer be on the map. The real danger for businesses and regular people would be not getting on board on time and losing the competitive advantages that FinTech offers.

ACKNOWLEDGMENT

This research received no specific grant from any funding agency in the public, commercial, or not-for-profit sectors.

REFERENCES

Abbasi, K. (2021). P2P Lending FinTech's and SME's Access to Finance. *Economics Letters*, (204). https://www.sciencedirect.com/science/article/abs/pii/S0165176521001671?via%3Dihub

Amsad, M. (2019). *ADBI Working Paper Series: Objectives of FinTech*. https://www.adb.org/sites/default/files/publication/533791/adbi-wp1016.pdf

Arner, D. W., Barberis, J. N., & Buckley, R. P. (2016). The Evolution of FinTech: A New Post-Crisis Paradigm? *Geo. J. Int'l. L.*, *47*, 1271.

Arner, Buckley, & Zetzsche. (2019). FinTech, Regtech and Systemic Risk: The Rise of Global Technology Risk. Systemic Risk in the Financial Sector: Ten Years after the Great Crash, 69.

Arner, D. W., Barberis, J. N., & Buckley, R. P. (2016). The Emergence of Regtech 2.0: From Know Your Customer to Know Your Data. *Journal of Financial Transformation*, *44*, 79. doi:10.2139srn.3044280

Arner, D. W., Zetzsche, D. A., Buckley, R. P., & Barberis, J. N. (2017). FinTech and RegTech: Enabling Innovation while Preserving Financial Stability. *Geo. J. Int'l. Aff.*, *18*, 47.

Bank for International Settlements. (2015). *Financial Inclusion Indicators*. https://www.bis.org/ifc/publ/ifcb38.pdf

BCG (FinTech Control Tower). (2021). *Number of FinTech startups worldwide from 2018 to 2021, by region* [Graph]. Statista. Retrieved March 19, 2023, from https://www-statista-com.ezproxy.myucwest.ca/statistics/8939 54/number-FinTech-startups-by-region/

Capgemini & EFMA. (2018). *Impact of non-traditional financial firms on selected banking products and services according to senior banking executives worldwide in 2018* [Graph]. Statista. Retrieved March 19, 2023, from https://www-statista-com.ezproxy.myucwest.ca/statistics/9468 86/impact-FinTech-banking-products-services-globally/

CFA Institute. (2023). *What is FinTech?* https://www.cfainstitute.org/en/research/foundation/2017/Fin Tech-and-regtech-in-a-nutshell-and-the-future-in-a-sandbox?s _cid=ppc_RF_Google_Search_FinTechandRegTech

Combe, C. (2006). *Introduction to E-Business: Management and Strategy*. Elsevier Ltd.

Davis, D. B. (2019). *Ransomware Activity Declines, But Remains Dangerous Threat*. Symantec Enterprise Blogs. Retrieved March 20, 2023, from https://symantec-enterprise-blogs.security.com/blogs/expert-perspectives/ransomware-activity-declines-remains-dangerous-threat

Deng, H., Dong, C., Xiao, Y., & Liu, Z. (2020). FinTech Integration in E-Business: A Systematic Review. *International Journal of Information Management*. Advance online publication. doi:10.1016/j.ijinfomgt.2020.102180

Feyen, E., Natarajan, H., & Saal, M. (2022). *FinTech and the Future of Finance Overview Paper*. The World Bank Group. https://documents.worldbank.org/curated/en/09945000516225011 0/P17300600228b70070914b0b5edf26e2f9f

FinTech Adoption Index. (2017). *The rapid emergence of FinTech*. Retrieved March 21, 2023, from https://assets.ey.com/content/dam/ey-sites/ey-com/en_gl/topics/megatrends/ey-megatrends-2020.pdf

Forbes. (2021). *How To Prevent A Data Breach In Your Company*. https://www.forbes.com/sites/forbesbusinesscouncil/2021/07/3 0/how-to-prevent-a-data-breach-in-your-company/?sh=c14fde718 da7

Forbes. (2023). *Uses of FinTech*. https://www.forbes.com/advisor/banking/what-is-FinTech/

Frost, J. (2020). *The economic forces driving FinTech adoption across countries*. Bank for International Settlements. https://www.bis.org/publ/work838.pdf

Gloor, P. (2012). *Making the e-Business Transformation*. Springer-Verlag. doi:10.1007/978-1-4471-0757-6

Harrison, P. (2022). *The FinTech Times*. https://theFinTechtimes.com/88-of-cloud-breaches-are-due-to-human-error-heres-how-to-avoid-data-breaches/

International Monetary Fund. (2019). *FinTech: The Experience So Far*. https://www.imf.org/en/Publications/Policy-Papers/Issues/201 9/06/27/FinTech-The-Experience-So-Far-47056

Jovarauskiene & Pilinkiene. (2009). E-Business or E-Technology? *Engineering Economics,* (1).

Lele, S. (2023). *FinTech 2.0: A new era of financial inclusion*. https://www.pwc.in/industries/financial-services/FinTech/Fin Tech-insights/FinTech-2-0-a-new-era-of-financial-inclusion.h tml#:~:text=The%20wider%20objective%20of%20FinTech,larger%20 goal%20of%20financial%20inclusion

Moreira-Santos, D., Au-Yong-Oliveira, M., & Palma-Moreira, A. (2022). FinTech Services and the Drivers of Their Implementation in Small and Medium Enterprises. *Information, 13*(9). https://doi-org.ezproxy.myucwest.ca/10.3390/info13090409

Murphy, D. J. (2022). *Fraud targeting FIS up 41% in 2021, mobile devices under attack.* CNP20-sm-100. Retrieved March 20, 2023, from https://news.cardnotpresent.com/news/fraud-targeting-fis-up-41-in-2021-mobile-devices-under-attack

Natsir, C. (2022). *The importance of accounting software for FinTech industry.* BusinessTech. Retrieved March 6, 2023, from https://www.hashmicro.com/blog/benefits-of-cloud-accounting-software-for-FinTech-industry/

Neykova, M., & Miltchev, R. (2019). Conceptual Approach To Introduce An Integrated Model Improving SMEs E-Business Technologies. *Management Theory and Studies for Rural Business and Infrastructure Development*, *41*(3), 381–399. doi:10.15544/mts.2019.31

Odinet, C. K., & College, O. (2018). Consumer BitCredit and FinTech Lending. *Alabama Law Review*, *69*, 781–858.

Pandya, A.-D., & Bhogal. (2001). Management of Engineering and Technology. *Portland International Conference*, *(1)*.

Security, I. B. M. (2021). *Cost of a Data Breach Report 2021.* https://www.ibm.com/downloads/cas/OJDVQGRY

Statista. (2022a). *Global consumer FinTech adoption rates 2015-2019, by category.* Statista Research Department. https://www.statista.com/statistics/1055356/FinTech-adoption-rates-globally-selected-countries-by-category/

Statista. (2022b). *Number of FinTech startups worldwide 2018-2021, by region.* Statista Research Department. https://www.statista.com/statistics/893954/number-FinTech-startups-by-region/

Team, C. F. I. (2022, December 7). *FinTech (Financial Technology).* Corporate Finance Institute. https://corporatefinanceinstitute.com/resources/wealth-management/FinTech-financial-technology/

Tharp, D. T. (2020). Potential Consumer Harm Due to Regulation on Financial Advisory Communication in the FinTech Age. *Financial Counseling and Planning*, *31*(1), 146–161. doi:10.1891/JFCP-18-00041

The World Bank Group. (2021). *Global FinTech-enabling regulations database.* https://www.worldbank.org/en/topic/FinTech/brief/global-FinTech-enabling-regulations-database

The World Bank Group and International Monetary Fund. (2019). *FinTech: The Experience So Far*. The World Bank Group. https://documents1.worldbank.org/curated/en/130201561082549144/pdf/FinTech-The-Experience-so-Far-Executive-Summary.pdf

Theaud, B. (2022). *How to choose the right FinTech for your business*. Entrepreneur. Retrieved March 6, 2023, from https://www.entrepreneur.com/money-finance/how-to-choose-the-right-FinTech-for-your-business/422790

Trificana, J. (2022, October 3). *What is FinTech? 6 main types of FinTech and how they work*. Plaid. Retrieved April 1, 2023, from https://plaid.com/resources/FinTech/what-is-FinTech/

ADDITIONAL READING

Alam, N., Gupta, L., & Zameni, A. (2019). FinTech Regulation. In *FinTech and Islamic Finance*. Palgrave Macmillan. doi:10.1007/978-3-030-24666-2_8

Elsaid, H. M. (2021). *A review of literature directions regarding the impact of FinTech firms on the banking industry*. Qualitative Research in Financial Markets. doi:10.1108/QRFM-10-2020-0197

Mention, A. (2019). The Future of FinTech. *Research Technology Management*, *62*(4), 59–63. doi:10.1080/08956308.2019.1613123

Moreira-Santos, D., Au-Yong-Oliveira, M., & Palma-Moreira, A. (2022). FinTech Services and the Drivers of Their Implementation in Small and Medium Enterprises. *Information, 13*(9), 409. doi:10.3390/info13090409

Pollari, I. (2016). The rise of FinTech opportunities and challenges. *JASSA: The Journal of the Securities Institute of Australia*, (3), 15–21. https://search.informit.org/doi/10.3316/ielapa.419743387759068

Sangwan, V. H., Prakash, P., & Singh, S. (2020). Financial technology: A review of extant literature. *Studies in Economics and Finance*, *37*(1), 71–88. doi:10.1108/SEF-07-2019-0270

Suryono, R. R., Budi, I., & Purwandari, B. (2020). Challenges and Trends of Financial Technology (FinTech): A Systematic Literature Review. *Information, 11*(12), 590. doi:10.3390/info11120590

KEY TERMS AND DEFINITIONS

Algorithmic Trading: An artificial intelligence that focuses on the buy and sell of stocks based on specific patterns.

Blockchain: A platform that uses a distributed database in which contains the most recent information and makes it available to an entire network.

Cryptocurrency: Pure digital kind of currency that has no backup by any physical commodity.

E-Commerce: Electronic commerce is the exercise of buying and selling of goods and services through the internet pages as websites and applications.

E-Wallet: Is a financial app or platform where secure money management services are provided allowing its user to send money, track transactions, make payments, and other related services.

Hedge Funds: An exclusive partnership between investors that run a high-risk high-reward investment.

Institutional Capacity: The ability combined with the skills that institutions, organizations, or jurisdictions have with the purpose to implement and execute public and private plans and contracts.

Mobile Payments: Refers to paying using a mobile device such as smartphones and tablets without the need for a physical currency or card.

Robo-Advisers: An artificial intelligence that suggests guidance based on each individual client situation.

Chapter 4

The Impact of Cryptocurrencies on the Financial Market:
National and International Monetary Systems

Phuong Nam Le
https://orcid.org/0000-0002-7578-8598
University Canada West, Canada

ABSTRACT

The emergence of cryptocurrencies has posed challenges to governments in managing the money supply. For years, governments have exercised monetary policy by controlling the supply of national currencies. However, cryptocurrencies are decentralized, meaning governments have little or no power to control them. This chapter provides a literature review on the impact of cryptocurrencies on (1) the national monetary policy, (2) the international monetary system, and (3) the role of cryptocurrency within the banking system. Research reveals that governments could consider developing their own cryptocurrency to maintain power and influence the money supply. Alternatively, they can use the legal framework to enable or disable cryptocurrency as legal tender within their jurisdictions. Due to its global nature, cryptocurrency can be used as an international payment method and become an integrated part of the FOREX market. Lastly, as cryptocurrency continues to gain popularity worldwide, regulations on crypto exchanges and issuers will be needed to avoid price bubbles.

DOI: 10.4018/978-1-6684-8368-8.ch004

INTRODUCTION

In the last decade, the topic of cryptocurrency has been of great interest to academics, business professionals and policymakers. These digital currencies were developed based on blockchain technology with the goal of being decentralized and global. Indeed, cryptocurrency users want to maintain privacy and avoid government intervention. As a result, there has been a question about the government's ability to continue maintaining its power to exercise monetary policy. Furthermore, it is vital to look at how cryptocurrency fits into our national and international financial systems. This book chapter will help to shed light on these matters. First, an overview of monetary policy, fiscal policy and the economic concept of money will be discussed. Then, the impact of cryptocurrency on government policies will be synthesized from the current literature. Second, we will look at how cryptocurrency can fit into the global monetary system. Lastly, we will examine the adaptation of cryptocurrency around the world.

CRYPTOCURRENCY AND MONETARY POLICY

The Basic of Monetary and Fiscal Policy

Let us start with the basic concepts of monetary policy. As we know, our economy is wildly fluctuating up and down. Economic fluctuation is represented by four stages in the business cycle: boom, recession, trough, and recovery. The first stage is boom means the economy is doing well, Gross Domestic Product (GDP) is growing, and there is high aggregate demand in the market. However, booming can potentially lead to inflation. When government tries to fight inflation, it will lower the total demand in the economy and can lead to a recession in which the economy is shrinking. In this stage, GDP will be reduced while the unemployment rate rises. When it reaches the bottom, we call this stage trough. After the trough stage, with the government's stimulation, the economy starts to recover, and we have the recovery stage. The four stages are shown in Figure 1.

Figure 1. Four stages of the business cycle

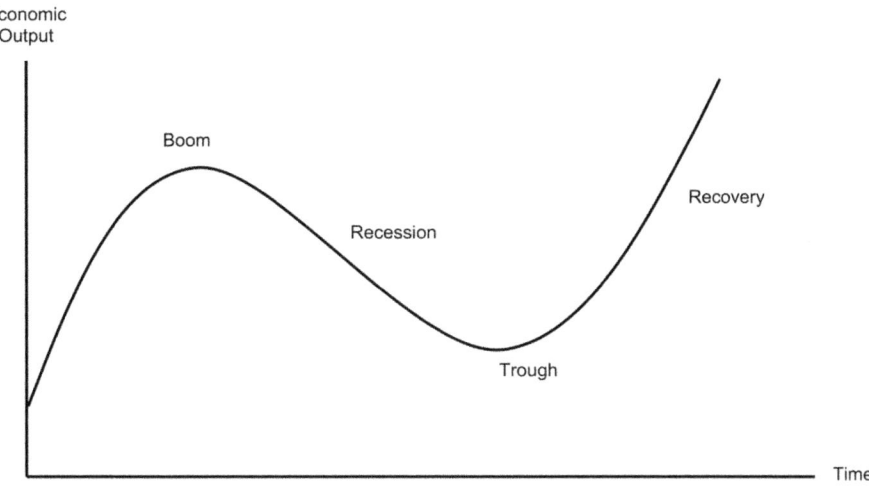

Economic fluctuation causes many problems; thus, the government needs to intervene to smooth it out. Figure 2 represents a perfect situation (green line) where the economy grows steadily and does not fluctuate at all. To achieve it, the government will need to use countercyclical policies, which include monetary and fiscal policies. Countercyclical means we go in the opposite direction of the business cycle. For example, if the economy expands too fast, these two policies will come together to slow it down and vice versa. We need the right amount of money supply in the economy to ensure it functions properly. The economy cannot grow with too little money supply, while too much money supply can cause inflation. Monetary policy refers to actions taken by the central banks to increase or decrease the money supply. For instance, increasing the money supply will help stimulate the economy. To increase the money supply, the central bank will implement an easy money policy by either lowering the interest rate or increasing private bank reserves (e.g., buying back government bonds or treasury bills). When the interest is low and bank reserve increases, credit is easier to obtain; thus, it will lead to an increase in demand. To fight inflation, central banks must implement the opposite tight money policy. The central bank will reversely increase interest rates and reduce reducing private banks' reserves. If the interest rate is high and low levels of bank reserves, credits become too expensive; businesses and individuals will cut down spending and increase savings. As a result, it will help to cool down the economy.

Fiscal policy is about managing government tax revenue and government spending. The total demand in the economy consists of five components: (1) consumer consumption spending, (2) business spending and investment, (3) government spending, (4) imports, and (5) exports. Of these five components, government spending is directly under the control of the government. During the recession, the aggregate demand in the economy is low. Thus, the government will increase their own spending to compensate for the low aggregate demand. At the same time, they will reduce taxes to allow business and individual to increase their spending. Contrarily, the government will lower aggregate demand during an economic boom with inflation risk by reducing their own spending and increasing taxes.

Figure 2. Applying the countercyclical policies

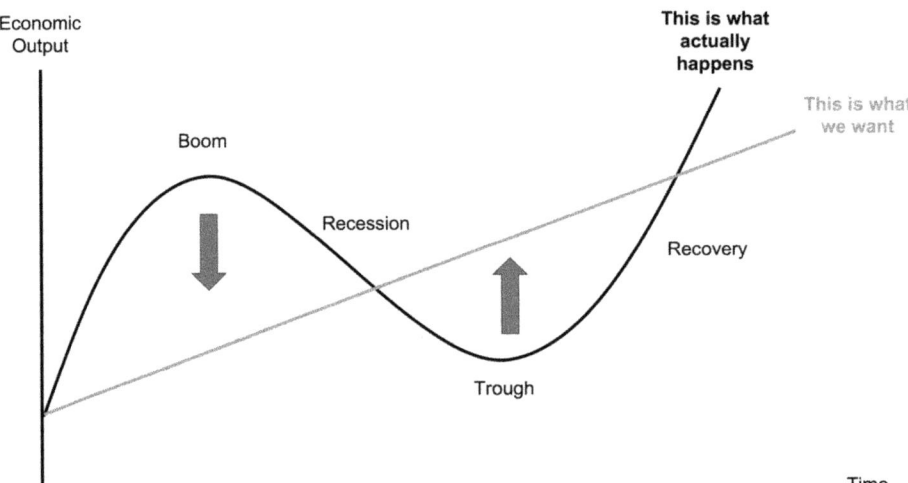

Although the countercyclical policies will not help to achieve the perfect situation, as shown in the straight line in Figure 2, they can significantly reduce the magnitude of fluctuation. Figure 3 shows the result of the policies. There is still some fluctuation, but the magnitude has reduced significantly.

Figure 3. Result of countercyclical policies

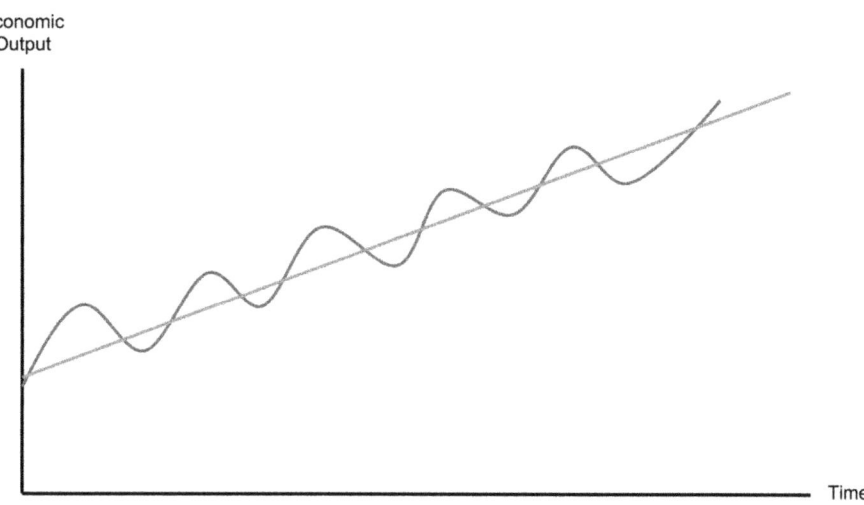

The following Table 1 shows interest rates set by central banks worldwide. The rate has increased significantly due to excessive inflation in 2022 following the pandemic (The Economist, 2022). Using the high-interest rate, governments around the world hope to bring inflation under control.

Table 1. Current central bank interest rates in selected countries as of January 29, 2023

Country	Current Rate	Country	Current Rate
United States	4.500%	Indonesia	6.500%
Australia	3.100%	Israel	3.750%
Chile	11.250%	Japan	-0.100%
South Korea	3.500%	Mexico	10.500%
Brazil	13.750%	New Zealand	3.500%
Great Britain	3.500%	Norway	2.750%
Canada	4.500%	Poland	6.750%
China	3.650%	Russia	7.500%
Czech Republic	7.000%	Saudi Arabia	5.000%
Denmark	1.900%	South Africa	7.250%
Europe	2.500%	Sweden	2.500%
Hungary	13.000%	Switzerland	1.000%
India	6.250%	Turkey	9.000%

Source: Central banks - summary of current interest rates (2023)

Table 2 shows the total government spending as a percentage of GDP from G20 countries. It is clear that government is a major spender in the economy. Therefore, the government can adjust its spending to significantly influence the country's total demand and inflation level. Table 3 shows government tax revenue as a percentage of revenue for the G20 nations. When government tax revenue is higher than its expenditure, it is said to have a budget surplus. Vice versa, when its expenditure is higher than tax revenue, it causes a budget deficit. During the economic boom, the government will likely run into a budget surplus because it can increase taxes and reduce spending to avoid inflation. However, a budget deficit will happen during a recession since the government will stimulate the economy by increasing its spending and cutting down on taxes.

Table 2. Government spending as a percentage of GDP from the G20 countries

Country	Spending (% of G.D.P. 2021)	Country	Spending (% of G.D.P. 2021)
Saudi Arabia	24.43	South Korea	18.16
France	24.25	Russia	17.77
UK	22.38	China	15.92
Australia	22.3	Argentina	15.84
Germany	22.14	USA	14.38
Canada	21.7	Turkey	13.06
Japan	21.42	Mexico	12.04
Italy	19.79	India	11.13
South Africa	19.65	Indonesia	9.14
Brazil	19.1		

Source: Theglobaleconomy.com (2021)

Table 3. Tax revenue as a percentage of GDP from the G20 countries

Country	Tax Revenue (% of G.D.P.)	Country	Tax Revenue (% of G.D.P.)
Saudi Arabia	8.6	South Korea	14.9
France	24.69	Russia	10.8
UK	24.73	China	8.1
Australia	22.61	Argentina	10.9
Germany	10.55	USA	9.9
Canada	13.3	Turkey	17.6
Japan	11.6	Mexico	14.3
Italy	24.8	India	12
South Africa	23.3	Indonesia	8.3
Brazil	13		

Source: The World Bank (n.d.)

The Evolution of Money and the Introduction of Cryptocurrency

Many thousand years ago, before having money, the barter system was the primary method for exchanging goods or services (Ritchie, 2022). In this system, goods will be directly traded for other goods. However, there are a couple of issues with the barter system. First, finding someone to complete the transaction is not always practical. For example, a person who has a dog and would like to get a pig would need to find someone else who has a pig and wants a dog. This transaction is quite hard to achieve because the person might be able to find someone with a pig but want something else rather than a dog. The other issue is how to value the goods. For instant, how many dogs are considered equivalent to a pig? Not all dogs are identical, and neither all pigs are the same. Thus, it is difficult to have a consistent ratio to trade. Even when we can specify, for example, two dogs equivalent to one pig, if one side only wants to trade a dog, the other side might not agree to trade half of the pig. Furthermore, it raises another issue, how do we store half of the pig? As the story illustrates, humankind needs something to solve the problem with the barter system, and money was invented.

There are three critical functions of money: (1) medium of exchange, (2) unit of account, and (3) store of value (Claeys, Demertzis, & Efstathiou, 2018). First, it is a medium of exchange in which people use money as an intermediary to exchange different goods or services. Someone with a dog can trade it for money and use the money to buy a pig. Second, it serves as the unit of account so we can easily measure the value of other items. For example, a dog is equivalent to 5 units of currency, while a pig can be 14 units of the same currency. Third, if we stored the value to use in the future using money, this function could not be achieved if we stored livestock or plants instead of money. One of the earlier forms of money was seashell (Wu, 2019). Seashell has been used for centuries as money, although they might not be the best compared to our standard today. Modern economists have stated that for something to be used as money, it should have the following characteristics:

- *Acceptability: Money is widely acceptable for liquidity*
- *Portability: Money is easy to carry*
- *Durability: Money is able to withstand the wear and tear*
- *Uniformity: Money has an interchangeable form*
- *Divisibility: Money is divisible into smaller denominations*
- *Scarcity: Scarce in nature, and the supply cannot be inflated easily*
- *Recognisability: Money is easily distinguished*
- *Stable Value: Money should have a stable value for daily transactions. (Crypto.com, 2020a)*

The following form of money in history is the metal coin. The early metal coin was found in China about 1000 BC. (Ritchie, 2022). Gold was one of the most popular metals used as money, especially for cross-border trade. The drawback of having metal money is that they are heavy to carry around. Thus, people deposited their gold coins at private banks and received bank notes which served as evidence that they owned gold at the bank. These banknotes were used as the medium of exchange without the need to withdraw gold from the bank. Thus, paper money was created. These earlier bank notes were backed by gold, meaning banks could only issue paper money based on the amount of gold they held. Although this gold backing is not used nowadays, the central bank can issue banknotes without holding any gold.

Two types of value are associated with money: intrinsic value and representative value (*Crypto.com*, 2020b). Intrinsic value is the value of the material that makes up money. Representative value is the value printed on the money. For example, we print $100 on 1 ounce of gold and print $100 on a piece of paper money. Both of them have the same representative value of $100. However, one ounce of gold will carry a much higher intrinsic value than paper money. Applying this concept to cryptocurrency, it has almost no intrinsic value but only representative value.

Modern currency can take many forms, from traditional coins and banknotes to newer forms such as credit cards and debit cards. Together with the development of e-commerce, online payment methods are also evolving, including digital wallets such as PayPal and mobile payment services like Apple Pay. In the last decade, we have observed rapid technology development in the financial service sector, resulting in a field called FinTech. As Goldstein, Jiang, and Karolyi (2019) stated, modern technologies have revolutionized the financial industry.

The newly created cryptocurrency is considered a subcategory of digital currency. Digital currencies are usually centralized and issued by public or private organizations (Chuen, Guo, & Wang, 2017). For example, there are digital currencies in the form of game tokens (e.g., World of Warcraft Gold). Users will need to use fiat money to purchase those digital tokens. Since these digital currencies can only be transacted within a specific platform, they cannot be used as legal tender. Cryptocurrencies are decentralized using blockchain technology (Chuen, Guo, & Wang, 2017). Blockchain technology helps to record transactions using a distributed ledger on the peer-to-peer network (PricewaterhouseCoopers, n.d.). Basically, it is a chain consisting of many data blocks. The hash value will link each block to previous blocks before and after. Each node on the network will have a copy of the same chain. Figure 4 illustrates the concept of the distributed ledger. This model will help prevent attackers from modifying the block's content since it will cause inconsistency with other copies of the chain on the network. Bitcoin was one of the first cryptocurrencies published in 2008 (Saksonova & Kuzmina-Merlino, 2019). Today there are thousands of different cryptocurrencies in the market. Table 4 provides a list of the top 10 cryptocurrencies by market capitalization.

Table 4. Top 10 cryptocurrencies by market capitalization as of Dec 2022

No.	Cryptocurrencies	Symbol	Market Cap (USD)
1	Bitcoin	BTC	$322,681,178,177
2	Ethereum	ETH	$145,228,570,927
3	Tether	USDT	$66,060,266,835
4	USD Coin	USDC	$44,941,949,846
5	BNB	BNB	$38,424,383,389
6	Binance USD	BUSD	$18,442,477,811
7	XRP	XRP	$17,786,516,630
8	Dogecoin	DOGE	$10,493,898,301
9	Cardano	A.D.A.	$9,182,816,278
10	Polygon	MATIC	$7,108,517,316

Source: Coinmarketcap.com (2022)

Figure 4. Distributed ledger

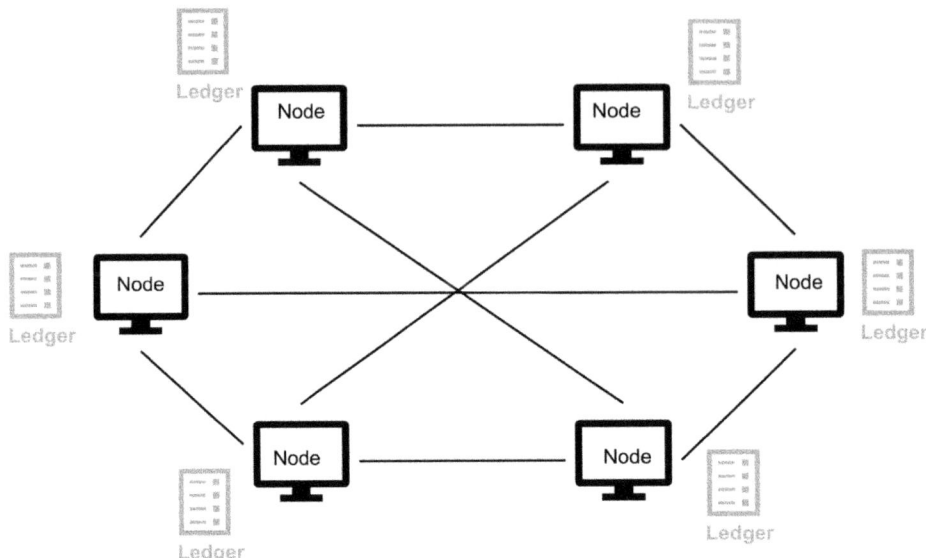

Currently, there are two methods for verifying transactions made with cryptocurrency: Proof-of-work (PoW) and Proof-of-state (PoS). Bitcoin has used PoW since its inception in 2008. The PoW method requires computer power to solve complicated mathematical functions to verify the transactions before adding a new block to the chain. When a transaction happens, a hash value (SHA-256) must be verified to avoid attackers tamping the transaction. Many computer systems in the network will compete to be the first ones to solve the math. The winner will be rewarded with new coins, and this process is also called coin mining. There is a downside to PoW, which will require extensive energy usage and causes environmental concerns. Proof-of-Stake (PoS) provides solutions to the excessive energy usage of PoW. Under the PoS model, a validator will be selected from the current coin owners to avoid competition in validating the transaction. In order to be selected, the coin owner will need to deposit coins as "stakes" in the coin network. After successfully validating a legitimate transaction, they will be rewarded. (Marquit, 2022). Otherwise, if they cheat the system, their coins will be destroyed. Ethereum has used proof-of-stake to verify its transaction (Ethereum.org, 2023).

There is a risk of a 51% attack on a cryptocurrency network. In theory, if a group controls more than 51% of computers solving the network's cryptographic puzzle, they can alter the creation of a new block in the Blockchain. Although, in reality, it is pretty hard to perform such type of attack due to the high cost of controlling an extensive computer network (Frankenfield, 2023).

How Will Cryptocurrencies Impact Monetary Policies?

As cryptocurrencies are decentralized, governments have little or no control over the supply of the currencies. Thus, it poses a challenge for central banks and threatens their monopoly power to exercise their monetary policies (Claeys, Demertzis, & Efstathiou, 2018). Moreover, the issuance of cryptocurrencies is automatic and transparent without political influence. Because of their digital form, cryptocurrencies are considered global in nature.

Claeys, Demertzis, and Efstathiou (2018) concluded that cryptocurrencies are not able to provide a decent monetary function compared to the official currencies issued by central banks. As stated earlier, for anything to be considered money, it needs to have three functions: (1) medium of exchange, (2) unit of account, and (3) store of value. In fact, the supply of cryptocurrencies cannot be responsive to various economic conditions. Its supply is fixed (e.g., bitcoin has a supply limit of 21 million) and inelastic. Thus, when demand change, it will cause volatility in the price of cryptocurrencies. When the value is unstable, it is hard for the public to use cryptocurrencies to fulfill the three functions of money. Since the value of cryptocurrencies fluctuates, it cannot be used to measure the value of other items. Cryptocurrencies can cause the prices of other items it measures to fluctuate too. Also, the market will only use the currency as a medium of exchange if it is relatively stable. Lastly, individuals or organizations that want to store their wealth would not choose cryptocurrencies due to their unpredictable value (Tomić, Todorović, & Čakajac, 2020). Thus, Claeys, Demertzis, and Efstathiou (2018) concluded that cryptocurrencies are more like speculative assets rather than actual money. In addition, the process of issuing cryptocurrencies is automated; thus, it is not possible to make sure the private issuers of these currencies are accountable to society if there is a situation of oversupply or undersupply (Claeys, Demertzis & Efstathiou, 2018). It is not the same as the government is responsible for the national economy through the supply of its traditional currencies.

Figure 5. Fluctuation in bitcoin price (in UDS) for the 5-year period ended on December 5, 2022
Source: Google Finance (2022)

Figure 6. Fluctuation in Ethereum price (in UDS) for the 5-year period ended on December 5, 2022
Source: Google Finance (2022)

Figures 5 and 6 show the fluctuation of the two most popular cryptocurrencies (Bitcoin and Ethereum) in the five-year period from the end of 2017 to the end of 2022. For Bitcoin, the peak at the end of 2021 is approximately 20 times the value at the end of 2018. For Ethereum, the magnitude is even more extensive; during the same period (end of 2018 to end of 2021), the value of this currency increased by more than 50 times.

Cryptocurrency creators have produced a potential solution for the volatility problem called "stablecoins." The goal is to create a cryptocurrency that is stable in value and does not fluctuate significantly. An example of "stablecoin" is "Basis." The mechanism behind "Basis" is ensuring its supply can match the change in demand so that the value can be relatively stable over time (Tomić, Todorović, & Čakajac, 2020). Indeed, this is still an idea but not very practical. For the supply to catch up with demand, the supply level of "Basis" needs to be tight to the Consumer Price Index of a currency area (e.g., the US, Eurozone). The concern is now CPI which country should be chosen since we have many jurisdictions around the world. Moreover, this goes against the global nature of cryptocurrencies (Claeys, Demertzis, & Efstathiou, 2018). Cryptocurrency should be global and decentralized. Moreover, this means that someone (governments or institutions) will monitor the supply of the currency. Thus, it will reduce the privacy feature of cryptocurrency.

Despite the shortcoming of cryptocurrencies, Claeys, Demertzis, and Efstathiou (2018) pointed out that cryptocurrencies can positively impact monetary policy if governments can develop procedures to enable or disable the use of cryptocurrencies as the medium of exchange. From the legal aspect, governments can deem a currency as legal tender. Thus, cryptocurrencies can be widely used if recognized by the government. For example, they can prevent using cryptocurrencies as a medium of exchange when they need to tighten monetary policy and allow using them when they try to loosen the policies. Although, this option can confuse consumers because sometimes the government will allow cryptocurrencies to be used; other times, they are not allowed.

While the ability of cryptocurrencies to fulfill the three functions of money is still in debate, it does have some impact on the economy. A study by Oh and Nguyen (2018) pointed out that privately issued cryptocurrencies increase the total money supply and lower interest rates. Using the IS-LM and MP model, Oh and Nguyen (2018) explained the impact of cryptocurrency on monetary policy. If cryptocurrencies are used alongside traditional money, there is an increase in the money supply. However, cryptocurrencies can also be considered a substitute for traditional money. According to economic theory, when people demand to buy more cryptocurrencies, the demand for traditional money will decrease. Thus, an increase in money supply (the addition of cryptocurrency to traditional currency) and a decrease in demand (people shift to use cryptocurrency instead of traditional currency) will cause lower interest rates. Consequently, it will lead to inflation, and the central bank will need to use its power to raise the interest rate back to control inflation. As seen in this illustration, the government and central bank are pretty passive in reacting. Therefore, like many other studies, Oh and Nguyen (2018) stated that cryptocurrencies could rival traditional currencies and central banks. The governments cannot control the supply of cryptocurrencies and weaken their power to exercise monetary policies. It is recommended that governments need to develop policies to prevent private parties from manipulating these cryptocurrencies.

Even though cryptocurrencies have existed for over a decade, they did not fully diminish the power of central banks to exercise their monetary policies. As pointed out by Tomić, Todorović, & Čakajac (2020), this situation might change when (1) a private cryptocurrency is widely accepted as a means of payment or (2) if countries begin to develop their own cryptocurrencies. On the one hand, if privately issued cryptocurrencies are used widely enough, it will reduce the central bank's power. For instance, to fight inflation, central banks can raise interest to reduce the money supply. Consumers and businesses can migrate to use cryptocurrencies instead of traditional currencies. Thus, the impact of the central bank's monetary policies can be significantly reduced. This situation has been evidenced in small economies where financial systems are based on foreign currencies (e.g., the US dollar) (Tomić, Todorović, & Čakajac, 2020). As the government tightens the supply of domestic currency, citizens shift to using foreign currencies instead for their daily transactions. Indeed, the monetary policy power could be unwillingly transferred to private cryptocurrency issuers, which can be risky for the economy.

On the other hand, the government can follow the technological trend by issuing its own cryptocurrencies. There are several good reasons for governments to consider this option. First, executing transactions using cryptocurrencies is easier and faster than using traditional currencies. Second, cryptocurrencies make it easier to receive an inflow of money for countries that heavily depend on remittance from overseas citizens. Third, cryptocurrencies can help countries to overcome international sanctions, such as in the case of Venezuela (Tomić, Todorović, & Čakajac, 2020). If the central banks introduce their own cryptocurrencies, there is not much change to their power to exercise monetary policy. The government will have control over their own digital currency. Thus, the other benefit of this option is that government can fight against the illegal use of cryptocurrencies for terrorist or criminal activities. However, it might impact personal privacy or freedom (Tomić, Todorović, & Čakajac, 2020), which is not consistent with the anonymous feature of other cryptocurrencies.

Bordo and Levin (2017) also discussed that digital currency issued by the central bank (Central Bank Digital Currency, CBDC) could be a better solution to the traditional currencies that are currently used. The government-issued digital currency can be less fluctuate compared to privately issued currencies. There are a couple of benefits regarding the three functions of money. According to the authors, it is the costless medium of exchange, a secure store of value and a stable unit of account (Bordo & Levin, 2017). The CBDC will help the market become more efficient and productive because transaction cost is low.

Additionally, with digital currency under control, the government can still exercise their monetary policies as with traditional currencies. To do this, it is critical that the central bank will need to determine the supply of their virtual currency. This is consistent with Tomić, Todorović, and Čakajac (2020). By using CBDC, the government can overcome the risk of losing control over monetary policies.

How About Cryptocurrencies' Impacts on Fiscal Policy?

Although cryptocurrencies will mainly impact monetary policies, they might also impact a nation's fiscal policies. As discussed earlier, fiscal policies include using government spending and taxation to smooth out economic fluctuations. If the government wants to reduce overall economic spending, it must collect more taxes from businesses and individuals to reduce consumption and business spending. However, Obu and Ukpere (2022) pointed out that cryptocurrencies can potentially enable tax evasion. Transaction through cryptocurrencies is usually under report. Therefore, it is hard for the government to keep track of income and collect the right amount of tax.

On the other hand, a reduction in government tax revenue can also hurt government spending. During the recession, governments sometimes want to stimulate the economy with their spending package. If their tax revenue is low, it will cause the government to run into a bad deficit. Thus, cryptocurrencies are weakening not only government monetary policy but also fiscal policies.

Tax on Cryptocurrencies

Xu (2019) stated that policy on cryptocurrency taxation is critical to ensure a clear and transparent tax system. Solodan (2019) looked at similar matters in some European nations. According to Solodan (2019), there is no consistent approach toward taxation on cryptocurrency among different nations. The author suggested that several types of taxes can be imposed on cryptocurrency, such as taxes on capital gains and taxes on income received through cryptocurrency. Within Europe, Great Britain (GB) is the leader in developing tax regulations related to cryptocurrency. They have tax regulations on businesses, individual income, and capital gain using cryptocurrency. The GB's primary goal is to avoid cryptocurrency being used for criminal activities.

CRYPTOCURRENCIES AND THE INTERNATIONAL MONETARY SYSTEM

Overview of the International Monetary System

The international monetary system consists of many policies and arrangements related to cross-border transactions and exchange rates (Santor, 2011). Hundreds of years ago, gold was used as the mean of payment for cross-border trade. Under the Gold Standard, currencies around the world were pegged to gold. As a result, the exchanges are determined relative to gold (Hill, Hult, McKaig, & Cotae, 2021). For example, if one ounce of gold can be purchased with ten units of currency A or twenty units of currency B, then the exchange rate will be 1 unit of currency A to 2 units of currency B. This system worked well until the late 1920s and early 1930s.

The Great Depression, which started in 1929, led to trade and currency wars. As the economies of many nations suffered economic chaos during the 1930s, countries tried to find a way to deal with the problem. Many governments believe an increase in exports and a reduction in imports can solve their economic problem. As a result, many nations raised trade barriers that led to the trade war. Currencies can be another weapon to achieve this goal; governments devaluate their own currency, hoping that their product will be cheaper and more competitive in foreign markets. Thus, a currency war started when all countries tried to do the same, devaluating their own currency (Lyons, 2012). Then, the second World War came in 1939 and ended in 1945. Toward the end of the War, the world leaders recognized that an international authority was needed to ensure stabilized order of the world currency and to avoid currency war from happening again. Thus, International Monetary Fund (IMF) was formed in 1944 during the Bretton Woods Conference. Nowadays, IMF has 190 member countries. Under the Bretton Woods system, all currencies are pegged to US dollars, and only US dollars can be used to redeem gold. This system was in place until it collapsed in the early 1970s (International Monetary Fund, n.d.). Due to the high oil price and the expensive War in Vietnam, people lost trust in the US dollar. Governments of many countries wanted to use the US dollar to redeem gold. US President Richard Nixon decided to temporarily suspend the dollar's convertibility to gold in 1971, which led to the collapse of the Bretton Woods system (International Monetary Fund, n.d.).

In the mid of 1970s, a new agreement was formed called the Jamaica Accords. This new agreement allowed currency values to float against each other. This system is still in place today. There are currently three approaches to the currency exchange rate: (1) free float exchange rate, (2) managed float, and (3) fixed exchange rate. First, some governments let their currencies float freely against other currencies. The exchange rates are, therefore, mainly determined by the demand and supply of that currencies. On the one hand, assuming all other factors remain constant, if the demand for a currency increases, its value will appreciate and vice versa. On the other hand, if the supply increase, the value of the currency will depreciate. This is consistent with the basic economic concept. Second, some governments might allow their currency to float against others but will be open to intervention if needed. There are a couple of instruments the central bank can use to intervene with the value of their currencies. They will try to influence the supply and demand of their currency. If the central bank wants to increase the demand for its national currency, it can use the foreign reserve to buy back its own currency. To exercise this policy, the central bank needs to hold a significant amount of foreign reserves. In the reverse situation, the central bank can use its currency to purchase foreign currencies to increase the supply and lower the value of its own currencies. China has implemented this tactic for many years to manipulate its Yuan for political and economic reasons (Howard, 2013). The purpose of currency manipulation is quite similar to the situation during the currency war in the first half of the twentieth century, which is to export more and import less. Third, other countries, usually smaller nations, might decide to peg their currencies to the value of other currencies, usually of major nations like the US dollar. In this case, the central banks will take appropriate actions to ensure their currency is somewhat fixed to the target currencies.

Discussing the international monetary system, we cannot ignore the concept of currency convertibility. Some country currencies can be convertible freely to other currencies, while others are non-convertible. Convertibility can also have an impact on the value of the currencies and their ability to be used as an international currency. Usually, convertible currencies can be used in the international payment system. Most advanced nations have convertible currencies (Santor, 2011). For cryptocurrencies, there is an equivalent concept called convertible virtual currency. According to the US Commodity Future Trading Commission, Bitcoin, among other cryptocurrencies, is an example of convertible virtual currency, meaning that it can be converted to other fiat currencies (The US Commodity Future Trading Commission, n.d.; Hayes, 2022).

How Does Cryptocurrency Fit Into the International Monetary System Today?

Potential Use of Cryptocurrency in International Trade

It is crucial to have a truly international currency to facilitate international payment. Currently, international trade transactions will have to deal with high bank fee and currency conversion, which is costly and delay the process (Melnyk, 2019).

Cryptocurrencies, in theory, can be international currencies to fulfill the function of international payment.

Due to a lack of trust in the international market, current international transactions are arranged in a complicated matter involving a Letter of Credit (L/C). For example, in a typical payment process in international trade, the buyer will need to get the L/C from their bank and send it to the foreign seller's bank. After the seller side is certain about the payment, they will ship the products. Lastly, using the Bill of Landing (B/L) and other documents as evidence of the shipment, the seller will get paid (Chang, Luo, & Chen, 2019). Using Blockchain, crypto-asset, and smart contracts can potentially replace the use of L/C. It is possible to set up a smart contract for international trade transactions. When an event triggers, payment will be released using cryptocurrency.

However, there are shortcomings; accounting standards like International Financial Reporting Standards (IFRS) or Generally Accepted Accounting Principles (GAAP) in some countries do not recognize these virtual currencies as cash. Due to the limitation to performing functions of money, as discussed earlier, it might not be appropriate to classify cryptocurrencies as cash on the company balance sheet. From an accounting perspective, cryptocurrencies are properties rather than cash or cash equivalent. In the future, there is a need for revised accounting standards to treat cryptocurrency appropriately as a currency.

FOREX Market

Cryptocurrency can be bought and sold in the exchange market for currency, just like any other currency. Similar to other fiat currencies, cryptocurrency prices are determined by the supply and demand of that particular currency. Businesses and individuals can easily convert cryptocurrency to other traditional currencies. Thus, we can view cryptocurrency as another alternative for the international payment. Moreover, cryptocurrency can have an impact on the foreign exchange market. For instance, research showed that cryptocurrency substantially impacts the Asian foreign exchange market. Corelli (2018) showed that cryptocurrencies are connected to some Asian fiat currencies (Thai Baht, Taiwan Dollar, and Chinese Yuan).

Component of Foreign Reserve

As discussed earlier, the government could use the foreign reserve to manipulate currency value. Moore and Stephen (2016) suggested that it is possible for central banks to hold cryptocurrencies within their international reserve portfolio among other foreign currencies. It is expected that cryptocurrencies will gain more popularity as the mean of international payment in the future. However, it might increase the volatility of the total reserve.

International Monetary Fund (IMF) and Cryptocurrency

It is possible that a government-backed cryptocurrency will destabilize the international monetary system (Goldsmith, 2019). Thus, Goldsmith called IMF to develop a strategy to avoid this issue in the future. The IMF is calling for consistent global standards and regulations related to cryptocurrencies. In addition, IMF suggests the world should focus more on stablecoins. The international institution also warns some emerging economies that they are on the edge of "generating risks to financial stability" due to cryptoization (Li, 2022). The IMF Deputy Managing Director said that the use of cryptocurrency can cause "capital outflows and loss of monetary sovereignty." According to Li (2022), to regulate the cryptocurrency market, the IMF gave several suggestions, including:

1. Cryptocurrency providers should be licensed, registered, and authorized.
2. There should be strict regulations on the crypto exchange.
3. Strong regulation is needed for stablecoins issuers to avoid a challenge to monetary and financial stability.
4. There should be regulations for financial institutions that want to engage in cryptocurrency.
5. The regulation should be consistent around the world.

Solutions to Deal With the Built-In Risk

Despite the potential usage as a means of international payment, Raza, Ahmed, and Aloui (2022) expressed that cryptocurrencies have built-in economic risk. This results from the enormous volatility in the price of the cryptocurrency, as pointed out by other researchers (Tomić, Todorović, & Čakajac, 2020; Claeys, Demertzis, & Efstathiou, 2018). In general, cryptocurrencies are more volatile than traditional fiat currencies such as the US dollar and Euro. Thus, the exchange rate between cryptocurrency and other currencies can fluctuate significantly. The other risk is that these currencies can be used for criminal activities (Corelli, 2018). Criminals can use cryptocurrency for international money laundering activities.

As suggested above, stablecoins can somewhat solve the problem of volatility. To issue stablecoins, a centralized institution will be responsible for issuing and redeeming cryptocurrencies. Moreover, the issued cryptocurrency will be backed by fiat currencies (Bains & Singh, 2022). It is just like paper monies was backed by gold in history. Moreover, there is a need to rebalance the privacy benefits and the costs of money laundering with cryptocurrency. We might need to accept that centralizing issued cryptocurrencies reduce some privacy to avoid criminal use of these currencies (Bains & Singh, 2022).

CRYPTOCURRENCIES AND THE BANKING SYSTEM

Cryptocurrency Regulation and Adoption in Different Countries

Sharma, Verma, and Sam (2021) pointed out that cryptocurrencies are gaining more popularity among people and are getting recognition from governments. According to the authors, it is possible in the future for cryptocurrency to be used as both a medium of exchange and an investable asset. It is also worth noting that tech-savvy nations are more open to accepting cryptocurrency than others. Different countries currently have different treatments for cryptocurrencies. Some countries consider them as virtual assets; others treat them as foreign currencies. Many countries have started to tax capital gain on cryptocurrency investment. The authors are confident that, in the long run, cryptocurrencies can replace fiat currencies to become the world's decentralized payment method (Sharma, Verma, & Sam, 2021).

North America and Europe are the leaders in developing policies and regulations regarding cryptocurrency. Most countries in these two regions either have (1) tax laws or (2) anti-money laundering related to cryptocurrency, or both (US Law Library of Congress, 2021). These legal frameworks can open the road for the broader acceptance of cryptocurrency in the future. For example, the United States and Canada have both types of laws. In the United States, the Internal Revenue Service (IRS) issued Notice 2014-21, stating that tax principles should be applied to cryptocurrency transactions. Any virtual currency received due to the sales of goods or services should be reported as part of gross income. In addition, virtual currency is considered property, not foreign currency. Thus, gains or losses realized from virtual currency trade will need to be reported. The US Department of the Treasury also introduced a legal framework to deal with potential money laundering activities (US Department of the Treasury, 2021). Similar treatment can be found in Canada. The Canada Revenue Agency (CRA) issued *a Guide for cryptocurrency users and tax professionals* (2021). This document explains the tax treatment for cryptocurrency transactions and capital gains or losses from trading cryptocurrency. The other legal document is *Money laundering and terrorist financing indicators— Virtual currency transactions (2021)* by the Government of Canada, which provides guidance to indicate red flags with money laundering and terrorist financing. Other countries may only have one of the two laws. For instance, Mexico only has a law on Anti-money laundering and anti-terrorism financing, while Brazil only has a tax law on cryptocurrency.

Nevertheless, 51 jurisdictions around the world have either absolute or implicit bans on transactions involving cryptocurrencies (US Law Library of Congress, 2021). Most countries that ban cryptocurrencies are in Africa and Asia. China is an example of countries that explicitly bans cryptocurrency. The Chinese government issued notice 237 in 2021 that banned the use of cryptocurrency due to the risk of financial and economic disorder and potential criminal activities (China Government Network, 2021). Some countries implicitly ban cryptocurrencies, such as Indonesia, Vietnam, Nigeria, and Bangladesh (US Law Library of Congress, 2021). These countries do not have laws that clearly ban cryptocurrency. However, through governments or central bank documents, it is understood that cryptocurrency is not allowed. De-Best (2023) conducted a survey in 56 countries regarding the adoption of cryptocurrency. Table 5 shows the percentage of respondents who owned or used cryptocurrency. It is interesting to see that cryptocurrency is popular in countries where it is explicitly or implicitly banned, like Nigeria, Vietnam, Turkey, and even China.

Table 5. Cryptocurrency adoptions in various countries from 2019 to 2022 by Statista (% of respondents)

No.	Countries	2019	2020	2021	2022	No.	Countries	2019	2020	2021	2022
1	Nigeria	28	32	42	45	29	New Zealand	6	5	11	15
2	Thailand	23	18	31	44	30	Norway	7	8	9	15
3	Turkey	20	16	25	40	31	Portugal	9	8	14	15
4	Argentina	16	14	21	35	32	Austria	7	7	10	14
5	United Arab Emirates	20	10	13	34	33	Canada	5	5	11	14
6	Philippines	15	20	28	29	34	Chile	11	12	14	14
7	Vietnam	22	21	27	27	35	Egypt	10	8	12	14
8	India	7	9	15	25	36	Lithuania	6	9	11	14
9	Singapore	9	10	11	25	37	Peru	15	16	13	14
10	Brazil	16	11	16	24	38	Romania	9	6	11	14
11	South Africa	16	18	21	24	39	Russia	9	7	9	14
12	Malaysia	6	12	16	20	40	Taiwan	10	5	10	14
13	Netherlands	9	10	15	20	41	Czechia	10	9	15	13
14	Saudi Arabia	14	11	12	20	42	Japan	3	4	4	13
15	Switzerland	10	11	16	20	43	Mexico	11	10	10	13
16	Indonesia	11	13	12	19	44	Serbia	9	7	11	13
17	Kenya	10	11	16	19	45	Denmark	8	4	11	12
18	Pakistan	6	6	14	19	46	Finland	4	5	7	12
19	South Korea	8	8	13	19	47	Germany	5	5	10	12
20	Australia	7	8	12	18	48	Hungary	11	6	9	12
21	Greece	11	11	13	18	49	Morocco	10	9	10	12
22	Colombia	18	15	15	16	50	Italy	7	5	8	11
23	Hong Kong	11	11	13	16	51	Poland	8	7	10	11
24	Spain	10	9	14	16	52	Sweden	4	5	9	11
25	United States	6	6	13	16	53	United Kingdom	5	5	7	11
26	Belgium	7	6	10	15	54	Israel	8	5	8	10
27	Dominican Republic	10	10	11	15	55	China	9	7	7	9
28	Ireland	8	10	13	15	56	France	5	6	7	9

Source: De-Best (2023)

CRYPTO BANKING AND PAYMENT CARD SERVICES

There is a network of cryptocurrency exchanges that allow customers to convert cryptocurrencies to fiat money or other assets. Customers need to transfer funds from their bank account to a crypto exchange account to purchase cryptocurrency. Table 6 shows the list of the top 10 crypto exchanges based on the trading volume.

Table 6. Top 10 crypto exchanges based on trading volume as of January 24, 2023

No.	Exchange	Trading Volume
1	Binance	$19,648,366,711
2	Upbit	$5,088,646,383
3	SuperEx	$3,983,258,682
4	CITEX	$3,017,926,067
5	Hotcoin Global	$2,914,054,481
6	IndoEx	$2,698,261,708
7	Coinbase Exchange	$2,241,920,384
8	P2B	$1,661,323,338
9	Bitrue	$1,537,681,736
10	OKX	$1,447,567,933

Source: CoinMarketCap (2023).

At this point, most banks do not have an account for depositing cryptocurrency. However, cryptocurrency holders can easily convert cryptocurrency into cash through a network of Crypto ATMs. Crypto ATMs are available for the holder to cash out. There are 38,342 Crypto ATMs around the world. The majority of them are in North America and Europe: 86.8% in the United States, 6.7% in Canada and 3.8% in Europe (Coinatmradar.com, n.d.).

Many banks are now becoming more crypto-friendly. For example, the US Provident Bank started to provide a line of credit for crypto-backed lending or crypto-mining operation (BankProv Annual Report, 2021). Similarly, another US bank, Silvergate, provides services to facilitate investors transferring their money to a crypto exchange network. They also provide lending backed by crypto assets (Benoit, 2022). However, following the fall of F.T.X., Silvergate and similar banks are negatively impacted. For an instant, in the last few months of 2022, two-thirds of Silvergate customers withdrew US$8 billion (Gerken, 2023). Earlier in 2023, the US Federal Reserve, Federal Deposit Insurance Corporation and the Office of the Comptroller of the Currency together issued a warning to financial institutions involved in cryptocurrency of potential legal risks or fraud (Liang, 2023). Thus, we might see a slowdown in crypto adoption across financial institutions.

There are several crypto credit cards in the market. These credit cards work the same way as any other traditional credit card. However, the rewards or cash back will be in the form of cryptocurrency. For example, the Crypto.com Visa card provides a means of payment, and cardholders can earn cash back in the form of CRO Token, a cryptocurrency created by Crypto.com (Crypto.com, n.d.). Another Visa card by Venmo allows users to choose to redeem their reward for several types of cryptocurrencies (Venmo, n.d.). Another example is the Binance Visa card that gives cash back by Binance coin (BNB) (Binance, n.d.).

Cryptocurrency as an Alternative Investment

Cryptocurrency has opened a new investment opportunity for investors. Investing in crypto assets is a new investment channel besides stocks, real estate, or other investment instruments. It is an innovation within the field of financial technology (FinTech). The decentralized model and disintermediation help to cut down transaction costs. Chuen, Guo, and Wang (2017) predicted that cryptocurrency could cause an investment bubble due to its lack of intrinsic value. Even if an intrinsic value exists for cryptocurrency, the price is going much faster than the intrinsic value, which makes it much riskier.

Capezza (2023) suggested that cryptocurrency can be used within the 401 (K) plan, which is a retirement plan in the United States. Cryptocurrencies help investors to diversify their investments. In 2022, the US Department of Labour issued guidance on including cryptocurrency in the retirement plan (Kramer & Tiemann, 2022). Aytekin and Ulusoy (2022) pointed out that interest in cryptocurrency investment has increased during the recession following the Covid-19 pandemic. Due to its global nature, cryptocurrency can be traded from anywhere; thus, it became a popular investment during the pandemic (Jabotinsky & Sarel, 2022). Even under lockdown, people can still purchase cryptocurrency easily. Many people believe that cryptocurrency can be a good hedge against political risk. Investors put fate in the decentralized nature of the cryptocurrency, which government or politicians will not be able to influence. However, there were problems with investing in cryptocurrencies during the pandemic, which is herding behaviour. Jabotinsky and Sarel (2022) pointed out that some people purchase cryptocurrencies because others are doing the same thing. This is an inherent risk with investing in cryptocurrencies. Herding is also a force that contributed to the massive increase in the value of cryptocurrencies from 2020 to 2021.

There has been disagreement on whether cryptocurrency can be a hedging tool. Many economies worldwide experience high post-pandemic inflation, according to

Jeffries, Johnson, and Staples (2022). The price of commodities has skyrocketed. One of the causes of high inflation is the shortage of supply. Moreover, the appreciation of cryptocurrency prices also contributes to the inflation level (Conlon, Corbet and McGee, 2021). There has been a suggestion of using cryptocurrency to hedge high inflation as an alternative to gold. "Inflation hedge refers to investments that protect investors from the declining purchasing power of money due to inflation" (Corporate Finance Institute, 2022). Contradictory, Conlon, Corbet and McGee (2021) pointed out that there is no clear evidence that cryptocurrencies like Bitcoin or Ethereum can be good hedging assets during inflationary times. A similar study by Smales (2022) also shared the same conclusion in his study conducted in the United States by saying that cryptocurrencies do not offer investors a tool to hedge inflation.

Cryptocurrency is still a high-risk investment. The price of many cryptocurrencies dropped significantly from late 2022 to early 2023. For instant, in September 2022, the Luna crypto network collapsed, which wiped out US$60 billion of digital assets. The value of TerraUSD stablecoin and Luna plummeted (Forbes Magazine, 2022). Then, in November 2022, FTX, a prominent crypto exchange, filed for bankruptcy. The reason FTX collapsed is due to the mismanagement of funds and fraud. The FTT crypto issued by FTX became worthless (Ramirez, 2023). Following the collapse of FTX, US$415 million of crypto has been hacked (Hoskins, 2023). Thus, although cryptocurrency can be an alternative investment, it is essential to realize that it is still a high-risk investment. Furthermore, new regulations will be developed in future years to avoid similar problems.

Lending With Cryptocurrency

One of the banking functions is lending which can possibly use cryptocurrencies. Lending is a critical activity in our modern economy. It helps to match capital to whoever needs them. Commercial banks will serve as the intermediary between depositors who earn interest and borrowers who pay the interest. With the new development of cryptocurrency, banks have more options to fulfill their lending function. However, the instability of cryptocurrency can be a barrier (Okoye & Clark, 2019). What if the loan is issued with a fixed interest rate, but then the value of the cryptocurrency fluctuates significantly? It can cause risk to both sides of the lending and borrowing process. For example, if the loan is issued with 5% interest per annum. On the one hand, during the term of the loan, if the value of the cryptocurrency appreciates, let us say, by 50%. Then there might be a risk for the borrower since they must repay with much more value.

On the other hand, if cryptocurrency depreciates by half, then the risk is on the lender's side because they receive much less than the value lent out. The other issue with crypto lending, as pointed out by Okoye and Clark (2019), is the trust problem because it is hard to track the identity of the parties involved in the transaction. Okoye and Clark (2019) suggested that cryptocurrency might need to be pegged to other assets, and central banks will need to be involved in managing these cryptocurrencies to ensure a stable value cryptocurrency. To solve the trust problem, the authors suggested that collateral and insurance be used.

Cryptocurrency and Islamic Banking System

Islamic banking provides financial services following Islamic law, which does not allow interest payment. Instead of paying interest, the borrower will share the profit with the lenders. In this case, both parties will share the risk (International Monetary Fund, 2017). Lawal (2019) pointed out that cryptocurrency can be a good fit for the Islamic banking system for several reasons. First, the ledger of all crypto transactions is transparent. Second, the authors argued that the supply of fiat money could be increased at the government's discretion; thus, it would cause inflation. At the same time, cryptocurrency can be deflationary in nature. Using cryptocurrency will be more confident and less risky than fiat currency, and this concept aligns well with Islamic law. Third, the creation of other currencies is based on debt which violates Islamic law, while the creation of cryptocurrency is not. Therefore, Lawal (2019) concluded that cryptocurrency is more halal (permissible under Islamic law) than other currencies. Lastly, cryptocurrency includes the component of risk sharing among the lender and borrower, which conforms with Islamic banking concepts. The top 9 countries that implement the Islamic banking concept include Saudi Arabia, Malaysia, UAE, Kuwait, Qatar, Indonesia, Turkey, Bahrain and Pakistan (Hirst, 2015). However, Most of these countries have an implicit ban on cryptocurrency, and Qatar has an absolute ban, except Malaysia, that have both tax law and anti-money laundering law.

CONCLUSION

Cryptocurrency is a new type of digital currency built upon the blockchain concept and distributed ledger. There is a need to examine the impacts of these new currencies on the government's ability to exercise monetary policy. Prior to cryptocurrency, by controlling the interest rate and supply of the national currency, the central bank could smooth out economic fluctuations to avoid problems such as inflation or recession. However, cryptocurrencies are decentralized, meaning the central bank has little or no power to control them. In this chapter, the author synthesized current literature on the topic to help answer the question of how cryptocurrency can impact government economic policy and how cryptocurrency can fit into our national and international monetary systems. First, previous literature has shown that cryptocurrency can challenge the government's ability to exercise its monetary policy. Therefore, governments could consider developing their cryptocurrency to maintain their power to influence the money supply. Also, they can use the legal framework to enable or disable the use of cryptocurrency as legal tender within their jurisdictions. If the government wishes to increase the money supply, it can allow cryptocurrency to be used alongside traditional currency. Other times, they can ban cryptocurrency from reducing the money supply. Second, due to the global nature of cryptocurrency, it can potentially be used as an international payment method. It is more convenient to complete international transactions using cryptocurrency combined with smart contracts. Cryptocurrency can become an integrated part of the FOREX market; it can be traded just like any of the traditional currencies. Moreover, the government could consider holding cryptocurrency within their foreign reserve. However, due to the risk of fluctuation in cryptocurrency value, policy maker will need to develop consistent regulations at the national and international levels. Third, the number of cryptocurrency asset holders has increased in the last couple of years. Especially during the pandemic, it became a popular investment instrument because of its virtual nature. Because of the lockdown in many countries and poor economic outlook, people switched to investing in cryptocurrency instead of traditional investment vehicles such as real estate or stock. The price of the cryptocurrency was inflated. During the second half of 2022, due to some scandals related to crypto exchange networks (Luna and FTX) and many economies that have reopened from the pandemic, there have been significant adjustments to the price of cryptocurrencies. Despite the recent crisis, cryptocurrency is expected to continue gaining more popularity worldwide. Regulations on crypto exchanges and crypto issuers will be necessary to avoid a similar financial crisis. Future research can look at factors that influence the government's implementation of its own cryptocurrency. Alternatively, researchers can study the technical infrastructure required for commercial banks to accept deposits and provide lending with cryptocurrency.

REFERENCES

Aytekin, B. A., & Ulusoy, T. A. (2022). A netnography study examined consumer perception towards cryptocurrency investment during the COVID-19 pandemic. *Business & Management Studies: An International Journal*, *11*(4), 1380–1396. doi:10.15295/bmij.v10i4.2151

Bains, P., & Singh, R. (2022). *Crypto's conservative coins*. IMF. https://www.imf.org/en/Publications/fandd/issues/2022/09/Basics-Crypto-conservative-coins-Bains-Singh

BankProv Annual Report. (2021). *Provident Bank*. https://s29.q4cdn.com/115418717/files/2021-Annual-Report_Provident-Bancorp-Inc_Web.pdf

Benoit, D. (2022, November 10). Crypto Bank Silvergate Capital's stock falls further. *The Wall Street Journal*. https://www.wsj.com/livecoverage/stock-market-news-today-11-09-2022/card/crypto-bank-silvergate-s-stock-falls-further-rQR1mdhX5s60V9Mzb5Iu#:~:text=Silvergate%20doesn't%20hold%20cryptocurrencies,cash%20out%20at%20any%20time.

Binance. (n.d.). *Binance Crypto Card*. https://www.binance.com/en/cards

Bordo, M. D., & Levin, A. T. (2017). Central bank digital currency and the future of monetary policy (No. w23711). National Bureau of Economic Research.

Capezza, M. (2023). Plan Distributions: Fiduciary Considerations for Cryptocurrency Investments in 401(k) Plans. *Journal of Pension Benefits: Issues in Administration*, *29*(4), 27–31.

Central banks - summary of current interest rates. (2023). *Global-rates.com*. https://www.global-rates.com/en/interest-rates/central-banks/central-banks.aspx

Chang, S. E., Luo, H. L., & Chen, Y. (2019). Blockchain-enabled trade finance innovation: A potential paradigm shift on using letter of credit. *Sustainability*, *12*(1), 188. doi:10.3390u12010188

China Government Network. (2021). *Notice on Further Prevention and Handling of Risks of Hype in Virtual Currency Trading*. http://www.gov.cn/zhengce/zhengceku/2021-10/08/content_5641404.htm

Chuen, D. L. K., Guo, L., & Wang, Y. (2017). Cryptocurrency: A new investment opportunity? *Journal of Alternative Investments*, *20*(3), 16–40. doi:10.3905/jai.2018.20.3.016

Claeys, G., Demertzis, M., & Efstathiou, K. (2018). *Cryptocurrencies and monetary policy*. EconStor. http://hdl.handle.net/10419/208013

Coinatmradar.com. (n.d.). *Bitcoin ATM geographical distribution*. https://coinatmradar.com/charts/geo-distribution/

CoinMarketCap. (2023). *Top Cryptocurrency Spot Exchanges.* https://coinmarketcap.com/rankings/exchanges/

Conlon, T., Corbet, S., & McGee, R. J. (2021). Inflation and cryptocurrencies revisited: A time-scale analysis. *Economics Letters, 206,* 109996. doi:10.1016/j.econlet.2021.109996

Corelli, A. (2018). Cryptocurrencies and Exchange Rates: A Relationship and Causality Analysis. *Risks, 6*(4), 111. doi:10.3390/risks6040111

Corporate Finance Institute. (2022). *Inflation Hedge.* https://corporatefinanceinstitute.com/resources/wealth-management/inflation-hedge/#:~:text=Inflation%20hedge%20refers%20to%20investments,in%20value%20during%20inflationary%20cycles

Crypto.com. (2020a). *The history of money – from barter to currency.* https://crypto.com/university/history-of-money-barter-to-bitcoin

Crypto.com. (2020b). *The history of money - From Fiat to Cryptocurrency.* https://crypto.com/university/history-of-money-fiat-to-cryptocurrency?utm_source=crypto.com+university&utm_medium=referral&utm_campaign=from+barter+to+currency&utm_content=evolution+from+fiat+to+cryptocurrency

Crypto.com. (n.d.). *Crypto.com Visa Card.* https://crypto.com/cards

De-Best, R. (2023). Share of respondents who indicated they either owned or used cryptocurrencies in 56 countries and territories worldwide from 2019 to 2022. *Statista.* https://www.statista.com/statistics/1202468/global-cryptocurrency-ownership/

Ethereum.org. (2023). *Proof-of-Stake.* https://ethereum.org/en/developers/docs/consensus-mechanisms/pos/

Forbes Magazine. (2022, September 20). *What really happened to Luna Crypto?* https://www.forbes.com/sites/qai/2022/09/20/what-really-happened-to-luna-crypto/?sh=1a7a684e4ff1

Frankenfield, J. (2023, January 3). *51% attack: Definition, who is at risk, example, and cost.* Investopedia. https://www.investopedia.com/terms/1/51-attack.asp#:~:text=for%20financial%20brands.-,What%20Is%20a%2051%25%20Attack%3F,power%20to%20alter%20the%20blockchain

Gerken, T. (2023, January 6). *US Bank Silvergate hit with $8bn in crypto withdrawals.* BBC News. https://www.bbc.com/news/technology-64176446

Goldsmith, J. (2019). The IMF Must Develop Best Practices before Government-Backed Cryptocurrencies Destabilize the International Monetary System. *Emory Int'l L. Rev., 34,* 595.

Goldstein, I., Jiang, W., & Karolyi, G. A. (2019). To FinTech and beyond. *Review of Financial Studies, 32*(5), 1647–1661. doi:10.1093/rfs/hhz025

Government of Canada. (2021). *Money laundering and terrorist financing indicators—Virtual currency transactions.* https://fintrac-canafe.canada.ca/guidance-directives/transac tion-operation/indicators-indicateurs/vc_mltf-eng

Hayes, A. (2022). *Convertible Virtual Currency.* Investopedia. https://www.investopedia.com/terms/c/convertible-virtual-cur rency.asp#:~:text=Convertible%20virtual%20currency%20is%20an ,as%20dollars%20via%20cryptocurrency%20exchanges

Hill, C., Hult, T., McKaig, T., & Cotae, F. (2021). *Global Business Today.* McGraw-Hill Ryerson Ltd.

Hirst, T. (2015). *These are the top 9 countries for Islamic finance.* World Economic Forum. https://www.weforum.org/agenda/2015/07/top-9-countries-islam ic-finance/

Hoskins, P. (2023). *FTX: Collapsed crypto exchange says $415m was hacked.* BBC News. https://www.bbc.com/news/business-64313624

Howard, L. (2013). Chinese Currency Manipulation: Are There Any Solutions? *Emory Int'l L. Rev., 27,* 1215.

International Monetary Fund. (2017). *Islamic finance and the role of IMF.* https://www.imf.org/external/themes/islamicfinance/#1

International Monetary Fund. (n.d.). *The end of the Bretton Woods System.* https://www.imf.org/external/about/histend.htm#:~:text=End%2 0of%20Bretton%20Woods%20system,-The%20system%20dissolved&tex t=In%20August%201971%2C%20U.S.%20President,the%20breakdown%2 0of%20the%20system

Jabotinsky, H. Y., & Sarel, R. (2022). How crisis affects crypto: Coronavirus as a test case. *The Hastings Law Journal.* Advance online publication. doi:10.2139srn.3557929

Jeffries, I., Johnson, R., & Staples, M. (2022). *How inflation is flipping the economic script in seven charts.* McKinsey & Company. https://www.mckinsey.com/featured-insights/inflation/how-inf lation-is-flipping-the-economic-script?cid=soc-web

Kramer, A. S., & Tiemann, B. J. (2022). When Are Cryptocurrencies Appropriate Investments for Retirement Plans and IRAs? US Labor Department Cautions 401(k) Plan Fiduciaries to Exercise Extreme Care. *Intellectual Property & Technology Law Journal, 34*(6), 3–6.

Lawal, I. M. I. M. (2019). The suitability of cryptocurrency in the structure of Islamic banking and finance. *Jurnal Perspektif Pembiayaan Dan Pembangunan Daerah, 6*(6), 639–648. doi:10.22437/ppd.v6i6.6603

Li, B. (2022, December 9). *Some key elements of crypto regulation.* International Monetary Fund. https://www.imf.org/en/News/Articles/2022/12/16/sp120922-som e-key-elements-of-crypto-regulation

Liang, A. (2023, January 4). *US regulators warn banks over cryptocurrency risks.* BBC News. https://www.bbc.com/news/business-64159452

Lyons, B. (2012). *Canadian Macroeconomics: Problems & Policies* (10th ed.). Pearson Prentice Hall.

Marquit, M. (2022). Proof of work vs. proof of stake: Why the difference matters | next advisor with time. *Time Magazine.* https://time.com/nextadvisor/investing/cryptocurrency/proof-of-work-vs-proof-of-stake/

Melnyk, N. (2019). *Cryptocurrency in international trade: accounting aspects.* Ternopil National Economic University. https://conf.ztu.edu.ua/wp-content/uploads/2019/06/156-1.pdf

Moore, W., & Stephen, J. (2016). Should cryptocurrencies be included in the portfolio of international reserves held by central banks? *Cogent Economics & Finance, 4*(1), 1147119. doi:10.1080/23322039.2016.1147119

Obu, O. C., & Ukpere, W. I. (2022). The Implications of the Incursion of Cryptocurrency on the Effectiveness of Fiscal Policy. *Review of Applied Socio-Economic Research, 23*(1), 134–150. doi:10.54609/reaser.v23i1.214

Oh, J. H., & Nguyen, K. (2018). The growing role of cryptocurrency: What does it mean for central banks and governments. *International Telecommunications Policy Review, 251*, 33–55.

Okoye, M. C., & Clark, J. (2019). Toward cryptocurrency lending. In *International Conference on Financial Cryptography and Data Security* (pp. 367-380). Springer. 10.1007/978-3-662-58820-8_25

PricewaterhouseCoopers. (n.d.). *Making sense of bitcoin, cryptocurrency and Blockchain.* https://www.pwc.com/us/en/industries/financial-services/fint ech/bitcoin-blockchain-cryptocurrency.html

Ramirez, D. (2023). *FTX Crash: Timeline, Fallout and What Investors Should Know.* Nerdwallet. https://www.nerdwallet.com/article/investing/ftx-crash#:~:te xt=FTX's%20crash%20has%20wide%2Dreaching,sinking%20prices%20and%20 financial%20troubles

Raza, S. A., Ahmed, M., & Aloui, C. (2022). On the asymmetrical connectedness between cryptocurrencies and foreign exchange markets: Evidence from the nonparametric quantile on quantile approach. *Research in International Business and Finance, 61*, 101627. doi:10.1016/j.ribaf.2022.101627

Ritchie, J. (2022). *The history of money: How our currency evolved from pelts to money.* MintLife Blog. https://mint.intuit.com/blog/investments/the-history-of-mone y/#:~:text=Before%20money%20was%20invented%2C%20people,were% 20used%20to%20pay%20armies

Saksonova, S., & Kuzmina-Merlino, I. (2019). Cryptocurrency as an investment instrument in a modern financial market. *Economy Bulletin of St. Petersburg University, 35*(2), 269–282. doi:10.21638pbu05.2019.205

Santor, E. (2011). *The International Monetary System: An Assessment and Avenue for reform.* Bank of Canada Review.

Sharma, D., Verma, R., & Sam, S. (2021). Adoption of cryptocurrency: An international perspective. *International Journal of Technology Transfer and Commercialisation, 18*(3), 247–260. doi:10.1504/IJTTC.2021.118863

SmalesL. A. (2022). *Cryptocurrency as an alternative inflation hedge?* https://ssrn. com/abstract=3883123

Solodan, K. (2019). Legal regulation of cryptocurrency taxation in European countries. *European Journal of Law and Public Administration, 6*(1), 64–74. doi:10.18662/eljpa/64

The Economist. (2022). *2022 has been a year of brutal inflation.* https://www.economist.com/finance-and-economics/2022/12/21/2 022-has-been-a-year-of-brutal-inflation

The U.S. Commodity Future Trading Commission. (n.d.). *Bitcoin Basics*. https://www.cftc.gov/sites/default/files/2019-12/oceo_bitcoinbasics0218.pdf

The World Bank. (n.d.). *Tax revenue (% of GDP)*. https://data.worldbank.org/indicator/GC.TAX.TOTL.GD.ZS

Theglobaleconomy.com. (2021). *Government spending, percent of GDP - Country rankings*. https://www.theglobaleconomy.com/rankings/government_size/G20/

Tomić, N., Todorović, V., & Čakajac, B. (2020). The potential effects of cryptocurrencies on monetary policy. *The European Journal of Applied Economics*, *17*(1), 37–48. doi:10.5937/EJAE17-21873

US Department of the Treasury. (2021). *Anti-Money Laundering and Countering the Financing of Terrorism National Priorities* https://www.fincen.gov/sites/default/files/shared/AML_CFT%20 Priorities%20(June%2030%2C%202021).pdf

US Internal Revenue Service. (2021). *Notice 2014-21*. https://www.irs.gov/pub/irs-drop/n-14-21.pdf

US Law Library of Congress. (2021). *Regulation of Cryptocurrency Around the World*. https://tile.loc.gov/storage-services/service/ll/llglrd/2021 687419/2021687419.pdf

Venmo. (n.d.). *Venmo Credit Card*. https://venmo.com/about/creditcard/

Wu, M. (2019, April 26). *Paying with shells: Cowrie shell money is one of the oldest currencies still collected today*. Ancient Origins. https://www.ancient-origins.net/history-ancient-traditions/shell-money-0011793

Xu, D. (2019). Free money, but not tax-free: A proposal for the tax treatment of cryptocurrency hard forks. *Fordham Law Review*, *87*(6), 2693–2723.

Chapter 5
Business Models in Financial Technologies

Mona Ebrahimi
Hamta Group–Hamta Business Corporation, Canada

ABSTRACT

The world of finance has been transforming alongside the rapid growth of technology significantly. FinTech companies have emerged as a consequence of technological developments in the financial sector. Despite the upward trends in the growth of FinTech, they definitely need a business model to survive and grow in the competitive market. A FinTech business model includes operating strategy, revenue sources, and intended customer base. FinTech organizations need to adopt approaches to ensure their services and products are available to their customers across different platforms and are not necessarily reliant on a convoluted sign-up process. This chapter reviews the main considerations in FinTech business models, and the success factors of a business model, and provides a guide to having a business model that wins in the market.

INTRODUCTION

Technology is making a significant impact on the financial sector and creates new competitors that play in a different playground, unlike traditional financial market players. As can be recognized from the name, FinTech is derived from finance and technology. The financial industry has always been influenced by technology as a facilitator tool to make advancements and simplify financial operations. The emergence of Automated Teller Machines can be identified as an instance of using technological innovations as financial solutions. Thus, the employment of

DOI: 10.4018/978-1-6684-8368-8.ch005

technological solutions in the financial market is not a new trend. New technologies are being introduced to the financial market at a pace that is faster than ever before. Both FinTech startups and technology firms are releasing technologies and products to the market which makes the competition in the market even tougher. The FinTech scope is widely covering diverse areas ranging from payments and money transfers to robo-advisors and cryptocurrencies (Murinde, Rizopoulos, & Zachariadis, 2022).

FinTechs are making a global revolution in the financial and technology sectors by focusing on providing pleasant experiences for customers to address their financial needs. Different FinTech startups are competing in the race to address customers' expectations and fill existing gaps left by traditional banks and financial institutions. FinTechs are recognized as being disruptive solution providers armed with digital approaches to address barriers and challenges in the market instead of traditional solutions. Technology has been an indispensable part of the financial industry for a long time; however, it has made a considerable impact in the past two decades through the emergence of FinTech. Recent breakthroughs in FinTech have transformed financial services and created significant shifts in business models and processes as well as consumer behavior and expectations. FinTechs are operating in various applications, from payment systems to investment and banking services (Murinde, Rizopoulos, & Zachariadis, 2022). Areas in which FinTech is expanded or is expected to be expanded include transactions, payments, funds, investment and wealth management, lending, and insurance. Focusing on the main factors that made FinTechs move steps ahead from traditional financial institutions are limited imposed regulatory burdens, cost reduction, and improved customer experience. Although Fintech startups are significantly important, limited theoretical insight is developed around this subject (Zavolokina, Dolata, & Schwabe, 2016).

FINTECH

Companies that employ technologies to offer financial services are recognized as FinTech companies. FinTech is also defined by the Financial Stability Board (FSB) as "technologically activated financial innovation, which could result in new business models, applications, processes or products with an associated material effect on financial markets and institutions and in the provision of financial services" (FSB, 2019).

Although the main focus of this definition is on the impact of FinTech in financial and banking institutions, it is worth considering that FinTech covers a broader range of innovative technologies in the financial sector with the aim of modernizing it or adding some value (Haddad & Hornuf, 2022). From the basic FinTech definition, it can be concluded that FinTech is focused not only on innovations in technology but also on shifts in business models. Employment of a new application that is provided by a FinTech company can make a significant impact on the business model of a financial institution and add value by decreasing the processing time or facilitating the process (Bellardini, Del Gaudio, Previtali, & Verdoliva, 2022). In addition, the unprecedented growth of digital transformation has led businesses to be encouraged to change their business models by employing FinTech services and products (Mărăcine, Voican, & Scarlat, 2020).

Financial sector has been recognized as one of the greatest spenders in terms of information technology (IT). Banks have been among the early organizations that decided to deploy computers and minimizeminimize the use of paper in financial transactions (Wardley, 2011). They have also been early adopters through the emergence of personal computers with the aim to develop their businesses as well as cutting costs and increasing efficiency. In the way of digital transformation, banks have spent massive budgets on IT projects to digitize transaction records, automate operations, and minimize dependency on human resources and associated errors as well (Taherdoost, Madanchian, & Ebrahimi, 2021). The efforts taken by banks and financial institutions through transforming digitally have ended up offering cheaper, faster, and customized services as well (Murinde et al., 2022). However, allocating massive budgets to develop hardware and software infrastructure to offer better services has not satisfied the value chains in banks and financial institutions through the years. Besides, considering the rapidly changing technologies, big organizations used to find it difficult to make shifts in their structures to respond to changes (Bellardini, Del Gaudio, Previtali, & Verdoliva, 2022). To clarify the context, it is also important to note that there is a significant distinction between digital transformation and digitalization. The focus area of digital transformation is not limited to moving paper-based and analog systems to a digital representation of data. However, it signifies changing the strategies and processes aiming to create value (Wardley, 2011). Thus, digital transformation comes with remarkable shifts in business models and heavily required budgets to stay competitive accordingly (Mărăcine et al., 2020). The rise of FinTechs through the path of digital transformation facilitates the way for banks and financial institutions to operate alongside emerging technologies, stay competitive, and be focused on their value chain. FinTechs provide the opportunity to facilitate, automate, and modify processes of financial services whether aiming for the customer-centricity objective (Bellardini et al., 2022).

The Growth of FinTechs

A broad range of activities from new technological breakthroughs to commercialized financial services are covered by FinTechs. Recent breakthroughs in technology including smartphones, sensors, and cloud computing have provided availability to access data and provide new experiences for customers. The rise of opportunities to collect data and access autonomous machines has influenced many industries substantially in terms of updating their outdated value chains with the aim to create profit and stay competitive in the market. Alongside these changes, the financial industry has been also involved with technological breakthroughs that eventually resulted in the emergence of financial technologies that are commonly known as FinTech (Murinde et al., 2022).

FinTech has emerged as a result of technological developments to provide users of financial services with solutions that help them to better manage their money and handle their finances. FinTechs not only target the consumers of financial services but also facilitate processes for financial institutions ranging from knowing their customers to recording transactions and booking associated documents through offering novel solutions. Thus, FinTechs address the needs of financial institutions and banks in terms of effectiveness and efficiency by filling existing gaps in their processes. How existing gaps may be addressed by different FinTech solutions to satisfy users' expectations are different for each respective type of FinTech service or product. Figure 1 shows a number of users' needs that have led to FinTech solutions to fill an existing gap in services.

Figure 1. FinTech solutions for user needs
Source: IMF (2019)

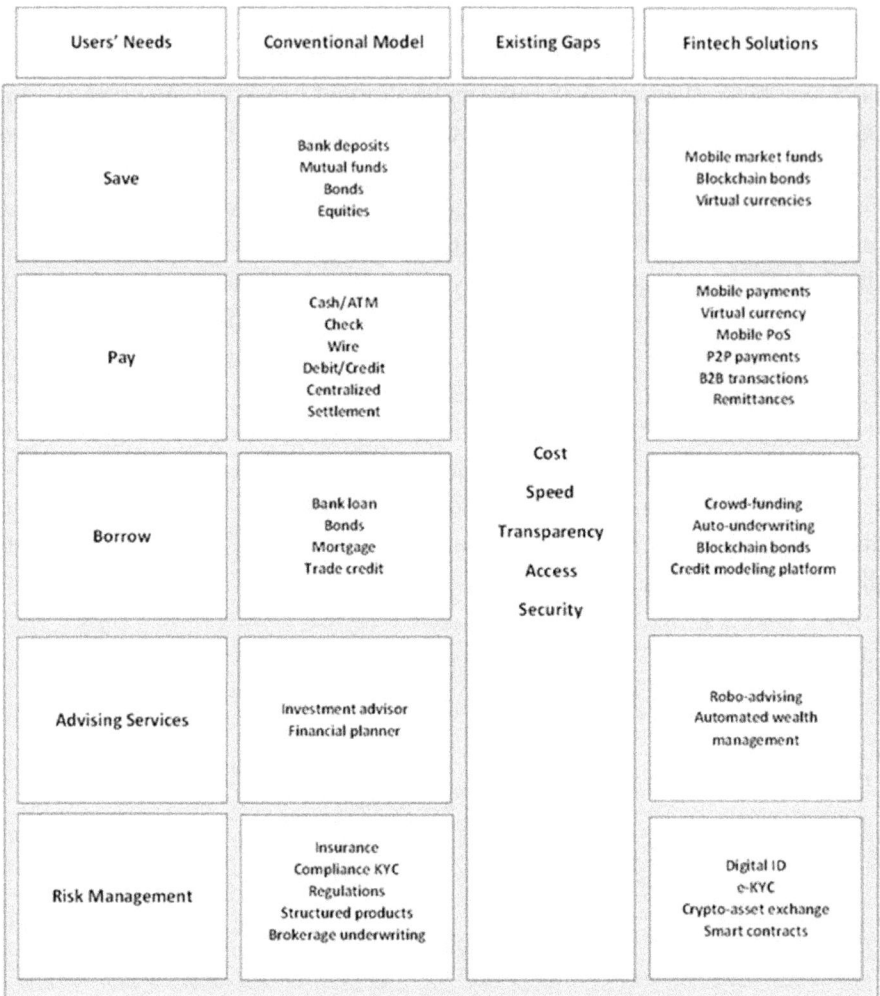

The deployment of technological solutions has always been a trend in the financial sector, however; there is a significant difference between the traditional way of investment in technologies and new FinTechs (Murinde et al., 2022). Traditional solutions are used to invest in technologies to automate solutions and lead to operations that are more cost-effective; however, FinTechs focus on making changes in the entire business process by revising business models and creating value accordingly. Entrepreneurs and investors have also been playing a critical role in the growth of FinTechs by being interested in taking advantage of this growing market (Bellardini et al., 2022).

On the other hand, financial institutions and banks need to walk alongside with their customers' preferences to use technological solutions. They have also been challenged to find solutions to recognize the segments of their customer and provide them with services and experiences that they enjoy (Haddad & Hornuf, 2022). As customers lost their trust and interest in financial institutions right after the financial crisis, FinTechs were new players that seemed to be a fresh start from customers' perspective and gaining more attention with establishing brand new neo banks, digital banks, and challenger banks. With the public perception that FinTechs offer better, more inclusive, and user-friendly services, FinTechs gained their share in the market (Mărăcine et al., 2020).

FinTech and FinTech Startups

Although FinTech is characterized differently in academia and commerce, it is generally referred to as making innovations in financial products and services (Temelkov, 2018). FinTechs are considered as adopted business models; however, they are regarded as an entirely different sector in other scenarios (Kim, Song, & Lee, 2016). In broader definitions, FinTech is referred to as any new process, product, service or business model that centers customers and aims to address their financial problems (Chuen & Teo, 2017). FinTechs leverage technological solutions including the Internet, mobile, social media, data analytics, artificial intelligence, and many other digital technologies (Dapp, 2017) to enrich their value propositions and disrupt the financial market. Thus, FinTechs can be an adopted business model by a financial institution or an individually established startup business. To clarify, FinTech is the application of digital technologies to innovate financial services; however, FinTech startups are businesses that are established to offer financial services and products to customers based on FinTech (Gimpel, Rau, & Röglinger, 2018).

The role of FinTechs to address customer expectations is indispensable in the financial value chain. Most FinTech startups address one specific financial problem; however, they are not typically financial firms. FinTechs are almost technology-driven companies or online businesses that are focused on financial solutions and collaborate with banks and financial institutions to offer products or services that are necessarily regulated (Dapp, 2017). FinTech startups have a deeper understanding of customer needs, they have less bureaucratic structures and dynamic teams that lead to reduced time-to-market in turn. Thus, FinTech startups have demonstrated to be more customer-centric with rates of long-term success. Considering the reasons for sustainable profit in FinTech startups, they are also attractive for traditional financial institutions to invest and collaborate aiming to reach out to a bigger customer segment and improve the experience of their existing customers as well (Gimpel et al., 2018).

Bank and FinTech Interaction

Many different industries have been influenced by digitalization in the past two decades leading to emergence of new innovations and growth opportunities for businesses (Zhang, van Gorp, & Kievit, 2022). Banking and finance sector as one of the most regulated and conservative economic sectors have also faced technology-driven solutions (Barba Navaretti, Calzolari, Mansilla-Fernández, & Pozzolo, 2018). Emergence of technological innovations and internet-based solutions enabled traditional financial firms to deliver more user-friendly and customer-centric applications to their customers and also attract new customers from other segments in the market that have been provided by FinTech startup solutions. Some of these solutions in payment systems, wealth management, foreign currency and other areas provided the possibility to entirely reshape traditional business activities in banks and financial institutions. Thus, banks had no choice but to accept the change in the market and embrace it. In this way, they are addressing higher levels of customers' expectations instead of simply providing them with buying and selling products (Temelkov, 2018).

Representation of FinTech sounds to be a serious challenge for banks and financial institutions that are following their traditional business models. Besides, the financial industry is heavily impacted by regulations that may avoid it to be flexible to dynamics of the rapidly changing market. However, the rising interest in FinTechs motivated banks and financial institutions to revise their business models by employing FinTech services and products as well. Although there is an upward trend in the interest of customers to use FinTech services, still some users are concerned with security issues of sharing their financial information with less well-known FinTechs and prefer to proceed with more recognized banks and financial institutions. This also highlights the importance of applying FinTech services by banks and financial services to improve their processes as well as ensuring their customers the privacy of their information (Bellardini et al., 2022). This is to some extent recognized as a paradox in the financial industry in which customers are not huge fans of banks but they still trust them to share their financial information and have their money (Shakhzodbek, Khurshidbek, & Shoxruxmirzo, 2022).

Considering the pitfalls and benefits of both FinTechs and financial institutions, the current status of the market dictates that the collaboration of financial institutions and FinTechs not only is a valuable deal for both sides but also it brings forward benefits for customers and leads to happy customers through providing innovative solutions. The interaction between banks and FinTechs should not be a game in which one loses and one wins. It is just a win-win game that leads to remarkable opportunities for both parties as well as eliminating time-consuming, complex, and expensive processes of technological developments in banks (Bellardini et al., 2022).

To make a balance in bank and FinTech interaction, banks will be pushed to have a forward-thinking perspective towards integration and FinTechs may need to rely on backward integration aiming to create a stable source of benefit for both parties (Bedjeti Baftijari & Nakov, 2020). On one hand, banks offer wider relationships with customers, stability, and access to the market. On the other hand, FinTechs offer interesting technological solutions and platforms with improved user experience. This two-way interaction eventually leads to a synergy that creates value for banks, FinTech companies, and their customers as well (Mărăcine et al., 2020). Although this interaction is profitable, it can be sustainable just in case the security of shared data is maintained and cybersecurity risks are considered with high priority.

Banks can engage with startups in some ways including investment, collaboration, in-house development, M&A, and FinTech programs (Bedjeti Baftijari & Nakov, 2020). If banks engage with FinTech companies through investment, they invest some of their capital in a FinTech start-up directly or indirectly. In this case, banks will be impacted by the successes and failures of the start-up as well. In the case of going through collaborations, banks provide the required platform for FinTech to test and implement its solutions through joint ventures (Hornuf, Klus, Lohwasser, & Schwienbacher, 2021). In-house development refers to cases in which banks develop FinTech solutions by themselves including contactless payment solutions and investment robots. Banks may also acquire a FinTech company aiming to access trending technologies in the market faster than their competitors as FinTech companies are almost agile in their processes (Shakhzodbek et al., 2022). This approach is recognized as M&A. Eventually, a FinTech program refers to the collaboration of some banks or stakeholders to come up with a FinTech solution that benefits them all. Each bank may decide to apply one or a combination of these ways to go through based on their advantages and disadvantages and the potential of the banks to adapt to new technologies and allocate the required budget and resources, and financial conditions. Over the years, banks have been recognized as giant money spenders in terms of technology; however, they seem to be slow to adapt to new technological shifts and sometimes resistant to change (Murinde et al., 2022). However, emergence of FinTech solutions can add value to the business models of banks by providing a better customer experience and personalized services (Vives, 2018).

Therefore, the competition in the financial markets that were almost dominated by regulated traditional institutions is enhanced to a great extent due to the existence of FinTechs. Fintechs are filling the customers' needs that were left as gaps in services provided by traditional financial institutions. Thus, they are likely to be adopted by users. On the other hand, banks have enough room to make improvements by adopting innovations in the market, making modifications in their business models or collaborating with FinTechs. Services and products offered by FinTechs are not very different from what is provided by banks in general; however, they offer them in a more innovative and productive way. Likewise, banks, FinTechs connect investors and lenders for investment opportunities but in a data-oriented approach that is expected to work more efficiently (Hornuf et al., 2021). FinTechs also deliver some pure services and products to their customers offering them a pleasant journey in their payments and online transactions; however, these services are also supported by banks at another level. While banks perform a bundle of financial activities and services, FinTechs only take the responsibility of delivering a few of them. In this case, banks and FinTechs complete the value chain and pave each other's ways to deliver quality services to their customers and add value to their own businesses as well (Vives, 2018).

Customer Experience in FinTech

One of the main success factors of FinTech startups is considering customer experience as the core element in their business processes. The level of customers' satisfaction is directly impacted by the experience that they achieve during using a product or service. Positive customer experience leads to customer experience accordingly. FinTech startups adopt business models that, unlike obsolete traditional models followed by banks and financial institutions, are focused on improving customer experience through innovative solutions. Robo-advisor is an example of digital FinTech solution that is mainly concentrated on a need from customers' side. Thus, it enhances customer experience through offering customized investment solutions to customers who have limited knowledge of investments. Considering customers' savings, objectives and risk appetite, robo-advisors offer the most appropriate portfolio that is tailored for each customer. The same happens when FinTech startups offer their insurance solutions in which they analyze customers' driving background history and the services provided by insurer firms to personalize the most cost-effective service for the customer (Barbu, Florea, Dabija, & Barbu, 2021).

Improvement in customer experience that is one critical factor in the success of FinTech startups is provided by employment of trending technologies such as big data analytics and blockchain. FinTechs have also demonstrated positive results in analyzing existing processes and addressing the gaps to make them faster, more productive or cost efficient. Digital wallets as an instance have facilitated the process of online shopping. As this solution was mainly leveraged based on a customer need, it was adopted by many people in the market. Being customer-centric and simplifying processes to meet customers' expectations are adopted approaches by FinTech startups leading to customer loyalty (Barbu, Florea, Dabija, & Barbu, 2021).

BUSINESS MODELS

Business models have been recognized as a popular area of analysis during recent years as they can clearly explain the reasons of failure or successes in different firms (Afuah & Tucci, 2000). Appropriate business models are likely to create sustainable value and competitive advantages and lead to higher financial benefits eventually (Amit & Zott, 2010). The competitiveness and profitability of businesses is identified by their business models. Appropriate business models are essential for a business to face challenges in the market and survive. While the idea of business models was initially limited to management studies, it was soon expanded to other fields of business (Zott, Amit, & Massa, 2011). Business models were primarily realized as strategies that are mainly based on the income statement and balance sheet of a business. However, companies employ a range of approaches and activities by reliance on their resources to create value for their stakeholders through their business models (Dorfleitner & Hornuf, 2019). There are different types of business models including strategic and operational business models (Osterwalder, 2004). While strategic business models focus on long-term objectives and milestones to create competitive advantage, operational business models focus on how to achieve these objectives (Casadesus-Masanell & Ricart, 2010). Business models consider a holistic perspective towards the business of the company and require steps to create value and address stakeholders' demands (Amit & Zott, 2001). A business model is defined as the method to classify existing types of business and a way to analyze the cost and benefit channels (Dorfleitner & Hornuf, 2019).

Fintech Business Models

As the certainty of changes in digital technologies is being expedited, some different factors are required to be taken into account to meet the dynamic nature of the market. FinTech is introducing new players, products and services and business models to the financial landscape. Business models that are limited to improving the efficiency in the value chain are not adequate to be competitive in this market since customers are also smarter about their financial situations and may not simply decide to change their behavior. Thus, methods should be considered to impact customers' behavior (Dorfleitner & Hornuf, 2019).

In this digital age, the number of people who have access to the Internet is undoubtedly larger than the number of people who have bank accounts. This provides a certain opportunity for FinTech companies to employ and make a huge market. To benefit from this huge market potential, FinTech companies need to be agile enough to respond to changes and trends in the market quickly. As more products and services become available through the Internet, the demand for secure

FinTech solutions that facilitate transactions for both sellers and consumers increase significantly as well. FinTechs are well-positioned solutions to address changing behaviors and habits of consumers (Taherdoost, 2023).

Therefore, FinTech business models are likely to converge towards business models of banks gradually. In case that this happens, it would be a matter of concern if FinTechs would still have their competitive advantage over banks and financial institutions. Besides, as FinTechs continue to develop their scope of activities, they need to apply more regulations as well. However, a gradual case by case approach towards expanding activities should be implemented in which regulations will be applied just in case that a service or product is carried out in practice. Thus, despite the fact that FinTechs are regulated for the products and services that they offer in the financial market, they are still excluded from general banking and financial regulations (Vives, 2018).

Another competitive advantage in FinTech business models is being granted by innovative technologies. FinTechs are also agile and adaptable to technological shifts and advancements. Moreover, they are more flexible to changes as they are not highly regulated of financial markets. FinTechs also unlike banks are not usually multi product with a wide range of customers with different needs; however, they are serving their specific segment. Thus, they can be more resilient to make changes in their business models in case that there is a new game in the market (Bedjeti Baftijari & Nakov, 2020).

Six Types of FinTech Business Models

FinTech startups have redefined customers' expectations about payment, lending, borrowing, investing and managing wealth. Based on the approaches and value propositions of fast growing FinTechs in the market, six basic business models have been developed in wealth management, payment, crowdfunding, capital market, loan and insurance services that are outlined in the following (Giglio, 2021).

Payment Business Model

As payments are more straightforward and commonly used in comparison to other financial services and products, it is more possible for FinTech startups with payment business models to acquire their customers. Not only are payment services being used on a regular basis by most of the individuals and businesses but also, they are the least regulated financial service. Retail, consumer and wholesale payments are main potential areas in the payment business model. Mobile wallets, digital currency solutions and real-time payments are solutions in this area that are provided to offer more convenience, quick and accessible payment services. FinTech startups are employing the opportunities provided by mobile devices including Near Field Communication (NFC), card and QR code reader solutions to offer mobile payment approaches (Giglio, 2021).

Wealth Management Business Model

Robo-advisors are one of the most recognized wealth managements FinTech business models as automated solutions that provide investment solutions for users. Robo-advisors work based on a combination of algorithms helping customers to invest their budget on a range of different assets referring to their risk appetite, budget and investment preferences. This business model is highly influenced by consumer behavior and changes in the demographics of the market. These advisors help customers to make a wise investment decision based on the collected data and make their profit out of the portfolios that they make (Giglio, 2021).

Crowdfunding Business Model

Crowdfunding FinTechs perform as mediators to raise funds aiming to create new products as venture capital or for charity purposes. In each crowdfunding project, three parties are involved including the project owner that is seeking for potential funds for the project, investors or contributors that may be interested to support the project and mediators that facilitate collaboration of two other parties through providing information about potential projects and investors (Giglio, 2021). There are three main models of crowdfunding including reward-based, donation-based and share-based crowdfunding.

In reward-based crowdfunding, the interest rate is set by the borrower based on his credit to repay it in a certain period. In donation-based crowdfunding; however, there is no monetary repayment as it is aimed for charity purposes. Share-based crowdfunding projects are also attractive for small and medium-sized enterprises as it provides entrepreneurs with the opportunity to reach investors that are interested to have shares in their project (Giglio, 2021).

Lending Business Model

Peer-to-Peer (P2P) FinTech business models that allow businesses and individuals to borrow and lend money directly with each other have found a major trend in the FinTech market. P2P FinTech startups are established based on an efficient structure that provides them with the opportunity to offer low interest rates. They also facilitate lending and borrowing processes to a great extent. FinTech startups are not the main beneficiaries of lending and borrowing money; however, they just match lenders and borrowers and collect fees from users. Thus, they do not have to meet capital market requirements associated with loan amounts that facilitate their processes accordingly. Although FinTech startups are being innovative in their lending and borrowing through employing new credit models, risk analysis, data sources and managing operating costs, the success or failure of their business is dependent on interest rates that are out of their control (Giglio, 2021).

Capital Market Business Model

Capital market business models cover a wide area including trade, investment, money exchange, research and risk analysis. In terms of trade, gone are the days those investors and trader had to wait in lines to place an order. FinTechs have made trading simple by providing platforms in which investors and traders are connected to each other to set buy and sell orders. Collecting data from the stock market, they have also offered a range of research and risk analysis solutions for buyers and sellers to gain an insight in real time before making a financial decision. FinTech startups have also facilitated foreign exchange transactions that used to be dominated by traditional financial institutions. Thus, users can trace prices in real time via simple accessible applications on their mobile devices. FinTechs offer foreign exchange transactions services at a lower cost comparatively and make their profit out of transactions as well (Giglio, 2021).

Insurance Services Business Model

The role of FinTechs in the insurance service business model is to work as a facilitator between customers and the insurer firms. They rely on data analytics to provide a pool of insurance offers for customers based on their history and preferences. In this case, FinTechs help customers to find the insurance services that best match to their needs and also market the services offered by insurance firms. Thus, FinTech startups that are based on insurance service business models are well-embraced by traditional insurance firms due to the sales platform that they provide. Considering the data that is collected from a wide range of customers attracted by FinTech startups, insurers can also improve their insurance risk analysis approaches that lead to better strategic solutions accordingly (Giglio, 2021).

Key Drivers of FinTech Business Model Success

As consumers' attitudes and habits are changing regarding the use of online solutions, there is a great opportunity for FinTech companies to position themselves in the market predominantly and flourish. Due to the fact that FinTech companies are usually agile startups, they are more flexible to adapt to customer's needs in real-time and provide them with their expected services (Bedjeti Baftijari & Nakov, 2020). However, some FinTechs fail and FinTechs survive and succeed in the competitive market due to a range of reasons. There is a different range of success stories about FinTech startups that have some key drivers in common including customization, cross-selling, resilience, risk management, agility, appropriate pricing, and innovation (Velazquez, Bobek, Vide, & Horvat, 2022).

Customization

Customer experience is a significant factor that is impacted not only by products and services offered by FinTechs but also the shifts in trends in the environment as well. As customers' consumption needs evolve due to various environmental reasons, their sense of satisfaction will be affected accordingly. Successful startups have noticed that the way to win their customers' heart is through understanding their needs and wants and then customizing services based on racing out to their touchpoints. Switching to Omni channel payments is an instance of understanding customers' needs by FinTech startups and addressing them aiming to provide a pleasant experience for customers. FinTechs are providing their customers with cutting-edge solutions that are tailored for their demands.

Cross Selling

One of the most effective techniques used by financial firms is to cross-selling products. This solution is based on understanding customers' needs and behaviors and providing them with products that add them some value through addressing their needs. One example of this approach is to analyze the needs of a customer who has a mortgage and sell them a line of credit. This tactic offers customers complementary products and makes them rely on one solution to address a range of different needs. Successful FinTech startups have made their way through becoming a single window in which customers can address many of their financial needs. Thus, they offer payments, lending, evaluating customers' credit score, insurance, wealth management and many other financial services in a fast paperless solution (Bedjeti Baftijari & Nakov, 2020).

Resilience

The dynamics of the market and rapid shifts in the economy have pushed FinTech startups to reconsider their value-adding processing and sources of revenue. Successful FinTech startups are resilient to these kinds of changes and economic pressures to cut their prices and increase their revenues as well. Such flexibility in FinTech startups to make positive changes in sources of cost and revenue is almost impossible to happen in giant financial institutions. In this way, business models adopted by FinTech startups can be inspiring for banks to build and focus on customer-centric and value-added processes in cases of change in market trends (Bedjeti Baftijari & Nakov, 2020).

Risk Management

FinTech startups have applied technology to minimize their risk. They are using the tools and technologies that they have in hand in collaboration with their partners' available technologies to mitigate their risks. Use of technology helps them to reach out to customers while considering precautionary measures, making some analysis about customers' behavior and preferences and making wise decisions that will not probably face the business with the risk of failure (Girling, 2022).

Agility

Customers are interested in faster services that address their needs in a timely manner even in case these services cost them more in terms of fees. To address this need, successful FinTech startups are delivering their services at a rapid pace with minimum or zero paperwork. As there is a lower level of complexity in the structure of FinTech startups and they are not extremely regulated, they can perform faster and be agile in innovative approaches (Girling, 2022). Relying on the agility concept, FinTech startups are focused on reaching their customers with respect to being agile and providing them with personalized services (Hendriyani & Raharja, 2019).

Appropriate Pricing

FinTech startups may not have plenty of financial supporters and founders with big budgets in comparison to big banks and financial institutions. Besides, there is a competitive market in the business that may lead to the financial failure of the startup in case of making false decisions. Thus, appropriate pricing and applying strategies to consider different financial aspects of the business is regarded as a critical success factor in FinTech business models (Neubert, 2020).

Innovation

The number of innovations made by FinTech startups is probably much bigger than the whole number of innovations by banks in their long-life cycle. The use of innovative solutions and technologies has facilitated the way financial services are provided to customers. Besides, FinTech startups have revolutionized the way to offer services to customers with their innovative approaches. FinTech startups have made specific innovations specifically in artificial intelligence, open banking, blockchain and mobile banking (Zhao, Li, Yu, Chen, & Lee, 2022).

INNOVATION IN FINTECH BUSINESS MODELS

FinTech startups commonly adopt disruptive innovations and technologies in their business models leading to major or minor shifts in their processes. The services that were traditionally provided by a single bank or financial institution, can be covered by a range of FinTech startups. However, FinTech startups have eliminated bureaucracy and complicated processes in their business models and have focused on value-added activities instead. They also tend to apply innovative approaches to keep their structure agile and add value to the chain (Murinde et al., 2022). The financial disintermediation by FinTech startups avoids the high dependency on traditional financial intermediaries such as financial institutions and banks. With the advent of FinTech in the financial value chain, the existing pipeline including investments, borrowing, saving and funding has become much more direct which will, in turn, enable modified strategic approaches to financial markets that are more adaptable to changes in the industry (Velazquez et al., 2022). This innovation in the business model, not only will bring more advantages for the founders but also leads to more relevant, powerful, and feasible financial decisions for clients. The income that is being gained in the FinTech market is getting back to the value chain and leading to the creation of more innovative solutions that will in turn add value to this market as well (Bedjeti Baftijari & Nakov, 2020). FinTech solutions that help to bypass existing currency laws and regulations in the financial market are making payment transactions much easier and faster. As the innovative solutions provided by FinTechs are relatively quick and straightforward, they are more likely to attract more customers to the business (Dorfleitner & Hornuf, 2019). Unlike banks and financial institutions that are commonly reliant on their conventional business models, FinTechs improve their business models aiming to create value for their customers and improve their experience (Murinde et al., 2022).

CONCLUSION

FinTech is growing fast due to new innovations in technology and changes in customers' behaviors. It has also attracted the attention of academics and regulators as well.

As an umbrella term, a wide range of financial technology solutions are covered by FinTechs; however, it mainly refers to any technological innovation that addresses a financial problem. Rapid developments in FinTech have made some impacts on the financial market and business models of banks and financial institutions. Considering the market conditions and employment of emerging technologies in FinTechs solutions, FinTech is expected to remain and grow in the market. As more individuals are interested in shifting their daily financial transactions to available online transactions, banks, and financial institutions are also getting interested to gain their share in this growing market. Banks and financial institutions need to accept the change and upcoming trends as they come up with the emergence of FinTech startups. When both banks and FinTech startups work together, a synergy will be created that is the result of integrating the advantages of both to cover their imperfections.

Many banks have made strategic decisions to invest in FinTech startups aiming to extend their banking services in a customer-centric manner. This motivates their existing customers to go on with their banking services and benefit from innovative FinTech solutions at the same time. In some other cases, FinTech startups and banks are partnered to maximize gains for both parties. FinTech startups considering the innovative technologies that they offer have already made their niche market and their collaboration with banks and financial institutions adds more value to banks and FinTech startups as well. Expectations for the future of FinTech are about double-edged consequences in which the structure of the market and business models will be influenced by market behavior aiming to maximize value for the users; however, it is likely to disrupt existing regulatory structures and accepted models of service in the market.

REFERENCES

Afuah, A., & Tucci, C. (2000). Internet Business Models and Strategies: Text and Cases. Academic Press.

Amit, R., & Zott, C. (2001). Value Creation in E-Business. *Strategic Management Journal, 22*(6-7), 493–520. doi:10.1002mj.187

Amit, R., & Zott, C. (2010). Business Model Innovation: Creating Value In Times Of Change. SSRN *Electronic Journal, 23.* doi:10.2139/ssrn.1701660

Barba Navaretti, G., Calzolari, G., Mansilla-Fernández, J., & Pozzolo, A. F. (2018). Fintech and Banking. Friends or Foes? SSRN *Electronic Journal.* doi:10.2139/ssrn.3099337

Barbu, C. M., Florea, D. L., Dabija, D.-C., & Barbu, M. C. (2021). Customer Experience in Fintech. *Journal of Theoretical and Applied Electronic Commerce Research*, *16*(5), 1415–1433. doi:10.3390/jtaer16050080

Bedjeti Baftijari, A., & Nakov, L. (2020). *An overview on managing changes for bank risks in times of fintech (r)evolution: A challenge or opportunity?* Academic Press. doi:10.1016/j.intfin.2021.101498

Bellardini, L., Del Gaudio, B. L., Previtali, D., & Verdoliva, V. (2022). How do banks invest in fintechs? Evidence from advanced economies. *Journal of International Financial Markets, Institutions and Money*, *77*, 101498. doi:10.1016/j.intfin.2021.101498

Casadesus-Masanell, R., & Ricart, J. (2010). From Strategy to Business Models and onto Tactics. *Long Range Planning*, *43*(2-3), 195–215. doi:10.1016/j.lrp.2010.01.004

Chuen, D., & Teo, E. (2017). *Emergence of FinTech and the LASIC Principles*. Academic Press.

Dapp, T. (2017). Fintech: The Digital Transformation in the Financial Sector. Academic Press.

Dorfleitner, G., & Hornuf, L. (2019). FinTech Business Models. In G. Dorfleitner & L. Hornuf (Eds.), *FinTech and Data Privacy in Germany: An Empirical Analysis with Policy Recommendations* (pp. 85–106). Springer International Publishing. doi:10.1007/978-3-030-31335-7_5

FSB. (2019). *Retrieved from Girling, P. X. (2022). Operational Risk Management: A Complete Guide for Banking and Fintech*. John Wiley & Sons.

Giglio, F. (2021). Fintech: A Literature Review. *European Research Studies Journal*, *24*(2B), 600–627. doi:10.35808/ersj/2254

Gimpel, H., Rau, D., & Röglinger, M. (2018). Understanding FinTech start-ups – a taxonomy of consumer-oriented service offerings. *Electronic Markets*, *28*(3), 245–264. doi:10.100712525-017-0275-0

Haddad, C., & Hornuf, L. (2022). How do fintech start-ups affect financial institutions' performance and default risk? *European Journal of Finance*, 1–32.

Hendriyani, C., & Raharja, S. u. J. (2019). Business agility strategy: Peer-to-peer lending of Fintech startup in the era of digital finance in Indonesia. *Review of Integrative Business and Economics Research*, *8*, 239–246.

Hornuf, L., Klus, M. F., Lohwasser, T. S., & Schwienbacher, A. (2021). How do banks interact with fintech startups? *Small Business Economics*, *57*(3), 1505–1526. doi:10.100711187-020-00359-3

Kim, J., Song, H., & Lee, C.-K. (2016). Effects of corporate social responsibility and internal marketing on organizational commitment and turnover intentions. *International Journal of Hospitality Management*, *55*, 25–32. doi:10.1016/j.ijhm.2016.02.007

Mărăcine, V., Voican, O., & Scarlat, E. (2020). The Digital Transformation and Disruption in Business Models of the Banks under the Impact of FinTech and BigTech. *Proceedings of the International Conference on Business Excellence*, *14*(1), 294-305. 10.2478/picbe-2020-0028

Murinde, V., Rizopoulos, E., & Zachariadis, M. (2022). The impact of the FinTech revolution on the future of banking: Opportunities and risks. *International Review of Financial Analysis*, *81*, 102103. doi:10.1016/j.irfa.2022.102103

NeubertM. (2020). Pricing Decisions of FinTech Firms. SSRN 3634459.

Osterwalder, A. (2004). *The Business Model Ontology – A Proposition in a Design Science Approach*. Academic Press.

Shakhzodbek, E., Khurshidbek, T., & Shoxruxmirzo, A. (2022). From bank to fintech and the power of network effects. *Boshqaruv Va Etika Qoidalari Onlayn Ilmiy Jurnali*, 14-16.

Taherdoost, H. (2023). Fintech: Emerging Trends and the Future of Finance. *Financial Technologies and DeFi: A Revisit to the Digital Finance Revolution*, 29-39.

Taherdoost, H., Madanchian, M., & Ebrahimi, M. (2021). Advancement of Cybersecurity and Information Security Awareness to Facilitate Digital Transformation: Opportunities and Challenges. Handbook of Research on Advancing Cybersecurity for Digital Transformation, 99-117.

Temelkov, Z. (2018). *Fintech firms opportunity or threat for banks?* Academic Press.

Velazquez, P. V., Bobek, V., Vide, R. K., & Horvat, T. (2022). Lessons from Remarkable FinTech Companies for the Financial Inclusion in Peru. *Journal of Risk and Financial Management*, *15*(2), 62. Advance online publication. doi:10.3390/jrfm15020062

Vives, X. (2018). *The Impact of Fintech on Banking*. Academic Press.

Wardley, P. (2011). Technological Innovation in Retail Finance: International Historical Perspectives. Routledge.

Zavolokina, L., Dolata, M., & Schwabe, G. (2016). The FinTech phenomenon: Antecedents of financial innovation perceived by the popular press. *Financial Innovation*, 2(1), 16. doi:10.118640854-016-0036-7

Zhang, J., van Gorp, D., & Kievit, H. (2022). Digital technology and national entrepreneurship: An ecosystem perspective. *The Journal of Technology Transfer*. Advance online publication. doi:10.100710961-022-09934-0 PMID:35602312

Zhao, J., Li, X., Yu, C.-H., Chen, S., & Lee, C.-C. (2022). Riding the FinTech innovation wave: FinTech, patents and bank performance. *Journal of International Money and Finance*, 122, 102552. doi:10.1016/j.jimonfin.2021.102552

Zott, C., Amit, R., & Massa, L. (2011). The Business Model: Recent Developments and Future Research. *Journal of Management*, 37(4), 1019–1042. Advance online publication. doi:10.1177/0149206311406265

Chapter 6

The Future of Cryptocurrency and Its Effect on Organizational Structure, Culture, and Change

Mitra Madanchian
Hamta Group–Hamta Business Corporation, Canada

ABSTRACT

Some of the constraints that cryptocurrencies now face, such as the fact that one's digital wealth might be lost in the event of a computer breakdown, may in the future be solved by technical advancements. Organizational structure, power distribution, and decision-making capacity are susceptible to disruption as a result of technological development. Consequently, culture will become fragile if executives do not take the essential steps to go ahead. Given that disruption will alter the present world, the time has come to comprehend blockchain and its consequences for corporate culture. This chapter discusses the future of cryptocurrencies and their impact on corporate culture and structure.

INTRODUCTION

Cryptocurrency, digital currency, is a new development in virtual currency. The advantages of digital money as a peer-to-peer means of trade and a store of value and assets are that it is decentralized and portable (Bohr & Bashir, 2014). This development, widespread interest, and widespread acceptance have posed a challenge to the current financial system. The 2008 financial crisis prompted the public to

DOI: 10.4018/978-1-6684-8368-8.ch006

doubt the dependability and trustworthiness of the current financial institutions and seek alternatives, such as digital banking systems (Vo & Xu, 2017). Cryptocurrency employs cryptographic techniques for the transfer of digital information to guarantee the authenticity of transactions (Farell, 2015). The purpose of cryptocurrencies is to eliminate the necessity for a central authority in business and financial transactions.

The study of the history of money revealed that the preferences of the people (according to their ideological and geographical culture and surroundings, etc.) affect the origin, process of change, and development of all types of currency. As a result, examining Bitcoin and cryptocurrency may need a sensitivity to public opinion, as it may have a big influence on the future of currency (Pakrou & Amir, 2016). From open innovation philosophy to open innovation culture, the inverted U-shaped curve of open innovation impacts, often known as the open innovation conundrum (Formica & Curley, 2018), should be overcome. During the 4th Industrial Revolution, the open innovation paradox is exploding, which is boosting the open innovation's complexity (Lee et al., 2018; Yun & Liu, 2019). In this circumstance, the need to comprehend culture, which might regulate the dynamics of open innovation, is increased.

Some of the limitations that cryptocurrencies face, such as the possibility of losing one's digital wealth in the case of a computer failure, may in the future be eliminated by technological advances. Due to technological advancement, decision-making, power distribution, and organizational structure ability are prone to disruption. Therefore, the culture will become weak if executives do not take the necessary measures to go forward. Given that disruption will transform the current global landscape, the moment has come to grasp blockchain and its effects on business culture. The future of cryptocurrencies and their influence on business culture and structure are discussed in this article.

CONCEPT OF CULTURAL EFFECTS

Culture impacts action by building a repertory or "toolkit" of styles, abilities, and habits from which individuals create "action strategies" (Swidler, 1986). "culture for open innovation dynamics" may take somewhat more effort than "the development of culture."

The trope of the day is to situate the cultural dilemma in the "beyond" domain. The "beyond" is neither a fresh outlook nor a departure from the past. The enduring mythologies of the middle years could be those of beginnings and ends. "Beyond" refers to a restless movement that has become popular everywhere, on all sides, in all directions, and back and forth (Grant & Mayer, 2009). If the idea that culture is a kind of innovation, is accepted, it is also likely that impression management goals increase the link between affiliative citizenship and altruistic goals by enticing staff members to demonstrate their altruism in ways that "do" and "look" good (Simon, 1993).

When a group is competing with other groups, altruism, which is defined in evolutionary economics as conduct that lowers an actor's fitness while boosting the fitness of others (in other words, it is a unique culture of economic behavior), raises the chances of the group surviving. In evolutionary economics, constrained rationality also results in the docile nature of economic actors, which benefits human fitness. Social influences (as a unique culture of economic behavior) often provide us counsel that is "for our benefit," along with the knowledge on which this advice is based (DiMaggio, 1997).

According to recent sociological studies, culture is now seen to be fractured between groups and inconsistent throughout its expressions as sophisticated rule-like systems that serve as resources that may be strategically used (Tomlinson, 1999). The latent variable perspective of culture as cohesive, integrated, and ambiguous has therefore been rejected by many sociologists in favor of descriptions of culture as a "toolkit," "repertoire," or collection of items that are diverse in function and content (Martin, 1992).

ORGANIZATIONAL STRUCTURE AND CULTURE

Despite the absence of a broadly accepted definition, researchers believe that culture is something that its members mainly share, which helps explain company success. Based on similar beliefs and standards, members of one organization are set apart from those of another via collective mind programming. Even before the company's members decide to accept its ideals, it was often created by the firm's founders. Although there are many different definitions of culture, it is apparent that each organization has its own unique culture, which is shown by the behavioral norms and shared experiences of its members as well as the company's top-down ideals and shared presumptions (Hope, 2003). An organization's positive culture may directly improve collaboration inside organizational units and coordination between organizational units, as well as indirectly improve a firm's performance (Hofstede & Hofstede, 2001). For instance, supply chain management or firm-level financial report disclosures rely on the relative importance of organizational culture (Galbreath, 2010). Corporate social responsibility (CSR) may benefit from a humanistic organizational culture (Ouchi & Wilkins, 1985). According to micro-analytic conceptions of organizational culture, culture is something that each person has and may be understood by exploring their unconscious minds or through cognitive processes like causal attribution, learning, and sense-making (Den Hartog & Verburg, 2004).

Building a solid business culture is a great strategy for changing employee behavior and raising productivity. Organizational culture may be impacted by human resource management (HRM) practices, and the prevailing culture may affect the HRM policies and practices that companies adopt. "A collection of basic beliefs, behavioral norms, artifacts, and behavioral patterns which influence how individuals in an organization interact with one another and invest their energy in their employment and the company as a whole" (Sørensen, 2002) is what is meant by organizational culture.

Businesses with a strong culture perform more consistently (less variably) in situations that are reasonably stable because their ability to capitalize on their core skills is improved by the alignment of their organizational aims and values. However, the advantages of strong cultures for dependability are lost in unstable circumstances. Different definitions of organizational culture include "a system of common values (that define what is essential) and standards that define suitable attitudes and actions for organizational members" A collection of values and rules that are generally accepted and firmly upheld across the company is referred to as having a strong culture (Kotter, 2008).

Organic structure and external orientation are often characteristics of entrepreneurial corporate cultures. It influences the firm's decision-making process for results, which includes organizational strategies and procedures. Said culture has the following crucial traits: (1) a flexible and risk-taking mindset, (2) a creative leadership style, (3) adaptable development-bonding mechanisms, and (4) a proactive attitude that is prepared to take on new challenges with a strategic focus (Deshpandé, Farley, & Webster Jr, 1993). Transformative leaders change their organizational cultures by first understanding them, realigning them with a new vision, and revising their shared norms, values, and assumptions (Hope, 2003). In contrast to transactional leaders, who operate within their organizational cultures by adhering to current norms, procedures, and rules.

The fundamental tenet of the functionalist anthropological definition of culture is that culture is a characteristic of groups and may be conceptualized as the collected knowledge that a particular group has gathered over the course of its history. Culture can be viewed as a set of fundamental beliefs that a particular group creates, learns, or develops to deal with its issues with internal integration and external adaptation. Once these beliefs have proven to be effective, they are to be passed on to new members as the right way to perceive, think about, and feel about those issues. It consists of three levels: artifacts, which are hard-to-understand organizational processes and structures; values, which are plans, objectives, and justifications; and implicit underlying assumptions taken-for-granted beliefs, perception patterns, mental motivations, and attitudes that serve as the foundation for behavior and values (Gassmann, Enkel, & Chesbrough, 2010).

STRUCTURAL CHANGE

Since the introduction of the cryptocurrency Bitcoin, businesses have been fascinated by the developing phenomenon of blockchain, a decentralized infrastructure that enables confirmed and tamper-resistant transactions across many network members (Beck, Müller-Bloch, & King, 2018). Blockchain's capacity to offer a "single truth" across agents without needing them to know or trust each other is of special interest to businesses and academics; this represents a fundamental change from trusting individuals to trusting algorithms (Antonopoulos, 2014).

Because data recorded in the blockchain cannot be changed, this shift in trust is feasible (Beck et al., 2018). This might lead to the elimination of time-consuming and expensive intermediaries in ownership verification and transaction processing. Blockchain's distinctive combination of technologically essential elements enables the shift in trust: distributed ledgers (a database maintained at various nodes rather than a central location), encryption and consensus processes to encrypt and secure the storage and updating of information, a potentially immutable audit trail, and smart contracts that automatically verify and enforce the terms of the agreement between users of blockchain applications (Du, Pan, Leidner, & Ying, 2019). A certain amount of flexibility is provided by blockchain in terms of the best consensus mechanism (including stakeholder-based and computer power-based approaches), the encryption method, built-in smart contracts, and the requirements for user participation, including permissioned blockchains, private blockchains, public blockchains, and fully open (Carson, Romanelli, Walsh, & Zhumaev, 2018). In contrast to private blockchains, which only permit nodes that have been preregistered by a central authority to read blockchain data, submit, and validate new information to be registered on the blockchain, public blockchains permit all nodes in a peer-to-peer network to read blockchain data and propose new data entries (Beck et al., 2018). For closed or semi-closed systems, where the majority of nodes are trusted, such as consortia made up of a small number of businesses, permissioned blockchains are more appropriate (Viriyasitavat & Hoonsopon, 2019).

The absence of real-world applications that go beyond prototypes and obstacles to adopting permissioned blockchain technology has been noted by many academics. For instance, van Hoek (Van Hoek, 2019) identifies financial limitations, a lack of managerial commitment, and opaque information disclosure policies as major obstacles to the successful implementation of permissioned blockchain. They also point to dependency on intra- and inter-organizational connections as a major barrier. Other academics include system-related obstacles such as security worries, dependability problems with systems, and the integration of blockchain into current IT structures (Beck et al., 2018; Wang, Singgih, Wang, & Rit, 2019). To assist firms in embracing blockchain, Lacity (Lacity, 2018) offers recommendations on how to develop practical governance models, how to address intellectual property problems, and how to tackle legislative ambiguity like industrial espionage risk.

Blockchain applications can only be used in situations where the transaction protocol can be developed to foresee and manage to coordinate all different user activities. That is why they need a deep familiarity with the cultural and social mechanisms supporting the processes that are being transferred from an external observer's perspective to a distributed, self-regulating system. The use of technology as a tool is often handled cautiously in reports. A decade before the blockchain, the Egan Report advised "to approach change by first defining and improving processes, then applying technology as a tool to support these process and cultural improvements" and "does not consider that technology on its own can provide the solution to the need for higher quality and efficiency in construction." (Belle, 2017).

The kinds of activity and coordination it enables should not be completely replicable by enterprises, markets, or hybrids if blockchain technology supports a unique organizational structure. The problem is that a significant portion of studies in this field do not represent innovative organizational strategies. For instance, when a centralized digital platform uses blockchain technology to expedite operations without affecting its level of influence and market power, the organizational structure remains the same. Despite any differences in the underlying technology, incentives, and governance remain the same. The relevant dynamics are still those of markets when a blockchain is utilized to run an exchange according to the same regulations that a conventional middleman would follow. However, there are grounds to think that the blockchain form might represent a unique structural option since it can carry out the following essential organizing tasks:

1. Freedom from institutional restrictions. Because blockchain-based organizations function digitally, they may be able to operate outside of geographical and legal boundaries or enable members to rely on superior institutional frameworks than the ones they are entrenched in (North, 1991).
2. Flexibility in management, where authority may be distributed more democratically or may be consolidated in the hands of a select few key developers. Additionally, work specialization and stakeholder incentive alignment are supported by the blockchain format (Aghion & Tirole, 1997).
3. Learning and adaptation, in which all participants' preferences and beliefs are combined through technology, and people change as a result of changes in their environment (Williamson, 1991). Similar to how financial markets gather data regarding demand and willingness to pay, blockchain systems with tradeable tokens may be used to crowdsource preferences, and collect views and expectations at scale (such as token curated registry) (Hayek, 1945).

4. Procedural and distributive justice, which allows for the transparent resolution of specific sorts of conflicts and the possibility of rewarding ecosystem contributors (Greenberg, 1990).

5. Agents are encouraged to work toward the organization's objectives since doing so will result in the greatest predicted advantages for them (Luu, Teutsch, Kulkarni, & Saxena, 2015). In particular, the blockchain form may advance the private-collective concept by adding financial incentives to complement reputation and reciprocity motives (Hippel & Krogh, 2003). This is a problem since financial incentives may supplant other, non-financial reasons for people to support a project.

CRYPTOCURRENCY IMPACTS

Consumers believe that there is a movement underway and that cryptocurrencies will become even more popular in the future, demonstrating the fact that bitcoin is not only a technology phenomenon but also deeply ingrained in the culture.

Worldwide lax monetary policy for more than 50 years has contributed to the development of a culture of excessive spending, high time preferences, and poor investment. Ordinary people are encouraged to spend their money as soon as they earn it and to save as little as possible when money is continually devalued. Parallel to this, unnaturally low-interest rates encourage additional borrowing and investment, which results in overproduction, excessive debt, and unwise investments. Due to weak monetary policy, both household and global debt have increased dramatically, and both nation-state and family savings have been discouraged. Because of this, economies are more brittle and susceptible to small shocks or slowdowns. By guaranteeing that people can save money easily, reducing the formation of excessive debt, and discouraging wanton overconsumption, bitcoin will play a big part in moderating and correcting these cultural tendencies.

Business pioneers and academics have shaped current management practices throughout the last century. Managers have been able to create organizations that are generally exclusive, hierarchical, and vertically integrated thanks to the key ideas, precepts, and practices. However, it seems blockchain that underpins digital currencies like bitcoin will have a significant impact on how businesses operate, including how they create value, how they are financed and run, and how they carry out essential tasks like motivating employees, accounting, and marketing. In certain circumstances, the software will make many managerial tasks unnecessary.

The development of technology is poised to upend organizational structure, power dynamics, and decision-making processes inside enterprises. Therefore, unless CEOs take the essential steps to advance, culture will become fragile. Addressing blockchain and its implications for corporate culture is essential given that disruption will transform the world as we know it.

The development of digital technology challenges centralized, control-focused companies and suggests substitute models that foster person (employee) centricity and strengthen democratic environments. Blockchain is given prominence in light of this information and is regarded as one of the most potent and pompous technologies that exemplify decentralization, peer-to-peer transactions, smart contracts, etc.

Smart contracts have the potential to automate business decision-making procedures. However, we do not completely understand how it would alter the capacity for making decisions in distributed and decentralized organizations. Understanding the potential impact of distributed ledger technology on decision-making is crucial because of this.

Blockchain: Transforming Culture

Additionally, flat organizational structures might be stimulated by blockchain inside enterprises. With the integration of all the participants in the organizational environment, such as workers, partners, consumers, and other stakeholders, apps created on the blockchain, for instance, would enable businesses to execute better, instantly, and intelligent judgments.

Blockchain will increase resource usage efficiency, transparency, decentralization, speed of transactions, and effectiveness, leading to the emergence of a new kind of organization known as a decentralized autonomous organization (DAO). It will have a significant influence on the organizational structure and make it even flatter than the holacratic structure.

The way business is conducted may alter if accountability and validation are established inside the internal organizational structure. Blockchain has the potential to change business culture and foster more stakeholder trust. Innovation and collaboration that may occur in an open economy free from administrative flaws.

Recently, blockchain research has spanned several fields, changing how various activities are seen (Miau & Yang, 2018). In reality, blockchain has transformed organizational dynamics in the industrial industry (Hughes, Park, Kietzmann, & Archer-Brown, 2019). In particular, Industry 4.0 technology has been incorporated into management processes like agile manufacturing or utilized in conjunction with other technologies, including additive manufacturing and robots, to boost business performance (Olsen & Tomlin, 2020).

It will be simple to get precise demand projections thanks to blockchain in South Carolina. This assists supply chains in reducing the hazards associated with the development of significant inventory stockpiles (Kamble, Gunasekaran, & Arha, 2019). Additionally, automated payments after a blockchain-based system's verification of a smart contract's terms raise inter-organizational confidence (Min, 2019).

The impacts of the blockchain on medium-sized and small enterprises are unknown, despite the perception that it is an innovation that derives advantages by being used in combination with all supply chain actors (Bavassano, Ferrari, & Tei, 2020). Because blockchain deployment depends on partners' consent and desire, some businesses could be hesitant to disclose crucial information for fear that other businesses would utilize it to their advantage (Montecchi, Plangger, & Etter, 2019).

Therefore, it could be interesting to find out if trust in technology can entirely take the place of trust in interpersonal interactions. In particular, how these novel decentralized organizational structures may provide trust and how they might be essential (Queiroz, Telles, & Bonilla, 2020).

With the creation of blockchain, the digital revolution, which got its start with the development of the internet, is now entering a new stage of growth. A new blockchain-based internet will usher in a period of the internet of value, which will reshape current business models through increased reliability and transparency of the data, whereas the pre-blockchain internet was dedicated to the internet of information function, which merely connects information providers with the consumers who use it (Tapscott & Tapscott, 2016). In reality, efforts to spread accurate and trustworthy information among customers existed well before blockchain. People publish product reviews with 5-star ratings on websites like Amazon to enlighten others and assist them in making better-informed decisions (Metzger & Flanagin, 2013). Users assess the items by exchanging data they have generated as customers, rather than only relying on data provided by service providers. Through a decentralized procedure that precludes one party from monopolizing information, blockchain innovation will assist in achieving a fairer and more objective consensus.

The 4th Industrial Revolution's foundational technologies, such as artificial intelligence (AI) and Internet of Things (IoT), are expected to be coupled with blockchain. Blockchain connections between IoT devices enable simple network participation by additional nodes without the need for a centralized infrastructure, lowering costs and enhancing scalability (Sun, Yan, & Zhang, 2016). Additionally, in the next IoT age, blockchain may be employed as a foundational technology for dependable and secure data transfer. For instance, in supply chain management, a blockchain IoT system links producers, sellers, and buyers through network nodes, offering transparent and trustworthy data in several activities associated with product consumption and supply (Saberi, Kouhizadeh, Sarkis, & Shen, 2019). As a foundational technology for data transfer and analysis between cars, service providers, and system administrators, blockchain technology may help the intelligent transport system (ITS traffic)'s flow run more smoothly when combined with AI technology (Yuan & Wang, 2016). When blockchain is integrated with other fundamental technologies, it is anticipated that more revolutionary and cutting-edge services will be developed shortly.

There is a lot of data to take in since there are many different cryptocurrencies accessible, each with its laws and values, such as Bitcoin, Ethereum, Litecoin, and Cardano. Cryptocurrency, often known as "peer-to-peer money," is changing how both people and corporations bank and perform their financial operations. This implies that for businesses that adopt a deliberate bitcoin strategy, various cost-saving and business development prospects may materialize. Everything is possible, from minimizing the risks associated with international commerce to dealing effortlessly across new and complex sectors.

Here are five ways that companies might utilize cryptocurrency to advance more quickly and how that can affect them:

- **Simplified Payroll Choice:** By running a worldwide company or manage a remote team, managing payroll for a group of workers who reside in various locations across the world may be a major problem. The costs associated with currency exchange are much less of a hardship than doing cross-border transactions. Instantaneous cross-border transactions with little to no costs are now possible thanks to cryptocurrencies. Cutting out banks may benefit the workforce greatly and save both the business and the employee money.

- **Lower Transaction Costs:** Cryptocurrency is very beneficial since it vastly enhances the capacity for processing payments. Cryptocurrencies may help consumers and companies save money by avoiding the exorbitant fees that many providers of financial services charge to process payments. The price of the transaction is very minimal when firms deal directly with the client and there is no middleman. For instance, small firms, who are more sensitive to little cost variations, might utilize this to engage in more advantageous competition and modify their product pricing.

- **Protect Client Privacy:** One of the largest drawbacks of digitalization continues to be the problem of cyber-security. A cryptocurrency's success is mostly because it is immune to governmental regulation. One of the most dependable data security solutions at the moment is blockchain. Blockchain technology may be able to reduce the effects of this loss of privacy. A peer-to-peer decentralized network with a public ledger may be used to provide reliable and transparent computing, as shown by Bitcoin and other blockchain-based digital currencies. Asymmetric cryptography is used by blockchain systems to safeguard user-to-user transactions. Each user in these systems has a public key and a private key. These cryptographically linked keys are made up of random sequences of numbers, making it theoretically impossible for one user to deduce another user's private key from their public key, protecting the anonymity of the consumer.

- **Reduce the Complexity of Cross-Border Transactions:** Cryptocurrencies also ease both local and international trade. With the use of cryptocurrency, many obstacles and restrictions to doing business internationally are eliminated, and accepting payments in other currencies is made easier. With the help of cryptocurrencies, doing worldwide business without giving up a significant portion of the profits or charging too much for the goods, is possible.

- **Broadening Reach:** Businesses may boost profits by entering new international markets. Due to the convenience and ease of utilizing cryptocurrencies like Bitcoin for transactions, it is probable to sell items internationally without giving up a piece of the earnings or overcharging the customers. Accepting cryptocurrency exposes the company to a whole new market, which is sure to have a beneficial effect on the sales, reputation, and bottom line.

Structure of the Present Organization

Currently, our organizational structure is either hierarchical, centralized, or both. With this strategy, high-level decision-making is handled by a centralized authority. It also provides a hierarchical structure where each member has a function that they should adhere to. Additionally, the whole system is bureaucratically standardized with a centralized authority making decisions and maintaining order throughout.

This method explains all aspects of an organization's existence, including its political, economic, and social aspects. Capitalism, in which one person grows wealthy, is a result of the centralized organizational system. Corporations are a prime illustration. There are other hierarchical and centralized institutions, such as banks and the financial sector, that make these firms function. They are essential to sustaining these businesses and making ensuring they can operate successfully and efficiently. Digital advancements are increasingly displacing traditional approaches in the present period. In addition to blockchain, other technologies will be essential in transforming enterprises. The following are some of these technologies:

- Technologies such as IoT, AI, nanotechnologies, and blockchain that work together to increase efficiency
- Cheaper and more powerful digital hardware
- Cloud-based services, such as automated algorithms and storage

Organizations will ultimately need to follow the digitalization process and gradually adapt. To modify the behaviors and attitudes, businesses should eventually adjust their hierarchical and centralized strategy.

The Impact of Blockchain on Organizations

The disruption caused by blockchain to businesses that adopt it quickly is now clear to everybody.

- Management

The administration of a company is improved by blockchain, but it is not the only benefit. To improve the effectiveness and efficiency of their procedures, they may incorporate blockchain. To achieve this, businesses should first digitize each process before switching to a contemporary blockchain platform.

- Increased Capital

Giving businesses an efficient means to obtain financing is another way that blockchain benefits businesses. With complete transparency, they may utilize the blockchain to seek money from a venture capitalist or conduct crowdsourcing.

- Marketing and Administration

By using blockchain technology, businesses may now get the most from their advertising money. They will no longer lose money due to fraud by using blockchain. They can detect and eliminate critical fraudulent behavior thanks to blockchain-powered advertising. The outcome will be a higher return on investment for the company.

- Cybersecurity

Organizations may more effectively safeguard their processes, data, and data secrets using blockchain. Organizations now spend a lot of money on cybersecurity. Whether the company is large or small, losing billions of dollars may result from the disclosure of trade secrets. Blockchain may assist businesses in enhancing their security. They may store data in addition to performing transactions. By doing so, they can ensure the integrity of the transactions and create unchangeable data.

- Accounting

The use of blockchain will also assist to enhance bookkeeping. The accounting department may be easily managed with the use of blockchain technology. In addition to handling several currencies, they are capable of managing complicated tax laws and large-scale activities. Blockchain can conduct complicated processes on top of the network and make them simpler. Additionally, it preserves the secrecy and anonymity needed to conduct such transactions.

- Legal Concerns

Smart contracts may be used to handle legal matters more effectively. Any company that interacts with other companies or end users will inevitably have to deal with legal issues. Organizations may better manage legal matters with the use of smart contracts. This is so that instead of defining legal contracts on paper, smart contracts do it in code. Both parties should sign the contract for the smart contract to take effect. It operates on conditions. All of these should be completed on a blockchain platform that saves all data in the most secure and immutable manner possible. All of these indicate that any organization's legal matters are managed quite well with the use of gathered data and smart contracts. Based on the data gathered, will streamline the whole procedure and safeguard the organization's interests.

- Leadership

Blockchain will fundamentally alter leadership, which is an essential component of every firm. Leaders will now adopt a clearer strategy because they respect the newly discovered openness. They will provide transparent criticism that everyone can see and appreciate. Because they can understand how their actions will affect the whole network, leaders will likewise be able to make better judgments. The blockchain is a vast network that connects many organizational divisions. He can put the correct ideas into action by getting the perfect eagle's eye perspective. Additionally, he may utilize the blockchain to promote new abilities and values so that every employee in the company feels appreciated.

- Personnel Management and Purchasing

The development of human resources and procurement will be one of the largest transformations that enterprises will experience. Human resources may be automated using blockchain to accept submissions and filter them using artificial intelligence. Additionally, the whole human resources department will function on top of the blockchain system, guaranteeing that the procedure is clear-cut and effective.

Candidates will have direct access to the system, and by simply logging in, they may check their status. The employment procedure as a whole will be made easier.

The use of smart contracts to compensate employees for their labor is also possible. It may set a prerequisite for the release of the money. Before agreeing to the terms of the smart contract, the worker may review them. The system will instantly disburse the money when the employee completes the assignment. Having the ability to pay employees in cryptocurrencies will be an additional perk.

Modification of Organizational Structure

The organization's design will undoubtedly be impacted by blockchain. The emphasis will now shift from an outdated hierarchical/centralized approach to one that is more decentralized. Organizations will become more efficient and independent by using DAO. It will undoubtedly alter the way the blockchain's organizational structure appears.

Decentralized autonomous organizations use smart contracts, distributed ledger technology, linked devices, analytics, and these technologies in their independent operations. To achieve this, users should install properly developed autonomous software that has immutable code. Each player will be properly positioned in the DAO according to their job. The only drawback is that once established, the rules cannot be changed. To provide the organization autonomy, this is crucial. Additionally, it will make sure that the consensus method takes care of data veracity and immutability and allow the various players to trust one another.

For society, cryptocurrencies provide both potential and hazards. On the one hand, if properly built, cryptocurrencies and the technology that powers them might be used to speed up, secure, and reduce the cost of transactions while also providing other social advantages (Cohen, 2018). A less obvious benefit is that they may make it harder for totalitarian regimes to expropriate funds, either indirectly or directly via currency inflation, depriving savers of a significant portion of their holdings. However, this is theoretically conceivable; see (Enserink, 2016). In this manner, a reliable cryptocurrency might promote more economic freedom and make it harder to finance autocracies. This may be modeled by choosing between two options: either using their local money or a cryptocurrency that is difficult to take (Stojanovic, 2006).

Both academic and lay groups are very interested in the interaction between society, culture, and technology. Does culture influence technology, or does technology influence culture? Or are technology and culture so intertwined that it is useless to talk about one without the other? While Shiller (Shiller, 2020) contends that cultural narratives inform economic trends, the socio-materialists (Orlikowski, 2007) hold that there is neither a social reality that is not material nor a material reality that is not also social, which would appear to support the latter view of culture, society, and technology. Another possibility is that, as complementary tangible objects, technologies will emerge from the fleeting and ephemeral soup of culture. Tax bills, customer service records, inventories, invoices, and numerous other records of money, value, and exchanges of worth were among the first written records of civilization that were discovered, for instance, in the ancient Sumerian civilization. The most plausible hypothesis is that written language developed out of the soup of Sumerian civilization as a requirement for recording value transfers, money, and other financial transactions (Schmandt-Besserat, 1977).

FUTURE DESIGNS FOR ORGANIZATIONS

Future forms of organization design will shift to a delegative type of design and decision-making with the advent of blockchain and smart contracts, in particular, as the availability of information IT therein allows self-governed actors to produce value. Through a global network of peer-to-peer actors working together seamlessly and in real-time to produce value for all engaged actors, blockchain technology helps the creation of value through smart contracts, consensus mechanisms, and cryptography.

The DAO

The most innovative organizational design at the moment is a DAO, which runs entirely on computer code and establishes governance without management or employees using smart contracts and distributed ledger technology. DAOs are intricate systems that function autonomously, adhere to compliance automatically, and fundamentally alter how organizations make decisions.

The DAO is a form of extreme organization design in which members can suggest changes to the organization and where technology itself controls how the activity is organized. By leveraging peer-to-peer collaboration and obviating the need for middlemen, these new organizations may eventually transform society. Numerous additional attempts to develop a successful DAO have been made, with more likely to do so shortly.

Strong Data Governance Focus

Even though blockchain does away with the requirement for trust in the absence of a centralized governing authority, data governance should be a top priority for any organization creating decentralized applications (dApps). Accuracy and reliability cannot be guaranteed; only the data's legitimacy can be. It is possible to write laws and rules into a blockchain such that they are automatically enforced, making governance simpler or almost automated. As a result, the distributed ledger may serve as a basis for legal claims over data, emphasizing the value of data ownership, transparency, and audibility (Zyskind & Nathan, 2015). A second new kind of organization architecture is made possible by big data, AI, smart contracts, and immutable blockchain records. Autonomous organizations with automated decision-making skills are the result. By using blockchain for various purposes, conventional organizations may already include certain characteristics of decentralized and autonomous organization design. However, when these two novel types of organizational design are joined, they may become DAOs.

How Decision Making Is Modified by Blockchain

Organizations exist in intricately interconnected contexts. Over time, the method of making decisions changed from being authoritative to being collaborative and even delegation. However, the introduction of distributed ledger technology in general, and smart contracts and consensus mechanisms in particular, will once again fundamentally alter the paradigm of decision-making (Beck et al., 2018).

Convergence Mechanism

Consensus-based decision-making has long been practiced by humans. It was first a notion used in politics and society, but it has now grown to be a significant aspect of computer science. Consensus algorithms make a guarantee that interconnected machines can function together independently without having to rely on one another and can go on operating even if some network nodes fail. Numerous consensus algorithms use various strategies to verify and authenticate items and transactions on a blockchain. By doing away with the need for trust between parties, choices may be taken, carried out, and assessed without the need for a centralized authority. As a consequence, whether it be machine-to-machine, human-to-machine, or human-to-human, transactions and decision-making are devoid of intermediaries.

Consensus is crucial in blockchains since there is no reliable central authority. Before a blockchain is implemented, network participants should agree on its governing principles, including how they should be applied. A network's nodes follow a predetermined algorithm, and the result should have the approval of a certain majority. Cryptography is also used by consensus methods to verify transactions (and, thus, decisions). The two most popular consensus algorithms at this time are Proof of Work (PoW) (PBFT) and Practical Byzantine Fault Tolerance (PBFT). Since new consensus algorithms are being created all the time, the environment probably will not look the same in a few years. With the advent of smart contracts, decision-making has been automated, and is now possible to be done decentralized and without a central authority.

Ricardian Contracts

The fact that smart contracts are not enforceable legally is still a concern. As a result, Ricardian Contracts have garnered increased attention. Because they are enforceable by law, Ricardian contracts vary from smart contracts. It stores the agreement between several parties in a language that is both human- and machine-readable (contrary to smart contracts, which only execute what is defined in an agreement). It is a legal document that anybody, not just attorneys, can read and comprehend. The fundamental benefit of a Ricardian contract is that any disputes between the parties may be resolved in court. Smart contracts, which simply consist of instructions based on what is specified in an agreement, prevent this from being achievable. Since they eliminate the need for human judgment, smart contracts, also known as Ricardian contracts, have an impact not just on contract law but also more widely on social contracts within society and companies. Smart contracts still need human decision-making when establishing the relevant parameters, even if once implemented on a blockchain, they eliminate the necessity for assessing, executing, or formulating choices made by management or workers. Multiple smart contracts paired with AI, large data analytics, and automated (strategic) decision-making provide a "fundamentally new paradigm for organizing activity" (Swan, 2015).

Smart Contracts

Since data on a blockchain is traceable, verifiable, and immutable, and since encryption ensures confidence between participants working on a blockchain, transactions, and decisions may be made without the need for a middleman. This eliminates the need for dependable centralized third parties, who often charge a fee for validating transactions. How players engage with one another and how choices are formed, carried out, and assessed are altered when middlemen are removed (Christidis & Devetsikiotis, 2016).

The phrase "smart contract" was initially used by Nick Szabo to describe "a computerized procedure that performs the provisions of a contract." It may be compared to a conventional agreement that is automatically and without discretion formed and executed by programming. Similar to computer programs that run on a blockchain to execute transactions or make decisions, smart contracts. Even though they are far more complex, "if this, then that" expressions may also be used for smart contracts. By selecting events or preconditions and specifying information about what should occur when those preconditions are satisfied, they are software programs that carry out certain transactions or choices that are decided upon by two or more actors. Once deployed, the protocol is then documented on a blockchain and will always run as soon as the prerequisites are satisfied.

Changing Organization Design

Not simply those connected to financial markets or "self-enforcing autonomous governance applications," smart contracts may allow a broad range of applications (Luu et al., 2015). As a consequence, there are almost no limits to what blockchain technology can do for businesses. It can help them develop novel, distributed goods, and services that will boost their productivity while also enabling more automated decision-making. dApps are a frequent term for such blockchain-enabled goods and services.

The Value of the Internet

In this "internet of value" (Tapscott & Tapscott, 2016) configuration, consumers create value by paying lower prices and having more free time, businesses create value by increasing efficiencies and lowering costs by utilizing the distributed ledger, smart contracts create value by carrying out specific tasks automatically, and miners generate wealth by verifying transactions. Together, these value-creating processes increase value creation for society as a whole.

When used to their full potential, these technology elements have the potential to change strategic management practices by introducing new types of organizational design that have an impact on organizations and inter-organizational relationships. Existing organizational designs continue to survive despite this. Organizations that do not employ distributed ledger technology, on the other hand, are unaffected; yet, those who do will undergo tremendous change.

dApps

A dApp has at least two distinguishing characteristics: 1) any protocol modifications should be accepted by consensus, and 2) the program should employ a cryptocurrency, or cryptographic token, that is created via a predetermined procedure (Swan, 2015). Thus, the decentralized organization is a new kind of organizational architecture made possible by consensus procedures and cryptographic primitives.

A company based on dApps is a decentralized company where choices are made by agreement among decentralized actors, trust between actors is generated via cryptography, and governance is incorporated into the code, connecting the code to the data (Shrier, Wu, & Pentland, 2016). Since the database is kept on hundreds of millions of distributed machines, dApps do not need to be maintained by a centralized authority. Because of its decentralized design, the network as a whole is protected against damage from a single instance of poor management leading to a point of failure (Shrier et al., 2016). Additionally, the use of blockchain and smart contracts allows an organization to manage and prevent opportunistic, directly affecting the behavior of the company, thanks to the trustless system based on cryptography (Morini, 2016).

NEW FORMS OF ORGANIZATION DESIGN

The way players inside an organizational network communicate with one another and make choices will alter as a result of new types of organization architecture based on smart contracts, consensus mechanisms, and encryption. Because blockchain both automates decision-making and lessens opportunism within networks, it has an impact on how actors interact with one another and changes decision-making capabilities even if an organization only partially adopts a DAO design. Industry partners may become more closely linked to one another as a consequence of sharing the same information across time and location. This increased connectivity increases the number of players and interactions inside a network, leading to collaborative community designs.

Decentralized and autonomous organization design will therefore be added as two additional types to this debate as a consequence of blockchain technology and smart contracts. These forms are distinct from previous talks on decentralized and autonomous organizations (Table 1), which achieved decentralization and autonomy through reorganizing human interactions and decision-making. According to the literature now in circulation, decentralized and autonomous organizations are those where confidence is built via connections and experience; decision-making is based on experience and seniority; and governance is formed by a board of directors.

Decentralization is defined as an organizational architecture that makes use of cryptographic primitives and consensus procedures to maintain confidence across decentralized actors throughout time and space. On the other hand, an autonomous organization is entirely managed by immutable code, where governance is built into the code and decision-making is automated via smart contracts. An autonomous organization should be decentralized, while a decentralized organization need not be autonomous.

Table 1. Current DAOs and conventional decentralized organizations

	Current DAOs	**Conventionally Decentralized Organizations**
Governance	Code embedding	Founded by the director's board
Decision-making	Smart Contracts	Seniority and skill
Reliance	Cryptography	Connections and experience

CONCLUSION

The potential for the loss of one's digital property in the event of a machine failure is one of the drawbacks of cryptocurrencies that may be overcome in the future by technical advancements. As technology develops, it has the potential to disrupt established systems of decision-making, power dynamics, and organizational capability. As a result, the culture will weaken if top leaders do not take action. The time has come to understand blockchain and its implications for corporate culture since disruption is set to drastically alter the present global scene. This article explored the potential of cryptocurrencies and their impact on the organizational structure and culture of businesses.

REFERENCES

Aghion, P., & Tirole, J. (1997). Formal and real authority in organizations. *Journal of Political Economy*, *105*(1), 1–29. doi:10.1086/262063

Antonopoulos, A. M. (2014). *Mastering Bitcoin: unlocking digital cryptocurrencies*. O'Reilly Media, Inc.

Bavassano, G., Ferrari, C., & Tei, A. (2020). Blockchain: How shipping industry is dealing with the ultimate technological leap. *Research in Transportation Business & Management*, *34*, 100428. doi:10.1016/j.rtbm.2020.100428

Beck, R., Müller-Bloch, C., & King, J. L. (2018). Governance in the blockchain economy: A framework and research agenda. *Journal of the Association for Information Systems*, *19*(10), 1. doi:10.17705/1jais.00518

Belle, I. (2017). The architecture, engineering and construction industry and blockchain technology. *Digital Culture*, *2017*, 279–284.

Bohr, J., & Bashir, M. (2014). *Who uses bitcoin? an exploration of the bitcoin community.* Paper presented at the 2014 Twelfth Annual International Conference on Privacy, Security and Trust. 10.1109/PST.2014.6890928

Carson, B., Romanelli, G., Walsh, P., & Zhumaev, A. (2018). Blockchain beyond the hype: What is the strategic business value. McKinsey & Company.

Christidis, K., & Devetsikiotis, M. (2016). Blockchains and smart contracts for the internet of things. *IEEE Access : Practical Innovations, Open Solutions, 4,* 2292–2303. doi:10.1109/ACCESS.2016.2566339

Cohen, J. (2018). Q&A: George Church and company on genomic sequencing, blockchain, and better drugs. *Science.*

Den Hartog, D. N., & Verburg, R. M. (2004). High performance work systems, organisational culture and firm effectiveness. *Human Resource Management Journal, 14*(1), 55–78. doi:10.1111/j.1748-8583.2004.tb00112.x

Deshpandé, R., Farley, J. U., & Webster, F. E. Jr. (1993). Corporate culture, customer orientation, and innovativeness in Japanese firms: A quadrad analysis. *Journal of Marketing, 57*(1), 23–37. doi:10.1177/002224299305700102

DiMaggio, P. (1997). Culture and cognition. *Annual Review of Sociology,* 23.

Du, W. D., Pan, S. L., Leidner, D. E., & Ying, W. (2019). Affordances, experimentation and actualization of FinTech: A blockchain implementation study. *The Journal of Strategic Information Systems, 28*(1), 50–65. doi:10.1016/j.jsis.2018.10.002

Enserink, M. (2016). *Evidence on trial.* American Association for the Advancement of Science. doi:10.1126cience.351.6278.1128

Farell, R. (2015). *An analysis of the cryptocurrency industry.* Academic Press.

Formica, P., & Curley, M. (2018). *Exploring the Culture of Open Innovation.* Emerald Bingley. doi:10.1108/9781787437890

Galbreath, J. (2010). Drivers of corporate social responsibility: The role of formal strategic planning and firm culture. *British Journal of Management, 21*(2), 511–525.

Gassmann, O., Enkel, E., & Chesbrough, H. (2010). The future of open innovation. *Research Management, 40*(3), 213–221.

Grant, A. M., & Mayer, D. M. (2009). Good soldiers and good actors: Prosocial and impression management motives as interactive predictors of affiliative citizenship behaviors. *The Journal of Applied Psychology, 94*(4), 900–912. doi:10.1037/a0013770 PMID:19594233

Greenberg, J. (1990). Organizational justice: Yesterday, today, and tomorrow. *Journal of Management, 16*(2), 399–432. doi:10.1177/014920639001600208

Hayek, F. A. (1945). The use of knowledge in society. *American Economic Review*, 519-530.

Hippel, E., & Krogh, G. (2003). Open source software and the "private-collective" innovation model: Issues for organization science. *Organization Science, 14*(2), 209–223. doi:10.1287/orsc.14.2.209.14992

Hofstede, G. H., & Hofstede, G. (2001). *Culture's consequences: Comparing values, behaviors, institutions and organizations across nations.* Sage.

Hope, O. K. (2003). Firm-level disclosures and the relative roles of culture and legal origin. *Journal of International Financial Management & Accounting, 14*(3), 218–248. doi:10.1111/1467-646X.00097

Hughes, A., Park, A., Kietzmann, J., & Archer-Brown, C. (2019). Beyond Bitcoin: What blockchain and distributed ledger technologies mean for firms. *Business Horizons, 62*(3), 273–281. doi:10.1016/j.bushor.2019.01.002

Kamble, S., Gunasekaran, A., & Arha, H. (2019). Understanding the Blockchain technology adoption in supply chains-Indian context. *International Journal of Production Research, 57*(7), 2009–2033. doi:10.1080/00207543.2018.1518610

Kotter, J. P. (2008). *Corporate culture and performance.* Simon and Schuster.

Lacity, M. C. (2018). *Enterprise blockchains: Eight sources of business value and the obstacles in their way.* https://walton. uark. edu/enterprise/downloads/blockchain/La cityBlockchainsExplained. pdf

Lee, M., Yun, J. J., Pyka, A., Won, D., Kodama, F., Schiuma, G., ... Jung, K. (2018). How to respond to the fourth industrial revolution, or the second information technology revolution? Dynamic new combinations between technology, market, and society through open innovation. *Journal of Open Innovation, 4*(3), 21. doi:10.3390/joitmc4030021

Luu, L., Teutsch, J., Kulkarni, R., & Saxena, P. (2015). Demystifying incentives in the consensus computer. *Proceedings of the 22nd ACM SIGSAC conference on computer and communications security.* 10.1145/2810103.2813659

Martin, J. (1992). *Cultures in organizations: Three perspectives.* Oxford University Press.

Metzger, M. J., & Flanagin, A. J. (2013). Credibility and trust of information in online environments: The use of cognitive heuristics. *Journal of Pragmatics, 59*, 210–220. doi:10.1016/j.pragma.2013.07.012

Miau, S., & Yang, J.-M. (2018). Bibliometrics-based evaluation of the Blockchain research trend: 2008–March 2017. *Technology Analysis and Strategic Management, 30*(9), 1029–1045. doi:10.1080/09537325.2018.1434138

Min, H. (2019). Blockchain technology for enhancing supply chain resilience. *Business Horizons, 62*(1), 35–45. doi:10.1016/j.bushor.2018.08.012

Montecchi, M., Plangger, K., & Etter, M. (2019). It's real, trust me! Establishing supply chain provenance using blockchain. *Business Horizons, 62*(3), 283–293. doi:10.1016/j.bushor.2019.01.008

MoriniM. (2016). From'Blockchain hype'to a real business case for Financial Markets. *Available at* SSRN 2760184.

Olsen, T. L., & Tomlin, B. (2020). Industry 4.0: Opportunities and challenges for operations management. *Manufacturing & Service Operations Management, 22*(1), 113–122. doi:10.1287/msom.2019.0796

Orlikowski, W. J. (2007). Sociomaterial practices: Exploring technology at work. *Organization Studies, 28*(9), 1435–1448. doi:10.1177/0170840607081138

Ouchi, W. G., & Wilkins, A. L. (1985). Organizational culture. *Annual Review of Sociology, 11*(1), 457–483. doi:10.1146/annurev.so.11.080185.002325

Pakrou, M., & Amir, K. (2016). The relationship between perceived value and the intention of using bitcoin. *Journal of Internet Banking and Commerce, 21*(2).

Queiroz, M. M., Telles, R., & Bonilla, S. H. (2020). Blockchain and supply chain management integration: A systematic review of the literature. *Supply Chain Management, 25*(2), 241–254. doi:10.1108/SCM-03-2018-0143

Saberi, S., Kouhizadeh, M., Sarkis, J., & Shen, L. (2019). Blockchain technology and its relationships to sustainable supply chain management. *International Journal of Production Research, 57*(7), 2117–2135. doi:10.1080/00207543.2018.1533261

Schmandt-Besserat, D. (1977). An archaic recording system and the origin of writing. *Syro-Mesopotamian Studies, 1.*

Shiller, R. J. (2020). *Narrative economics: How stories go viral and drive major economic events.* Princeton University Press.

Shrier, D., Wu, W., & Pentland, A. (2016). Blockchain & infrastructure (identity, data security). *Massachusetts Institute of Technology-Connection Science, 1*(3), 1–19.

Simon, H. A. (1993). Altruism and economics. *The American Economic Review, 83*(2), 156–161.

Sørensen, J. B. (2002). The strength of corporate culture and the reliability of firm performance. *Administrative Science Quarterly*, *47*(1), 70–91. doi:10.2307/3094891

Stojanovic, S. D. (2006). Pricing and hedging of multi type contracts under multidimensional risks in incomplete markets modeled by general Itô SDE systems. *Asia-Pacific Financial Markets*, *13*(4), 345–372. doi:10.100710690-007-9049-6

Sun, J., Yan, J., & Zhang, K. Z. (2016). Blockchain-based sharing services: What blockchain technology can contribute to smart cities. *Financial Innovation*, *2*(1), 1–9. doi:10.118640854-016-0040-y

Swan, M. (2015). Blockchain thinking: The brain as a decentralized autonomous corporation [commentary]. *IEEE Technology and Society Magazine*, *34*(4), 41–52. doi:10.1109/MTS.2015.2494358

Swidler, A. (1986). Culture in action: Symbols and strategies. *American Sociological Review*, *51*(2), 273–286. doi:10.2307/2095521

Tapscott, D., & Tapscott, A. (2016). *Blockchain revolution: how the technology behind bitcoin is changing money, business, and the world*. Penguin.

Tomlinson, J. (1999). *Globalization and culture*. University of Chicago Press.

Van Hoek, R. (2019). Exploring blockchain implementation in the supply chain: Learning from pioneers and RFID research. *International Journal of Operations & Production Management*, *39*(6/7/8), 829–859. doi:10.1108/IJOPM-01-2019-0022

Viriyasitavat, W., & Hoonsopon, D. (2019). Blockchain characteristics and consensus in modern business processes. *Journal of Industrial Information Integration*, *13*, 32–39. doi:10.1016/j.jii.2018.07.004

Vo, N. N., & Xu, G. (2017). *The volatility of Bitcoin returns and its correlation to financial markets*. Paper presented at the 2017 International Conference on Behavioral, Economic, Socio-cultural Computing (BESC). 10.1109/BESC.2017.8256365

Wang, Y., Singgih, M., Wang, J., & Rit, M. (2019). Making sense of blockchain technology: How will it transform supply chains? *International Journal of Production Economics*, *211*, 221–236. doi:10.1016/j.ijpe.2019.02.002

Williamson, O. E. (1991). Comparative economic organization: The analysis of discrete structural alternatives. *Administrative Science Quarterly*, *36*(2), 269–296. doi:10.2307/2393356

Yuan, Y., & Wang, F.-Y. (2016). *Towards blockchain-based intelligent transportation systems.* Paper presented at the 2016 IEEE 19th international conference on intelligent transportation systems (ITSC).

Yun, J. J., & Liu, Z. (2019). *Micro-and macro-dynamics of open innovation with a quadruple-helix model* (Vol. 11). MDPI.

Zyskind, G., & Nathan, O. (2015). *Decentralizing privacy: Using blockchain to protect personal data.* Paper presented at the 2015 IEEE Security and Privacy Workshops. 10.1109/SPW.2015.27

Chapter 7
FinTech and Change Management:
Challenges and Necessities

Frida Lizbeth Ponce Pulido
University Canada West, Canada

ABSTRACT

FinTech refers to the integration of information technology and financial services. Over the years, digital transformation went from being perceived as an option to becoming a competitive advantage and a necessity for any organization to survive in such a hyper-competitive business market. A successful digital transformation goes beyond complying exclusively with the technical requirement and thrives on delivering sustainable outcomes. Change management's core motive is to sustain change by guiding and supporting individuals through change and adaptation to further contribute to the organization's success and outcomes. Many authors have contributed by proposing management models, starting with Kurt Lewin in 1947. This chapter aims to analyze nine change management models to identify necessities and challenges faced by individuals, organizations, and industries, such as FinTech, when embarking on a digital transformation journey.

INTRODUCTION

Although technology is not new within the financial services industry, the integration of traditional financial services and information technology, an industry better known as FinTech, has revolutionized the way the industry operates and delivers services. Goldstein et al. (2019) propose that, what makes this technological revolution of

DOI: 10.4018/978-1-6684-8368-8.ch007

financial services so special, is the accelerated pace at which technologies are tested and implemented. Despite the accelerated pace at which FinTech initiatives are emerging and growing, a standard definition has yet to be provided. However, Patrick Schueffel (2016) recently proposed defining it as "a new financial industry that applies technology to improve financial services."

In recent years change has been the only constant, and digital disruptions are continuously changing the game's rules. Chaanoun et al. (2022) affirm that, for organizations to thrive and take advantage of the opportunities that technology poses, they must shift to an agile mindset and adapt their business strategies to the fast-moving environment through digital transformation initiatives. "Digital transformation is the most important catalyst behind the fintech phenomenon" (Nicoletti, 2007). Stolterman and Fors (2004) define *digital transformation* as how digital technologies change and influence how humans live and interact with a world that is "increasingly experienced with, through, and by information technology." Furthermore, digitalization, meaning the digital transformation of companies, is socially the most remarkable transformational trend influencing individuals' everyday life and organizations' everyday operations (Budde et al., 2022).

Digital transformation complexity derives from the necessity to manage change, given that these initiatives imply change and adoption of new technologies, processes, and, most importantly, a shift in organizational culture. Therefore, digital transformation success cannot be judged by a successful implementation but rather by its sustainability after implementation (Pacolli, 2022). The Fintech industry, as the result of a digital transformation, has faced challenges due to employees' resistance to change attributed to the fear of the unknown and substitution, challenges that can be addressed through change management.

Over the years, starting with Lewin's model in 1947, a series of change management models have been published to guide organizations during this endeavor. In this research, nine selected frameworks will be analyzed to identify omissions and areas of opportunity to consider every factor that may affect change implementation and sustainability. Critical components of change management, such as diagnosing the company's state before planning the change, the planning phase, training efforts, and evaluating both training and change management actions, are not consistently included in the existing models, thus, posing a great area for improvement.

FINANCIAL TECHNOLOGY, FINTECH

FinTech is the term used to describe the integration of financial services and information technology. According to the CFA Institute, FinTech refers to "the use of technology to deliver financial services." Following that idea, Dorfleitner et al. (2017)

claimed that what characterizes FinTech firms is the delivery of application-oriented and internet-based services, meaning that these organizations place technology at the core of their business models (Broby, 2019). Moreover, Anne-Laure Mention (2019) sets the discussion of whether FinTech should be considered as a mechanism to disrupt the financial services industry, a business model that organizations should adopt to thrive, or a product itself supported by interdisciplinary collaboration with technologies like cloud computing, artificial intelligence, machine learning, blockchain, Robotic Process Automation, Internet of Things, among many others.

The future of the FinTech industry is promising due to its innovative nature. It sets an open space for entrepreneurship, democratizes access to financial services, and facilitates disintermediation. However, the industry has been facing challenges mainly related to law, privacy, and regulatory enforcement (Philippon, 2016), along with stakeholders' perception of the security and reliability of the data used by businesses (Bofondi & Gobbi, 2017). "FinTech companies have to be trusted in order to be accepted" (Broby, 2019). Goldstein et al. (2019) stressed that the digital transformation of traditional financial services has raised people's and industries' concerns about whether a new market equilibrium is going to be met or if industries such as banking will be replaced by data-driven e-commerce and FinTech enterprises.

FinTech firms, compared to traditional financial organizations, have extra competitive pressure since they are expected to procure a more direct engagement with their customers. In fact, that closeness was pointed out by Nicoletti (2017), affirming that customers are now perceived as a user of financial services thanks to the company's customer-centric approach. A customer-oriented approach increases the flexibility and speed at which customers access information and services through technology-enabled devices regardless of their location, making them less dependent on physical interactions, thus, enabling firms to address the immediacy crisis exposed by Parise et al. (2016).

The novelty of FinTech, compared to traditional financial services, creates a direct association with obstacles due to the high degree of innovative disruption. Denier and Spacek (2021) concluded that these obstacles are related to a lack of strategies and management support, lack of market knowledge and product diversity, poor employee and customer inclusion and participation, and failure to communicate the benefits of digital transformation. Organizations must be aware of the importance of bringing people, systems, processes, and structures to cooperate to overcome challenges successfully and become digital.

CHANGE MANAGEMENT

Managing change has become increasingly important for organizations to sustain and exploit the benefits that transformation initiatives can bring. However, the debate on what factors affect transformation initiatives and, therefore, must be considered when managing change is still ongoing. Sirkin et al. (2005) highlight how change management efforts have shifted from focusing on the technical component of change to soft issues like motivation, leadership, and organizational culture. Furthermore, Thomas Lauer (2021) sustains that the human factor must be the priority of any change initiative, arguing that the success of its implementation depends on the active support of those involved and affected by the change.

Tim Creasey, CIO of Prosci, refers to change management as a structured and intentional approach that supports individuals during the change to ensure organizational success. This discipline is a process and competency for leaders in entitling skills that facilitate change and increases organizational effectiveness (Creasey). Similarly, Lauer (2021) defines *change management* as managerial techniques directed toward people to adapt the internal environment to the ever-changing external environment through strategic management.

In recent years, particular emphasis has been placed on skilled and committed leaders to empower people and increase the chances of acceptance and successful implementation of sustainable changes. Roger Gill (2002) proposed a leadership model where leaders must empower, motivate, and inspire people by shaping and communicating the vision and strategy for the potential change and developing a "culture of sustainable shared values." The most common barriers organizations identify when implementing change are the need for more management support and resistance to change. Therefore, the critical challenge has been finding effective ways to remove those barriers and facilitate the transition process led by top management (Budde et al., 2022).

There is a vast list of change management models that propose a series of steps to successfully implement change within organizations, everyone differing in their manner of approaching change. Bernard Burnes (2009), who sees change as a feature of organizational life, exposed two approaches: planned change and emergent change; the first change model published in 1947 by Kurt Lewin followed a planned change approach. However, the accelerated pace at which organizations must adapt to change has made the emergent change approach more popular. Kotter's eight-stage model is an example of adaptability, being initially published in 1996 and further adapted in 2014 to create a culture of speed and agility, maintain eight stages, and rephrase and adapt some concepts to the world's current situation. Differences like the top-down or bottom-up approach can be identified along the models, as well as the emphasis on managing the transition process rather than the change alone; for example, William Bridges' and Colin Carnall's models.

Change Management Models

Change is a complex process and even more when several people is involved. For that reason, many authors have contributed to the organizational change field to alleviate the challenges that organizations face when making changes to systems, structures, and processes by proposing change or transition management models. The following change management frameworks present different approaches to how organizations can lead people through change. Change management models can differ from top-down to bottom-up approaches, planned to emergent change, and change-oriented to transition-oriented.

Kurt Lewin's Three-Step Model

The first change management model corresponds to Kurt Lewin, a psychologist whose main concern was understanding and solving social conflict through the study of individuals' behavior in group dynamics. Lewin (1951) proposed that making change is not about setting a goal and reaching it; change is moving "from the present level to the desired one" to reach what he called "quasi-stationary equilibrium." Lewin's model is based on a planned change approach, defined by Burnes (2009) as a "change that was consciously embarked upon by an organization."

The model presented in Figure 1 starts by *unfreezing* the current state of the organization, meaning that. The *change* stage, also referred to as the moving stage, comprehends the implementation of the change. Here is where people work on getting adapted to the new processes, systems, and structures to move to the final stage. Freezing or refreezing the change aims to consolidate the outcomes and reach again the "quasi-stationary equilibrium" that Lewin proposes as the ideal state.

Figure 1. Kurt Lewin's planned change model

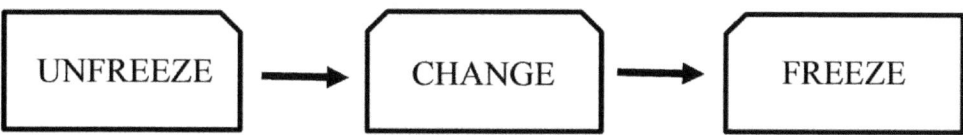

GE's Change Acceleration Process

In the late 80s, a change management model was created out of Jack Welch's dissatisfaction with the pace at which the employees of the organization were adopting a new program. After analyzing previous projects, a group of consultants concluded that, despite a strong technical strategy, most of the projects or initiatives failed to address the people side of change. The commitment was such that they created the so-called 'change effectiveness equation' where: *Effectiveness of a solution = Quality of the solution x acceptance of the solution.* In other words, if the strategy is not accepted by those being affected by the change, regardless of the quality of the strategy, it cannot be considered effective (Von Der Linn, 2009).

The group of consultants developed a process, displayed in Figure 2, that organizations can use as a framework for the successful implementation of the change. The model's first four steps aim to accelerate the adoption of change, starting by establishing the need for authentic and committed leadership to *lead change*. The author claims that if employees perceive a lack of commitment from leadership, chances are high for the initiative to fail. Then, leadership must ensure that there is a *shared need*, meaning the reasons for the change are clearly communicated and understood by stakeholders to reduce resistance. In order to create a shared need, *shaping a vision* is needed to inform the stakeholders how they will be impacted and how things are going to work after the implementation of the change, emphasizing behavioral terms, not business results. Finally, after leadership brings everyone on board by creating a shared need and vision of the change, *mobilizing commitment* by leveraging the early adopters will help leaders to build momentum and continue to fight resistance.

Once the acceptance of change is accelerated, leadership must take action towards *making changes last* by developing a strategy for implementation based on the observed conducts and results from the early adopters and celebrating small wins. *Monitoring the process* is vital to creating benchmarks and identifying potential issues, as well as recognizing positive outcomes. In the end, *changing systems and structures* to support the business's new state and make change last by identifying how they affect and influence an individual's behavior is critical to avoid people pushing back to the old state.

Figure 2. Change acceleration process

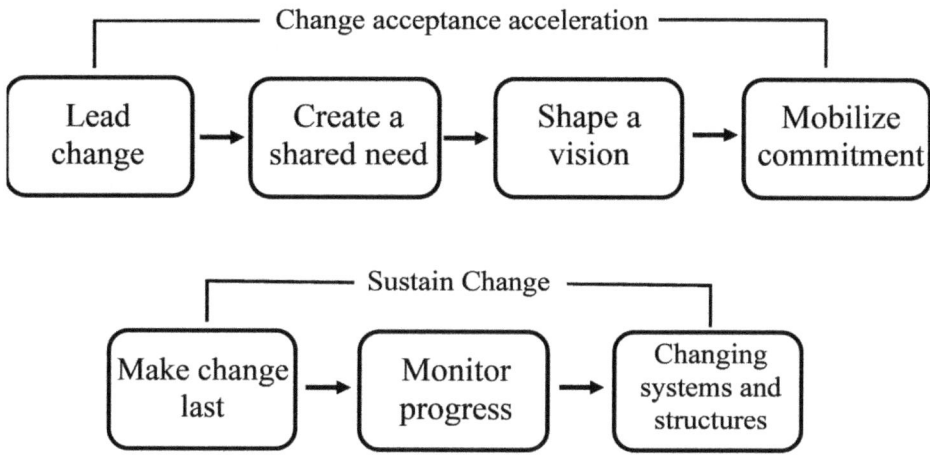

Kotter's Eight-Stage Process

John P. Kotter (1996) published a model to address change in any organization acknowledging that major changes will not happen easily. He identified eight common barriers, exposed in Figure 3, that undermine transformation and must be eliminated to change processes and strategies while improving their quality, effectiveness, and efficiency.

The model starts by gaining cooperation through *creating a sense of urgency*, a concept so appreciated by the author that an independent publication was made by him in 2008 addressing the concept. In the book, he proposes four tactics to create a sense of urgency: 1) bring the outside in, 2) behave with urgency every day, 3) find opportunity in crises, and 4) deal with NoNos, referring to people who undermine and discredit the change and try to convince the rest to join them. Lowering complacency is critical to elevate urgency.

Kotter believed that to develop the right strategy and communicate it to a large audience, *building a strong guiding coalition* in the early stages, with a high level of trust and a well-established shared objective, is needed. Thereby, *developing a vision and strategy* will be easier. The purpose of the vision is to provide direction for change, motivate people, and coordinate actions in a faster and more efficient manner. To exploit the power of the vision, *communicating the change vision* is crucial to creating a common understanding of the direction, goals, and objectives of the change, creating a shared desire for it.

After communicating the change vision, the author suggested taking action to *empower employees for broad-based action* by removing structural barriers, providing training, aligning the systems with the vision, and confronting those who undercut the need for change. Acknowledging that major changes take time, he recommends generating *short-term wins* to appreciate and reinforce the change, embrace self-recognition and give time to celebrate the wins, continuously test the vision against changing conditions, improve performance, increase visibility to retain top management support, and build momentum.

Finally, *consolidating gains and producing more change*, and *anchoring new approaches in culture* to avoid regression. It includes modifications to norms and shared values. Managers must be aware that changing key people might be needed to change the culture; thus, open communication is vital.

Figure 3. Kotter's eight-step model

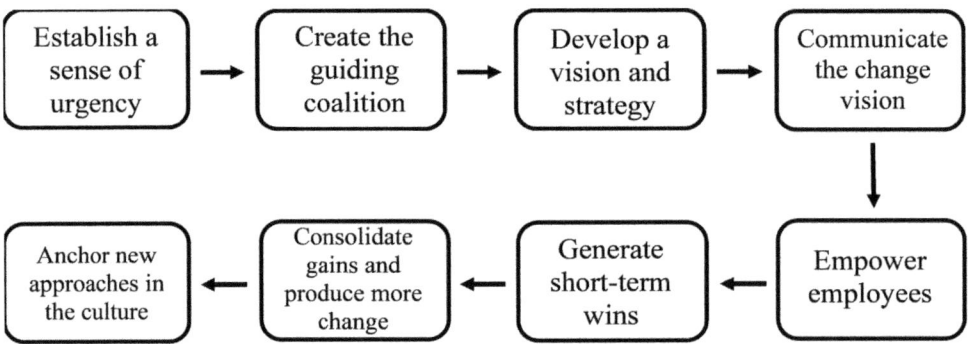

Joyce's MegaChange Model

William F. Joyce introduced a new transformation model in 1999 called *MegaChange model* (Figure 4), a model whose main assumption is human capability rather than limitation. He believes that assuming people's capability sets the bar higher for organizational performance. The model aims to transform the way every member of the organization thinks, acts, and cooperates by transforming the organizational culture, resulting in the optimization of not only the organization but also individual performance, ability, and satisfaction (Joyce, 1999). The author adjudicates the need for a MegaChange to market *hypercompetition*, a term introduced by Richard D'Aveni, referring to "an environment in which advantages are rapidly created and eroded" (D'Aveni, 1994). Furthermore, Joyce states that in a hyper-competitive market, enterprises must be adaptive, nimble, and fleet to survive.

The first stage of Joyce's model consists of "empowering the workforce" in the early stages of change. For that instance, five actions are suggested: a) embrace workforce empowerment in the strategy and mission statements, b) provide necessary financial support, c) constantly provide the rationale for change, d) support flexible implementation, and e) display emotion for the changing concept. In addition, a performance model, used as a tool for empowerment, was developed to support the actions beforementioned. The performance model establishes that *performance = motivation x Ability x Understanding*, forcing the three variables to be present for effective work performance.

The second stage is called "engaging systems," meaning redesigning the firm's processes with the active participation of the empowered workforce; Joyce refers to this stage as a knowledge-based empowerment effort. He advocates that the most knowledgeable workers of the process that is going to be changed must participate in the design of the new processes. The two main actions taken in this stage are workforce-driven policy changes and workforce-driven large systems changes, orchestrated by the so-called tool "change council."

Third, "reforming structures" consist of restructuring, reengineering, and reforming policies, processes, and systems to remove obstacles toward enhanced performance. The actions taken to reform structures imply a) reducing departmentation, b) eliminating rules, c) expanding roles, d) increasing spans, and e) delayering. Tools provided to facilitate this task include role negotiation and a RAMMPP matrix.

Fourth and last, "remaking the strategy." The final stage takes the outcomes and lessons from the first three stages to conduct a) strategic planning and strategy formulation and b) strategy formation. The new strategy must provide direction and create motivation through establishing goals and facilitating coordination by sharing the goals and maintaining consistency towards realization. According to the author, creating a shared meaning transforms goals into motivational and directional goals.

Figure 4. MegaChange model

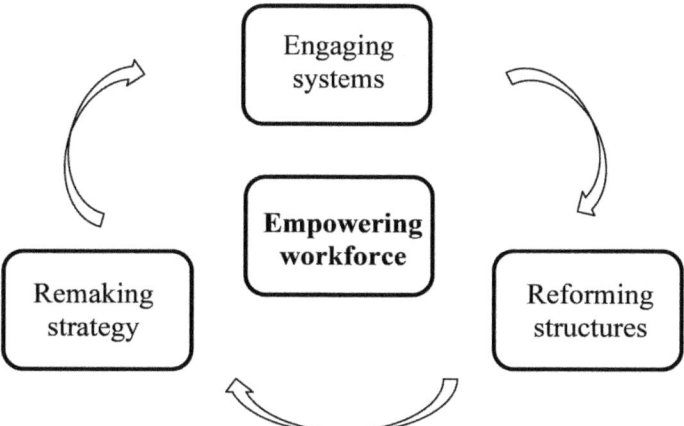

Kirkpatrick's Change Management Model

Donald Kirkpatrick proposed a systematic approach to managing change effectively in 2001. The model aims to achieve the highest degree of acceptance when implementing change within an organization by analyzing possible reactions through empathy so that effective communication and participation are present during the process (Kirkpatrick, 2001).

The author developed seven steps, displayed in Figure 5, to ensure changes will be accepted based on the best decisions. The model suggests that organizations must initiate by *determining the need or desire for change*; this decision can come from top management or employees that identify the necessity. Second, *prepare tentative plans* to implement the change. In this step, the author emphasizes the importance of being open to suggestions and feedback and recommends brainstorming sessions. Third, *analyze what possible reactions* people might have towards the change, varying between negative, neutral, and positive.

Then, managers must move to *make the final decision*, whether through group problem-solving or top management decisions, ensuring that the rate of acceptance is the highest. Followed by *establishing a timetable* for change implementation considering the degree of resistance to change and adjusting the pace to get everyone on board. Once the decision is made, step six consists of *communicating the decision*; Kirkpatrick describes this action as telling and selling the plan and encourages being open to suggestions and analyzing the reactions. Finally, taking action *to implement the change* ensures constant monitoring and evaluation of the plan to detect any issue; in case of existence, going back to step four is suggested as a starting point.

Figure 5. Kirkpatrick's change management model

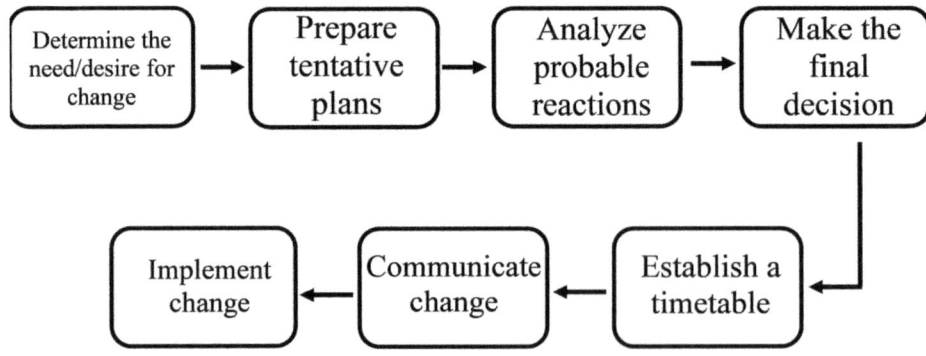

ADKAR Model

ADKAR model's purpose is to build awareness, create desire, develop knowledge, foster ability, and reinforce change, named after the initials of the 5 steps comprehended in the framework illustrated in Figure 6. This model was developed by the owner of Prosci Inc., Jeff Hiat, in 2003. Hiatt's model approaches change from an individual perspective. "To effect change in our organizations, businesses, and communities, we must first understand how to effect change one person at a time." (Prosci b).

Jeff M. Hiatt (2006) puts emphasis on the strict order of the elements and the fact that the lifecycle of his model takes place after identifying the necessity of change. Awareness comes first place; it represents the individual's understanding of why the change is necessary, the benefits of its implementation, the consequences of not doing it, and how it will benefit the individual. Desire must be influenced through intrinsic motivators depending on each person, and its purpose is to gain support from every individual and engagement with the proposed change. Developing knowledge consists of providing the individual with the answers to what is going to happen, why it is necessary, who will be affected and involved, and how the change is going to happen. Ability, as defined by the author, is "turning knowledge into action," a person's capability to execute change following the established standards. Finally, reinforcing change is represented by people's ability to sustain change through time regardless of the internal and external factors affecting them.

Figure 6. ADKAR model

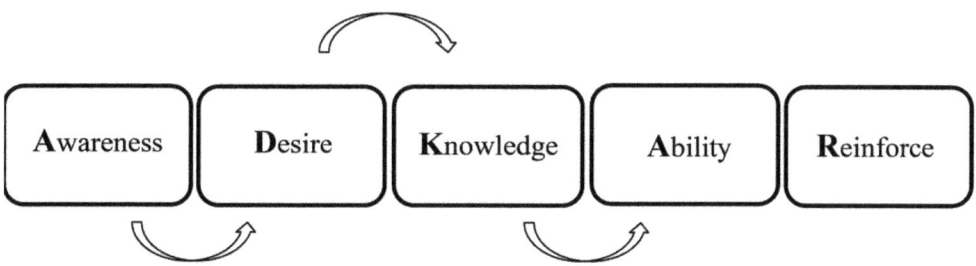

William Bridges' Transition Model

"It isn't the changes that do you in, it's the transition... Change is situational, Transition is psychological" (Bridges W., 2009, p. 3).

The model described in this section is more behavioral-oriented since its focus is on managing the transition process that people in the organization go through when change happens. The author poses that a change without a transition process is just a rearrangement; indeed, he claims that "unmanaged transition makes change unmanageable."

The transition process was clustered into three stages visible in Figure 7. In the beginning, people go through a sentiment of letting go, accepting that things are ending to move through the second phase, called the neutral zone. The neutral zone must be seen as the core of any transition process, and it is where leaders must encourage people to innovate and create a new identity that will contribute to their growth and the company as well; when managed correctly, the entrance to the third phase, referred to as the new beginning will be graceful and smothering generating the perfect environment to act toward the change. William Bridges (2009) about the difference between managing change and transitions: "With change, you naturally focus on the outcome that the change produces... with transition is not the outcome but the ending that you'll have to make to leave the old situation behind."

Figure 7. Bridges' transition process

Kotter's Dual Operating System

John P. Kotter (2014) proposed a change management model that aims to strategically accelerate change by creating a culture of speed and agility that allows people to do more in less time, consisting of a network and a hierarchy. The model consists of eight steps, referred to by the author as accelerators, presented in Figure 8. He poses it as "purposeful expansion in scale, scope, and power of the smaller, informal networks that accomplish tasks faster and cheaper than hierarchies can."

The model consists of a network system, described by the author as a dynamic structure due to its openness to change, characterized by fostering innovation and creativity, along with individualism, since there are no bureaucratic layers. And a hierarchical system is designed to improve the efficiency of day-to-day work by making incremental changes and managing strategic initiatives that help the organization address foreseeable modifications. One of the principles set by the author states that for the dual system to work, there must be "An inseparable partnership between the hierarchy and the network, not just an enhanced hierarchy" (Kotter, 2014).

Kotter positions the *establishment of a sense of urgency* at the top of the hierarchy, describing it as a crucial action to keep people excited, the operating system working orderly, and leaders focused on single opportunities to procure the network growth. He refers to the members of the *guiding coalition* as volunteers, each of whom will represent one department or level from the hierarchy. From there, the guiding coalition focus will be *forming a strategic vision and change initiatives* that will provide direction for the dual system, robust enough to take advantage of big opportunities. The vision intention is to present a picture of success and the information needed for decision-making; thus, it must be feasible and easy to communicate and understand. A memorable and authentic vision and strategy will allow the guiding coalition to *enlist the volunteer army*, i.e., gain people's buy-in and initiate shared commitment to change by communicating the vision and strategy.

Understanding that the volunteers are change leaders must be the main driver for the guiding coalition to facilitate everyone's work by *removing barriers*. Volunteers from the network work closely to meet the goals and identify potential initiatives that align with the vision and strategy. The importance of *generating and celebrating short-term wins* relies on confirming and increasing the visibility of the benefits resulting from the decisions and actions of everyone participating in the change initiative. Kotter (2012) claims that short-term wins should be "obvious, unambiguous, and clearly related to the vision."

To *sustain change*, organizations should strive to identify and complete related change initiatives (sub-initiatives) in a successful manner to sustain momentum and keep people going. According to the author, when momentum is lost, volunteers tend to go back to their hierarchical roles, resulting in the hierarchy outweighing the network. Lastly, volunteers must incorporate the initiative into their daily activities to *institute changes* to send the organization into what Kotter (2012) calls a strategically better future.

Figure 8. Kotter's eight-step model

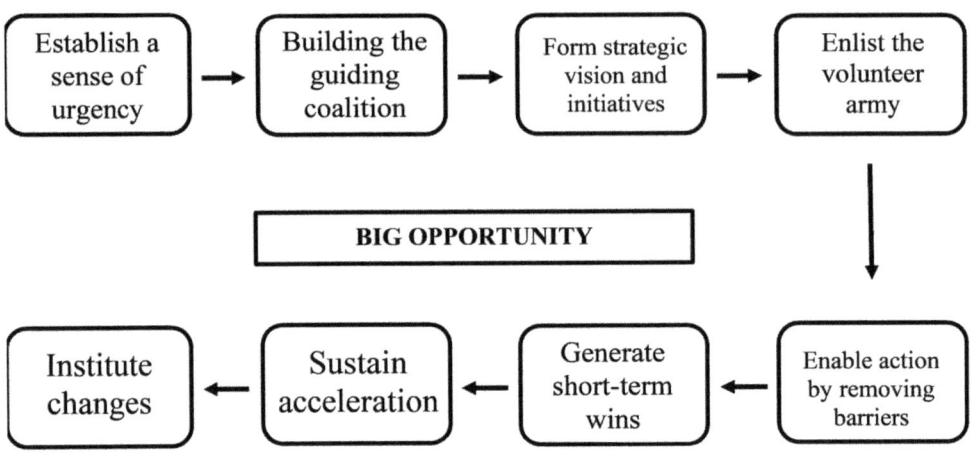

Collin Carnall's Model

Collin Carnall (1986) published the book Managing Strategic Change: An Integrated Approach, where he proposed a model supporting the idea that change can be disturbing as well as disruptive, thus successful organizational change requires managers to have a series of skills to manage transitions while dealing with organizational cultures and complying with organizational change politics.

The first skill is the ability to lead people through a learning and adaptation process, referred to as "managing transition to effectiveness." Second, empathy, defined by the author as the "sensitivity to cultural differences, and the struggle to understand them and to communicate in an intelligible fashion, is essential." Third, regarding political skills, Carnall emphasizes the importance of managers' sensitivity toward political processes to gain buy-in from the rest. Once managers are aware of the skills they must develop to lead effective change, Carnall encourages them to analyze how people will experience the change and how they can help them to cope with it. For that instance, five stages were identified and analyzed through *the coping cycle* (Figure 9).

When change emerges, people go through a stage of *denial*, possibly feeling overwhelmed and finding difficulty understanding why change is needed and minimizing the impact that it can have. *Defense* comes after the denial stage; here, people can feel frustrated, leading to defensive behavior; the manager must ensure time and space to let them assimilate the change. People start to let go and enter the *discarding* stage when they recognize the need for change and that it is inevitable. With recognition comes the *adaptation* stage; individuals are open to experimentation and begin to test the new systems, processes, and structures, as well as themselves. Finally, *internalization,* "now the new behavior becomes part of the normal behavior" (Carnall, 1986). After testing the new systems, processes, and structures, people come to accept and incorporate them into their routines.

"The key point is that only by synthesizing the management of transitions, dealing with organizational cultures, and handling organizational politics constructively can we create the environment in which creativity, risk-taking, learning, and the rebuilding of self-esteem and performance can be achieved" (Carnall, 1986).

Figure 9. The coping cycle

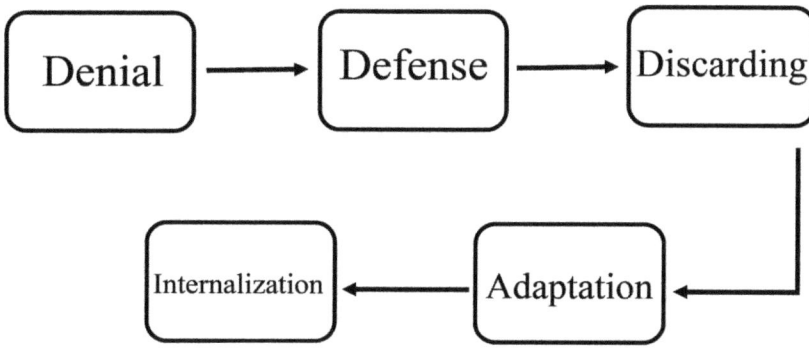

DISCUSSION

Moran and Brightman (2001) define *change management* as a continuous process where organizations renew their direction, structure, and capabilities to meet the evolving needs of external and internal customers. Fintech enterprises, on the other hand, are under massive pressure to transform their business models from a product-centric to a customer-centric approach in order to sustain competitiveness. Therefore, the importance of accompanying digital transformation with change management.

The COVID-19 pandemic has accelerated digital transformation adoption and the Fintech industry growth due to the need for digital connectivity to replace interactions between consumers and providers. Given that digital transformation is the primary driver of Fintech companies, the challenges faced by this industry are similar, if not the same, as any organization embarking on a digital journey. In 2008, Erich Chan pointed out a series of barriers commonly experienced in digitalization initiatives including, but not limited to, lack of knowledge and skills, lack of sense of urgency, lack of motivation and professional advice, lack of attitude toward change, the ambiguity of guidelines, implementation and maintenance costs, inconsistent support, and outcome uncertainty (Chan, 2008).

The increased awareness of established financial institutions of the growth that the FinTech industry has been experiencing in recent years has led banks like Goldman Sachs, Citi, and JP Morgan to invest in this sector. Yet, it has been observed that these investments were made with a strategic intention rather than solely to generate returns (Mention, 2019; CBInsights, 2018). Therefore, to effectively manage change, organizations must take a strategic approach to identify the need for change, set clear goals and objectives, properly communicate with stakeholders, and provide employee training and support.

The change management models described in the previous section provide a structured approach to implementing change while reducing resistance to it within organizations. Hence, facilitating the adoption of financial technology. There is a striking pattern that these models follow. First, they suggest that organizations must create a shared need and sense of urgency for change. For that instance, a guiding coalition must be formed to spread the vision and strategy, so stakeholders develop a desire for change.

Nevertheless, Ashta and Biot-Paquerot (2018) affirm that due to the speed at which the banking and financial institutions world is changing, a sense of urgency already exists, and organizations have put together a guiding team by this time. However, the pace of technological advancements is so fast that any new vision or strategy the team agrees upon is likely to need to be updated by the time it is implemented. For that reason, FinTech can be best described as evolutionary rather than revolutionary (Broby, 2019).

The benefits have been identified and continue to increase as technology advances. Faster, cheaper, and more secure digital transactions, along with more customized services, are part of the list of benefits brought by FinTech (Broby, 2019). On the other hand, cybersecurity, legal, financial, regulatory, and operational risks have also been exposed (Vucinic, 2020). Nevertheless, the potential benefits of FinTech have been demonstrated to outweigh the risks in the medium to long term (Mention, 2019). However, FinTech has also raised the need for new skills not traditionally associated with financial services, including computer programming languages, database management, Artificial Intelligence, Machine Learning, Robot Automation Processing, pattern recognition, and visualization, among others (Broby, 2019).

After communicating the change established by some models, the next step is mobilizing commitment and empowering the workforce to build momentum toward its implementation. Even Kotter's eight-accelerators model mentions enabling action by removing barriers. Despite these calls for action, none of the models explicitly mention *training* as a step toward change implementation. However, as mentioned before, digital transformation initiatives, and in this case, the incorporation of information technology into traditional financial services, represent a scenario where employees must be trained and upskilled in new technologies to support their transition process and remove fears of the unknown and substitution, facilitating that way the adoption of financial technology while providing a sense of self-actualization that will be transformed into empowerment.

Two models are included in the analysis centered on managing the transition process rather than the change process. Bridges (2009) advocates that transition is a psychological process that should be prioritized to implement sustainable change successfully. Moreover, Carnall (1986) affirms that changes that considerably impact the workforce, such as changes brought by FinTech, affect their self-esteem and performance too. Therefore, understanding how people involved and affected by the change feel when it is communicated through the coping cycle explained by Colin Carnall will help rebuild their self-esteem and boost their performance. In 1943, Abraham Maslow introduced a theory of human motivation; he stated that once psychological, safety, and love and belonging needs are met, self-esteem will be built, leading to individuals' self-actualization, resulting in motivated people. Training efforts will help to rebuild the workforce's self-esteem and motivate them to foster change.

Sartori et al. (2018) define training as educational initiatives that organizations undertake to enhance the skills of their workers geared towards fostering a culture of lifelong learning and improving job performance. Furthermore, Sartori and Scalco (2014) believe that training, development, and innovation are interrelated activities. For that reason, including training as one of the steps in any business model is essential to reduce resistance to change and empower the workforce. Yet, a thorough assessment of the organization's state is vital to understanding what and why change is needed, which resources are available and what needs to be added, what skills and competencies the employees already have, and what others need to be improved through training. This assessment is called the diagnosis and planning phase by Ibrahim and Benabdelhadi (2022).

Finally, the authors of the models analyzed in this paper mention the need to make change last after its implementation by monitoring the change outcomes, i.e., focusing on monitoring and evaluating the changes brought by incorporating technology in the financial sector. However, evaluating the outcomes of the change management efforts is essential to sustain those changes. Monitor and evaluate the communication between stakeholders, the progress and success (or failure) of the training sessions and assess the degree of resistance from the employees to take timely action and ensure adherence to the intended goals.

This scenario creates an urgency for a more robust framework to leverage the adoption of financial technology by traditional financial institutions. As beforementioned, most of the analyzed models have things in common, like initiating change by creating a shared sense of urgency, building a strategy based on a new vision, and implementing and reinforcing change, the majority fails to address three critical components of change management suggested by Ibrahim and Benabdelhadi (2022) based on the work of authors like Vandangeon-Derumez (1998), Autissier et al. (2014), Kotter and Schlesinger (1983), Giroux (1996). Toumsin (2005), and Collin and Porras (2000), are presented below.

1. **Diagnosis and Planning Stage:** A psychosociological and cultural assessment of the organization's state is necessary to understand where the organization is positioned and therefore build a strategy accordingly while determining the scope of the change.
2. **Leverage Stage:** Once the diagnosis and plan stage is completed, a plan for communicating the change, providing training, and managing resistance to change must take place. According to Lauer (2021) the failure of change processes can be attributed to resistance from stakeholders whether based on a psychological reaction against the unknown or a perceived loss of freedom, or due to misunderstandings derived from a lack of communication.
   a. **Communication:** Appropriate communication of the change influences stakeholders' attitudes towards change, facilitating its acceptance.
   b. **Training:** Providing the necessary resources and tools to upgrade the skills that were affected by the change will alleviate the stress experienced by the stakeholders while ensuring full exploitation of the new processes and systems.
   c. **Manage Resistance to Change:** "Individuals or groups can react very differently to change, from passively resisting to it, aggressively trying to undermine it, to sincerely embracing it... Many managers underestimate the variety of reactions to change and their power to influence those responses" (Kotter & Schlesinger, 2008).
3. **Evaluation Stage:** Monitoring and evaluating the outcomes of the actions implemented in the leverage stage is key to determining the degree of ownership developed by the people involved and affected by the change. Ensure that they are informed and have a vast understanding of the change and its implications, thus adhering to and participating in the change process.

Including diagnosis and planning, leverage, and evaluation phases are essential because FinTech is here to stay (Mention, 2019). To remain competitive, financial institutions operating under traditional business models must incorporate emerging technologies. Otherwise, they will face substitution by FinTech startups increasingly gaining market share. However, only some formulas will work for some organizations. Hence, diagnosing the firm's state will facilitate identifying necessary changes and prioritization and tailoring the plan that would best fit the conditions and resources available within the firm. In addition, these procedures will improve the organization's skill inventory management, allowing for accurate exploitation and actualization of the existing skills among employees. Lastly, evaluating the outcomes of the change management efforts will allow leaders to correct or reinforce actions taken for further implementation.

CONCLUSION

FinTech is a rapidly growing industry that combines financial services with information technology to provide innovative, customer-oriented solutions. It is an industry that is set to revolutionize the traditional financial services industry, but it also faces challenges related to regulation, data privacy, and stakeholder trust. FinTech companies have extra competitive pressure as they are expected to have a more direct engagement with their customers, which has led to a customer-centric approach that emphasizes flexibility, speed, and access to financial services. To overcome the obstacles related to innovative disruption, organizations must be aware of the importance of bringing people, systems, processes, and structures together to cooperate in digital transformation successfully. As the FinTech industry continues to grow and develop, it will be fascinating to see how it shapes the financial services industry's future and transforms how we access and use financial services.

Change management is crucial for organizations to navigate the ever-changing external environment and sustain growth successfully. The human factor must be prioritized, focusing on soft issues such as motivation, leadership, and organizational culture. Effective change management requires skilled and committed leaders who can empower, motivate, and inspire people by communicating a clear vision and strategy for change. Various change management models exist, each with their approach, from planned change to emergent change, top-down or bottom-up, emphasizing managing the transition process rather than just the change itself.

It is important to note that change management is not a one-size-fits-all solution. Organizations must choose the most suitable change management model to implement sustainable changes and ensure long-term success. It is a continuous process that involves renewing an organization's direction, structure, and capabilities to meet evolving internal and external customer needs. The challenges faced by the FinTech industry are similar to any organization embarking on a digital journey, including a lack of knowledge and skills, sense of urgency, motivation and professional advice, attitude towards change, the ambiguity of guidelines, implementation and maintenance costs, inconsistent support, and outcome uncertainty. Therefore, organizations must take a strategic approach to identify the need for change, set clear goals and objectives, communicate with stakeholders, and provide training and support to employees to manage change effectively.

There is no doubt that a solid change management framework is necessary to ensure a suitable environment for implementing change where every person involved and affected can achieve a sense of ownership. The ownership of the change or appropriation of the process, as defined by Proulx (2001), refers to how an individual adapts and integrates the newly acquired knowledge and skills into his day-to-day work. Revel (2004) claims that a participatory change is an accomplished change. Therefore, Green et al. (2020) emphasize prioritizing the individual's needs; the authors affirm that "once individuals have the motivation to do something different, the whole world can begin to change."

The existing change management models provide a series of steps that comprehend the actions taken once the decision has been made until the change is implemented. However, ignoring the importance of diagnosing the organization's situation before planning the change can lead to failure. Furthermore, the omission of considering training activities in the change management plan can increase resistance to change and negatively impact the overall organization's performance. Lastly, concentrating efforts on monitoring and evaluating the outcomes of the digital transformation and leaving behind the evaluation of the change management actions can undermine the sustainability of the change.

The benefits of Fintech, such as faster, cheaper, and more secure digital transactions, along with more customized services, have been demonstrated to outweigh the risks in the medium to long term (Mention, 2019; Broby, 2019). However, the transition process towards digital transformation requires employees to be trained and upskilled in new technologies to support their process, remove barriers to enable action (Kotter, 2014), and facilitate the adoption of financial technology while providing a sense of self-actualization that will be transformed into empowerment to acquire a culture of change and continuous learning.

FinTech has disrupted and revolutionized the way organizations competing in the financial industry create and deliver services and products; at the same time, the boundaries of the industry have been expanded (Philippon, 2016), it has opened the door to the creation of competitors from outside the traditional financial sector (Goldstein et al., 2019), triggering that way resistance to change from those operating under the traditional business models. With questions about what the future looks like for the traditional industry and to what extent human interactions will be reduced, people must recognize the need to do and become digital. Nevertheless, an appropriate change management model can set the basis to communicate and persuade stakeholders about the need and positive impact that the change poses, along with guiding them through the transition process to ensure acceptance, success, and sustained change.

ACKNOWLEDGMENT

I acknowledge Dr. Hamed Taherdoost for the support, expertise, and insightful feedback provided throughout the research and writing process of this publication.

REFERENCES

Ashta, A., & Biot-Paquerot, G. (2018). FinTech evolution: Strategic value management issues in a fast changing industry. *Strategic Change*, *27*(4), 301–311. doi:10.1002/jsc.2203

Autissier, D., Johnson, K. J., & Moutot, J. M. (2014, January 1). La conduite du changement pour et avec les technologies digitales. *Question(s) de Management*, *3*(7), 79-89. doi:10.3917/qdm.143.0079

Bofondi, M., & Gobbi, G. (2017). The big promise of FinTech. *European Economy*, *2*, 107–119.

Bridges, W. (2009). *Managing Transitions: Making the most of change* (3rd ed.). Nicholas Brealey Publishing.

BrobyD. (2019). *Strategic Fintech*. Center for Financial Regulation and Innovation.

Budde, L., Benninghaus, C., Hänggi, R., & Friedli, T. (2022). Literature review on organizational change and digital transformation. *MDPI*, *2*, 463–483. doi:10.3390/digital2040025

Burnes, B. (2009). *Managing Change* (5th ed.). Pitman Imprint.

Cameron, E., & Green, M. (2020). *Making Sense of Change Management* (5th ed.). Kogan Page Limited.

Carnall, C. A. (1986). Managing Strategic Change: An Integrated Approach. *Long Range Planning*, *19*(6), 105–115. doi:10.1016/0024-6301(86)90103-2

CBInsights. (2018). The Fintech 250: The top fintech startups of 2018. *Research Briefs*. https://www.cbinsights.com/research/fintech-250-startups-most-promising/

Chaanoun, J., Rahmouni, A., & Alaoui, M. (2022). Literature review on organizational change and digital transformation. *International Journal on Optimization and Applications*, *2*(3).

Chan, E. S. (2008). Barriers to EMS in the Hotel Industry. *International Journal of Hospitality Management*, *28*(2), 187–196. doi:10.1016/j.ijhm.2007.07.011

Creasy, T. (n.d.). *An Introduction to Change Management: What it is and why it makes a difference in your organization.* Prosci, Inc.

D'Aveni, R. A. (1994). *Hypercompetition* (1st ed.). The Free Press.

Diener, F., & Spacek, M. (2021, January 1). Digital Transformation in Banking: A Managerial Perspective on Barriers to Change. *Sustainability*, *13*(2032), 2032. Advance online publication. doi:10.3390u13042032

Dorfleitner, G., Hornuf, L., Schmitt, M., & Weber, M. (2017). *Definition of FinTech and Description of the FinTech Industry.* Springer. doi:10.1007/978-3-319-54666-7_2

Gill, R. (2002). Change Management—Or change leadership? *Journal of Change Management*, *3*(4), 307–318. doi:10.1080/714023845

Goldstein, I., Jiang, W., & Karolyi, A. (2019). To Fintech and Beyond. *Review of Financial Studies*, *32*(5), 1647–1661. Advance online publication. doi:10.1093/rfs/hhz025

Hiatt, J. M. (2006). *ADKAR: A Model for Change in Business, Government, and Our Community* (1st ed.). Prosci Learning Center Publications.

Ibrahim, A. K., & Benabdelhadi, A. (2022). Organizational Change Management of Digital Administration. *International Journal of Human Resource Management*, *3*(2), 339–356. doi:10.5281/zenodo.639041

Joyce, W. F. (1999). *MegaChange* (1st ed.). The Free Press.

Kirkpatrick, D. L. (2001). *Managing Change Effectively.* Butterworth-Heinemann.

Kotter, J. P. (1996). *Leading Change.* Harvard Business School Press.

Kotter, J. P. (2012). Accelerate! *Harvard Business Review.* PMID:23155997

Kotter, J. P. (2014). *Accelerate: Building strategic agility for a faster-moving world.* Harvard Business Review Press.

Kotter, J. P., & Schlesinger, L. A. (2008, July-August). Choosing Strategies for Change. *Harvard Business Review.* PMID:10240501

Lauer, T. (2021). *Change Management: Fundamentals and Success Factors.* Springer., doi:10.1007/978-3-662-62187-5

Lewin, K. (1951). *Field Theory in Social Science.* Harper and Brothers Publishers NY.

Mention, A. L. (2019). The Future of FinTech. *Research Technology Management, 62*(4), 59–63. doi:10.1080/08956308.2019.1613123

Moran, J. W., & Brightman, B. K. (2001). Leading Organizational Change. *Career Development International, 6*(2), 111–118.

Nicoletti, B. (2017). *The Future of Fintech* (1st ed.). Palgrave Macmillan. doi:10.1007/978-3-319-51415-4

Pacolli, M. (2022). Importance of Change Management in Digital Transformation Sustainability. *Elsevier, 55*(39), 276-280.

Philippon, T. (2016). *The FinTech Opportunity*. National Bureau of Economic Research. doi:10.3386/w22476

Prosci, Inc. (n.d.a). *What is Change Management?* https://www.prosci.com/

Prosci, Inc. (n.d.b). *The Prosci ADKAR Model.* Prosci Learning Center Publications.

Proulx, S. (2001). Usages des technologies d'information et de communication: Reconsidering the field of study? *Proceedings of the National Congress of UNESCO CIS.*

Revel, M. (2004). Un changement mesuré? *XV AGRH Convention, Montreal, Canada. AGRH.*

Sartori, R., Costantini, A., Ceschi, A., & Tommasi, F. (2018). How Do You Manage Change in Organizations? Training, Development, Innovation, and Their Relationships. *Frontiers in Psychology, 9*, 313. Advance online publication. doi:10.3389/fpsyg.2018.00313 PMID:29662463

Sartori, R., & Scalco, A. (2014). Managing organizational innovation through human resources, human capital and psychological capital. *European Journal of Business and Management, 14*(2), 63–70. doi:10.18374/EJM-14-2.5

Schueffel, P. (2016). Taming the Beast: A Scientific Definition of Fintech. *Journal of Innovation Management, 4*(4), 32–54. doi:10.24840/2183-0606_004.004_0004

Sirkin, H., Keenan, P., & Jackson, A. (2005, November 1). The Hard Side of Change Management. *Harvard Business Review, 83*(10). Advance online publication. doi:10.1109/EMR.2014.6966953 PMID:16250629

Stolterman, E., & Fors, A. C. (2004). Information Technology and the Good Life. IFIP International Federation for Information Processing, 143, 687-692. doi:10.1007/1-4020-8095-6_45

Vandangeon-Derumez, I. (1998). *La dynamique des processus de changement.* Thèse de Doctorat en Sciences de Gestion.

Von Der Linn, B. (2009, January 25). *Overview of GE's Change Acceleration Process (CAP).* Bob Von Der Linn's Change Management and Human Performance Technology Blog. Retrieved January 22, 2023, from https://bvonderlinn.wordpress.com/2009/01/25/overview-of-ges -change-acceleration-process-cap/

Vucinic, M. (2020). Fintech and Financial Stability Potential Influence of FinTech on Financial Stability, Risks and Benefits. *Journal of Central Banking Theory and Practice, 2*(2), 43–66. doi:10.2478/jcbtp-2020-0013

World Bank Group. (2022). *Fintech and the Digital Transformation of Financial Services: Implications for Market Structure and Public Policy.* International Bank for Reconstruction and Development.

Chapter 8
The Criminal Side of Cryptocurrency

Angelo Kevin Brown
Arkansas State University, USA

ABSTRACT

As cryptocurrency (crypto) has become more and more popular, so has crypto-related crime. There has been a lack of academic research on crypto-related crime, but it is becoming more prevalent in the last couple of years. Crypto-related crime became especially significant in the impact it had on victims and the awareness of these crimes in the media and the government in late 2019 and early 2020 as various criminal organizations and criminal opportunities opened up as cryptocurrency became mainstream. The common crimes related to cryptocurrency include fraud, theft, and money laundering. In 2021 estimates of crypto-related crime were estimated to be as high as $14 billion, which is a small fraction of a percent of the cryptocurrency transactions that were around $15.8 trillion in 2021. The purpose of the chapter is to provide a detailed account of the common crypto-related crimes and scams that have occurred and to evaluate the effectiveness of enforcement of these crimes.

INTRODUCTION

As Bitcoin is one of the most popular cryptocurrencies it is also one of the most exploited by criminals (Leuprecht et al., 2022). Cryptocurrencies have various vulnerabilities that allow criminals to exploit them and the people who use them. The enforcement of cryptocurrency fraud and scams has also been limited due to the difficulty in tracking and prosecuting the offenders and the lack of law enforcement expertise and laws related to cryptocurrencies.

DOI: 10.4018/978-1-6684-8368-8.ch008

A major way that blockchains like Bitcoin can be exploited is through one issue known as a transaction malleability problem (De Filippi, 2014). The transaction malleability problem is an aspect of blockchain that opens up a vulnerability to the cryptocurrencies by the alternation of a cryptographic hash, especially the digital signature that identifies a transaction of cryptocurrency. The exploitation can be used to change the ID of a transaction before the transaction has been confirmed and a hacker can trick a computer system into sending multiple transactions through manipulation of the ID. This is considered a top vulnerability of blockchains like Bitcoin (Liu et al., 2017). The issue became known around 2011 by the Bitcoin community. The largest Bitcoin exchange in 2014 was Mt. Gox which was targeted by a transaction malleability, and the company soon lost $100s of millions because of this and later had to close the site down (Rajput et al.,2014).

In 2020 various well-known Twitter accounts were hacked including Apple, Barack Obama, Bill Gates, Elon Musk, Jeff Bezos, Joe Biden, Kanye West, Uber, and over 100 others (Rosengren, 2022). The scammers had hacked the accounts to send posts to the millions of followers to transfer Bitcoin into a wallet and the victims were told that their contribution would be doubled (Anderson & Saleh, 2021). There were around 320 transactions that occurred after the fraudulent posts, and victims sent over $110,000 worth of Bitcoin. Twitter had become aware of the attack and had created a statement a few hours after and stopped the hackers from creating any more messages.

There are many different black markets online on the regular web and on the dark web which often use cryptocurrency transactions (Leuprecht et al., 2022). The crimes that are supported through cryptocurrency exchanges include illegal pornography such as child pornography and revenge porn, illicit drugs, counterfeit pharmaceutical drugs, murder for hire, weapons trafficking, terrorism funding, counterfeit luxury goods, and much more (Han et al., 2020). Funding through cryptocurrency gives law enforcement and intelligence agencies a difficult time investigating and finding out who these people are because of the decentralized and anonymous nature of cryptocurrencies. When criminal organizations that use websites to sell illegal goods online are shut down by law enforcement they often open up again which can have a new name, or can be in a new country, as the ability to run a website anywhere in the world with an internet connection makes it difficult to shut down these criminal organizations.

Crypto Fraud and Scams

Most cryptocurrency frauds are cyber-enabled crimes. These crimes allow the perpetrator to use technology to increase the reach of the offense (McGuire & Dowling, 2013). For example, many of these frauds have been used before the invention of cryptocurrency like the Ponzi schemes which occurred in the 1920s by Charles Ponzi (Jacobs & Schain, 2011) but criminals can increase anonymity and reach through the use of cryptocurrency (Choi et al., 2022).

Crypto scams have even hit the mainstream media with the story of Gerald "Gerry" Cotton. Cotton was suspected of stealing about $250 million through a cryptocurrency scam and later reportedly died in India. Cotton was the founder of QuadrigaCX, and at the time there was no official bank account as there was no system of managing cryptocurrency. While Cotton was wanted for crimes he was diagnosed with septic shock, perforation, peritonitis, and intestinal obstruction and died a day later on December 9th, 2018 in Jaipur India. At the time of his death, he was supposedly the only person who had the password to the wallet with all the cryptocurrency. There was a lot of controversy over the death and if the death was real, factors that made it suspicious was that he had signed a will just 12 days before his death leaving his entire estate to his wife Jennifer Robertson. The story became a Netflix original documentary called "Trust No One: The Hunt for the Crypto King".

Cryptocurrency fraud had become a serious issue internationally. Many governments started to warn about these scams and have tried to gather data to report on the occurrence. Government agencies that track these crimes have had difficulties as many people do not report these crimes when they are victimized. In the last couple of years, the complexities and rates of these scams have increased. Researchers have identified at least 47 unique types of scams being used (Trozze et al., 2022). Ransomware and pump-and-dump schemes have been some of the most lucrative scams.

Scam Tokens

The creation of scam tokens increased in the last couple of years. In 2022 there was about an average of 350 scam tokens created each day according to Solidus Labs an organization that tracks cryptocurrency tokens, they counted 117,629 scam tokens created in the year, an increase of about 41 percent compared to 2021 (Coghlan, 2022). The scam tokens come from various serious but Build N Build (BNB) Chain and the Ethereum networks have been reported to harbor the most. One of the most common scams related to these tokens was the honeypot, where a token contract does not permit the buyer to resell the token (Agarwal et al., 2022). An infamous example of the honeypot was the Squid Game token.

A pump-and-dump scam involved a fake charity to entice customers called Save the Kids token (Barry, 2021). A pump-and-dump scam has been used for decades but has gotten a new variety with cryptocurrency. Pump and dump in general is a type of securities fraud where the scammers create an artificially inflated price of a stock or in the case of cryptocurrency an inflated token. The scammers give a false impression of the worth of the asset so that they can sell it at a high price and dump off the asset making the value fall significantly which makes the victims lose money. This has become common in the cryptocurrency market as it is generally an unregulated market compared to traditional investments like stocks and bonds (De Filippi, 2014). There have been various organized pump and dump scams that were organized through social media platforms including Discord, Telegram, Twitter, and Reddit.

The scammers marketed the Save the Kids token as a charity token. The scammers stated that each coin would provide a percentage of the transaction fee to a charity for kids. The token was supported by various well-known Youtubers and influencers including the rapper RiceGum who has had over 10 million subscribers and billions of views. The token used an anti-whaling mechanism to help stop the larger investors from trading a large portion of their tokens. The token originally was said to allow an investor who owned more than .5 percent of the tokens to be defined as a "whale" which meant they could only trade 20 percent of their supply in 24 hours, but this was later changed as the code had been updated allowing for these "whales" to sell all of their tokens without the limitations. Most of the marketing was targeted toward the youth who followed YouTubers. Once the token had crashed after the top holders sold off the majority of their tokens, Binance who supposedly received the donations had stated they had not received any donations from Save the Kids or other altcoins.

Romance scammers have been commonly attempting to gain cryptocurrency through deception. The Federal Trade Commission (FTC) has established that romance scammers have stolen about $139 million in 2021. The amount stolen of cryptocurrency through romance scams was about five times as much as it was just a year before and on average each victim lost about $9,700 (Roth, 2022). The scammers use dating apps like Tinder and social media apps including Facebook and Instagram to target victims to send money to fake profiles (BBC, 2022).

Romance scams are often a type of catfish scam where profiles are made using pictures of people taken from the internet to trick people. The perpetrators often tell the victim that they are in a crisis and need money to get out of their crisis and that they will pay the victim back. An infamous example of a romance scam was the Netflix true crime documentary called the Tindler Swindler, where Shimon Hayut known as Lev Leviev had used Tinder to manipulate women out of money. Hayut has claimed to become a successful and legit businessman after the scams as he started trading in Bitcoin.

Scammers also have attempted to hold private data for ransom in exchange for Bitcoin. In 2020 a Finnish company Vastaamo had its data stolen from hackers. The hackers reportedly stole 40,000 patient files and were holding them for ransom for around $500,000 worth of Bitcoin (40 Bitcoin). The company refused to give the Bitcoin for ransom and the hackers attempted to extort the individual patients directly (Rosengren, 2022).

Energy Theft and Factories

Cryptocurrencies need electricity to operate. Some criminals engage in electricity theft to mine cryptocurrency. Some large cases of these crimes include the arrest of six Malaysian men in February of 2021 who were accused of stealing about $2 million in electricity for their Bitcoin mining operations. Malaysia has had various crackdowns on cryptocurrency mining schemes and in July 2021 they destroyed a reported 1,069 mining systems that were reportedly stealing electricity. Later in July of 2021, the Ukrainian government found an underground cryptocurrency farm that was illegally stealing electricity for an estimated 259,000$ a month.

Some of the criminals operate in well-organized groups including in fraud factories. Fraud factories are often operated out of Asia including prior operations that have operated in Cambodia, Laos, Thailand, and Myanmar by Chinese gang members. These fraud factories often trick Africans into traveling to Asia and then force them into slavery and into scamming people into purchasing cryptocurrencies. The gang members threatened their hostages in various ways including the threat of selling their organs or forcing them into prostitution.

A fraud factory operation that operated out of Mynamar had used mostly people from Kenya and Uganda and was used to target young victims from African and Western nations. The scams are usually based on fake social media profiles and dating profiles where human-trafficked victims attempt to build trust with people online and scam them into fake romantic relationships where they will ask for cryptocurrency. This scam is also known as pig butchering. After a victim died from an attempted organ harvest the Kenyan government conducted an investigation and was able to rescue 76 human trafficking victims. The operations often are conducted in Myanmar as the Kachin conflict makes the region difficult to get to and difficult to investigate human trafficking and associated crimes.

Money Laundering

Money laundering is when money is gained through illegal means and is made to look like it was gained through legitimate means. Money laundering usually goes through three phases of laundering include placement, layering, and integration. The first step is when illegally obtained currency is introduced into a financial system, next the currency is moved around in several steps to make it difficult to trace, and lastly, It is incorporated further into the legitimate financial system (Bartoletti et al., 2021).

Investment Scams

Investment scams usually advertise high-interest rates for investors. A common investment scam is a Ponzi scheme. In these scams, the returns on investments are paid to the earlier investors by the funds invested by the newer investors. The scam continues until the perpetrator can no longer find new victims, this has been used with people who invest in cryptocurrency. The majority of investors in Ponzi schemes end up losing most of their investment.

There have been many similar Ponzi-like schemes in the crypto market including Bitconnect. Bitconnect operated in various countries including the United Kingdom (UK) and the United States (US) before it was given a cease and desist order by the Texas State Securities Board in 2018 and was soon shut down after Bitconnect had raised over $2.5 billion. Bitconnect had peaked at around $525 before plummeting down below $1. Through a federal investigation, the US Securities and the Federal Exchange Commission (SEC) sued the company and the founder Satish Kumbhani for the scheme that defrauded American investors an estimated $2 billion.

OneCoin another Ponzi scheme and a pyramid scheme was defined as 'one of the biggest scams in history' by the *Times* as the fraud had gained an estimated $4 billion. The part of the company that made it a pyramid scheme was that it did not have an actual product but recruited new people to invest. OneCoin which is a centralized currency had created false databases to simulate transactions that were not registered by a real blockchain. They claimed to be involved in selling educational materials for cryptocurrency trading, which was reported to be plagiarized from other sources according to a lawsuit filed. OneCoin was based in Bulgaria but had been registered in Belize and Dubai. Countries like these especially Belize have been used by Americans as a tax haven as they have less tax liability and are assumed to be less likely to investigate money laundering than the US government. By 2016 various governments were aware that this company was a scam including the Italian Antitru Authority described the company as an "illegal pyramid sales system".

The Chinese government was also involved in the prosecution and enforcement of the OneCoin scam and was able to recover around $267 million. The founder Ruja Ignatova also known as the Cryptoqueen was wanted by US authorities, but she was unable to be found and became a top ten most wanted fugitive by the Federal Bureau of Investigations (FBI) with a $100,000 reward. Other involved parties have been on the run or arrested including her brother Konstantin who was arrested in 2019 and pleaded guilty to money laundering and fraud and faced a maximum of 90 years in prison. Ignatova was born in Bulgaria and immigrated to Germany as a child and had various arrests and crimes related to fraud including a conviction in 2012 that she was involved with her father in illegal business practices. In 2013 she was involved in a multi-level marketing scheme known as BigCoin.

Ponzi scams on cryptocurrencies have been detected by analyzing the transactions made. Machine learning has been used to help identify such scams by looking at previous Ponzi scam datasets and the factors that they have in common which include contracts that distribute the money among financiers, money received only from other financiers, financiers making profits when other investors contribute enough, the later financiers who join the higher their risk of losing their money (Bartoletti et al., 2021).

An initial coin offering (ICO) is a strategy used for crypto to create funds before they are officially put on the market, which is like an Initial Public Offering (IPO) that shares use before they go public. Like IPOs many ICOs are legitimate but criminals exploit these and create fake advertisements and fraudulent currencies. In 2017 it was reported that about 80 percent of ICOs were fraudulent with about $150 million spent on them. A major fraudulent ICO was Pincoin which launched in 2018 and had $660 million raised.

A large scam known as PlusToken began in 2018. The scam operated mostly in China and South Korea. The scam started off offering monthly payments to the user's wallets. The PlusToken had risen in 2019 to be worth over $2 billion before the arrest of the operators who were six Chinese citizens who were arrested in the South Pacific island of Vanuatu. By the end of the investigation over a hundred, different people were arrested according to China's Ministry of Public Security.

Rug Pull

Rug pull scams have been used to scam investors by inviting investors to help invest in a new nonfungible token (NFT) or other coins to pump it up. As the funds increase and the scammers have access to the victims invested the money they leave and take the money. The scammers code the currency so that the investors cannot sell it so they have valueless currency. This scam occurred with the Squidcoin scam which the Squidcoin went from being worth a penny to around $90 and peaked at about $2,856. As the price peaked the money disappeared which led to the token being worthless and the scammers taking around $2.5 million from the victims (Dickens, 2021).

Exchange Scam

In early 2022 an exchange platform called Wormhole had last over $300 million after a cyber attack by crypto scammers. This was one of the largest attacks of the year of cryptocurrency stolen that totaled more than $1 billion in the last year. A common bitcoin investment scheme occurs when fake investment managers claim that they can help manage people's cryptocurrency investments and promise that the investors can make money. The investors make an upfront payment fee to pay the manager, but the fees are just stolen and the scammers often request more personal information and gain access to the victim's entire crypto assets.

Cryptojacking

Different cryptocurrencies have different levels of security and vulnerabilities. Cryptojacking has been a major form of crypto crime. This type of theft is when a person hijacks a computer to mine cryptocurrency that they do not own. This can be done through various methods including through a website or software like Coinhive. Coinhive was becoming popular in 2017 to mine but was eventually shut down in 2019.

When successful cryptojacking malware is intended for the victim to be unaware they were 'jacked'. The malware can slow down or crash the computer that it is jacking and covertly mining bitcoin or other cryptocurrencies. One large case of cryptojacking occurred with E-Sports Entertainment which was suspected of hijacking around 14,000 computers, another case occurred when Yahoo Europe used an ad that contained malware that infected millions of computers for bitcoin mining.

According to The European Union Agency for Law Enforcement Cooperation (Europol), Bitcoin was used in about 40 percent of illegal transmissions in the European Union (2015 report). This is likely due to more people using cryptocurrency, more scams of cryptocurrency users, and the government becoming more aware of such issues. The cryptocurrency scams do not seem to be slowing down anytime soon.

Exit Scams

Exit scams have been another cryptocurrency fraud. The use of a centralized market escrow permits a market to close and leave with the buyer's cryptocurrency. A notable case of his was with Evolution. The process of exit scams usually happens after the vendors have created a good reputation and have sold enough items to have accumulated a significant amount of escrow funds and then exit before having to compete in the market. Evolution was brought down by Operation Onymous which was a law enforcement operation that was directed by the FBI and Europol.

Onymous also had various other law enforcement agencies to aid in the operation including the Drug Enforcement Agency (DEA), U.S. Department of Homeland Security (DHS), Immigration and Customs Enforcement (ICE), and The European Union Agency for Criminal Justice Cooperation (Eurojust). This operation brought down hundreds of websites that were involved with crypto-related crimes including the Silk Road 2.0 and seized $1,000,000s in cryptocurrencies and other assets.

Onymous consisted of law enforcement agencies from 17 countries and there were 17 arrests made including a software developer who was infamously known as Defcon. During the Silk Road 2.0, it was also targeted by hackers and they lost $2.7 million through exploited transaction malleability. Soon after the arrests and seizures are just a couple hours a new Silk Road was activated known as Silk Road 3.0 showing the difficulty in stopping the Silk Road and other illicit markets. Onymous was seen as a success by the agencies involved with DHS stating that they stopped a black-market site that allowed for "murder-for-hire".

The closure of the Silk Road had little if any impact on the illicit drug market. The sales of illegal drugs online had increased as the Silk Road closed. There have been many others who sold drugs online and have inspired a popular Netflix series called *How to Sell Drugs Online (Fast)*, and a Netflix documentary called *Shiny Flakes: The Teenage Drug Lord*. The series is inspired by the true story of Maximilian Schmidt who was arrested and sentenced to seven years in prison. Schmidt had started selling drugs for crypto as a child until his arrest after having sold thousands of pounds of drugs worth $1,000,000s. It is suspected that Schmidt still has over $1,000,000 worth of Bitcoin that law enforcement was unable to seize. This has been a serious issue for authorities when they arrest suspects and get a conviction the cryptocurrencies can be difficult to seize as they would other assets.

With the effort of governmental task forces, the anonymity of cryptocurrency no longer is as strong as it once was. The punishment that some of these criminals received may act as a deterrent for some would-be offenders. Ulbricht who was the creator of the Silk Road was given a double life sentence plus 40 years in prison in February 2015. Once Ulbricht was arrested on August 21st, 2014 and he was given no bail which is usually given to those who are suspected of serious violent or sexual crimes. He was convicted of all charges of money laundering, conspiracy to commit computer hacking, and conspiracy to traffic narcotics. This a severe sentence as the average sentence length for murder in the US in 2016 was 40.6 years, the average for rape/sexual assault was 12.2 years, and for manslaughter was 10.1 years (Kaeble, 2018).

Ransomware

Ransomware has been used to hack victims' computers and to demand money in the form of cryptocurrency to allow the victims to gain access to their computers. The hackers use a type of malware that holds the computer 'hostage' (Musiala et al., 2020). One such way victims get tricked is through an upgrade scam. Crypto software is constantly upgraded and scammers attempt to imitate a legitimate upgrade so that a person will accept a fake upgrade and the scammers can access their crypto and private keys. This occurred when scammers took advantage of the Ethereum merge

Crytpo Loggers are another type of crypto scammer who attempts to steal information about a victim's wallet through a crypto service through the use of malware. Crypto loggers attempt to get the private key to necessitate a transfer of the funds from a victim's account to theirs.

A SIM-swap scam is a newer scam that has become more common recently. A SIM swap is when a person gets access to a person's SIM card from their phone and uses it to access information from the phone. If a person can successfully Sim-swap then one can often access the crypto wallets and other information to steal the crypto.

Crypto Wallet

Wallets are a way that crypto users can manage their currency. Some scammers have created fraudulent wallet services where they can take a person's entire wallet or take a small percentage at a time. Other fake wallet scammers wait until their wallet exceeds a certain amount and that deposit all the money to another wallet (Bartoletti et al., 2021).

A related scam to the fake wallet is a fake exchange (Horch et al., 2022). This is when a scammer creates a fake exchange to trick people into purchasing cryptocurrencies. The scammers often offer competitive prices and they manipulate users to believe their exchanges are cheap and easy to use.

Impersonation

The impersonation of government officials or celebrities was yet another way criminals have tried to obtain cryptocurrency. This scam was often perpetrated by scammers who were pretending to be federal agents. Other scams would use the image of a celebrity that is well known to use their name to sell a product with cryptocurrency or have people invest in c cryptocurrency.

Some celebrities have been accused of allegedly supporting crypto scams. Such cases include the influencers and boxers Jake and Logan Paul, Mark Cuban, Kim Kardashian, Floyd Mayweather, and many others. The Paul brothers were accused of supporting a pump-and-dump scheme for the token SafeMoon and a class-action lawsuit was filed against the company (Franceschi-Bicchierai, 2022). The Paul brothers are defendants in the case for their role in the scheme. A lawsuit was filed against Kim Kardashian, Floyd Mayweather, and former Boston Celtic Paul Pierce for their promotion and or involvement in the EthereumMax token. These issues related to people promoting scam tokens have led to governments acknowledging that there needs to be more regulation of crypto.

Blackmail

The use of blackmailing has occurred with the demand for cryptocurrency for ransom, especially Bitcoin (Choi et al., 2022). These scams often involve the scammer having hacked or claiming to have hacked the victim's webcam and that they have video of them that they will release unless they get paid through Bitcoin. This type of scam can also fall into sextortion, which is one of the most successful types of crypto scams (Flodmark & Jakum, 2022). A sextortion email that became widespread in 2018 used the threat of releasing videos of the victim performing sexual acts that were recorded through the email. The scammers didn't have any videos but were still able to con people into paying.

Phishing

Phishing has been used to generate cryptocurrency. Phishing is when a scammer sends a fraudulent email, message, or link that is created to manipulate the victim so that they reveal information to the scammer or hack the victim's computer with ransomware to gather personal information. Phishing websites have been used to collect wallet keys, steel passcodes, and more. One such website stole up to $4 million of MIOTA tokens up until it was discovered in 2018. A common way to lure victims is to have a link that brings a person to a fake website, and that allows the scammers to steal account information. The fake websites can make people believe they are on a legitimate website like Amazon, a governmental website, or a bank's website. The famous film producer Seth Green was a victim of this type of scam when his Bored Ape NFTs were stolen (Guadamuz, 2022). Eventually Green was able to get his Bored Apes back but reports indicate he paid $260,000 for the return of the Bored Apes (Hogg, 2022).

Counterfeit Goods

The ability to sell counterfeit luxury goods has been exploited through the transaction of cryptocurrencies (Hemantha, 2022). The counterfeit goods industry is about $1 trillion a year and the amount that is transferred by blockchain peaked in 2021. The scammers have especially exploited the pre-owned luxury goods market which is valued at about $32.6 billion.

Luxury brands have been attempting to fight counterfeiters by using their blockchain technologies. The companies have been testing using a unique identifier for each product so that it can be traced from the raw material to the secondhand market (Tramatm, 2022). This can help provide digital proof to the potential buyer of the product's authenticity through a smart tag system.

A trust tag can give real-time location tracking and update each transaction with a time stamp through each step to provide a layer of trust. Various luxury brands have implemented this technology including Cartier, Christian Dior, Louis Vuitton, and Prada. One system is called Aura which is used by Louis Vuitton, Prada, and other companies it was the first blockchain system platform to track the history and authenticity of luxury goods with the help of Microsoft in assisting the platform (Akhtar, 2021).

ENFORCEMENT

One of the largest seizures of cryptocurrency occurred in 2021 according to the United States Department of Justice (DOJ). In November 2021 law enforcement agents seized over 50,000 Bitcoins that were hidden in the home of James Zhong who was later found guilty of using the Silk Road in acquiring Bitcoin. The Silk Road is a marketplace on the darknet that functions as a marketplace for the black market including the selling of illegal products including weapons, drugs, counterfeit items including currency, stolen credit card information, forged documents like passports, and other illegal goods (Martin, 2014).

The original Silk Road was investigated through the Silk Road Task Force which used various agencies in the US and abroad including the DEA. The task force agencies including a DEA agent (Carl Mark Force) and a Secret Service agent (Shaun Bridges) had attempted to extort the founder of the Silk Road Ross Ulbricht for Bitcoin. The agents had faked the killing of an informant to pressure Ulbricht into giving bitcoins. Force had pleaded guilty to his involvement in money laundering, obstruction of justice, and extortion under the color of official right and was sent to federal prison. Bridges also plead guilty to depositing about $800,000 worth of bitcoins to his account and was also guilty of money laundering of cryptocurrency and was also sent to federal prison.

Darknet users often use cryptocurrency to help with the anonymity of their activities so that they are less likely to be caught (Choi et al., 2022). Bitcoin has been a major cryptocurrency used in these markets. Law enforcement operations have caused serious issues with some of these markets for example the Bloomsfield Market had to close because the operators of the site were arrested by authorities. Bloomsfield was set up by the former Silk Road drug market users and was used to sell illegal drugs and other products.

In 2018 there was growing concern that terror groups including al-Qaeda (the group behind the September 11th, 2001 attacks) were using the Darknet and Bitcoin to fund their organization (Irwin, & Milad, 2016). As terrorist organizations need secrecy to be successful the ability of anonymity and cryptocurrency exchange has been an important factor to current terrorist groups (Whyte, 2019). It also gives criminal groups protection from being scammed by other criminals because of the financial security that blockchains like bitcoin provide.

Terror groups are known to operate with significant funding from donors. Donors are often at risk of being charged with a crime if they are caught funding terror groups so the higher the perceived risk for a would-be donor the less likely they will donate. Cryptocurrency helps reduce that risk for donors. The challenge terror groups like the Islamic State of Iraq and Syria (ISIS) have are that cryptocurrencies are limited in their usability and acceptability as a currency in the regions that they operate (Abboushi, 2017).

The vendors that terror groups like ISIS interact with often prefer cash as bitcoin and other cryptocurrencies are not practical in most of the middle east. There are other limitations with cryptocurrencies for terror groups and organized crime including the lack of reliability of cryptocurrencies, their constant fluctuation in price, and volume can be limited. Many cryptocurrencies have a low volume which makes the transfer of large amounts expensive and noticeable. As transactions are often posted publicly through blockchain networks they can be identified by law enforcement as suspicious (Dion-Schwarz et al., 2019).

Government agencies have continued to put more resources into stopping cryptocurrency-related crimes. Recently the FBI acknowledged a Crypto Task Force at the Munich Cyber Security Conference on February 17th, 2022. The task force named Virtual Asset Exploitation Unit (VAXU) to better investigate cryptocurrency and to be better able to seize virtual assets. A statement made by the task force helped detail their goals "Ransomware and digital extortion, like many other crimes fueled by cryptocurrency, only work if the bad guys get paid... The currency might be virtual, but the message to companies is concrete: if you report to us, we can follow the money and not only help you but hopefully prevent the next victim."

The United Nations (UN), and international cooperation have used significant efforts in attempting to reduce crypto terrorism financing through the Global Coordinated Programme on Detecting, Preventing and Countering the Financing of Terrorism (CFT Programme) of the United Nations Counter-Terrorism Centre (UNCCT) within the United Nations Office of Counter-Terrorism (UNOCT) and other methods (Dion-Schwarz, et al., 2019). The UN has passed various resolutions with the support of the international community to counter the funding, especially Resolution 2462 (2019). The UN has analyzed terror attacks that are related to crypto funding and the number has significantly increased (Shukla, 2022).

The Financial Action Task Force (FATF) is a multi-agency group that investigates suspected terror group funding (Choo, 2015). This task force has made it a priority to check to ensure that nations are implementing annual anti-money laundering and anti-terrorist financing laws regarding criminal organizations and specifically terrorism.

In 2015 there were various reports about ISIS using crypto wallets to fund terrorism, ones such claim was from Deutsche Welle who stated they had evidence of a Bitcoin wallet connected to ISIS that was worth $10s of millions. Another report by Ghost Security Group which is an anti-terror group of hacktivists claimed that they found transactions of Bitcoin owned by ISIS operatives. The reported worth of these wallets was estimated to be up to $15 million (Irwin, & Milad, 2016).

Zcash is an important currency regarding terrorism and organized crime as it is a departure compared to traditional cryptocurrencies in regards to the technical infrastructure. Zcash which was launched in 2016 does not allow for transactions to be in the visible blockchain so it has a higher level of privacy. The transactions are viewable to those possessing the view key and the originator because it uses the Zero Knowledge Succient Arguments of Knowledge (ZK-SnARKs). The ability for Zcash to be transferred online can make it very difficult for law enforcement and intelligence agencies to know about the funding of terror groups.

Bitcoin has been a popular way to purchase child pornography. Europol has a cybercrime unit that has helped investigate and arrest people who have been buying illegal material like child pornography. There are at least 30 websites known to exclusively accept Bitcoin for its pornography. There has even been a deep web crowdfund to support a child pornography website (Cook, 2014).

Victims

During the COVID-19 epidemic, there was a significant increase in the use of cryptocurrencies, crypto scams, and victims of scams (Barry, 2021). These included various types of scams the buyer was thought to be buying protective equipment, and donations scams (National Services Scotland, 2020).

Victims of crypto scams are unlikely to get their crypto back after it has been stolen. There is very little crime control in the crypto market, especially in the beginning (Mackenzie, 2022). As this market has been largely unregulated it has been open to manipulation and scams have been normalized with many victims who are ready to invest in speculative opportunities.

The crypto market is prescribed as *responsibilized* where an investor has a loss even when a victim of a crime is to write it off (Mackenzie, 2022). There are various reasons for this but the main factors include the lack of law enforcement dedicated and trained to deal with crypto crimes and the confidentiality of crypto in general (Read, 2022).

The theft of cryptocurrency can happen to a person by a roommate or a person that is on the other side of the planet. Many perpetrators that victimized Americans are from other countries. US law enforcement agencies will usually not investigate these crimes where the perpetrator is thought to be in another country unless the amount stolen is very high and even then it may not be seriously investigated.

Local law enforcement usually does not have the resources to conduct international investigations so these crimes are usually handled by federal law enforcement such as the FBI (Moggridge & Montasari, 2022). Victims can report to various non-law enforcement agencies. The main agencies that victims of crypto scams report to include the FTC, Securities and SEC, Commodity Futures Trading Commission (CFTC), Internet Crime Complaint Center, and the crypto exchange platform that was used by the victim. Federal and state agencies have tried to educate and warn potential victims about scams and what red flags to look out for.

CONCLUSION

The research and knowledge of cryptocurrency scams are incomplete as there are few public databases about such crimes (Bartoletti et al., 2021). Governments, corporations, and other agencies are constantly trying to fight crypto crime. It seems that the vast majority of crypto crime goes away without any investigation and that this will continue for some time.

The prevention of crypto crime is important. Education is an important factor, as educated investors seem to be significantly less likely to be victimized. Improved reporting systems need to be established so more scams can be reported to authorities and blockchain platforms. Current public data sources on scams related to cryptocurrency are unreliable and incomplete. An improved dataset can help improve scam detection systems. This can help improve resource detection systems for non-technical investors to be warned of potential fraudulent websites and platforms.

REFERENCES

Abboushi, S. (2017). Global Virtual Currency–Brief Overview. *Journal of Applied Business & Economics, 19*(6).

Agarwal, R., Thapliyal, T., & Shukla, S. (2022). Analyzing malicious activities and detecting adversarial behavior in cryptocurrency based permissionless blockchains: An Ethereum usecase. *Distributed Ledger Technologies: Research and Practice.*

Akhtar, T. (2021). Louis Vuitton, Cartier, Prada to Use Bespoke Blockchain to Tackle Counterfeit Goods. *CoinDesk.* https://www.coindesk.com/business/2021/04/20/louis-vuitton-c artier-prada-to-use- bespoke-blockchain-to-tackle-counterfei t-goods/

Anderson, C., & Saleh, T. (2021). Investigating cyber attacks using domain and DNS data. *Network Security, 2021*(3), 6–8. doi:10.1016/S1353-4858(21)00028-3

Barry, T. M. (2021). # NotFinancialAdvice: Empowering the Federal Trade Commission to Regulate Cryptocurrency Social Media Influencers. *Ohio St. Bus. LJ, 16*, 279.

Bartoletti, M., Lande, S., Loddo, A., Pompianu, L., & Serusi, S. (2021). Cryptocurrency scams: Analysis and perspectives. *IEEE Access : Practical Innovations, Open Solutions, 9*, 148353–148373. doi:10.1109/ACCESS.2021.3123894

BBC. (2022). The Kenyans lured to become unwitting 'love' fraudsters. *BBC.* https://www.bbc.com/news/world-africa-63654637

Choi, J., Kim, J., Song, M., Kim, H., Park, N., Seo, M., & Shin, S. (2022). A Large-Scale Bitcoin Abuse Measurement and Clustering Analysis Utilizing Public Reports. *IEICE Transactions on Information and Systems, 105*(7), 1296–1307. doi:10.1587/transinf.2021EDP7182

Choo, K. K. R. (2015). Cryptocurrency and virtual currency: Corruption and money laundering/terrorism financing risks? In *Handbook of digital currency* (pp. 283–307). Academic Press. doi:10.1016/B978-0-12-802117-0.00015-1

Coghlan, J. (2022). *350 new 'scam tokens' were created every day this year.* Solidus Labs.

Cook, J. (2014). Paedophiles Have Created A Deep Web Version Of Kickstarter To Crowdfund Child Porn. *Business Insider.* https://www.businessinsider.com/pedophiles-have-created-a-de ep-web-version-of-kickstarter-to-crowdfund-child-porn-2014-11

De Filippi, P. (2014). Bitcoin: a regulatory nightmare to a libertarian dream. *Internet Policy Review, 3*(2).

Dickens, S. (2021). Squid Game meme coin crashes by 99.9% after developers pull the plug. *Yahoo!* https://www.yahoo.com/now/squid-game-meme-coin-crashes-13190 8065.html

Dion-Schwarz, C., Manheim, D., & Johnston, P. B. (2019). *Terrorist use of cryptocurrencies: Technical and organizational barriers and future threats.* Rand Corporation. doi:10.7249/RR3026

Flodmark, A., & Jakum, M. (2022). *Characterizing Bitcoin Spam Emails: An analysis of what makes certain Bitcoin spams generate millions of dollars.* Linköping University.

Franceschi-Bicchierai. (2022). Meet the Blockchain Detectives Who Track Crypto's Hackers and Scammers. *Vice News.* https://www.vice.com/en/article/xgd9zw/meet-the-blockchain-d etectives-who-track-cryptos-hackers-and-scammers

Guadamuz, A. (2022). These are not the apes you are looking for. *Communications of the ACM, 65*(9), 20–22. doi:10.1145/3548761

Han, W., Duong, V., Nguyen, L., & Mier, C. (2020, May). Darknet and bitcoin de-anonymization: Emerging development. In 2020 Zooming Innovation in Consumer Technologies Conference (ZINC) (pp. 222- 226). IEEE.

Hemantha, Y. (2022). Embracing block chain technology in supply chain to combat counterfeiting luxury and fashion brands. *Asian Journal of Management, 13*(2), 145–150.

Hogg, R. (2022). Seth Green pays $260,000 ransom for a stolen Bored Ape Ethereum NFT meant to feature in his new TV show. *Business Insider.* https://www.businessinsider.com/seth-green-pays-260000-return-stolen-bored-ape-ethereum-nft-2022-6

Horch, A., Schunck, C. H., & Ruff, C. (2022). Adversary Tactics and Techniques specific to Cryptocurrency Scams. *Open Identity Summit 2022.*

Irwin, A. S., & Milad, G. (2016). The use of crypto-currencies in funding violent jihad. *Journal of Money Laundering Control, 19*(4), 407–425. doi:10.1108/JMLC-01-2016-0003

Jacobs, P., & Schain, L. (2011). The never ending attraction of the Ponzi Scheme. *Journal of Comprehensive Research, 9*, 40–46.

Kaeble, D. (2018). *Time Served in State Prison, 2016 (NCJ 252205).* US Department of Justice, Bureau of Justice Statistics.

Leuprecht, C., Jenkins, C., & Hamilton, R. (2022). Virtual money laundering: policy implications of the proliferation in the illicit use of cryptocurrency. *Journal of Financial Crime.*

Liu, Y., Liu, X., Zhang, L., Tang, C., & Kang, H. (2017). An efficient strategy to eliminate malleability of bitcoin transaction. In *2017 4th International Conference on Systems and Informatics (ICSAI)* (pp. 960-964). IEEE.

Mackenzie, S. (2022). Criminology towards the metaverse: Cryptocurrency scams, grey economy and the technosocial. *British Journal of Criminology*, *62*(6), 1537–1552. doi:10.1093/bjc/azab118

Martin, J. (2014). Lost on the Silk Road: Online drug distribution and the 'cryptomarket'. *Criminology & Criminal Justice*, *14*(3), 351–367. doi:10.1177/1748895813505234

McGuire, M., & Dowling, S. (2013). Cyber crime: A review of the evidence. Research Report 75.

Moggridge, E., & Montasari, R. (2022). A Critical Analysis of the Dark Web Challenges to Digital Policing. In *Artificial Intelligence and National Security* (pp. 157–167). Springer. doi:10.1007/978-3-031-06709-9_8

Musiala, R. A. Jr, Goody, T. M., Reynolds, V., Tenery, L., McGrath, M., Rowland, C., & Sekhri, S. (2020). *Cryptocurrencies: Forensic techniques to meet the challenge of new fraud and corruption risks | FVS eye on fraud*. AICP.

National Services Scotland. (2020). *NHS counter fraud services rolling COVID-19*. Intelligence alert no. 14. Author.

Rajput, U., Abbas, F., Hussain, R., Eun, H., & Oh, H. (2014, August). A simple yet efficient approach to combat transaction malleability in bitcoin. In *International Workshop on Information Security Applications* (pp. 27-37). Springer.

Read, C. L. (2022). No More Duffel Bags Full of Cash. In *The Bitcoin Dilemma* (pp. 113–119). Palgrave Macmillan. doi:10.1007/978-3-031-09138-4_11

Rosengren, K. (2022). *Contribution of Open-Source Intelligence to Social Engineering Cyberattacks*. Turku University.

Roth, E. (2022). *Romance scammers collected $139 million in crypto last year*. The Verge.

Shukla, S. (2022). UN Says Crypto Use in Terror Financing Likely Soaring. *Bloomberg*. https://www.bloomberg.com/news/articles/2022-10-31/un-finding-more-cases-where-crypto-involved-in-terror-financing

Trama, T. (2022). Brands are introducing new Blockchain Technologies to fight Counterfeit. *Lexology*. https://www.lexology.com/library/detail.aspx?g=a1559142-01a7 -400e-97f9-31ef6a853640

Trozze, A., Kamps, J., Akartuna, E. A., Hetzel, F. J., Kleinberg, B., Davies, T., & Johnson, S. D. (2022). Cryptocurrencies and future financial crime. *Crime Science*, *11*(1), 1–35. doi:10.118640163-021-00163-8 PMID:35013699

Whyte, C. (2019). Cryptoterrorism: Assessing the utility of blockchain technologies for terrorist enterprise. *Studies in Conflict and Terrorism*, 1–24. doi:10.1080/1057 610X.2018.1531565

Chapter 9
Cryptocurrency Adoption

Kochar Sahibpreet Singh

 https://orcid.org/0009-0003-6414-0854

University Canada West, Canada

ABSTRACT

This chapter examines how familiarity influences the adoption and how education may increase cryptocurrency users. This project will use a systematic approach highlighting the growth of acceptance of cryptocurrency from 2017 to 2023 using a mixed methods approach since there has been little research on how individuals have embraced and accepted cryptocurrencies. Due to a lack of study, this study examines cryptocurrency adoption, its drivers, and its hazards. This study's outcomes will be a form of Literature Review for future research, increase knowledge of cryptocurrency acceptance, and help in cryptocurrency adoption.

INTRODUCTION

Cryptocurrency is a digital or virtual currency that operates independently of a central bank. It works on a decentralized platform, meaning any single entity, such as a government or financial institution, does not control it. Transactions are verified and recorded on a public ledger called a blockchain, which makes the currency transparent and immutable (Popper, 2015). The first and most well-known cryptocurrency is Bitcoin, created in 2009 by an anonymous person or group using Satoshi Nakamoto's pseudonym. Since then, thousands of other cryptocurrencies have emerged, including Ethereum, Litecoin, and Ripple.

Cryptocurrencies can be bought and sold on digital exchanges and used to purchase goods and services from merchants who accept them as payment. The value of a cryptocurrency is determined by supply and demand and can be subject

DOI: 10.4018/978-1-6684-8368-8.ch009

to volatility due to its decentralized nature and lack of regulation (Buterin, 2014). It is also often known as "digital money." In 2009, it was first introduced as a novel kind of monetary exchange.

During the last few years, the Cryptocurrency market and its acceptance have advanced rapidly. Cryptocurrencies rely on cryptography to transmit digital information to guarantee the security and authenticity of transactions. It is believed to be a game-changer for digital money and finance (Pilkington, 2018). The original idea behind cryptocurrency was to create decentralized digital money that could be traded freely between users online, replacing traditional fiat (flat) cash. It takes on some of the most prominent features of currency. According to Eikmanns and Sandner, in their Harvard published papers of 2017, Bitcoin is money since it may be used as a medium of trade, a unit of account, and a store of value.

According to https://www.statista.com, There are now 8685 traded cryptocurrencies, and the total market cap of all cryptocurrencies is $1.18 trillion. A total of $480 billion has been invested in Bitcoin (BTC) as of Jan 2023, giving Bitcoin a market share of 40.55%. From 2023 to 2030, the worldwide cryptocurrency industry is projected to increase from a valuation of $67 trillion at a CAGR (compound annual growth rate) of 66.5% (Statista, 2023). Hence, it is safe to say that the cryptocurrency market has expanded exponentially.

This study aims to fill a gap in the existing literature by investigating "the elements determining the user's desire to embrace cryptocurrency."

1. To determine how the awareness model can inspire a change in utility usage for an individual. What are the factors that influence the adoption of cryptocurrency?
2. To what extent does awareness influence the adoption of cryptocurrency?
3. How does cryptocurrency awareness differ among different demographic groups worldwide?
4. What are the implications of this study for future cryptocurrency adoption?

BACKGROUND

The conceptual idea behind creating cryptocurrency was to create a decentralized and secure system for conducting digital transactions without the need for intermediaries like banks or governments. The founder of Bitcoin, the first and most well-known cryptocurrency, outlined this concept in his white paper published in 2008, stating that "A purely peer-to-peer version of electronic cash would allow online payments to be sent directly from one party to another without going through a financial institution" (Nakamoto, 2008).

The significance of cryptocurrency lies in its potential to disrupt the traditional financial system and offer a more democratic and accessible alternative to traditional banking (Huang & Liu, 2017). Any central authority does not control cryptocurrencies, and their transactions are secured by cryptography, making them highly resistant to fraud and hacking (Nakamoto, 2008). This allows for greater financial autonomy for individuals and businesses, especially those in developing countries with limited access to traditional banking services. Additionally, the transparency and immutability of cryptocurrency transactions offer opportunities for increased efficiency and reduced costs in various industries, such as supply chain management and voting systems. (Ghazinoory et al., 2021).

Cryptocurrencies have the potential to save third-world countries in several ways. One of the most significant advantages of cryptocurrency is its ability to provide financial services to people who do not have access to traditional banking services. (Saeed & Tugrul, 2019). In many third-world countries, much of the population does not have access to essential financial services such as bank accounts, credit cards, and loans. Cryptocurrencies can provide an alternative way to transact and store value without relying on banks or other financial intermediaries.

Another way that cryptocurrencies can help third-world countries is by reducing the costs of financial transactions. High fees, long processing times, and bureaucratic red tape often plague traditional financial systems. Cryptocurrencies can provide a faster, cheaper, and more efficient way to send and receive money, especially across borders.

Finally, cryptocurrencies can help third-world countries by promoting financial inclusion and economic growth. By providing access to essential financial services, cryptocurrencies can help people save money, build credit, and invest in their futures. This can increase economic activity, job creation, and higher living standards (Kim & Kim, 2019).

In recent years, cryptocurrency has gained traction as a viable investment option and a decentralized method of online purchases and payments, bypassing traditional financial institutions (Saeed & Tugrul, 2019). The conceptual idea and significance of cryptocurrency to uplift developing countries and form a new form of currency parrel to the existing economic system were lost to the view of new technology that might revolutionize how we make business and exchange money (Mensah & Mwakapesa, 2022).

From ING International Survey that the average cryptocurrency adoption rate in Europe and North America is 7.2%, more than twice the global average of 3.1%. Given the increasing awareness and bullish sentiments around cryptocurrencies, the adoption rate will grow in the next few months. In 2018, the estimated cryptocurrency awareness among European and North American markets was 59.8%*. In addition, the IE Center for Governance of Change 2019 estimates cryptocurrency awareness to be 67.7%.

This 13.2% increase in awareness is explained by a rise in cryptocurrency users across all demographics, especially so within these groups:

1. Males,
2. Younger adults below age 35,
3. Highly educated, as well as
4. Highly affluent.

A quarter of cryptocurrency holders in these countries already purchase cryptocurrency goods and services. High-value cryptocurrency transactions (over USD 1,000) dominated the European and North American markets, accounting for 48% and 66% of transactions, in contrast to global transaction sizes (38%). (ING International Survey, 2018).

REASON FOR DELAYED ADOPTION AND PROBLEMS WITH CRYPTOCURRENCY

Despite the advantages offered by cryptocurrency, there are also several challenges associated with its adoption. One of the main challenges is the lack of regulation, which has led to several controversies and scams in the industry (Wang et al., 2015). Cryptocurrencies are not backed by any government or financial institution, which makes them highly volatile and unpredictable. This has resulted in several instances of market manipulation and fraud. Security is also a significant concern, as hackers can exploit vulnerabilities in the system to steal digital assets. Another challenge is perceiving cryptocurrency as a tool for illegal activities, such as money laundering and drug trafficking. (Eom & Kim, 2020).

However, the significant issues and controversies include:

1. **Security:** While blockchain technology has been praised for its security features, cryptocurrency exchanges and wallets have been hacked numerous times, resulting in the loss of millions of dollars. In 2019, the QuadrigaCX exchange collapsed after its founder died, taking $190 million worth of customer funds with him. This incident highlighted the cryptocurrency industry's lack of regulation and oversight and the need for better security measures to protect users' funds (Böhme et al., 2015).
2. **Volatility:** Cryptocurrencies are known for their high volatility, with prices often fluctuating rapidly and unpredictably. This makes them risky investments

and can lead to significant losses for investors. For example, in 2017, the price of Bitcoin surged from around $1,000 to almost $20,000 before crashing back down to around $3,000 in 2018 (Briere et al., 2015).

3. **Regulatory Challenges:** Cryptocurrencies operate in a legal gray area, with many governments and regulators unsure how to classify and regulate them. Some countries have banned or restricted cryptocurrencies, while others have embraced them. This lack of regulatory clarity has created uncertainty for businesses and investors. It has also made it easier for cryptocurrencies to be used for illegal activities such as money laundering and terrorism financing (Narayanan et al., 2016).

4. **Environmental Concerns:** Cryptocurrency mining, the process of verifying transactions and adding them to the blockchain, requires significant energy. This has led to concerns about the environmental impact of cryptocurrencies, particularly Bitcoin. According to one estimate, Bitcoin mining uses as much electricity as the entire country of Argentina (Krause et al., 2018).

Most people and businesses still depend on more conventional payment methods, which has resulted in the relatively gradual adoption of cryptocurrencies. Research conducted by Cambridge University estimates that the number of people utilizing bitcoin will exceed 100 million by 2020, increasing from around 10 million in 2013 to that amount. Despite this increase, most consumers and organizations still rely on conventional payment methods such as credit cards, debit cards, and bank transfers. The delayed acceptance of bitcoin may be attributed to several problems, including a lack of knowledge of the underlying technology, worries over security, and a lack of confidence in the institutions behind it.

Several different aspects play a role in the proliferation of cryptocurrencies. Security is one of the primary motivating factors for the widespread acceptance of cryptocurrencies. Cryptocurrencies use decentralized systems; transactions are recorded on a public ledger maintained by a network of computers rather than being controlled by a single entity. Because of this, there is no longer a need for intermediaries such as banks, which makes financial transactions much quicker, less expensive, and more secure.

Potential Methods for Creating an Adoption Model

To create an effective adoption model for cryptocurrency, there must be a clear understanding of the barriers to adoption and the potential solutions for overcoming them. One of the main challenges to cryptocurrency adoption is the need for more education and awareness. Therefore, a vital component of any adoption model should be an educational outreach program designed to inform people about the technology and its potential uses (Stoltenberg & Wagener, 2021).

Another critical factor in creating an adoption model is developing an infrastructure conducive to cryptocurrency use. This includes providing a secure platform for users to store their cryptocurrency and resources such as tutorials and customer support to help users navigate the technology. Additionally, it is essential to ensure that the infrastructure is compatible with existing payment systems and compliant with relevant regulations.

The Adoption Model of Cryptocurrency Hinges on Network Effects

Network effects are shown by a 'good' if the value of a new service resulting from adopting the 'good' grows in proportion to the number of previously accepted users (Varian, 2017). This creates a self-reinforcing cycle of increasing value for the 'good' as more people accept it. The inverse of this positive feedback loop is also possible: a "death spiral" in which the item or service gradually disappears because it never reaches a critical mass of customers.

Unlike growing returns to scale, which have to do with the cost decreasing or the quality improving with the number of units produced, network effects are a demand-side phenomenon, according to Varian (2017), "Network effects are attributable to value increasing with the number of units sold."

More individuals joining a system strengthens security since the agreement binds more people. Since merchants and consumers benefit from increased transaction volume, there is a positive feedback loop between the two factors. Because of the "developer network effect," the forum will be more accessible; more people will be inspired to build compatible applications with widely used platforms. A widely used venue will attract additional media integration, giving users access to more valuable features.

If money is measured in the same unit that prices are determined in, then keeping track of one's financial resources is much simpler. The term for this phenomenon is the "unit of account network effect," It happens when a stable, widely accepted currency is utilized as the standard for monetary transactions (San Martín & Camarero, 2018).

More significant amounts of money may be exchanged into and out of a currency on the exchanges because of the increased market depth. The spreading impact on the market occurs when a currency with a higher market value has a lower spread on currency exchanges. This allows for more speedy and accurate currency conversions. There is an effect known as "intrapersonal single-currency preference," wherein users already familiar with a currency are more likely to use it for other transactions because it requires less cognitive load and results in a smaller total liquid balance across all cryptocurrencies without incurring interchange fees. To avoid paying excessive fees and conversion rates, most people prefer to use the same currency as others around them when making regular transactions.

A "network effect" arises when increased exposure to a product or service results from increased usage. Popular systems also have more knowledgeable users. As a result, they worry less about being taken advantage of by dishonest individuals who attempt to sell them something harmful that they do not understand. Because of the "regulatory legitimacy network effect," authorities are less likely to launch a revenge assault on a public figure. According to the "diffusion of innovations" concept, there is an initial group of innovators and early adopters, then a larger group of early and late majority users, and finally a smaller group of laggards. This model considers several factors to predict the rate at which bitcoin will be adopted. These factors include the rate at which new users will adopt the technology, the rate at which existing users will leave, and the knowledge and understanding of cryptocurrency across different demographics (San Martín & Camarero, 2018).

ADOPTION MODELS OF CRYPTOCURRENCY

Several models have been presented to comprehend the adoption of cryptocurrencies. This research focuses on

1. The Technology Acceptance Model (TAM),
2. Technological-Organizational-Environmental (TOE) Framework,
3. Unified Theory of Acceptance Technology (UTAT),
4. Technology Adoption Life Cycle (TALC).

If businesses are authorized to use the most current technology and automation, they may improve the efficacy of their operations, reduce their overall expenditures, and increase customer satisfaction. Introducing cryptocurrency opens the way for several choices advantageous to the area's growth, such as manufacturing innovative new products and services.

The findings from the World Economic Forum and the National Institute of Standards and Technology in the United States support this conclusion. To provide a complete and accurate picture of the global implications of cryptocurrency in the Technology Acceptance Model (TAM), the Unified Theory of Acceptance and Technology (UTAT) and the Structural Equation Awareness Modeling (SEAM) from other regions should also be included. These models may generate incredible innovations for expanding cryptocurrency and constructing a parallel financial system, narrowing the wealth gap.

1.   Technology Acceptance Model (TAM)

Davis (1989) was the first person to suggest what is now known as the Technology Acceptance Model (TAM), which has since become a viral tool for explaining how people accept and use new technologies. According to this concept, technology adoption is impacted by two primary factors: its perceived utility and simplicity. The term "perceived usefulness" refers to how a person feels that utilizing a particular piece of technology would improve the quality of their life or their performance at work.

The adoption of cryptocurrency can be analyzed using the technology adoption model (TAM), a widely used framework for understanding the factors that influence the adoption of new technologies. According to the TAM, technology adoption is influenced by two main factors: perceived usefulness and perceived ease of use. Perceived usefulness refers to how a technology is perceived as helpful in achieving a specific goal or task. Perceived ease of use refers to the extent to which a technology is understood and user-friendly. Cryptocurrency adoption can be divided into four stages: awareness, interest, evaluation, and adoption. In the awareness stage, individuals become aware of the existence of cryptocurrency through various channels, such as news articles, social media, and word of mouth. In the interest stage, individuals become interested in cryptocurrency and start researching and learning more about it. In the evaluation stage, individuals evaluate cryptocurrency's perceived usefulness and ease of use and decide whether to adopt it. In the adoption stage, individuals.

Figure 1 shows Bitcoin adoption drivers in Malaysia's internet economy (Chen, X.et al., 2022) predict cryptocurrencies' growth. Social Influence (SI), transparency (TR), pricing value (PV), traceability (TRA), and attitude (AT) were examined via customer satisfaction. The five TAMs/theory models provide key aspects and moderating influences. This resulted in the following framework, which served as the basis for the research framework.

Expectations, product performance, and cognitive comparisons determine customer happiness. This study found that better customer satisfaction mediates the association between SI, TRA, PV, TR, AT, and online cryptocurrency adoption.

Figure 1. TAM research framework
Source: Chen et al. (2022)

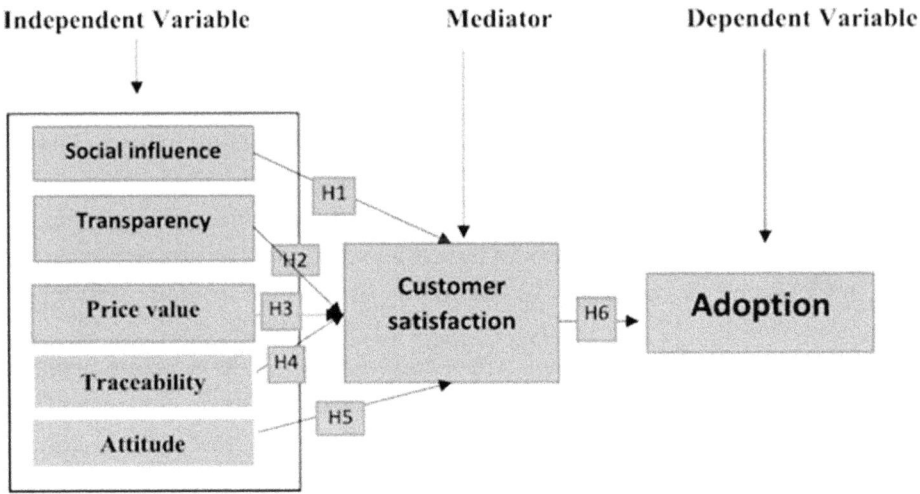

The inclination of consumers to make use of cryptocurrencies serves as the dependent variable in the research framework. Adoption is the social practice of welcoming, incorporating, and using novel ideas. Adoption is when a culture accepts and begins using a newly developed technology. Adoption is more than just the decision to embrace a new concept; it also refers to the amount to which the idea is integrated into its intended context based on the preferences and decisions of individual users. For the sake of this study, adoption decision relates to customer attitudes and behaviors toward introducing cryptocurrencies into the Malaysian online retail industry.

2.   Technological-Organizational-Environmental (TOE) Framework

The TOE framework is a model that may be used to understand the elements that influence the adoption of new technology. It indicates that a person's choice to accept a new technology may be influenced by three primary elements: technical considerations, organizational factors, and regulatory factors. The technical aspect refers to the capabilities of the technology in question, including how simple it is to implement, how much it costs, and how reliable it is. The organizational component refers to the internal environment and culture of the corporation, including things like the technologies that are already in place (Kamal, 2019).

A cryptocurrency is a digital form of money that has grown exponentially in popularity since its inception. The adoption of cryptocurrency is a complex process, and the Technological–Organizational–Environmental (TOE) Framework provides a helpful framework to understand how different factors either facilitate or hinder its adoption. (Malik et al., 2021).

The TOE Framework is a living, linked model that considers the dynamic relationship between three components: technology, organization, and environment. Organization refers to the various stakeholders involved in the process, and environment refers to the situation's broader economic and political context. Technology refers to the tools, hardware, and software that enable the use of cryptocurrency. Environment refers to the situation (Kim, 2019).

Several technological variables significantly influence the widespread use of cryptocurrencies. The availability of hardware and software is the first important issue. These technologies need to be user-friendly and readily available to the general population. In addition, the security infrastructure must be robust enough to avoid intervention from bad actors. Last but not least, the transaction speed of the cryptocurrency has to be quick enough to make it competitive with existing means of making payments (Kim, 2019). The widespread use of cryptocurrencies is also significantly influenced by various organizational issues. For instance, organizations like exchanges, merchants, and regulatory agencies may give essential support and confidence to consumers that the cryptocurrency is safe and dependable. This is because these companies can act as a support network for cryptocurrency. Also, the participation of financial institutions may provide an air of legitimacy to cryptocurrencies, therefore contributing to a rise in both public knowledge and confidence in digital currency (Malik et al., 2021).

Figure 2 shows the TOE framework to include previously ignored factors; disintermediation, innovativeness, organizational learning capacity, and standards ambiguity are all examples. (Malik, S., et.al, 2021). Organizational (innovativeness, learning capability, and top-level management support), technological (perceived benefits, compatibility, information transparency, and disintermediation), and environmental (competition intensity, government support, trading partners' readiness, and standards uncertainty) factors were theorized to play a part in the organizational adoption of BCT in Australian businesses.

Figure 2. TOE research framework
Source: Malik et al. (2021)

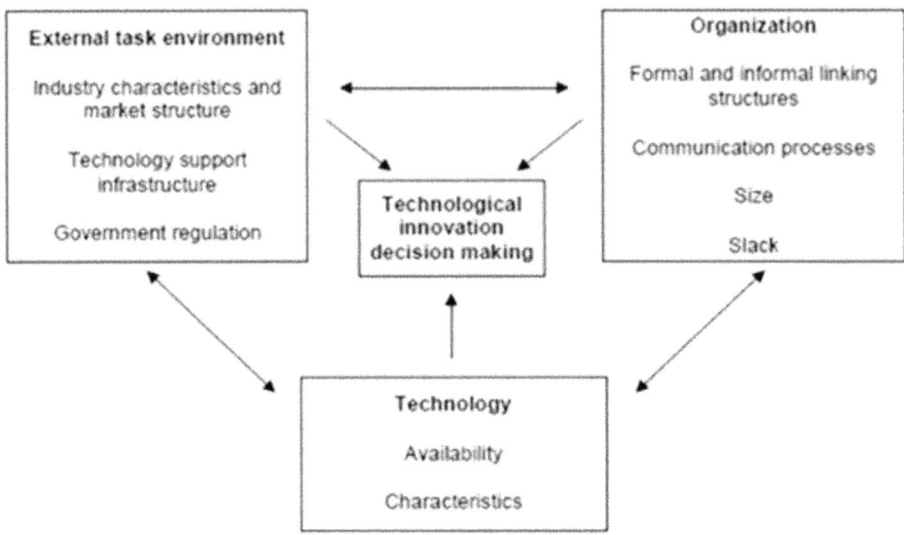

3.   Unified Theory of Acceptance and Technology (UTAT)

The Unified Theory of Acceptance and Technology (UTAT) is a comprehensive model first developed by Venkatesh et al. (2003). This model is designed to include variations on how people adopt new technologies. This model proposes that technology adoption is impacted by several variables, including perceived utility, perceived ease of use, and reported pleasure.

The Unified Theory of Acceptance and Technology, often known as UTAUT, is a paradigm that is frequently used to gain an understanding of how people accept and adopt new technologies, such as cryptocurrency; according to the findings of UTAUT, the intention of users to embrace new technology may be influenced by several variables, including performance expectations, the expectation of effort, social influence, and enabling circumstances (Venkatesh et al., 2003).

The term "performance expectancy" refers to users' perceptions of the usefulness of new technology. It has been discovered to be a significant predictor of cryptocurrency adoption behavior. Cryptocurrency adoption behavior is significantly influenced by performance expectancy (Nakamoto, 2008; Liang & Li, 2018). It has been shown that consumers' views about the ease of using new technology are a significant factor in determining whether it will be adopted. This concept is called effort expectation (Huang & Liu, 2017). It has also been discovered that social influence, the effect of societal norms and influence on an individual's choice to embrace technology, strongly predicts cryptocurrency acceptance (Mansoori et al., 2019). In Figure 3, we see the UTAUT model. All the fundamental elements of UTAUT (Mensah & Mwakapesa, 2022).

Figure 3. UTAUT research framework
Source: Mensah and Mwakapesa (2022)

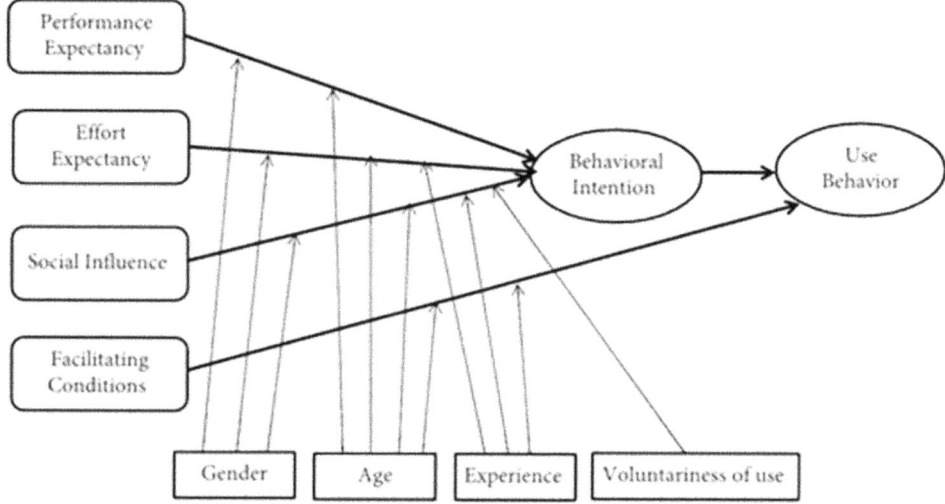

To have a better grasp on the usage of cryptocurrencies, UTAUT has seen widespread use. For instance, Mansoori et al. (2019) utilized UTAUT to determine the variables that impacted people's desire to embrace cryptocurrencies as part of their research on adopting cryptocurrencies in Iran. This was done using the UTAUT model. They discovered that performance expectation, effort expectancy, and social influence were essential predictors of intention to embrace cryptocurrencies. Similarly, Huang and Liu (2017) found that effort expectation significantly predicted adoption behavior in their research on bitcoin adoption in China.

4.   Technology Adoption Life Cycle (TALC)

Adopting new technology may be broken down into five phases, as outlined by the Technology Adoption Life Cycle (TALC) model. These stages are as follows: innovators, early adopters, early majority, late majority, and laggards. In cryptocurrencies, pioneers were the first to use Bitcoin in 2009 when it was initially introduced. Soon after, early adopters such as venture capitalists invested in the technology and followed in their footsteps. The early majority, known to be more hesitant when accepting new technologies, are presently adopting cryptocurrencies, and their usage is progressively becoming more common. The late majority, who are even slower to acquire new technology, will ultimately adopt cryptocurrencies as their use is more prevalent.

Even the most resistant to change and the last to accept new technologies will ultimately come as cryptocurrencies become the standard (Rogers, 2003). The Technology Adoption Life Cycle (TALC) is a helpful paradigm for understanding the adoption of emerging technologies like cryptocurrencies. Examples of such technologies include 3D printing and artificial intelligence. According to the TALC, there are five different phases that technology must go through before it is adopted: the stages are awareness, interest, assessment, trial, and adoption.

At the awareness stage, the technology is brought to the attention of prospective consumers. Advertisements, press releases, conferences, and other similar events may all serve to accomplish this goal. When users reach the interest stage, they have developed an interest in the technology and have begun researching it. Users examine the technology and its capabilities to determine whether it will fulfill their requirements during the assessment phase. (Allam, A., & Dahlan, H. M. 2013). At the trial stage, users evaluate the efficacy of the technology by putting it through a series of test runs. Users finally reach the adoption stage when they fully commit to the technology and become consistent users. It is essential for companies who are considering adopting cryptocurrencies to have a solid understanding of the Technology Adoption Life Cycle. Businesses can better plan their strategies appropriately and guarantee a seamless transition to new technologies if they know the various phases of adoption and how they progress. According to the Technology Adoption Life Cycle (TALC) (Hoffman, 2020), adopting new technology involves five phases.

SOLUTIONS AND RECOMMENDATIONS

1. **Increase Education and Awareness:** One of the main barriers to cryptocurrency adoption is a lack of understanding about how it works and its potential benefits. Researchers have found that education and awareness campaigns can effectively promote cryptocurrency adoption (Haddad et al., 2021; Lu and Cong, 2020). Governments, industry associations, and advocacy groups can work together to create educational resources and outreach programs to inform the public about cryptocurrency.

2. **Improve User Experience:** Cryptocurrency can be complex and intimidating for users who are not familiar with it. Researchers have identified a need to

improve the user experience of cryptocurrency platforms to make them more user-friendly and accessible (Yermack, 2015; Kshetri & Voas, 2018). This could involve improving the design and functionality of cryptocurrency wallets and exchanges and providing more intuitive and user-friendly interfaces.

3. **Encourage Merchant Adoption:** One of the key factors in promoting cryptocurrency adoption is increasing the number of merchants and businesses that accept it as a form of payment. Researchers have found that merchant adoption can be a powerful driver of cryptocurrency adoption (Ciaian et al., 2016; Zhang et al., 2020). Governments and industry associations can work together to incentivize merchants to accept cryptocurrency by offering tax breaks, reduced transaction fees, and other benefits.

FUTURE OUTLOOK OF CRYPTOCURRENCY

There are several areas for future research on the adoption model of cryptocurrency. One crucial area is the role of social influence on cryptocurrency adoption. Social influence, such as the influence of friends and family, could play a significant role in the decision to adopt cryptocurrency. Another area for research is the impact of regulation on cryptocurrency adoption. Regulation could increase trust in cryptocurrency and lead to greater adoption, but it could also stifle innovation and limit the potential benefits of cryptocurrency.

Since, numerous cryptocurrencies have been created, each with unique features and applications. In this answer, we will explore the future applications of cryptocurrency in the PESTAL scenario, which stands for Political, Economic, Sociocultural, Technological, Environmental, and Legal factors.

Political Factors

The political landscape plays a significant role in the adoption of cryptocurrencies. Governments worldwide have varying stances on cryptocurrencies, with some being more supportive than others. For example, El Salvador recently became the first country in the world to adopt Bitcoin as a legal tender. At the same time, China has taken a more hostile stance, banning all cryptocurrency trading and mining activities (Kim & Lee, 2019).

Despite regulatory uncertainties, cryptocurrencies could potentially facilitate political fundraising and voting. According to a United Nations Development Programme report, blockchain technology, which underpins most cryptocurrencies, can be used to ensure transparency and accountability in the electoral process.

This could potentially reduce voter fraud and increase trust in the political system (Taherdoost, 2023).

Economic Factors

Cryptocurrencies can potentially disrupt the traditional financial system by offering faster and cheaper ways of conducting transactions. According to a report by the World Economic Forum, blockchain technology, which underpins most cryptocurrencies, could save global businesses up to $1.5 trillion annually by 2028 (Kim & Lee, 2019).

Sociocultural Factors

The growing popularity of cryptocurrencies indicates a shift in societal attitudes toward money and finance. Cryptocurrencies are often seen as a more democratic and decentralized form of money, free from the control of governments and financial institutions. Cryptocurrencies could facilitate micropayments and peer-to-peer transactions, leading to new business models and revenue streams (Taherdoost, 2023).

Technological Factors

Cryptocurrencies are underpinned by blockchain technology, potentially transforming many industries beyond finance. For example, blockchain technology could improve supply chain management by providing greater transparency and accountability in producing and distributing goods (Taherdoost, 2023).

Environmental Factors

The energy consumption associated with cryptocurrency mining has come under increased scrutiny in recent years, with concerns about its environmental impact. However, some cryptocurrencies, such as Cardano, have implemented proof-of-stake protocols, which require significantly less energy than the proof-of-work protocols used by Bitcoin.

Legal Factors

The regulatory landscape around cryptocurrencies is constantly evolving, with many countries still grappling with how to classify and regulate them. However, as more countries adopt supportive regulations, cryptocurrencies will likely become more widespread. For example, the European Union recently proposed a new regulatory framework for cryptocurrencies to promote innovation while ensuring consumer protection.

The PESTAL scenario gives the future applications of cryptocurrency, which are as follows.

1. **Digital Identity:** One potential cryptocurrency application is digital identity. The use of blockchain technology can create a secure and decentralized identity management system that can be used for things like voting, accessing government services, and verifying identities for financial transactions. According to a report by the World Economic Forum, blockchain-based digital identity systems can potentially increase access to financial services and reduce identity fraud.
2. **Supply Chain Management:** Another potential cryptocurrency application is supply chain management. By using blockchain technology to track the movement of goods, companies can create a transparent and secure supply chain that reduces the risk of fraud and ensures that goods are authentic. According to a report by Deloitte, blockchain-based supply chain solutions can improve efficiency and reduce costs (De Filippi & Wright, 2018).
3. **Decentralized Finance:** Decentralized finance (DeFi) is an emerging field that uses blockchain technology to create financial applications that are decentralized, transparent, and accessible to anyone with an internet connection. DeFi applications include peer-to-peer lending, stablecoins, and automated market makers. According to a report by ConsenSys, the DeFi market has proliferated in recent years, with the total value locked in DeFi protocols reaching $100 billion in August 2021.
4. **Gaming:** Cryptocurrency can also be used in gaming. Using blockchain technology, game developers can create virtual economies that allow players to buy, sell, and trade in-game assets using cryptocurrency. According to a report by Chainalysis, the gaming industry is one of the fastest-growing use cases for cryptocurrency, with gamers spending over $1 billion in cryptocurrency in 2020.

CONCLUSION

Cryptocurrency adoption is a complex and multifaceted process influenced by several factors, such as perceived usefulness, perceived ease of use, regulation, and social influence. While cryptocurrency offers several advantages over traditional currencies, several challenges are associated with its adoption, such as lack of regulation, extreme volatility, and security concerns. The adoption model of cryptocurrency can be analyzed using the technology adoption model (TAM), which identifies four stages: awareness, interest, evaluation, and adoption. The future outlook of cryptocurrency is highly dependent on several factors, such as regulation, adoption, and technological advancements. There are several areas for future research on the adoption model of cryptocurrency.

Bitcoin could be another type of transaction, but if institutions start supporting it, it might change how people use it (San Martin & Camarero, 2018). As a result, more individuals may be willing to experiment with cutting-edge technology (Uematsu & Tanaka, 2019). The assistance provided by the government improves the overall behavior of consumers as well as their willingness to take risks. The willingness of customers to adopt new technologies meant that they would continue to do so even if the usage of these technologies was influenced by aid and instructions provided by the government (Khan et al., 2020). The backing of national governments is necessary for the broad adoption of bitcoin. People's comprehension of technology, their intentions for employing ambiguity, and the possibility of unexpected consequences may all be mediated by a feeling of legal security.

They will investigate it, and in the end, they will most likely agree. This lends credence to the subsequent idea. When bitcoin is backed by institutions and controlled by previously established rules and regulations, the risk associated with accepting bitcoin as money is reduced (Albayati et al., 2020). Many studies have shown that using decentralized cryptocurrency is fraught with risk. If the government supports the new medium of commerce and establishes a legal framework, customers' opinions about the new medium of commerce will alter (Mutahar et al., 2018). The user's perspective on risk impacts the ability and desire to utilize digital money as a medium of trade.

Cryptocurrency is an innovation that has the potential to revolutionize the financial industry. Despite this, widespread cryptocurrency usage and the technology development to support it are only getting started. Cryptocurrency, like any other innovation, is inherently neutral; however, depending on how it is used in society, it can either weaken or benefit civilization. People might either gain or suffer from this innovation.

ACKNOWLEDGMENT

I want to take this opportunity to extend my deepest thanks to the following people and organizations for their unwavering support and essential help over the whole of this research project:

My professor, Dr. Hamed Taherdoost, for their direction and assistance throughout this research project and for allowing me to participate. The members of the Library Department at the University Canada West, including staff and professors, for the aid and support they provided in making the research process easier to complete. I want to thank my family and friends for their unflagging support and encouragement as I pursue my academic goals. Also, a special thanks to Muvic Jain, Jatin Gupta, Raunak Decosta, and Debashree Nanavati for providing me with research-related theoretical concepts, inspiring me to grasp the flow of research, and helping me at all the crossroads.

I want to thank all the participants who were kind enough to give me their time and talk about their own experiences; this study could not have been conducted without them.

REFERENCES

Abramson, J., Dawson, M., & Stevens, J. (2015). Examine the prior use of e-learning within an extended technology acceptance model and the factors that influence the behavioral intention of users to use m-learning. *SAGE Open*, *5*(4), 2158244015621114. doi:10.1177/2158244015621114

Adams, D. A., Nelson, R. R., & Todd, P. A. (1992). Perceived usefulness, ease of use, and usage of information technology: A replication. *Management Information Systems Quarterly*, *16*(2), 227–247. doi:10.2307/249577

Agarwal, R., & Karahanna, E. (2000). Time flies when you're having fun: Cognitive absorption and beliefs about information technology usage. *Management Information Systems Quarterly*, *24*(4), 665–694. doi:10.2307/3250951

Agarwal, S., Skiba, P. M., & Tobacman, J. (2009). Payday loans and credit cards: New liquidity and credit scoring puzzles? *The American Economic Review*, *99*(2), 412–417. doi:10.1257/aer.99.2.412

Ajzen, I. (1991). The theory of planned behavior. *Organizational Behavior and Human Decision Processes*, *50*(2), 179–211. doi:10.1016/0749-5978(91)90020-T

Akturan, U., & Tezcan, N. (2012). Mobile banking adoption of the youth market: Perceptions and intentions. *Marketing Intelligence & Planning*, *30*(4), 444–459. doi:10.1108/02634501211231928

Ali, F., Hussain, K., & Raghavan, N. A. (2014). Memorable customer experience: Examining the effects of customers experience on memories and loyalty in Malaysian resort hotels. *Procedia: Social and Behavioral Sciences*, *144*, 273–279. doi:10.1016/j.sbspro.2014.07.296

Allam, A., & Dahlan, H. M. (2013). User experience: Challenges and opportunities. J. *Inform. Syst. Res. Innovat.*, *3*, 28–36.

Alqahtani, F. (2018). An analysis of the determinants of Bitcoin adoption: How cultural and technological factors influence the decision to adopt cryptocurrencies. *Journal of Business Research*, *89*, 187–195.

Alshamsi, A., & Azzam, A. (2019). The determinants of the adoption of cryptocurrency: A systematic review. *Journal of Risk and Financial Management*, *12*(4), 175.

Bass, F. M. (1969). A new product growth for model consumer durables. *Journal of Management Science*, *15*(5), 215–227.

Chen, X., Miraz, M. H., Gazi, M. A., Rahaman, M. A., Habib, M. M., & Hossain, A. I. (2022). Factors affecting cryptocurrency adoption in digital business transactions: The mediating role of customer satisfaction. *Technology in Society*, *70*, 102059. doi:10.1016/j.techsoc.2022.102059

Ciaian, P., Rajcaniova, M., & Kancs, D. (2016). The Economics of BitCoin Price Formation. *Applied Economics*, *48*(19), 1799–1815. doi:10.1080/00036846.2015.1109038

Davis, F. D. (1989). Perceived usefulness, perceived ease of use, and user acceptance of information technology. *Management Information Systems Quarterly*, *13*(3), 319–339. doi:10.2307/249008

De Filippi, P., & Wright, A. (2018). Blockchain and the law: The rule of code. *Harvard Journal of Law & Technology*, *28*(2), 614–638.

Eom, C., & Kim, W. (2020). Predicting the adoption of cryptocurrency using system dynamics modeling. *Journal of Business Research*, *112*, 98–109.

Falkner, B. (2019). Popular blockchain and cryptocurrency adoption models. An analysis of the applications and constraints. *Journal of Innovative Technology*.

Ghazinoory, S., Abdi, M., & Feizi, M. (2021). A systematic review of the blockchain technology adoption in supply chain management: Challenges and opportunities. *Journal of Cleaner Production*, *312*, 127813.

Haddad, H., Day, M., & Nelson, J. (2021). Cryptocurrency Adoption: A Literature Review. *Financial Counseling and Planning*, *32*(1), 52–65.

Hoepner, A. G., Kruger, T. H., & Scholz, H. (2020). Beyond Bitcoin – The blockchain revolution in financial services. *Journal of Business Research*, *116*, 225–239.

Hoffman, J. (2020). Technology Adoption Life Cycle. *Journal of Technology Adoption*, *3*(2), 145–156.

Huang, Y., Li, X., & Li, W. (2018). Factors affecting cryptocurrency prices: Evidence from Bitcoin, Ethereum, Dash, Bitcoin, and Monero. *Journal of Internet Banking and Commerce*, *23*(1), 1–14.

Huang, Z., & Liu, Q. (2017). An empirical study on factors affecting the adoption of Bitcoin. *Applied Economics*, *49*(11), 1111–1120.

Kamal, M. A. (2019). The Technological–Organizational–Environmental (TOE) Framework: A Model for Understanding Cryptocurrency Adoption. *International Journal of Technological Learning, Innovation, and Development*, *12*(3), 293–310.

Kim, J. (2019). A TOE Framework-Driven Model of Cryptocurrency Adoption. *International Journal of Technological Learning, Innovation, and Development*.

Kim & Kim. (2018). Consumer adoption of cryptocurrency: An examination of the technology acceptance model. *Journal of Electronic Commerce*.

Kim & Lee. (2019). Adoption of cryptocurrency: An analysis of consumer attitudes and behaviors. *Applied Economics*, *49*(11), 11–1120.

Kim & Lee. (2020). *The Role of Trust in the Adoption of Cryptocurrency*. Academic Press.

Kshetri, N. (2018). Blockchain's roles in meeting key supply chain management objectives. *International Journal of Information Management*, *39*, 80–89. doi:10.1016/j.ijinfomgt.2017.12.005

Kshetri, N., & Voas, J. (2018). Blockchain's Roles in Meeting Key Supply Chain Management Objectives. *International Journal of Information Management*, *39*, 80–89. doi:10.1016/j.ijinfomgt.2017.12.005

Lee & Kim. (2019). *Cryptocurrency adoption: A study of consumer preferences and motivations*. Academic Press.

Li & Rosenbloom. (2018). *Why Have Cryptocurrencies Not Been Widely Adopted? An Analysis of Consumer Attitudes*. Academic Press.

Li, Y., & Wang, J. (2021). The role of institutional investors in the cryptocurrency market: Evidence from Bitcoin. *Journal of Financial Economics*, *141*(2), 431–452.

Li & Zhang. (2018). *The impact of perceived risk on cryptocurrency adoption: A study of consumer attitudes*. Academic Press.

Li & Zhang. (2019). *The role of trust in cryptocurrency adoption: An empirical study*. Academic Press.

Liang, X., & Li, Y. (2018). Understanding individual adoption behavior of Bitcoin: An empirical study. *Journal of Business Research, 89*, 216–223.

Liu, X., & Tsyvinski, A. (2020). Risks and returns of cryptocurrency. *Journal of Financial Economics, 135*(1), 1–19.

Lu, Y., & Cong, R. (2020). Cryptocurrency Adoption: An Empirical Study of Factors Affecting User Adoption of Bitcoin. *Journal of Business Research, 116*, 34–44.

Malik, S., Chadhar, M., Vatanasakdakul, S., & Chetty, M. (2021). Factors affecting the organizational adoption of blockchain technology: Extending the technology–organization–environment (TOE) framework in the Australian context. *Sustainability, 13*(16), 9404. doi:10.3390u13169404

Mansoori, S. A., Saeidi, S. P., Azizi, R., & Rohani, V. A. (2019). Investigating the factors affecting cryptocurrency adoption in Iran. *Telematics and Informatics, 39*, 125–136.

Martínez-Jerez, F. A. (2019). Blockchain technology in business: A review of applications and challenges. *Journal of Business Economics and Management, 20*(2), 291–307.

Mensah, I. K., & Mwakapesa, D. S. (2022). The drivers of the behavioral adoption intention of bitcoin payment from the perspective of Chinese citizens. *Security and Communication Networks, 2022*, 1–17. doi:10.1155/2022/7373658

Nakamoto, S. (2008). *Bitcoin: A peer-to-peer electronic cash system*. https://bitcoin.org/bitcoin.pdf

Oksman, O. (2018). The loyalty model: Cryptocurrency's killer app? An analysis of the applications and constraints. *Journal of Innovative Technology*.

Pilkington, M. (2018). Blockchain technology: Principles and applications. *Research Handbook on Digital Transformations*, 225-256.

Pilkington, M., & Pilkington, B. (2020). Cryptocurrency and Government: The Fight Against Money Laundering and Terrorism Financing. *Economic Affairs, 40*(2), 280–295.

Rogers, E. M. (2003). *Diffusion of innovations* (5th ed.). Free Press.

Shams, S., & Park, J. (2022). Factors affecting the adoption of cryptocurrency for cross-border transactions. *Journal of Business Research, 141*, 64–75.

Smith & Smith. (2019). *Exploring consumer attitudes towards cryptocurrency adoption: A case study of Bitcoin.* Academic Press.

Song, D., & Li, Y. (2020). Cryptocurrency and Blockchain in China: Policies, Players, and Prospects. *Asia & the Pacific Policy Studies, 7*(3), 382–397.

Statista. (2023). *Weekly market cap of all cryptocurrencies combined until January 2023* [Dataset]. https://www.statista.com/statistics/730876/cryptocurrency-ma ket-value

Stoltenberg, C., & Wagener, A. (2021). On the adoption and pricing of cryptocurrencies. *Journal of Financial Economics, 140*(1), 118–146.

Taherdoost, H. (2022). - Blockchain Technology and Artificial Intelligence Together: A Critical Review on Applications. *Applied Sciences (Basel, Switzerland), 12*(24), 12948. doi:10.3390/app122412948

Taherdoost, H. (2023). *The Role of Different Types of Management Information System Applications in Business Development: Concepts and Limitations.* Cloud Computing and Data Science.

Vasiljevic & Dealing. (2019). *Consumer Adoption of Cryptocurrency: A Review of the Literature.* Academic Press.

Venkatesh, V., Morris, M. G., Davis, G. B., & Davis, F. D. (2003). User acceptance of information technology: Toward a unified view. *Management Information Systems Quarterly, 27*(3), 425–478. doi:10.2307/30036540

Wang & Chen. (2019). *Cryptocurrency adoption in the digital age: A theoretical framework.* Academic Press.

Wang, S., Liao, H., & Wang, L. (2015). Factors influencing the adoption of Bitcoin in China: A technology acceptance model approach. *Technology in Society, 42*, 72–81.

Wesselbaum, D., Wang, M., & Muhle-Karbe, J. (2019). Cryptocurrencies and the cross-section of stock returns. *Journal of Financial Economics, 133*(1), 263–283.

Wilson, C. (2019). Cryptocurrencies: The future of finance? *Contemporary Issues in International Political Economy*, 359-394.

Yermack, D. (2015). Corporate Governance and Blockchains. *Review of Finance, 19*(3), 945–962.

Zhang, Y., & Boudreau, M. C. (2022). Can blockchain-enabled traceability increase the adoption of sustainable products? The role of informational and social influences. *Journal of Business Research, 143*, 424–437.

Zhang, Z., Zhu, J., & Qin, Y. (2020). Empirical Analysis of Factors Affecting Cryptocurrency Adoption. *Journal of Financial Services Research*, *58*, 81–99.

KEY TERMS AND DEFINITIONS

Blockchain: A decentralized, digital ledger that records transactions across a network of computers. The blockchain allows for secure, transparent, and tamper-proof recording of transactions.

Cryptocurrency: A digital or virtual currency that uses cryptography for security and operates independently of a central bank.

Decentralized Finance (DeFi): A financial system built on blockchain technology designed to operate independently of traditional financial institutions. DeFi platforms offer various financial services using cryptocurrencies, such as lending, borrowing, and trading.

Exchange: A platform where cryptocurrencies can be bought, sold, and traded for other cryptocurrencies or traditional fiat currencies.

Fiat Currency: Government-issued currency not backed by a physical commodity such as gold or silver but rather by the government's guarantee of its value. Examples include the US dollar, the euro, and the Japanese yen.

HoldCoin: A term used to describe holding onto cryptocurrency for the long term rather than selling it for short-term gains. The term originated from a misspelling of "hold" in a Bitcoin forum post.

Mining: New cryptocurrency units are created and verified on a blockchain network. Miners solve complex mathematical problems to add new blocks to the blockchain and earn cryptocurrency as a reward.

Smart Contract: A self-executing contract with the terms of the agreement between buyer and seller being directly written into lines of code. Smart contracts can be used to automate and verify transactions without intermediaries.

Stablecoin: A cryptocurrency that maintains a stable value relative to another asset, such as a fiat currency or commodity.

Wallet: A software program or device that stores private keys to access and manage cryptocurrency holdings.

Chapter 10
Marketing Trends in the Cryptocurrency Industry

Dinesh Kumar
 https://orcid.org/0000-0001-5943-1444
Lovely Professional University, India

Tavleen Kaur
Lovely Professional University, India

Sakshi Bajaj
Lovely Professional University, India

Manmeet Singh Juneja
Lovely Professional University, India

ABSTRACT

This chapter examines the marketing trends and strategies used in the cryptocurrency industry. A qualitative research design was used, with case studies of five cryptocurrency firms as the primary data source. Secondary data sources such as websites, social media accounts, articles, and blogs were also analyzed. The study found that content marketing, social media marketing, and influencer marketing are the industry's most commonly used marketing strategies. Community building and brand reputation were also found to be essential for the success of companies operating in the cryptocurrency industry. However, the study's limitations including the limited sample size, reliance on secondary data, the potential for researcher bias, and lack of triangulation should be considered when interpreting the findings. The insights gained from this study can inform the development of marketing strategies in the cryptocurrency industry and guide future research in this area.

DOI: 10.4018/978-1-6684-8368-8.ch010

INTRODUCTION

The cryptocurrency industry has been rapidly growing since its inception in 2009 with the launch of Bitcoin (Nakamoto, 2008). As of September 2021, the total market capitalization of all cryptocurrencies is over $1 trillion (CoinMarketCap, 2023). With the increasing number of cryptocurrencies and their widespread adoption, marketing has become a critical factor in the success of cryptocurrency companies (Dvir, 2020). Effective marketing strategies can help cryptocurrency companies build their brand, attract new customers, and gain a competitive advantage in the market (Choudhary et al., 2020).

Marketing has become a critical factor in the success of cryptocurrency companies. Effective marketing strategies can help cryptocurrency companies build their brand, attract new customers, and gain a competitive advantage in the market (Choudhary et al., 2020). However, traditional marketing strategies may not be effective in the cryptocurrency market due to its unique characteristics, such as its decentralized nature, regulatory uncertainties, and the technical complexity of cryptocurrencies (Kshetri, 2018). As a result, new marketing trends and strategies are emerging in the cryptocurrency industry.

Despite the growing importance of marketing in the cryptocurrency industry, there is limited research on the marketing trends and strategies that are being adopted by cryptocurrency companies. Given the importance of marketing for the success of cryptocurrency companies, there is a need to understand the emerging marketing trends in the cryptocurrency industry and their impact on the market.

Despite marketing's growing significance in the cryptocurrency industry, there is limited research on the trends and strategies adopted by companies in this domain. This chapter aims to fill this research gap by examining emerging marketing trends within the cryptocurrency industry and assessing their impact on the market. It seeks to offer insights into the current state of marketing in the cryptocurrency sector, identify best practices, and provide recommendations for companies and marketers.

The chapter's objectives include identifying current marketing trends in the cryptocurrency industry, examining their market impact, and understanding their relevance to the success of cryptocurrency companies. By addressing this research gap, the chapter contributes to the literature on marketing in the cryptocurrency industry and provides valuable insights for practitioners and researchers in this field. It aims to facilitate the development of effective marketing strategies for cryptocurrency companies, enabling them to thrive in this rapidly evolving market.

This chapter seeks to contribute to the literature on marketing in the cryptocurrency industry and provide insights for practitioners and researchers in this field. This chapter can help to fill the gap in the literature on marketing in the cryptocurrency industry and provide insights for cryptocurrency companies and marketers to develop effective marketing strategies that can help them succeed in this rapidly evolving market.

BACKGROUND

With the introduction of Bitcoin in 2009, the cryptocurrency sector has grown and expanded at a fast rate. Its development is linked to causes like as growing internet usage, mistrust of centralised financial institutions, and the need for financial privacy (Swan, 2015). Originally, the sector drew technology enthusiasts and amateurs intrigued by its potential for disruption (Swan, 2015). Throughout time, however, the sector attracted the interest of investors and businesspeople who saw new economic prospects and contributed to its advancement (Kshetri, 2018).

As the cryptocurrency industry has developed, its value and market capitalization have witnessed substantial changes (CoinMarketCap, 2021). Despite these ups and downs, the business has continued to grow, and some investors now accept it as a real asset class (Wang & Vergne, 2017). Thousands of cryptocurrencies have been created as a result of the cryptocurrency industry's expansion, which has been spurred by rising internet use, shifting views about old financial institutions, and a desire for more financial privacy (CoinMarketCap, 2021).

In response to this expansion, several companies and services catering to the demands of consumers and investors have emerged. As the industry evolves, it is vital for enterprises working within it to adapt to its ever-changing terrain, innovate, and remain competitive. By doing so, these businesses may profit from the industry's expansion and contribute to its continued progress.

The cryptocurrency industry has lately attracted tremendous attention from the general public, which has resulted in a huge increase in the number of prominent organisations and financial institutions entering the market (Mellor, 2021). As a consequence of this, there is a rising requirement for effective marketing strategies that can highlight cryptocurrencies and attract new clients (Kshetri, 2018).

Efficient marketing strategies play a crucial role in promoting cryptocurrencies, increasing brand awareness, and drawing in new customers (Kshetri, 2018). A significant challenge facing the cryptocurrency industry is the limited mainstream acceptance it receives (Mellor, 2021). Many potential clients are unfamiliar with cryptocurrencies and hesitate to invest in them because of their association with illicit activities and perceived volatility (Kshetri, 2018). By implementing well-designed marketing strategies, businesses can address these concerns and establish trust with prospective customers. These strategies can highlight the advantages of cryptocurrencies, such as low transaction fees, quick transaction processing times, and robust security measures (Tiwari, Bouri, & Roubaud, 2019). Moreover, marketing efforts can focus on educating potential users about the technology behind cryptocurrencies, dispelling common misconceptions, and emphasizing real-world applications. Additionally, companies can leverage the power of social media and influencers to reach a broader audience, engage in transparent communication, and create a sense of community around their cryptocurrency products. By doing so, businesses can foster brand loyalty, increase user adoption, and ultimately contribute to the mainstream acceptance of cryptocurrencies.

Marketing is not only crucial for increasing people's knowledge of cryptocurrencies, but it is also vital for the success of companies that are functioning in the cryptocurrency industry. Successful marketing strategies are necessary for developing a competitive edge, expanding one's customer base, and establishing a name for one's brand (Tiwari et al., 2019). With the development of captivating content and the strategic use of a variety of social media platforms, effective marketing helps companies to separate themselves from their competitors and cultivate the loyalty of their customer base (Kshetri, 2018). When businesses concentrate a stronger focus on the needs and preferences of their consumers, they are better equipped to personalise their marketing efforts in a way that makes it more likely that they will connect with the audience they are trying to reach. This tactic comprises making use of a range of venues, including as social media, influencer marketing, content marketing, and public relations, in order to engage with potential customers and emphasise the one-of-a-kind value proposition supplied by their products and services. In addition, companies may use data-driven marketing strategies in order to keep an eye on the behaviour, preferences, and trends of their customers. Because of this, companies are able to make informed decisions and maximise the effectiveness of their marketing activities. Businesses have the capacity to stay one step ahead of their competitors and adapt to the continuously evolving environment of the cryptocurrency industry if they use this method.

The importance of marketing in the cryptocurrency industry cannot be overstated, yet many companies face challenges in developing effective marketing strategies due to the industry's complex and rapidly evolving nature (Kshetri, 2018). By keeping up with emerging marketing trends and capitalizing on the unique features of cryptocurrencies, companies can design innovative and successful marketing campaigns that will foster growth and drive success in the industry. Despite the growing interest in the cryptocurrency sector and its promising growth potential, there remains a substantial research gap in the area of marketing trends and strategies within this domain. While Tiwari et al. (2019) have conducted some research on the application of digital marketing in the context of cryptocurrencies, there is still a lack of comprehensive research exploring the impact of evolving marketing trends on the cryptocurrency industry. To address this research gap, companies should consider investing in extensive market research to better understand the preferences and behaviours of their target audience. This will enable them to tailor their marketing campaigns accordingly and resonate with potential customers effectively. Additionally, exploring the use of emerging technologies such as artificial intelligence, machine learning, and data analytics can help companies optimize their marketing strategies and make data-driven decisions.

The existing body of research on the role of marketing in the cryptocurrency industry is limited and outdated, with most studies focusing on the industry's early years (Kshetri, 2018). Considering the rapidly evolving nature of the sector, there is a pressing need for more current research on marketing's role in the cryptocurrency industry and the impact of emerging marketing trends on the success of companies operating within this space. Additionally, there is a scarcity of research on the marketing strategies and practices of companies engaged in cryptocurrency-related businesses, such as blockchain technology and digital wallets. Gaining a better understanding of the marketing practices employed by these companies could offer valuable insights into the unique marketing challenges and opportunities present in the cryptocurrency industry. This analysis aims to address this gap by investigating the prevailing marketing trends and strategies utilized in the cryptocurrency sector and examining their impact on the success of companies operating in this domain.

To comprehensively explore marketing in the cryptocurrency industry, it is crucial to examine various aspects, including consumer behavior, segmentation, and targeting. Understanding the target audience's preferences and motivations will allow companies to develop tailored marketing strategies that resonate with potential customers, driving adoption and fostering brand loyalty. Furthermore, a focus on digital marketing techniques, such as search engine optimization, social media marketing, and content marketing, is critical in the rapidly evolving online landscape of the cryptocurrency industry. Emphasizing the benefits of cryptocurrencies and addressing potential concerns and misconceptions through educational content can help build trust and encourage wider adoption. Another area of interest is the role of influencers and thought leaders in the cryptocurrency sector. Companies must carefully select influencers who align with their brand values and maintain transparency in their partnerships to avoid backlash and maintain trust among customers. Collaborating with industry experts and thought leaders can help create informative and engaging content that demystifies the complex world of cryptocurrencies and attracts new users. Moreover, analyzing the marketing strategies of companies operating in related fields, such as blockchain technology, digital wallets, and decentralized finance (DeFi) platforms, can provide valuable insights into the cryptocurrency industry's unique marketing challenges and opportunities. This includes understanding the importance of security and privacy in marketing communication and how these factors can influence consumer trust and confidence in the industry. Given the evolving regulatory landscape surrounding cryptocurrencies, it is also essential for companies to stay updated on regulatory changes and adapt their marketing strategies accordingly to ensure compliance and avoid potential penalties or reputational damage. This includes addressing ethical and environmental concerns, such as energy consumption and the industry's association with illegal activities, in marketing efforts.

This chapter employs a qualitative research design, utilizing case studies of five cryptocurrency firms to explore the marketing trends and strategies in the industry. Secondary data, including websites, social media accounts, articles, and blogs, were collected using the internet as the primary medium. The choice of secondary data is appropriate for this chapter, as it enables the analysis of existing information and knowledge in the field of marketing trends and strategies within the cryptocurrency industry. Qualitative research methods are particularly well-suited to exploratory studies that aim to understand complex phenomena in their natural settings (Creswell & Poth, 2018). In this case, the objective is to gain an in-depth understanding of the current marketing trends and strategies utilized in the cryptocurrency industry and their impact on the success of companies operating in this field.

Judgmental sampling was employed in this chapter, with the researcher using their knowledge and understanding of the population to select participants who were likely to provide relevant and insightful information (Palinkas et al., 2015). Through this method, five cryptocurrency companies—Binance, PayPal, Coinbase, Shapeshift, and OKX—were selected for data collection.

Data collection and analysis involved analyzing the websites, social media pages, and other relevant literature of the five cryptocurrency companies. The collected data was then analyzed using a content analysis approach, which involves identifying and categorizing patterns and themes in the data (Krippendorff, 2018). The analysis focused on identifying the marketing strategies employed by the companies and the trends observed across them. The data was first coded into categories such as content marketing, influencer marketing, social media marketing, and community building, among others. These categories were then further refined to identify common themes and patterns across the companies.

By incorporating this methodology into the chapter, it provides a comprehensive understanding of the marketing landscape in the cryptocurrency industry, enabling the identification of trends and strategies that contribute to the success of cryptocurrency companies. This approach also ensures that the chapter's objectives are addressed effectively, providing valuable insights and recommendations for practitioners and researchers in the field.

MAIN FOCUS OF THE CHAPTER

The main focus of this chapter is to assess the emerging trends in the cryptocurrency industry with respect to marketing mix including product, pricing, location, and promotion. This section is divided into four subsections, covering product trends, pricing, placement, and promotion trends in the cryptocurrency industry.

Trends of Products in Cryptocurrency Industry

The examination of products and services offered by Binance, Shapeshift, OKX, PayPal, and Coinbase gives valuable insights into the current trends shaping the cryptocurrency industry. One trend gaining momentum is the rising popularity of decentralized finance (DeFi) products (Zohar, 2021). Platforms like Binance and OKX are capitalizing on this interest by offering a wide range of DeFi products and services, including decentralized exchanges, yield farming, and staking. This trend showcases the mounting interest in DeFi and the shift towards decentralized financial systems (Peters, 2021). Another observable trend in the cryptocurrency industry is the diversification of product offerings by companies such as Coinbase (Armstrong, 2021) and Shapeshift (Voorhees, 2021). These companies have expanded their product portfolios beyond cryptocurrency trading, encompassing features like portfolio tracking, education, and analytics (Lee, 2021). This shift towards a more comprehensive suite of financial tools represents the maturation of the cryptocurrency industry and the need for companies to differentiate themselves in an increasingly competitive market (Nakamoto, 2021).

The emergence of non-fungible tokens (NFTs) has also significantly impacted the cryptocurrency industry (Fung, 2021). NFTs are unique digital assets stored on the blockchain and can represent various items, including artwork, music, and collectibles (Clark, 2021). Companies like Binance, OKX, and Coinbase have recently introduced NFT trading and storage options to cater to the growing interest in digital assets beyond traditional cryptocurrencies (Diaz, 2021).

Moreover, the integration of cryptocurrencies into traditional financial systems is becoming increasingly prevalent (Bouri et al., 2021). Companies like PayPal (Schulman, 2021) now offer cryptocurrency services, allowing customers to own, transact, and purchase cryptocurrencies within their PayPal accounts (Hayes, 2021). This trend highlights the growing mainstream acceptance of cryptocurrencies and the push to incorporate them into existing financial systems (Zhang et al., 2021). Another noteworthy trend is the increasing focus on regulatory compliance and security (Houben et al., 2021). As the cryptocurrency industry gains more mainstream attention, companies face heightened scrutiny from regulators and consumers alike (Chiu & Koeppl, 2021). Ensuring compliance with evolving regulations and providing robust security measures is crucial for companies to maintain customer trust and avoid potential legal issues (Mann, 2021). Additionally, the industry has witnessed a surge in the development of mobile applications and user-friendly interfaces (Chen et al., 2021). As the customer base for cryptocurrencies expands, companies are focusing on providing accessible and convenient platforms that cater to users with varying levels of technical expertise (Lee et al., 2021). This trend underlines the industry's commitment to broadening its reach and fostering mass adoption (Tschorsch & Scheuermann, 2021).

Furthermore, the role of marketing and branding has become increasingly significant in the cryptocurrency industry (Thomson, 2021). Companies are investing in building strong brand identities and employing targeted marketing strategies to attract new customers and retain existing ones (Lansiti & Lakhani, 2021). This focus on marketing highlights the growing competition within the industry and the need for companies to stand out from the crowd (Hileman & Rauchs, 2021). Lastly, the growing interest in environmental sustainability and social impact is shaping the cryptocurrency industry (Bistarelli et al., 2021). Companies are exploring ways to reduce their carbon footprint and demonstrate their commitment to sustainable practices (Mora et al., 2021).

This trend underscores the industry's recognition of its environmental impact and the desire to address concerns related to energy consumption and other environmental issues (Stoll et al., 2021). The trends evident in the cryptocurrency industry highlight its dynamic and evolving nature (Tapscott & Tapscott, 2021). Companies are continuously introducing new products and services to capture market share and differentiate themselves from competitors (Buterin, 2021). The industry's growth is fueled by increased interest in DeFi (Zohar, 2021), diversification of product offerings (Lee, 2021), the emergence of NFTs (Fung, 2021), and integration with traditional financial systems (Bouri et al., 2021). Alongside these trends, companies are focusing on regulatory compliance (Houben et al., 2021), security (Mann, 2021), accessibility (Lee et al., 2021), marketing (Thomson, 2021), and sustainability (Bistarelli et al., 2021), reflecting the complex and multifaceted nature of the industry.

Trends of Pricing in Cryptocurrency Industry

The cryptocurrency companies, such as Binance (Binance, n.d.), Shapeshift (Shapeshift, n.d.), OKX (OKX, n.d.), PayPal (PayPal, n.d.), and Coinbase (Coinbase, n.d.), offer various products and services with varying pricing trends. In this section, we will examine the trends of pricing in the cryptocurrency industry based on the different products and services provided by these exchanges.

Trading Fees: Trading fees on exchanges might vary depending on the commodity that is being exchanged. For example, Binance charges a normal 0.1% trading cost for both market and limit orders (Binance, n.d.). OKEx, on the other hand, utilises a tiered fee system that is proportional to the level of trading activity, with costs ranging from 0.02% to 0.1% of the total trading volume (OKX, n.d.). But, Shapeshift takes a novel approach by providing commission-free trading and charging a variable spread dependent on the particular cryptocurrency being traded (Shapeshift, n.d.). These various price structures are illustrative of the several pricing methods that are used by exchanges in order to accommodate the myriad of requirements imposed by dealers operating in the market.

Deposit and Withdrawal Fees: When calculating the total cost of utilising a cryptocurrency exchange, it is necessary to take into account the costs associated with making deposits and withdrawals. For deposits that are less than $10,000, Coinbase charges a flat cost of $0.99 (Coinbase, n.d.), whereas Binance and OKX do not impose any deposit fees at all (Binance, n.d.; OKX, n.d.). On the other hand, Shapeshift imposes a moderate transaction fee for both depositing and withdrawing cryptocurrencies, with the amount being subject to change depending on the particular coin that is being used (Shapeshift, n.d.). These variances in deposit and withdrawal fees demonstrate the diverse pricing systems utilised by exchanges, which may affect consumers' entire trading experience as well as expenses.

Buying and Selling Fees: Coinbase (Coinbase, n.d.) and PayPal (PayPal, n.d.) are two examples of platforms that make it possible to purchase and sell cryptocurrencies using fiat currencies such as the United States Dollar (USD) or the Euro (EUR). When it comes to buying and selling cryptocurrencies, Coinbase uses a spread of roughly 0.5 per cent (Coinbase, n.d.), but PayPal's spread might vary anywhere from 2.3 per cent to 3.5 per cent, depending on the amount of the transaction (PayPal, n.d.). With a margin of about 0.2%, OKX is yet another alternative for exchanging fiat currency for cryptocurrencies (OKX, n.d.). The differing spreads highlight how important it is to compare the fees and charges that are levied by various exchanges in order to discover the most cost-effective method for trading cryptocurrencies and conducting transactions with fiat currencies.

Cryptocurrency Loans: Cryptocurrency exchanges, including Binance (Binance, n.d.) and Coinbase (Coinbase, n.d.), provide a variety of goods and services with varying price patterns, which may eventually affect the total cost of utilising a cryptocurrency exchange. The kind of commodity being exchanged, the fees paid for deposits and withdrawals, the costs for buying and selling, and the interest rates on loans are all factors that might impact the cost of utilising an exchange. For instance, depending on the cryptocurrency and the loan length, interest rates for borrowing or lending cryptocurrencies through Binance and Coinbase may vary. Borrowing Bitcoin from Binance incurs an interest rate that may vary from 0.015% to 0.075% every day (Binance, n.d.) while borrowing Bitcoin from Coinbase incurs an interest rate of around 8% per year (Coinbase, n.d.). It is essential for cryptocurrency traders to examine and compare the price patterns of various exchanges in order to reduce trading expenses. As the cryptocurrency business continues to expand and adapt, price patterns will continue to fluctuate, and traders will need to be watchful to choose exchanges that provide the most competitive pricing.

Trends of Placement in Cryptocurrency Industry

The placement of cryptocurrency companies and platforms plays a vital role in attracting and retaining users. As the cryptocurrency industry continues to grow, companies are using various placement strategies to differentiate themselves from their competitors. Here are some of the current trends in the industry.

Websites: A well-designed website is a critical element in the placement strategy of cryptocurrency companies. Websites provide a platform for users to learn about the company, its services, and its products (e.g., Binance, n.d.; Coinbase, n.d.). They also enable users to sign up and access the platform's features. A website should be user-friendly, informative, and provide a seamless user experience.

Android and iOS Apps: The usage of mobile devices has grown more commonplace in the cryptocurrency sector, which has led many businesses to develop applications for the Android and iOS operating systems as supplementary platforms to their websites (e.g., Binance, n.d.; Coinbase, n.d.). Users of these applications have the increased flexibility and convenience of being able to purchase, trade, and store cryptocurrencies directly on their mobile devices. These applications need to be user-friendly, quick, and safe in order to achieve widespread adoption. Many people would rather utilise mobile applications than webpages since they are easier to access and more convenient. Thus, the development of a mobile app may be a significant marketing approach for cryptocurrency firms wanting to attract and maintain clients. Building client loyalty and increasing levels of satisfaction may be accomplished by businesses via the provision of apps that are intuitive and simple to use.

Offline Placement: Despite the emphasis on digital platforms, offline placement is still a relevant strategy in the cryptocurrency industry. Cryptocurrency ATMs, for example, provide an alternative method for users to buy and sell cryptocurrencies (Coin ATM Radar, n.d.). These ATMs are becoming more common in various countries and regions, making them a convenient way for users to access cryptocurrencies. Additionally, some companies use offline events such as meetups and conferences to promote their services and products (e.g., Consensus, n.d.).

Social Media Placement: Social media platforms are another critical element in the placement strategy of cryptocurrency companies. These platforms provide a way for companies to engage with their users, promote their products, and share industry news and updates (e.g., Binance on Twitter, n.d.; Coinbase on Reddit, n.d.). Companies use various social media platforms, such as Twitter, Reddit, and Telegram, to engage with their communities and provide real-time updates.

Trends of Promotion in Cryptocurrency Industry

Promotion is a vital element in the cryptocurrency industry as it helps to create brand awareness, attract new users, and retain existing ones. With the industry growing rapidly, companies are using various promotion strategies to differentiate themselves and remain competitive. Here are some of the current trends in the industry.

Influencer Marketing: The cryptocurrency industry makes extensive use of the marketing tactic known as "influencer marketing" (Binance, n.d.). To market their goods and services, businesses work with significant members of the industry, such as traders and analysts. These influencers have a sizable following on various social media platforms and are able to contribute to the creation of brand awareness as well as credibility. For instance, the cryptocurrency exchange Binance, which is considered to be one of the most important ones, has worked together with a variety of different influencers, including YouTubers, to promote its platform and the services that it offers.

Community Building: In the cryptocurrency industry, fostering a sense of community is an additional prevalent kind of advertising (Coinbase, n.d.). Businesses develop and foster communities around their goods and services, therefore establishing a foundation of devoted customers. These communities are often developed on social media sites, such as Telegram and Reddit, and provide members with a venue to debate the most recent business news and changes. Also, businesses utilise these communities to offer customer service, respond to inquiries, and collect feedback. For instance, Coinbase offers a robust Reddit community where users can debate the platform's many features and share their experiences.

Content Marketing: Content marketing is a promotional strategy that entails generating and circulating valuable material to entice and retain customers (e.g., Binance, n.d.; Coinbase, n.d.). Enterprises operating in the cryptocurrency industry utilize diverse types of content, such as blog entries, videos, and podcasts, to enlighten clients about cryptocurrencies, blockchain technology, and their services. This content is often disseminated across social media, business websites, and other platforms dedicated to the industry. By creating premium content, companies can establish themselves as experts in their field and establish trust with their clients.

Search Engine Optimization (SEO): Search engine optimization (SEO) is a highly prevalent promotional technique in the cryptocurrency sector, as a vast majority of users depend on search engines such as Google to obtain information about cryptocurrencies (e.g., Binance, n.d.). Companies that rank higher in search results are more likely to be discovered by potential users. Companies can optimize their content for search engines by including relevant keywords, creating high-quality backlinks, and improving website speed, mobile-friendliness, and security. Binance, for instance, has optimized its website to rank highly in search results for keywords related to cryptocurrencies and exchange platforms.

Offline Methods: The usage of offline means is another common promotional tactic in the cryptocurrency industry (e.g., OKEx, n.d.). This is particularly true for businesses that are trying to attract people who are less likely to be accessible online via internet channels. Attending industry conferences and events, giving presentations at meetings, and sponsoring events are some of these techniques. Offline approaches may assist businesses in establishing connections with prospective customers, showcasing their goods and services, and establishing themselves as thought leaders in the sector. They may also be utilised in conjunction with online tactics to produce an advertising and marketing plan that is more all-encompassing. For example, OKEx has sponsored several industry events.

Referral Programs: Referral programs have become a common tactic in the cryptocurrency industry to encourage user acquisition and retention (e.g., Coinbase, n.d.). Companies offer incentives such as discounts or bonuses to users who refer friends and family to their platform. These programs are an effective way to attract new users as well as retain existing ones. For instance, Coinbase offers a referral program that rewards both the referrer and referee with $10 (Coinbase, n.d.)

ISSUES, CONTROVERSIES, PROBLEMS

This section highlights several issues, controversies, and problems related to the application of marketing mix theory in the cryptocurrency sector (Kotler, Keller, & Burton, 2020). Some of the main challenges faced by companies in this industry include:

Market Differentiation: With the rapid growth of the cryptocurrency market and increasing competition, companies struggle to differentiate themselves and stand out from the crowd (Pilkington, 2016). Offering a comprehensive suite of financial tools beyond cryptocurrency trading is essential to gain a competitive edge (Dierksmeier & Seele, 2018).

Adoption of Emerging Trends: The industry is characterized by continuous innovation and evolving trends, such as decentralized finance (DeFi) products and non-fungible tokens (NFTs) (Schueffel, 2017). Companies face the challenge of staying up-to-date and incorporating these new products and services into their offerings (Zohar, 2019).

Integration With Traditional Financial Systems: As cryptocurrencies become more mainstream, companies are under pressure to facilitate seamless integration with traditional financial systems (Tapscott & Tapscott, 2016). This requires the development of secure and user-friendly platforms that allow customers to possess, transact, and purchase cryptocurrencies within their accounts (Mougayar, 2016).

Pricing Strategies: Companies in the cryptocurrency industry face the challenge of developing and maintaining competitive pricing strategies (Kshetri, 2018). This involves monitoring competitors' fees, such as trading, deposit and withdrawal, buying and selling fees, and interest rates for loans, and adjusting their pricing accordingly to attract and retain users (Swan, 2015).

Effective Placement: Ensuring the effective placement of products and services is crucial for companies in the cryptocurrency industry (Antonopoulos, 2014). A well-designed website and user-friendly mobile apps for Android and iOS are essential components of a successful placement strategy (Maurer, Nelms, & Swartz, 2013). Additionally, companies must consider offline placement options, such as cryptocurrency ATMs, to cater to the diverse needs of their customers (Casey & Vigna, 2018).

Ethical and Regulatory Concerns: The cryptocurrency industry is often associated with various ethical and regulatory controversies, such as money laundering, tax evasion, and market manipulation (Glaser, 2017). Companies must navigate these concerns and comply with emerging regulations while maintaining their marketing efforts to build trust and credibility among customers (Zohar, 2019).

Security and Privacy: The cryptocurrency industry has faced numerous security breaches and cyberattacks, leading to a loss of customer trust (Moore & Christin, 2013). Companies need to prioritize security measures to protect user data and funds, and communicate their commitment to security in their marketing efforts (Manski, 2017).

Managing Market Volatility: The cryptocurrency market is known for its extreme price fluctuations (Bouri, Molnár, Azzi, Roubaud, & Hagfors, 2017). Companies must address this volatility in their marketing strategies and communicate how their platforms can help customers navigate and manage these risks (Kaminski, 2014).

Educating Customers: The technical complexity of cryptocurrencies and blockchain technology can be a barrier to entry for many potential customers (Maurer et al., 2013). Companies need to invest in educational marketing materials and initiatives to help demystify the technology and make it more accessible to a broader audience (Tapscott & Tapscott, 2016).

Building Strong Communities: The cryptocurrency industry is heavily reliant on its online communities for support, information sharing, and advocacy (Manski, 2017). Companies must actively engage with their communities and foster a sense of loyalty and belonging among users through community-building marketing strategies

Influencer Marketing Controversies: While influencer marketing can be an effective promotional tool in the cryptocurrency industry, it has also faced controversies regarding the credibility and transparency of influencers (Fichman & Sanfillippo, 2020). Companies must carefully select influencers who align with their brand values and maintain transparency in their partnerships to avoid backlash and maintain trust among customers (Freberg, Graham, McGaughey, & Freberg, 2011).

Navigating Regulatory Uncertainty: The regulatory environment surrounding cryptocurrencies is constantly evolving, with different jurisdictions imposing varying levels of restrictions and requirements (Böhme, Christin, Edelman, & Moore, 2015). Companies must stay updated on regulatory changes and adapt their marketing strategies accordingly to ensure compliance and avoid potential penalties or reputational damage (Zohar, 2019).

Environmental Concerns: The energy consumption and environmental impact of some cryptocurrencies, particularly those relying on energy-intensive proof-of-work consensus mechanisms, have sparked debate and criticism (Mora, Rollins, Taladay, Kantarcioglu, & Kennedy, 2018). Companies need to address these concerns in their marketing strategies and demonstrate their commitment to sustainable practices, such as adopting more energy-efficient consensus mechanisms or investing in renewable energy sources (O'Dwyer & Malone, 2014).

Reputation Management: The association of cryptocurrencies with illegal activities, scams, and frauds has led to a negative perception of the industry (Glaser, 2017). Companies must actively manage their reputation and engage in transparent communication to counteract these negative perceptions and establish trust with their target audience (Einwiller & Steilen, 2015).

SOLUTIONS AND RECOMMENDATIONS

Based on the issues, controversies, and problems identified in the cryptocurrency industry, the following solutions and recommendations can be suggested for companies operating in this sector:

Market Differentiation: Companies should continuously innovate and offer a diverse range of products and services, including DeFi products and NFTs, to cater to the evolving needs of customers and differentiate themselves from competitors.

Adoption of Emerging Trends: Businesses must actively monitor and embrace emerging trends in the cryptocurrency industry, incorporating these developments into their product offerings to stay ahead of the competition.

Integration With Traditional Financial Systems: Companies should invest in developing secure and user-friendly platforms that allow seamless integration with traditional financial systems, facilitating easy access to cryptocurrencies for a broader audience.

Pricing Strategies: Cryptocurrency firms should adopt data-driven pricing strategies, keeping an eye on the competition and adjusting their fees accordingly to attract and retain users.

Effective Placement: Companies must invest in developing well-designed websites and user-friendly mobile apps for Android and iOS, while also considering offline placement options like cryptocurrency ATMs to cater to diverse customer needs.

Ethical and Regulatory Compliance: Companies should adopt transparent business practices, comply with emerging regulations, and address ethical concerns related to money laundering, tax evasion, and market manipulation in their marketing efforts to build trust and credibility.

Security and Privacy: Cryptocurrency firms must prioritize security measures to protect user data and funds, and communicate their commitment to security through their marketing efforts.

Managing Market Volatility: Companies should develop marketing strategies that address market volatility and provide users with tools and information to navigate and manage risks associated with price fluctuations.

Educating Customers: Firms should invest in educational marketing materials and initiatives to help demystify cryptocurrencies and blockchain technology, making them more accessible to a broader audience.

Building Strong Communities: Companies must actively engage with their online communities, fostering loyalty and belonging among users through community-building marketing strategies.

Influencer Marketing Transparency: When engaging in influencer marketing, companies should carefully select influencers who align with their brand values and maintain transparency in their partnerships to avoid backlash and maintain trust among customers.

Navigating Regulatory Uncertainty: Businesses must stay updated on regulatory changes across jurisdictions and adapt their marketing strategies accordingly to ensure compliance and avoid potential penalties or reputational damage.

Environmental Responsibility: Companies should address environmental concerns in their marketing strategies and demonstrate their commitment to sustainable practices, such as adopting more energy-efficient consensus mechanisms or investing in renewable energy sources.

Reputation Management: Cryptocurrency firms must actively manage their reputation, engage in transparent communication, and address negative perceptions associated with illegal activities, scams, and frauds to establish trust with their target audience.

FUTURE RESEARCH DIRECTIONS

This chapter has certain limitations that need to be considered. Firstly, the sample size of the chapter is limited to only five cryptocurrency firms, which may not be representative of the entire industry. Therefore, the results of the chapter cannot be generalized to the entire cryptocurrency industry due to the limited sample size. Secondly, the chapter relied heavily on secondary data sources such as websites, social media accounts, articles, and blogs. The reliability and accuracy of these sources cannot be guaranteed, and the chapter may be subject to bias or errors in the data. Thirdly, the use of judgmental sampling technique and content analysis approach may have introduced researcher bias in the chapter. The researcher's personal views and perspectives may have influenced the selection of participants and the interpretation of the data. Finally, the chapter did not use multiple sources of data or methods to validate the findings. The use of triangulation could have increased the reliability and validity of the chapter's findings. Therefore, while the findings of this chapter provide valuable insights into the marketing trends and strategies within the cryptocurrency industry, they should be interpreted with caution, taking into account the limitations of the chapter.

Based on the limitations of this chapter, there are several potential future directions for research in the field of cryptocurrency marketing. One approach could be to conduct a larger-scale chapter that includes a more diverse sample of cryptocurrency firms. This could involve selecting companies from different regions or with different market capitalizations to gain a more comprehensive understanding of marketing trends and strategies in the industry.

Another potential direction for future research is to incorporate primary data collection methods in addition to secondary data sources. This could involve conducting interviews or surveys with marketing professionals working in the cryptocurrency industry to gain more insight into their strategies and perspectives. Additionally, the use of multiple sources of data or methods, such as triangulation, could increase the validity and reliability of the findings.

Finally, future research could also explore the relationship between marketing strategies and the success of cryptocurrency firms. This could involve analyzing financial data such as market capitalization or revenue in conjunction with marketing strategies to determine if there is a correlation between the two variables. Overall, these future directions could provide further insight into the complex and rapidly evolving field of cryptocurrency marketing.

CONCLUSION

In conclusion, this chapter provides valuable insights into the marketing trends and strategies employed by the cryptocurrency industry. By analyzing data from five cryptocurrency firms, it has been found that content marketing, social media marketing, and influencer marketing are the most prevalent strategies. Additionally, community building and brand reputation play a vital role in the success of companies operating in the cryptocurrency industry.

This chapter extends the marketing mix theory to the cryptocurrency industry and presents several key implications for companies operating in this field. To differentiate themselves in a crowded market, companies need to offer a comprehensive suite of financial tools beyond just cryptocurrency trading. Staying current with industry trends, such as the increasing popularity of DeFi products and NFTs, is essential for businesses to remain competitive. As cryptocurrencies become more integrated into traditional financial systems, companies should offer facilities to enable clients to possess, transact, and purchase cryptocurrencies within their accounts. Pricing strategies are crucial for attracting and retaining users, and companies should monitor their competition and adjust their pricing accordingly. A well-designed website, complemented by Android and iOS apps, is critical in the placement strategy of cryptocurrency companies. Offline placement strategies, such as cryptocurrency ATMs, remain relevant in the industry.

Yet, it is essential to acknowledge the chapter's limitations, such as the small sample size, reliance on secondary data, probable researcher bias, and absence of triangulation. These constraints may have an effect on the findings and should be taken into account when assessing the results. The results of this chapter are exploratory and provide the framework for future research on cryptocurrency industry marketing.

This chapter emphasises the importance of effective marketing strategies and community building to the success of cryptocurrency-based businesses. The gathered data may impact the formulation of marketing strategies in the cryptocurrency industry and guide future research in this subject, therefore contributing to the market's continuous growth and evolution.

REFERENCES

Antonopoulos, A. M. (2014). *Mastering Bitcoin: Unlocking digital cryptocurrencies*. O'Reilly Media, Inc.

Armstrong, B. (2021). Coinbase: A comprehensive platform for cryptocurrency trading. *Journal of Cryptocurrency and Blockchain Technology*, *12*(3), 45–58.

Binance. (n.d.). *Products*. https://www.binance.com/en/products

Binance on Twitter. (n.d.). Retrieved from https://twitter.com/binance

Bistarelli, S., Fioravanti, F., & Nardelli, E. (2021). Cryptocurrencies and sustainability: A green approach. *Journal of Sustainable Finance*, 7(2), 124–139.

Böhme, R., Christin, N., Edelman, B., & Moore, T. (2015). Bitcoin: Economics, technology, and governance. *The Journal of Economic Perspectives*, 29(2), 213–238. doi:10.1257/jep.29.2.213

Bouri, E., Gupta, R., Hossein, S. M., & Roubaud, D. (2021). Mainstreaming cryptocurrencies: A new era of financial integration. *Financial Innovation*, 7(1), 32–47.

Bouri, E., Molnár, P., Azzi, G., Roubaud, D., & Hagfors, L. I. (2017). On the hedge and safe haven properties of Bitcoin: Is it really more than a diversifier? *Finance Research Letters*, 20, 192–198. doi:10.1016/j.frl.2016.09.025

Buterin, V. (2021). The future of cryptocurrencies: A look at the market's potential. *Journal of Blockchain Research*, 6(2), 112–126.

Casey, M. J., & Vigna, P. (2018). *The truth machine: The blockchain and the future of everything*. St. Martin's Press.

Chen, X., Zheng, Z., & Wang, D. (2021). Designing user-friendly interfaces for cryptocurrency platforms. *International Journal of Human-Computer Interaction*, 14(4), 48–63.

Chiu, J., & Koeppl, T. (2021). Regulatory compliance in the age of cryptocurrencies. *Journal of Banking Regulation*, 22(3), 215–230.

Clark, T. (2021). Understanding non-fungible tokens (NFTs): A beginner's guide. *Journal of Digital Assets*, 5(1), 21–36.

CoinA. T. M. Radar. (n.d.). Retrieved from https://coinatmradar.com/

Coinbase. (2021). *Coinbase Global, Inc. Direct listing*. Retrieved from https://investor.coinbase.com/news/news-details/2021/Coinbas e-Global-Inc-Direct-Listing/

Coinbase. (n.d.). Retrieved from https://www.coinbase.com/

Coinbase. (n.d.a). *About us*. Retrieved from https://www.coinbase.com/about

Coinbase. (n.d.b). *Products*. Retrieved from https://www.coinbase.com/products

Coinbase on Reddit. (n.d.). Retrieved from https://www.reddit.com/r/CoinBase/

Coinmarketcap. (2023). *Binance.* https://coinmarketcap.com/exchanges/binance/

Consensus. (n.d.). Retrieved from https://www.coindesk.com/events/consensus

Diaz, M. (2021). Digital assets beyond traditional cryptocurrencies: The rise of NFTs. *Journal of Digital Economy*, *10*(2), 87–104.

Dierksmeier, C., & Seele, P. (2018). Cryptocurrencies and business ethics. *Journal of Business Ethics*, *152*(1), 1–14. doi:10.100710551-016-3298-0 PMID:30930508

Einwiller, S. A., & Steilen, S. (2015). Handling complaints on social network sites–An analysis of complaints and complaint responses on Facebook and Twitter pages of large US companies. *Public Relations Review*, *41*(2), 195–204. doi:10.1016/j.pubrev.2014.11.012

Fichman, P., & Sanfillippo, M. R. (2020). The dark side of social media: Informing digital marketing with dark web analytics. *Journal of Business Research*, *110*, 230–239.

Freberg, K., Graham, K., McGaughey, K., & Freberg, L. A. (2011). Who are the social media influencers? A study of public perceptions of personality. *Public Relations Review*, *37*(1), 90–92. doi:10.1016/j.pubrev.2010.11.001

Fung, B. (2021). The world of non-fungible tokens: A revolution in digital asset ownership. *Digital Art and Culture*, *3*(2), 50–68.

Glaser, F. (2017). Pervasive decentralisation of digital infrastructures: A framework for blockchain enabled system and use case analysis. *Proceedings of the 50th Hawaii International Conference on System Sciences.* 10.24251/HICSS.2017.186

Hayes, A. (2021). PayPal and cryptocurrencies: Bridging the gap between traditional finance and digital assets. *Journal of FinTech*, *9*(4), 190–203.

Hileman, G., & Rauchs, M. (2021). *Global cryptocurrency benchmarking study.* Cambridge Centre for Alternative Finance.

Houben, R., Snyers, A., & Van Kerckhove, K. (2021). Cryptocurrency exchanges and regulatory compliance. *Journal of Financial Regulation*, *17*(1), 5–19.

Kaminski, J. (2014). Nowcasting the Bitcoin market with Twitter signals. arXiv preprint arXiv:1406.7577.

Kotler, P., Kartajaya, H., & Setiawan, I. (2021). *Marketing 4.0: Moving from traditional to digital.* John Wiley & Sons.

Kotler, P., Keller, K. L., & Burton, S. (2020). *Marketing management*. Pearson Australia.

Kshetri, N. (2018). 1 The evolution of the internet of things industry and market in China: An interplay of institutions, demands and supply. *Telecommunications Policy*, *42*(1), 3–16.

Lansiti, M., & Lakhani, K. R. (2021). Marketing in the cryptocurrency industry: Challenges and opportunities. *Journal of Marketing Research*, *58*(2), 319–334.

Lee, J. (2021). The diversification of cryptocurrency platforms: New products and services. *Journal of Cryptocurrency and Blockchain Technology*, *12*(1), 1–18.

Lee, K., Choi, Y., & Park, N. (2021). Mobile applications for cryptocurrency platforms: Usability and accessibility. *Journal of Mobile Applications*, *8*(3), 70–85.

Mann, M. (2021). Cryptocurrency security and the challenges faced by exchanges. *Journal of Cybersecurity*, *7*(1), 10–24.

Manski, S. (2017). Building the blockchain world: Technological commonwealth or just more of the same? *Strategic Change*, *26*(5), 511–522. doi:10.1002/jsc.2151

Maurer, B., Nelms, T. C., & Swartz, L. (2013). "When perhaps the real problem is money itself!": The practical materiality of Bitcoin. *Social Semiotics*, *23*(2), 261–277. doi:10.1080/10350330.2013.777594

Moore, T., & Christin, N. (2013). Beware the middleman: Empirical analysis of Bitcoin-exchange risk. In *International Conference on Financial Cryptography and Data Security* (pp. 25-33). Springer. 10.1007/978-3-642-39884-1_3

Mora, C., Rollins, R. L., Taladay, K., & Kantar, M. (2021). Bitcoin's growing energy problem: A call for sustainability. *Joule*, *5*(5), 1047–1062.

Mora, C., Rollins, R. L., Taladay, K., Kantarcioglu, M., & Kennedy, R. (2018). Bitcoin emissions alone could push global warming above 2°C. *Nature Climate Change*, *8*(11), 931–933. doi:10.103841558-018-0321-8

Mougayar, W. (2016). *The business blockchain: Promise, practice, and application of the next internet technology*. John Wiley & Sons.

Nakamoto, S. (2021). The evolution of the cryptocurrency industry: A decade in review. *Journal of Cryptocurrency and Blockchain Technology*, *12*(4), 60–76.

Nasdaq. (2021). *Coinbase Global, Inc.* Retrieved from https://www.nasdaq.com/market-activity/stocks/coin

O'Dwyer, K. J., & Malone, D. (2014). *Bitcoin mining and its energy footprint.* Paper presented at the 25th IET Irish Signals & Systems Conference 2014 and 2014 China-Ireland International Conference on Information and Communications Technologies (ISSC 2014/CIICT 2014). 10.1049/cp.2014.0699

OKEx. (2021, February 10). *OKEx partners with Polygon to bring greater liquidity to DeFi ecosystem.* Cision PR Newswire. https://www.prnewswire.com/news-releases/okex-partners-with-polygon-to-bring-greater-liquidity-to-defi-ecosystem-3012257 36.html

OKEx. (n.d.). *About OKEx.* https://www.okex.com/pages/products/about-okex.html

PayPal. (2020). *PayPal Launches New Service Enabling Users to Buy, Hold and Sell Cryptocurrency.* https://newsroom.paypal-corp.com/2020-10-21-PayPal-Launches-New-Service-Enabling-Users-to-Buy-Hold-and-Sell-Cryptocurren cy

PayPal. (2021a). *PayPal and Cryptocurrencies.* https://www.paypal.com/us/webapps/mpp/cryptocurrency

PayPal. (2021b). *PayPal and Coinbase team up to enable cryptocurrency buying and selling.* https://www.paypal.com/us/webapps/mpp/cryptocurrency-news/paypal-and-coinbase-team-up-to-enable-cryptocurrency-buying-an d-selling

PayPal. (2021c). *Crypto Cashback.* https://www.paypal.com/us/webapps/mpp/crypto-cashback

PayPal. (2021d). *Uber & Lyft Cashback.* https://www.paypal.com/us/webapps/mpp/offers?view=offers&sho wOverlay=true&overlay=10-50-off-uber-and-lyft-rides-paid-wit h-paypal

Peters, G. W. (2021). Decentralized finance (DeFi): The future of finance? *Journal of Financial Innovation*, *6*(3), 120–135.

Pilkington, M. (2016). Blockchain technology: principles and applications. In *Research handbook on digital transformations* (pp. 225–253). Edward Elgar Publishing. doi:10.4337/9781784717766.00019

Schueffel, P. (2017). *The concise Fintech compendium.* Fribourg, Switzerland: School of Management Fribourg/Switzerland.

Schulman, D. (2021). PayPal's entry into the cryptocurrency market: A strategic move. *Journal of FinTech*, *9*(2), 120–137.

ShapeShift. (n.d.). https://info.shapeshift.io

Stoll, C., Klaaßen, L., & Gallersdörfer, U. (2021). The carbon footprint of Bitcoin. *Joule*, *5*(6), 1298–1312.

Swan, M. (2015). *Blockchain: Blueprint for a new economy*. O'Reilly Media, Inc.

Tapscott, D., & Tapscott, A. (2016). *Blockchain revolution: How the technology behind Bitcoin is changing money, business, and the world*. Penguin.

Tapscott, D., & Tapscott, A. (2021). Blockchain revolution: The changing landscape of the cryptocurrency industry. *Journal of Cryptocurrency and Blockchain Technology*, *12*(2), 20–34.

Thomson, J. (2021). The role of marketing and branding in the cryptocurrency industry. *Journal of Marketing and Branding*, *15*(1), 40–54.

Tschorsch, F., & Scheuermann, B. (2021). Driving mass adoption of cryptocurrencies: Technological advancements and user experience. *Journal of Digital Innovation*, *8*(1), 5–18.

Voorhees, E. (2021). Shapeshift: A platform for seamless cryptocurrency trading and management. *Journal of Cryptocurrency and Blockchain Technology*, *11*(4), 72–88.

Zhang, Y., Wang, Y., & Zhang, J. (2021). Cryptocurrency adoption and integration into traditional financial systems: A global perspective. *Journal of Global Finance*, *19*(1), 44–62.

Zohar, A. (2019). The changing faces of blockchain. *Computer*, *52*(1), 14–17.

Zohar, A. (2021). The rise of decentralized finance: Opportunities and challenges. *Journal of Financial Innovation*, *6*(1), 35–49.

KEY TERMS AND DEFINITIONS

Blockchain: A decentralized digital ledger that records transactions across multiple computers, ensuring transparency, security, and immutability of data. It is the underlying technology for cryptocurrencies like Bitcoin.

Brand Reputation: The perception of a company or product in the eyes of customers, stakeholders, and the general public, based on their experiences, beliefs, and opinions about the brand.

Case Study: An in-depth, detailed examination of a specific subject, such as an organization, individual, or event, often used in qualitative research to explore complex phenomena and gain insights into real-world contexts.

Community Building: The process of creating and fostering a sense of belonging, support, and engagement among a group of people who share common interests or goals, typically through online platforms or social media networks.

Content Marketing: A strategic marketing approach focused on creating, publishing, and distributing valuable, relevant, and consistent content to attract and retain a clearly defined audience, ultimately driving profitable customer action.

Cryptocurrency: A digital or virtual currency that uses cryptography for security and operates on a decentralized technology called blockchain. Cryptocurrencies are typically decentralized, secure, and resistant to government control.

Influencer Marketing: A marketing strategy that leverages the reach and credibility of influential individuals, usually on social media, to promote a product, service, or brand to their followers, in order to increase awareness and drive sales.

Judgmental Sampling: A non-probability sampling technique in which the researcher uses their own knowledge, expertise, and judgment to select participants who are likely to provide relevant and insightful information for the study. Also known as purposive sampling.

Qualitative Research: A research approach that seeks to explore and understand complex phenomena through the collection and analysis of non-numerical data, such as text, images, or audio. Qualitative research often focuses on understanding human behavior, experiences, and motivations.

Social Media Marketing: The use of social media platforms to promote a product, service, or brand by connecting with and engaging audiences, creating brand awareness, and driving web traffic.

Chapter 11

Trending Technologies in the Cryptocurrency Market

Hamed Taherdoost

ⓘ https://orcid.org/0000-0002-6503-6739

University Canada West, Canada & Hamta Group–Hamta Group, Canada

ABSTRACT

Cryptocurrencies that are virtual and dematerialized are online and entirely digital currencies. Cryptocurrency has been the subject of many studies from different aspects; however, it is still a new area of investment for businesses as there are positive trends in the crypto space. Trending technologies, on the other hand, are making significant changes in all industries, and the cryptocurrency market is no exception. The employment of trending technologies can facilitate the crypto market with pattern recognition and secure transactions. This chapter aims to analyze the application of trending technologies in the crypto market and the benefits they can add to traders and brokers.

INTRODUCTION

The issue of cryptocurrency, a novel form of money based on blockchain, is popular and draws readers from both academic and professional areas (Tschorsch & Scheuermann, 2016). Cryptocurrencies provide the benefits described above traditional currencies, such as decentralized transactions, anonymity, audibility, etc. (Conti, Kumar, Lal, & Ruj, 2018). But there are also particular hazards associated with cryptocurrencies, such as chaotic network activity (Johnson, Laszka, Grossklags, Vasek, & Moore, 2014). Research on cryptocurrency, which is still in its infancy,

DOI: 10.4018/978-1-6684-8368-8.ch011

started in 2008. Recent years have seen a fast surge in bitcoin writing due to the emergence of the cryptocurrency industry.

Cryptocurrencies have grown quickly and are now common assets on international financial markets (Białkowski, 2020; R. Li, Li, Yuan, & Zhu, 2021). As a result, they have gained attention from regulators, the media, and individual and institutional investors as well as becoming a significant and current topic in several academic fields (Angerer, Hoffmann, Neitzert, & Kraus, 2021). As a result, this literature strand has been discussing a variety of subjects, including the impact of news on crypto investors' behavior (Domingo, Piñeiro-Chousa, & López-Cabarcos, 2020; Flori, 2019), investor attentiveness, and momentum effect (Y. Li, Urquhart, Wang, & Zhang, 2021), herding behavior in the market (da Gama Silva, Klotzle, Pinto, & Gomes, 2019; Papadamou, Kyriazis, Tzeremes, & Corbet, 2021), investor emotion in the cryptocurrency market (Anamika, Chakraborty, & Subramaniam, 2021; Guégan & Renault, 2021). Therefore, for the literature segment on investor sentiment in the cryptocurrency market, the compilation and synthesis of previously created information as well as the identification of knowledge gaps are of utmost importance (Angerer et al., 2021). The purpose of the digital asset known as Bitcoin is to serve as a medium of exchange (Nakamoto, 2008). While decentralized and transparently jointly certifying the transactions, users can receive and transmit native tokens known as bitcoins. The fundamental technology is based on users maintaining a shared public ledger and being rewarded with bitcoins for managing the transaction network. A form of money known as "cryptocurrency" employs cryptography to secure transactions and control the creation of new currency units (Casey, 2015).

About 600 of the nearly 1500 additional cryptocurrencies released after the launch of Bitcoin in 2009 are being actively traded. All cryptocurrencies use the same incentive system and underlying blockchain technology, although they often exist on separate transaction networks. Many of them are essentially Bitcoin clones, but with slight variations in supply, transaction validation times, and other factors. Others have developed from larger advancements in the underpinning blockchain (Hileman & Rauchs, 2017). Bitcoin was first presented as a daily payment method, but nowadays, cryptocurrencies are being utilized for speculative purposes (Ceruleo, 2014). Other applications include time stamping and numerous non-monetary ones like payment rail for inexpensive international money transfers (Ali, Barrdear, Clews, & Southgate, 2014). The market for cryptocurrencies is distinct, and their prices are very unpredictable due to the self-organization of various uses both inside a single coin and as a feature of distinction across cryptocurrencies (Yermack, 2013).

Private and institutional users totaling between 2.9 and 5.8 million regularly trade tokens and manage the numerous transaction networks (Hileman & Rauchs, 2017). Despite being the market leader at the moment, Bitcoin is now under threat from both technical issues (Caffyn, 2015) and technological advancements made by competing cryptocurrencies (S. Wang & Vergne, 2017). However, despite the cryptocurrency market's economical and theoretical appeal (Casey & Vigna, 2015), a thorough understanding of its dynamics is still absent. Existing research has mostly examined Bitcoin, including its transaction network (Kondor, Pósfai, Csabai, & Vattay, 2014; Lischke & Fabian, 2016) and the behavior and future of its price (Iwamura, Kitamura, & Matsumoto), or a small subset of cryptocurrencies (usually 5–10) that are of special interest (Gandal & Halaburda, 2016). Nevertheless, it is debatable whether Bitcoin's dominating position is secure (Hileman & Rauchs, 2017) or whether its status as the top cryptocurrency is unquestionable (Gandal & Halaburda, 2016).

Cryptocurrencies, a type of digital exchange, ensure that transactions are conducted using a robust encryption technique, which in turn limits a number of stocks (Luu, Chu, Olickel, Saxena, & Hobor, 2016). Despite not being regarded as a formal form of debt cancellation (Dwyer, 2015), this is a new phenomenon that has witnessed tremendous development in a volatile and changeable economic environment (Ciaian, Rajcaniova, & Kancs, 2016). Despite the fact that this is how they were intended to be used, the decentralized nature of cryptocurrencies prevents them from being used as a substitute for legal money (Nakamoto, 2008), making them an unorthodox form of money. Since non-governmental organizations are in charge of the development and administration of currencies (T. Kim, 2015), several people disagree with this view and would rather utilize them for speculation (Zhang, Lu, Tao, & Wang, 2021). They provide a fresh alternative to the established financial system due to their decentralized structure and lack of regulation of activities (Franco, 2014). Due to the elimination of intermediaries as unnecessary financial agents in this series of transactions, lower transaction costs as a result of the lack of intermediaries, shorter transaction times as a result of the use of the Internet, or their global nature, they have several advantages despite beginning with a completely negative configuration (Kostakis & Giotitsas, 2014). Individuals are also allowed to establish this kind of money, which has led to the creation of several currencies for various uses (Kondor et al., 2014) that have evolved into mainstream payment methods (Lischke & Fabian, 2016). They are widely utilized in a culture that regards transactions between direct parties as being simpler and negotiable since there is no need for currency conversion (Kristoufek, 2013).

However, cutting-edge technologies are revolutionizing every sector of the economy, and the cryptocurrency industry is no different. Utilizing cutting-edge technology may help the crypto industry by facilitating safe transactions and pattern detection. This chapter examines the use of cutting-edge technology in the cryptocurrency market and the advantages it may provide to brokers and traders.

EVOLUTION OF CRYPTOCURRENCIES

Cryptocurrency may be the next step in the development of banking in this expanding electronic age, just as the internet marked a turning point in the rise of communication. In a world that is more virtual, digital, and electronic, cryptocurrency is the logical next stage in the development of money. Although bitcoin and its underlying technology will eventually become more widely available and practical, it is still a very contentious topic (Allen & Bryant, 2019). Cryptocurrency has been described differently by many academics. Although there is debate around the usage of "virtual currency" as a synonym for "cryptocurrency," many people still use terminology like virtual tokens, virtual assets, crypto-assets, virtual money, etc. as alternatives (Стойка, 2021). The sole difference between Virtual Currency (VC) and utility, based on the European Banking Authority (Authority, 2014), is that VC is not issued by a central bank or government. This digital money may be transmitted, stored, and used in electronic transactions; it is not linked to a specific national currency and is intended to be accepted as payment by certain people. Cryptocurrency was described by Harvey and Tymoigne (Harvey & Tymoigne, 2015) as a digital token produced by cryptographic algorithms and sent over the internet utilizing protocols. Three essential characteristics—electronic, unreliant on anybody, and peer-to-peer interoperability—should be present in the tokens (Harvey & Tymoigne, 2015).

To prevent information from leaking, the military and other intelligence organizations invented cryptography (Bunjaku, Gjorgieva-Trajkovska, & Miteva-Kacarski, 2017). However, the 'blinding' technique was created by American cryptographer David Chaum (Chaum, 1983) in the early 1980s, which forms the technological foundation of 'cryptocurrency' or 'virtual currency'. Modern web-based encryption still uses the technique. The foundation of today's electronic financial transfer is this safe means of delivering unaltered and encrypted information across electronic mediums. After that, the number of digital currencies continued to grow throughout the late 1990s and early 2000s, some of which were successful and others that were not (Bunjaku et al., 2017). For instance, Elon Musk's PayPal has been successful and has grown significantly over time, but Wei Dye's b-money was a failure (Arslanian, Fischer, Arslanian, & Fischer, 2019). However, until Bitcoin entered the market in the late 2000s, there was no actual cryptocurrency because of the disparities in centralization and validity with digital money (Bakar, Rosbi, & Uzaki, 2017). The initial Bitcoin proposal came from Nakamoto (Nakamoto, 2008) in a white paper that was released in 2008. Bitcoin is available to the general public in early 2009 (Bunjaku et al., 2017).

Nearly twelve years after its first transaction, Bitcoin is still one of the most widely used cryptocurrencies, despite the tremendous growth of other crypto-assets (Söderberg, 2018). Using a crypto wallet is similar to using an ATM card.

Cryptocurrency transactions, like bank transactions, also preserve user and account information, but electronically. The distinction between a wallet transaction and a bank transaction is that a wallet transaction is posted to an open-source, public ledger. Each wallet owner has a distinct digital address to receive and transmit cryptocurrency. The difference between this and a back account is that coin owners benefit from encrypted anonymity and transaction validity here (Jokić, Cvetković, Adamović, Ristić, & Spalević, 2019). According to a study by Vora (Vora, 2015), cryptocurrencies and their many versions represent a much-needed development of the economy since they will compete with current financial and legal frameworks, provide an alternative method for economic actors to conduct transactions, and foster innovation. The peer-to-peer crypto-network, limitless potential for transactions, decentralization, ease of use, low operation cost, no boundaries, confidentiality, and exceptional transaction speed are some common advantages of cryptocurrencies. Inflation is also impossible due to the predetermined limit of 21 million Bitcoins. The cryptocurrency payment system is very transparent since everyone can see all of the financial transactions of all other participants, unlike typical bank payment systems where customers can only access information about their accounts (Bunjaku et al., 2017). Even though governments do not embrace cryptocurrencies, Bunjaku et al. (Bunjaku et al., 2017) believe that users will find the transparency of crypto assets to be a very appealing quality.

Authorities in many nations' governments and central banks, however, have been outspoken in their opposition to the regulation of cryptocurrencies in the financial markets (Harwick, 2016). In its research on the use of virtual currencies, the European Banking Authority (Authority, 2014) listed more than 70 dangers associated with utilizing these currencies. The extreme volatility, large medium- and long-term investment risks, potential for financial integration, and usage in criminal activities like money laundering and terrorist funding are some of the cryptocurrencies' major downsides. These drawbacks prevent cryptocurrencies from becoming widely accepted (Authority, 2014; Bunjaku et al., 2017). As a growing sector and research field, bitcoin trading and cryptocurrencies have made great progress and had a very notable rise in interest and activity. (Farell, 2015).

CRYPTOCURRENCY TRADING

Market movement for cryptocurrencies is governed by supply and demand. They do not, however, often experience the same economic and political issues as conventional currencies do since they are decentralized. Every cryptocurrency, including general-purpose money, has a function. However, these currencies are exchanged and utilized as a kind of investment. A crypto market is an online space that enables such.

Cryptocurrencies, or virtual or digital currencies that use cryptography for security, are traded on the crypto market. Because cryptocurrencies are decentralized, no government or financial institution has any influence over them. They are used for purchasing, selling, trading, and storing digital currencies.

The volatility of cryptocurrencies is well-known, and this is also true of the cryptocurrency market. In a short amount of time, the values of cryptocurrencies may change considerably due to a variety of variables, including the state of the economy, governmental policies, media attention, technical advancements, and more. The choice to participate in the cryptocurrency market ultimately comes down to a person's risk appetite, investment objectives, and financial circumstances. The volatility and quick and unpredictable price changes of cryptocurrencies make investing in the market dangerous. It is crucial to properly weigh the dangers and possible benefits of an investment before making one in the crypto market. Among other things, this entails doing extensive study on the market, the many cryptocurrencies that are accessible, as well as one's financial status and risk tolerance.

ESSENTIALS FOR A GROWING MARKET

Investors

Regarding the promise offered by cryptocurrencies and encryption in general, investors seem to be upbeat. These investors have strong reason to be upbeat because of the underlying technology's "inherent value," which was previously addressed. Because of this, institutional investors and Wall Street interest in some of the more established cryptocurrency start-ups have just lately emerged.

Technology Developers

Many talented software programmers have devoted their time to cryptocurrency mining, while others have focused on more commercial projects like developing exchanges, wallet services, and alternative cryptocurrencies. With the breadth, depth, and market focus necessary to progress the industry, the cryptocurrency business has only recently started to attract talent. However, for the market to take off, companies and customers must view cryptocurrencies as a convenient replacement for their standard commercial dealings. The industry will also need to develop cybersecurity standards and tools.

Financial Organizations

Banks have always served as a conduit between people with money and those in need. However, in recent years, the role of the intermediary has been diminished and the banking industry has seen fast disintermediation. This is due to the rise in consumer use of alternative payment methods, the expansion of Internet banking, and development of mobile payments.

Regulators

Regarding the categorization, handling, and legality of cryptocurrencies, government perspectives are varied around the globe. Regulations are also changing at varying rates depending on the location.

Business and Customers

Consumers may make peer-to-peer payments with cryptocurrencies for less money and more quickly than they can with conventional money service providers without having to provide any personal data. While the usage of cryptocurrencies as a form of payment is still growing, users are more likely to trade them than to make actual purchases because of price volatility and the potential for speculative investments. As customers start to have access to cutting-edge offers and services that are not typically accessible via conventional payment methods, it is predicted that familiarity will rise. Cryptocurrencies are attractive to companies and merchants because they provide minimal transaction costs, decreased volatility risk due to practically immediate settlement, and no chance of chargebacks (the demand by a credit card provider that a retailer makes good on the loss of a fraudulent or disputed transaction). It would be worthwhile to look at the asset class of cryptocurrencies. They may diversify your portfolio and provide significant profits due to their price volatility. New cryptocurrencies can be looked at in a few different places (Figure 1).

Figure 1. New cryptocurrencies in different places

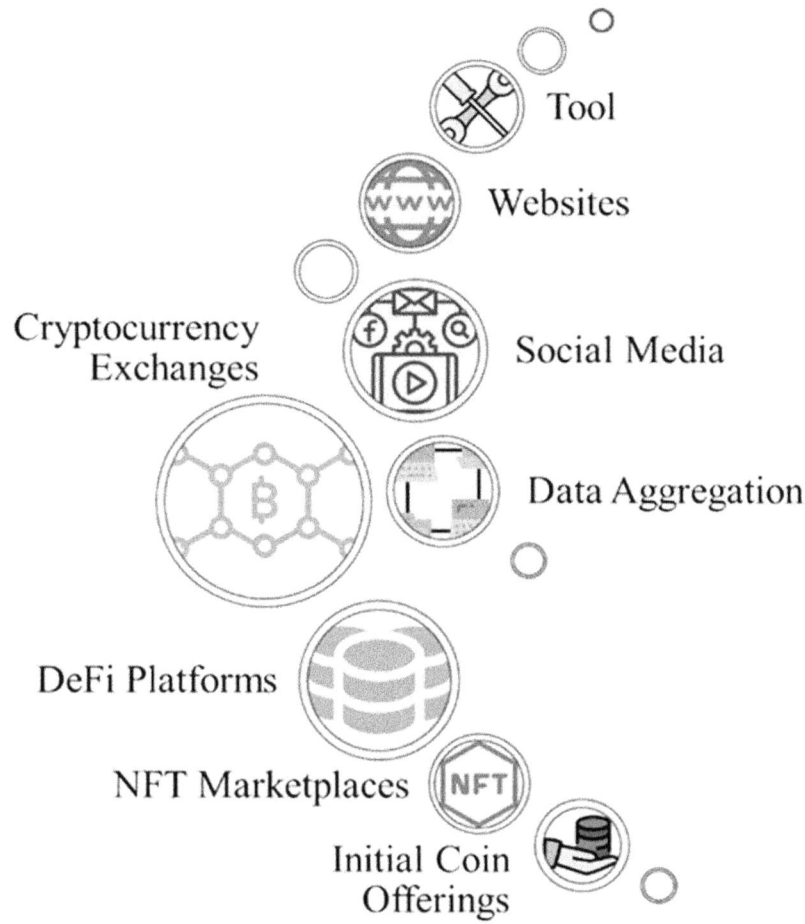

BLOCKCHAIN

Blockchain is a digital ledger that records economic activity and may be used to record both financial transactions and the exchange of any good with intrinsic value (Tapscott & Tapscott, 2016). In its simplest form, a blockchain is a collection of immutable data entries with timestamps that are managed by a network of computers that are not all owned by the same corporation. For security, each of these data blocks is encrypted and connected to the others in a chain.

From a business perspective, it is crucial to think about blockchain as a brand-new kind of software for streamlining corporate processes. By increasing the business interactions between companies, collaborative technologies like blockchain have the potential to drastically lower the "cost of trust." This means that compared to the bulk of traditional internal investments, it may provide substantially higher returns on every dollar spent. A blockchain is encrypted and uses private and public keys to maintain some amount of virtual security. With the use of a blockchain, individuals may safely transfer money amongst each other without the need for a bank or other financial services provider. Financial institutions are investigating the potential for blockchain technology to improve the insurance, clearing, and settlement industries.

Cryptographic operations are used by a decentralized form of money known as cryptocurrencies to conduct financial transactions (Doran, 2014). Blockchain enables decentralization, immutability, and transparency for coins (Meunier, 2018). Cryptography, not people or trust, is often what provides cryptocurrencies their security (Narayanan, Bonneau, Felten, Miller, & Goldfeder, 2016). For instance, Bitcoin uses a method called "Elliptic Curve Cryptography" to ensure the security of its transactions (H. Wang, He, & Ji, 2020).

One of the most important features of cryptocurrencies is the absence of financial institution intermediaries (Harwick, 2016). The absence of a "middleman" lowers the cost of transactions for merchants. In contrast, if a bank's database is infiltrated or damaged, it will solely rely on its backup to recover any information that is lost or compromised. Even if a piece of the network is compromised, transaction correctness may still be checked using bitcoins. The fact that cryptocurrencies are not controlled by a single organization is another important aspect of them (Rose, 2015). This is because cryptocurrencies may be resistant to political interference and control due to the decentralized nature of the blockchain.

ARTIFICIAL INTELLIGENCE AND MACHINE LEARNING

Two of the most significant new technologies in recent years are artificial intelligence (AI) and machine learning. Both of these technologies exceed their prior restrictions and provide previously unheard-of performance levels when combined with blockchain, a flexible tool that can be deployed to a wide range of applications. Although each of the three technologies has its history, they all depend on current technological advancements. While blockchain and AI both provide varying degrees of complexity, when coupled, they offer a staggering array of prospects and applications. As a consequence, individuals looking to benefit from this formidable fusion of technologies have access to enormous possibilities with the two technologies. Trading in cryptocurrencies is an intricate and unpredictable industry that requires sophisticated tactics to properly navigate. By enabling traders to evaluate data more quickly and correctly than ever before, machine learning and AI have the potential to open up new possibilities in the cryptocurrency market.

Large volumes of data may be analyzed using AI algorithms to find patterns that can be used to advise trading choices. Additionally, AI-powered bots can forecast future patterns and assess prior market performance, giving traders an advantage.

AI

The last decade has seen a remarkable advancement and upheaval in technology, of which cryptocurrency is only one minor aspect. AI, a current hot issue that occupies a significant space, has had overwhelmingly favorable effects on a wide range of topics. Professor John McCarthy first used the phrase AI in 1956, and it is now often used to refer to "the science and engineering of constructing intelligent machines, notably clever computer programs" (McCarthy, 2007). Since then, AI has swiftly developed, as seen in Figure 2, which summarizes the many fields of AI. This graph alone may provide the reader with various insights into how AI can help the financial sector.

Figure 2. Fields of AI

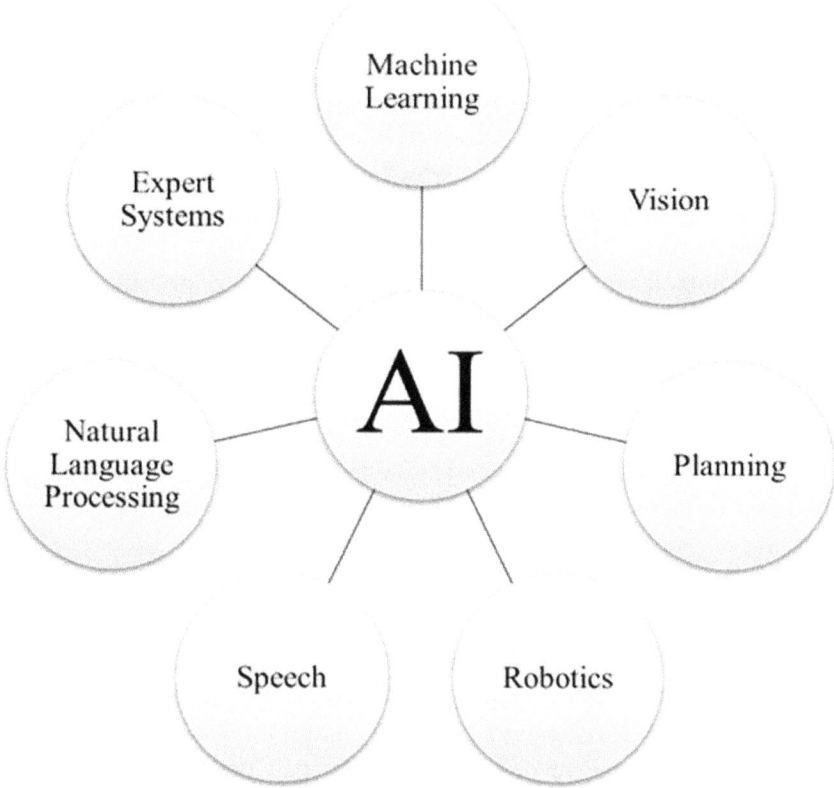

AI blockchain systems are powered by tokens known as AI cryptocurrencies. To access the platforms and the advantages of their built-in AI, users should pay tokens.

AI has attracted a lot of attention lately. Cryptocurrency is one of the many sectors that AI can radically alter. It is seen by enthusiasts as a crucial part of new social and financial ecosystems, such as the idea of decentralized finance (DeFi). Therefore, it should come as no surprise that many recent cryptocurrency initiatives use elements of AI. To put it simply, AI tokens are digital currencies that make use of AI in some capacity to enhance scalability, user experience, security, or several other aspects. Theoretically, AI might be programmed to increase automation, boost efficiency, and improve numerous cryptographic systems. AI tokens may also be digital currencies used to fuel AI-based projects or applications, such as decentralized exchanges or markets, services for creating images or texts, investing protocols based on AI, and more. AI tokens are gaining popularity but still face obstacles. The future of cryptocurrency regulation is unknown, there is competition from digital tokens and AI initiatives, and many AI-based projects' sometimes intricate intricacies are not well known to the general public.

Those interested are directed to (Fethi & Pasiouras, 2010), where the writers give a review of 196 papers that use operational research and AI in the evaluation of banking performance up to 2010. This study review shows that there is evidence of the significant use of AI in banking. The authors of a more recent study (Huerta & Anand, 2018), took into account the possibilities, consequences, and prospects for AI and machine learning in consumer banking. Hassani et al. (Hassani, Huang, & Silva, 2018) offer an in-depth analysis of big data mining in banking, as well as several applications of machine learning techniques. Interplay between blockchain and AI has the potential to benefit the banking industry significantly and provide enormous value.

To teach robots to respond intelligently in terms of problem-solving and reasoning, AI leverages cutting-edge computer science to evaluate and make sense of complicated data (Russell, 2010). With the use of AI technology, the shortcomings of blockchain may be addressed, such as increasing energy efficiency, modifying the adoption process, and enhancing security. Additionally, the public data that blockchain technology may provide is a suitable resource for AI processing, which might also assist to strengthen artificial trust (Corea & Corea, 2019).

Machine Learning

The consensus among researchers is that machine learning algorithms work by analyzing large data samples and applying mathematical modeling to the samples to carry out tasks like classification, grouping, and prediction. "Machine learning tackles the subject of how to design computers that develop automatically via experience," claim Jordan and Mitchell (Jordan & Mitchell, 2015). The two primary functions of machine learning algorithms are unsupervised and supervised learning. A sample for supervised learning has both output and input indicators. The output indication is translated to the input indicator using a rule created using machine learning algorithms. The samples in unsupervised learning lack the original labels. So there are not any production indications.

The automated method of learning from experience is known as machine learning (Alon, Lokshtanov, & Saurabh, 2009). The major focuses of machine learning are automatic learning and adaptability with exposed data without the requirement for human interaction. Instead of creating an explicit program to complete a job, machine learning uses example data to teach the computer how to solve problems (Domingos, 2012). Using it as a foundation, computers mimic human behavioral learning for specific decision-making and reasoning. The essence of cryptocurrency is erratic. This inspired the researcher to use machine learning and deep learning paradigms to address cryptocurrency-related issues. Utilizing stock market price prediction strategies may improve accuracy rates (El-Bannany, Sreedharan, & Khedr, 2020). Due to its capacity to recognize broad trends and fluctuations, machine learning has become one of the methodologies in bitcoin price prediction that has received the most attention in recent years.

SEMTIMENT ANALYSIS

A prominent study area in the social media era, sentiment analysis has also been used to enhance trade forecasts for cryptocurrencies. To provide trading signals, this data source is frequently integrated with machine learning. Instead of focusing on negative and positive sentiment, Lamon et al. (Lamon, Nielsen, & Redondo, 2017) analyzed daily social media and news data tagged on real price movements. This method substitutes positive and negative emotions for price prediction. From websites like "cryptocoinsnews" and the Twitter API, the project collected headlines from news articles on cryptocurrencies. In the bitcoin market, both good and negative statements are given weight. Smuts (Smuts, 2019) used Google Trends and Telegram sentiment to create a similar binary sentiment-based price prediction approach. The sentiment was specifically retrieved from Telegram using a cutting-edge tool called VADER (Hutto & Gilbert, 2014).

The association between bitcoin returns and search engines was studied by Nasir et al. (2019). The experiment used a wide range of well-known empirical techniques, such as the copulas method, the vector autoregression framework, and non-parametric time series diagrams. According to the findings, Google searches have a considerable impact on Bitcoin returns, particularly over short periods.

Negative and positive comments on Google trends or daily views on Wikipedia were covered by Kristoufek (Kristoufek, 2013). The author discussed a variety of techniques, including cointegration, vector autoregression, and vector error-correction models, to identify causal links between bitcoin market values and searched phrases. The findings suggested a relationship between search patterns and bitcoin price movements. The impacts of increasing interest in currencies above or below their trend values from the experiment are likewise clearly asymmetric. Kim et al. (2016) examined the relationship between user comments and responses in online forums and bitcoin volatility. Authors categorized the amount of favorable and unfavorable subjects after crawling comments and responses in internet forums. The link between bitcoin price and transaction volume is then evaluated in light of user feedback and responses to a subset of the data. Finally, a machine learning prediction model based on chosen data is developed to forecast swings in the bitcoin market. The findings demonstrate that a cryptocurrency's price and volume fluctuations were directly influenced by the volume of gathered data and active community activity.

Dynamic topic modeling and the Hawkes model were used by Phillips and Gorse (2018) to analyze the connections between themes and fluctuations in cryptocurrency prices. The Latent Dirichlet Allocation (LDA) model, which implies that each document includes many subjects to varying degrees, was utilized by the authors for topic modeling. The authors suggested that the links may be included in real-time cryptocurrency trading after the experiment revealed that certain subjects often anticipate various sorts of price fluctuations in the cryptocurrency market. Flori (2019) used a Bayesian framework to create diverse investing strategies in the Bitcoin market by fusing objective information with subjective assumptions. The outcome demonstrates that news and media attention seem to affect Bitcoin demand and broaden the pool of possible investors, likely causing price exuberance and upward-downward market dynamics. Similar findings were obtained when Garcia and Schweitzer (2015) and Colianni et al. (2015) used sentiment analysis technologies in the bitcoin trading space. Garcia and Schweitzer (2015) used multidimensional analysis and impulse analysis in the algorithmic trading of Bitcoin and social signals of sentiment impacts. The findings supported the long-held belief that sentiment on transaction-based social media platforms may lead to a profitable return on investment. On Twitter Sentiment Analysis for bitcoin trading, Colianni et al. (2015) cleansed data and used supervised machine learning methods including support vector machines, Naive Bayes, and logistic regression, etc.

IMPLICATIONS

As a relatively new concept, cryptocurrency is still evolving through a period of rapid technological development and innovation. Its price changes make it more difficult for individuals to speculate on it concurrently. If people grow more used to cryptocurrencies, there's a chance that over time, they'll become less volatile. However, given the present situation, it is difficult to forecast how volatile cryptocurrencies will be. Economists are still unconvinced that cryptocurrencies will serve as a reliable public store of wealth. All other industry items would likewise tend to have variable pricing if bitcoin begins to be used as a fiat currency and is linked to all other industry products since the merchant will not understand what the price of Bitcoin will be the following day.

With its growing demand in the first half of the previous lustrum, decline in the middle, and eventual balance in the latter part, the history of cryptocurrencies has never been anything less than a drama. The fact that investors are bidding on a volatile currency always amuses them with cryptocurrency. Cryptocurrency has always offered enormous rewards to those who were willing to accept the risk connected with its downside, but if you invest in any kind of financial security anywhere in the world that offers significant returns, you can bet that it will eventually experience a slump as well. Even said, the situation with cryptocurrencies is quite different from that of conventional financial products since they offer some very outstanding development prospects that have the potential to completely overhaul the current financial system.

Conglomerates and large enterprises are growing in every country in the globe in the digital age of globalization and international trade, and even small-scale industries aren't holding back from extending their operations abroad. To function and maximize their profits while offering customers superior quality and a wide selection of items that they are unable to obtain in the local markets, manufacturers and producers are acquiring foreign money and the newest forms of equipment from international marketplaces. Transfers and payments internationally are now necessary. According to market dynamics, cryptocurrencies are likely to displace the traditional financial system. The booming demand for e-commerce in the marketplace is not being sufficiently met by the conventional financial system; it takes a long time to transact values and may only transfer money to a limited extent, and even then, it is bound by strict regulations. In addition to these problems, they impose exorbitant fees on these kinds of transactions. On the other hand, Bitcoin can transmit large sums of money in a matter of seconds thanks to its rapid and simple method of transaction. The conventional banking system will fall short of expectations when a firm that operates worldwide needs emergency funding from a cross-border corporation. Consequently, cryptocurrencies have a great chance to take over this platform for international financial transfers and currency conversion.

To prevent the value of the cryptocurrency from rising by producing them in large quantities, the production of cryptocurrencies has been limited to a certain quantity. This value proposition enables the rarity of cryptocurrencies. According to the rules of supply and demand, a product will often have a higher price on the market if there is less demand for it and greater supply. In the same way that gold and other commodities are traded on the market, cryptocurrencies may also be classified as commodities. Over the last ten years, the popularity of cryptocurrencies has grown significantly. Due to this acceptance and international trading of cryptocurrencies, investors gained confidence from this popularity. Future-proofing bitcoin on the foundation of gold may enable it to become the global standard, bringing all other currencies into line with the value of cryptocurrency.

Despite their popularity, cryptocurrencies are still a rather young and unproven technology. To realize its full potential, several issues should be resolved. One of the biggest issues is the lack of rules. Cryptocurrency is not subject to the same scrutiny and regulation as conventional financial institutions since it works outside of them. This has led to worries about fraud, money laundering, and other illegal activities. Lack of acceptability by the general public is another issue. Even if Bitcoin and other cryptocurrencies have increased in value, there is still limited acceptance of them as a means of payment. People find it challenging to utilize them in their everyday life as a result. Scalability is the last problem to be addressed. The cryptocurrency's underlying blockchain technology can only handle a certain number of transactions per second. This can cause pricey expenditures and protracted transaction delays.

It has gained a lot of popularity and value recently and has the potential to upend established financial institutions. For it to realize its full potential, however, there are still issues that must be resolved. It will be fascinating to observe how bitcoin develops over the next several years since it is a constantly evolving field.

FUTURE DIRECTIONS

There is a sizable body of work that use natural language processing technologies for sentiment analysis with the ultimate objective of exploiting news and media content to boost the effectiveness of bitcoin trading techniques.

A larger volume of media input for sentiment analysis (such as adding video sources), updating the baseline model of natural language processing to perform more robust text preprocessing, using opinion dynamics, neural networks in label training, transaction fees, extending samples in terms of the holding period, and user reputation research is all potential research directions.

Research on long- and short-term trading shows that there are big variations in trading cryptocurrencies over long and short periods. When managing a position for weeks or months, long-term traders may achieve bigger gains but also have more control over risk. In long-term strategies, risk management is essential because the lengthening of the holding time, which is inversely correlated to the trader's risk, makes it necessary. On the other hand, the risk and most crucial risk management both increase with the length of the horizon. Cost takes precedence over risk in the formulation of a plan the shorter the horizon, the greater the cost, and the lower the risk. When holding durations are shorter than a week, automated algorithmic trading may be used in short-term trading. By using wavelet technology to analyze bubble regimes (Phillips & Gorse, 2018) and taking price explosiveness (Bouri, Shahzad, & Roubaud, 2019) hypotheses into account, researchers may distinguish between short-term and long-term trading in cryptocurrency trading.

The focus of the current study is mostly on highlighting the distinctions between long-term and short-term bitcoin trading. Long-term trading saves time by using just basic technical indicators and trend tracing for market research. Because each transaction uses a tiny position, short-term trading may reduce total risk. However, short transaction times and market noise (interference) may add to the stress of short-term trading. Exploring trading signal extraction, time series analysis, portfolio management applications, the connection between a severe market collapse and a little price decline, derivative pricing in the bitcoin market, etc., may also be of interest.

Correlation between cryptocurrencies and other assets: Due to the uncontrollable impacts of monetary policy and economic cycles, cryptocurrencies always have a negative correlation to broad financial market movements. There are connections between cryptocurrencies and other financial markets that may be utilized to forecast the direction of the cryptocurrency market (Castro, Tito, Brandão, & Gomes, 2020). Given the features of cryptocurrencies, further study is still needed to determine their association with other assets. Principal component analysis, the interaction between cryptocurrencies and other currencies under severe situations, and other research areas might lead to breakthroughs (i.e., financial collapse).

The cryptocurrency market bubbles (Cheung, Roca, & Su, 2015), the relationship between cryptocurrency bubbles and indicators like the volatility index (VIX) (Enoksen & Landsnes, 2019), a "panic index" to measure the implied volatility of the S&P500 Index Options, and spillover effects in the cryptocurrency market (Luu Duc Huynh, 2019). have all been the subject of research on bubbles and crashes. Additional research on bubbles and crashes in cryptocurrency trading could examine the relationship between the process of bubble formation and financial collapse, conduct a coherent analysis (from bubble formation to bubble bust aftermath analysis), analyze bubble theory using microeconomics, test out various industrial or physical models to study bubbles in the cryptocurrency market, and debate the pros and cons of each model (like using demand and supply graph to simulate the bubble burst and simulate the generation of bubbles).

In the conventional financial market, using game theory or agent-based modeling in trading is a hot study topic. This strategy might also be useful for trading in cryptocurrency markets. Research into the links between the construction of a specific currency's transaction network and its price has expanded significantly in recent years, as has an interest in user identification (Juhász, Stéger, Kondor, & Vattay, 2018). It is possible to uncover new characteristics in price prediction and get closer to comprehending financial bubbles in cryptocurrency trading if there is a thorough grasp of these networks. According to a study by McLean and Pontiff (McLean & Pontiff, 2016), scholarly articles are where investors learn about stock market mispricing. Similarly, research publications in the field may have an impact on bitcoin market forecasting. One possibility is to experiment with new pricing techniques based on real-time market developments. Another tipping point in the pricing process is the growing share of educated traders in the bitcoin market (looking for a balance between trading research literature and alpha trading).

CONCLUSION

Generating an excessive amount of cryptocurrency would drive down its value, thus its creation is limited. This is the basic tenet of the cryptocurrency's value proposition. According to the principles of supply and demand, a commodity's market price will rise if there is an excess of supply relative to demand. Much like gold and other commodities, bitcoin may be categorized as a marketable good. The previous ten years have been rough for the financial system as a whole due to the meteoric rise of cryptocurrency use. Thanks to this success, traders and investors all around the world have begun to trade and accept cryptocurrencies.

Virtual, decentralized cryptocurrencies exist only in digital form on the internet. Even though cryptocurrency has been the focus of several academic investigations from a variety of angles, it remains uncharted territory for commercial investment despite encouraging developments in the crypto industry. However, emerging technologies are reshaping every sector of the economy, and the bitcoin industry is no different. Using cutting-edge technology may help the crypto market in several ways, including safe transactions and pattern detection. The purpose of this chapter was to examine how certain cutting-edge technologies are being used in the cryptocurrency market, and what kind of value they provide to investors and intermediaries. This chapter covered the evolution of cryptocurrencies, the need for an expanding market, blockchain, AI, and machine learning technologies, and sentiment analysis.

REFERENCES

Ali, R., Barrdear, J., Clews, R., & Southgate, J. (2014). The economics of digital currencies. *Bank of England Quarterly Bulletin*.

Allen, B., & Bryant, S. K. (2019). The market for cryptocurrency: How will it evolve? *Global Economy Journal*, *19*(03), 1950019. doi:10.1142/S2194565919500192

Alon, N., Lokshtanov, D., & Saurabh, S. (2009). Fast fast. *Automata, Languages and Programming: 36th International Colloquium, ICALP 2009, Rhodes, Greece, July 5-12, 2009, Proceedings, Part I, 36*.

Anamika, C. M., & Subramaniam, S. (2021). Does sentiment impact cryptocurrency? *Journal of Behavioral Finance*, 1–17.

Angerer, M., Hoffmann, C. H., Neitzert, F., & Kraus, S. (2021). Objective and subjective risks of investing into cryptocurrencies. *Finance Research Letters*, *40*, 101737. doi:10.1016/j.frl.2020.101737

Arslanian, H., Fischer, F., Arslanian, H., & Fischer, F. (2019). The basics of cryptography and encryption. The Future of Finance: The Impact of FinTech, AI, and Crypto on Financial Services, 89-93.

Authority, E. B. (2014). *Eba opinion on virtual currencies*. Available on https://www. eba. europa. eu/documents/10180/657547/EBA-Op-2 014-08+ Opinion+ on+ Virtual+ Currencies. pdf

Bakar, N. A., Rosbi, S., & Uzaki, K. (2017). Cryptocurrency framework diagnostics from Islamic finance perspective: A new insight of Bitcoin system transaction. *International Journal of Management Science and Business Administration*, *4*(1), 19–28. doi:10.18775/ijmsba.1849-5664-5419.2014.41.1003

Białkowski, J. (2020). Cryptocurrencies in institutional investors' portfolios: Evidence from industry stop-loss rules. *Economics Letters*, *191*, 108834. doi:10.1016/j.econlet.2019.108834

Bouri, E., Shahzad, S. J. H., & Roubaud, D. (2019). Co-explosivity in the cryptocurrency market. *Finance Research Letters*, *29*, 178–183. doi:10.1016/j.frl.2018.07.005

Bunjaku, F., Gjorgieva-Trajkovska, O., & Miteva-Kacarski, E. (2017). Cryptocurrencies–advantages and disadvantages. *Journal of Economics*, *2*(1), 31–39.

Caffyn, G. (2015). *What is the bitcoin block size debate and why does it matter.* http://www.coindesk. com/what-is-the-bitcoin-block-size-deba te-and-why-does-it-matter/

Casey, M. J., & Vigna, P. (2015). Bitcoin and the digital-currency revolution. *The Wall Street Journal, 23.*

Casey, P. V. M. J. (2015). *The Age of Cryptocurrency: How Bitcoin and Digital Money Are Challenging the Global Economic Order Hardcover.* Academic Press.

Castro, J. G., Tito, E. A. H., Brandão, L. E. T., & Gomes, L. L. (2020). Crypto-assets portfolio optimization under the omega measure. *The Engineering Economist, 65*(2), 114–134. doi:10.1080/0013791X.2019.1668098

Ceruleo, P. (2014). *Bitcoin: A rival to fiat money or a speculative financial asset?* Academic Press.

Chaum, D. (1983). Blind signatures for untraceable payments. *Advances in Cryptology: Proceedings of Crypto, 82.*

Cheung, A., Roca, E., & Su, J.-J. (2015). Crypto-currency bubbles: An application of the Phillips–Shi–Yu (2013) methodology on Mt. Gox bitcoin prices. *Applied Economics, 47*(23), 2348–2358. doi:10.1080/00036846.2015.1005827

Ciaian, P., Rajcaniova, M., & Kancs, A. (2016). The economics of BitCoin price formation. *Applied Economics, 48*(19), 1799–1815. doi:10.1080/00036846.2015. 1109038

Colianni, S., Rosales, S., & Signorotti, M. (2015). Algorithmic trading of cryptocurrency based on Twitter sentiment analysis. *CS229 Project, 1*(5), 1-4.

Conti, M., Kumar, E. S., Lal, C., & Ruj, S. (2018). A survey on security and privacy issues of bitcoin. *IEEE Communications Surveys and Tutorials, 20*(4), 3416–3452. doi:10.1109/COMST.2018.2842460

Corea, F., & Corea, F. (2019). The convergence of AI and blockchain. *Applied artificial intelligence: Where AI can be used in business,* 19-26.

da Gama Silva, P. V. J., Klotzle, M. C., Pinto, A. C. F., & Gomes, L. L. (2019). Herding behavior and contagion in the cryptocurrency market. *Journal of Behavioral and Experimental Finance, 22,* 41–50. doi:10.1016/j.jbef.2019.01.006

Domingo, R.-S., Piñeiro-Chousa, J., & López-Cabarcos, M. Á. (2020). What factors drive returns on initial coin offerings? *Technological Forecasting and Social Change, 153,* 119915. doi:10.1016/j.techfore.2020.119915

Domingos, P. (2012). A few useful things to know about machine learning. *Communications of the ACM*, *55*(10), 78–87. doi:10.1145/2347736.2347755

Doran, M. D. (2014). *A forensic look at bitcoin cryptocurrency.* Utica College.

Dwyer, G. P. (2015). The economics of Bitcoin and similar private digital currencies. *Journal of Financial Stability*, *17*, 81–91.

El-Bannany, M., Sreedharan, M., & Khedr, A. M. (2020). A robust deep learning model for financial distress prediction. *International Journal of Advanced Computer Science and Applications*, *11*(2). Advance online publication. doi:10.14569/IJACSA.2020.0110222

Enoksen, F. A., & Landsnes, C. J. (2019). *What Can Predict Bubbles in Cryptocurrency Prices?* University of Stavanger.

Farell, R. (2015). *An analysis of the cryptocurrency industry.* Academic Press.

Fethi, M. D., & Pasiouras, F. (2010). Assessing bank efficiency and performance with operational research and artificial intelligence techniques: A survey. *European Journal of Operational Research*, *204*(2), 189–198. doi:10.1016/j.ejor.2009.08.003

Flori, A. (2019). News and subjective beliefs: A Bayesian approach to Bitcoin investments. *Research in International Business and Finance*, *50*, 336–356. doi:10.1016/j.ribaf.2019.05.007

Franco, P. (2014). *Understanding Bitcoin: Cryptography, engineering and economics.* John Wiley & Sons. doi:10.1002/9781119019138

Gandal, N., & Halaburda, H. (2016). Can we predict the winner in a market with network effects? Competition in cryptocurrency market. *Games*, *7*(3), 16. doi:10.3390/g7030016

Garcia, D., & Schweitzer, F. (2015). Social signals and algorithmic trading of Bitcoin. *Royal Society Open Science*, *2*(9), 150288. doi:10.1098/rsos.150288 PMID:26473051

Guégan, D., & Renault, T. (2021). Does investor sentiment on social media provide robust information for Bitcoin returns predictability? *Finance Research Letters*, *38*, 101494. doi:10.1016/j.frl.2020.101494

Harvey, C., & Tymoigne, E. (2015). Do cryptocurrencies such as Bitcoin have a future. *Retrieved*, (July), 10.

Harwick, C. (2016). Cryptocurrency and the problem of intermediation. *The Independent Review, 20*(4), 569-588.

Hassani, H., Huang, X., & Silva, E. (2018). Digitalisation and big data mining in banking. *Big Data and Cognitive Computing, 2*(3), 18. doi:10.3390/bdcc2030018

Hileman, G., & Rauchs, M. (2017). *2017 global cryptocurrency benchmarking study.* Available at *SSRN* 2965436.

Huerta, J. M., & Anand, A. (2018). Machine learning and artificial intelligence in consumer banking. *Journal of Digital Banking, 3*(1), 22–32.

Hutto, C., & Gilbert, E. (2014). Vader: A parsimonious rule-based model for sentiment analysis of social media text. *Proceedings of the international AAAI conference on web and social media.* 10.1609/icwsm.v8i1.14550

Iwamura, M., Kitamura, Y., & Matsumoto, T. (2014). Is Bitcoin the Only Cryptocurrency in the Town? *Economics of Cryptocurrency.*

Johnson, B., Laszka, A., Grossklags, J., Vasek, M., & Moore, T. (2014). *Game-theoretic analysis of DDoS attacks against Bitcoin mining pools.* Paper presented at the Financial Cryptography and Data Security: FC 2014 Workshops, BITCOIN and WAHC 2014, Christ Church, Barbados. 10.1007/978-3-662-44774-1_6

Jokić, S., Cvetković, A. S., Adamović, S., Ristić, N., & Spalević, P. (2019). Comparative analysis of cryptocurrency wallets vs traditional wallets. *Ekonomika, 65*(3), 65-75.

Jordan, M. I., & Mitchell, T. M. (2015). Machine learning: Trends, perspectives, and prospects. *Science, 349*(6245), 255–260. doi:10.1126cience.aaa8415 PMID:26185243

Juhász, P. L., Stéger, J., Kondor, D., & Vattay, G. (2018). A bayesian approach to identify bitcoin users. *PLoS One, 13*(12), e0207000. doi:10.1371/journal.pone.0207000 PMID:30543629

Kim, T. (2015). The predecessors of bitcoin and their implications for the prospect of virtual currencies. *PLoS One, 10*(4), e0123071. doi:10.1371/journal.pone.0123071 PMID:25919027

Kim, Y. B., Kim, J. G., Kim, W., Im, J. H., Kim, T. H., Kang, S. J., & Kim, C. H. (2016). Predicting fluctuations in cryptocurrency transactions based on user comments and replies. *PLoS One, 11*(8), e0161197. doi:10.1371/journal.pone.0161197 PMID:27533113

Kondor, D., Pósfai, M., Csabai, I., & Vattay, G. (2014). Do the rich get richer? An empirical analysis of the Bitcoin transaction network. *PLoS One, 9*(2), e86197. doi:10.1371/journal.pone.0086197 PMID:24505257

Kostakis, V., & Giotitsas, C. (2014). The (A) political economy of bitcoin. *tripleC: Communication, Capitalism & Critique. Open Access Journal for a Global Sustainable Information Society, 12*(2), 431–440-431–440.

Kristoufek, L. (2013). BitCoin meets Google Trends and Wikipedia: Quantifying the relationship between phenomena of the Internet era. *Scientific Reports, 3*(1), 3415. doi:10.1038rep03415 PMID:24301322

Lamon, C., Nielsen, E., & Redondo, E. (2017). Cryptocurrency price prediction using news and social media sentiment. *SMU Data Sci. Rev, 1*(3), 1–22.

Li, R., Li, S., Yuan, D., & Zhu, H. (2021). Investor attention and cryptocurrency: Evidence from wavelet-based quantile Granger causality analysis. *Research in International Business and Finance, 56*, 101389. doi:10.1016/j.ribaf.2021.101389

Li, Y., Urquhart, A., Wang, P., & Zhang, W. (2021). MAX momentum in cryptocurrency markets. *International Review of Financial Analysis, 77*, 101829. doi:10.1016/j.irfa.2021.101829

Lischke, M., & Fabian, B. (2016). Analyzing the bitcoin network: The first four years. *Future Internet, 8*(1), 7.

Luu, L., Chu, D.-H., Olickel, H., Saxena, P., & Hobor, A. (2016). Making smart contracts smarter. *Proceedings of the 2016 ACM SIGSAC conference on computer and communications security*. 10.1145/2976749.2978309

Luu Duc Huynh, T. (2019). Spillover risks on cryptocurrency markets: A look from VAR-SVAR granger causality and student'st copulas. *Journal of Risk and Financial Management, 12*(2), 52. doi:10.3390/jrfm12020052

McCarthy, J. (2007). *What is artificial intelligence*. Academic Press.

McLean, R. D., & Pontiff, J. (2016). Does academic research destroy stock return predictability? *The Journal of Finance, 71*(1), 5–32. doi:10.1111/jofi.12365

Meunier, S. (2018). Blockchain 101: What is blockchain and how does this revolutionary technology work? In Transforming climate finance and green investment with Blockchains (pp. 23-34): Elsevier.

Nakamoto, S. (2008). Bitcoin: A peer-to-peer electronic cash system. *Decentralized Business Review*, 21260.

Narayanan, A., Bonneau, J., Felten, E., Miller, A., & Goldfeder, S. (2016). *Bitcoin and cryptocurrency technologies: a comprehensive introduction*. Princeton University Press.

Nasir, M. A., Huynh, T. L. D., Nguyen, S. P., & Duong, D. (2019). Forecasting cryptocurrency returns and volume using search engines. *Financial Innovation*, *5*(1), 1–13. doi:10.118640854-018-0119-8

Papadamou, S., Kyriazis, N. A., Tzeremes, P., & Corbet, S. (2021). Herding behaviour and price convergence clubs in cryptocurrencies during bull and bear markets. *Journal of Behavioral and Experimental Finance*, *30*, 100469. doi:10.1016/j.jbef.2021.100469

Phillips, R. C., & Gorse, D. (2018). Mutual-excitation of cryptocurrency market returns and social media topics. *Proceedings of the 4th international conference on frontiers of educational technologies*. 10.1145/3233347.3233370

Rose, C. (2015). The evolution of digital currencies: Bitcoin, a cryptocurrency causing a monetary revolution. *International Business & Economics Research Journal*, *14*(4), 617–622. doi:10.19030/iber.v14i4.9353

Russell, S. J. (2010). *Artificial intelligence a modern approach*. Pearson Education, Inc.

Smuts, N. (2019). What drives cryptocurrency prices? An investigation of google trends and telegram sentiment. *Performance Evaluation Review*, *46*(3), 131–134. doi:10.1145/3308897.3308955

Söderberg, G. (2018). Are Bitcoin and other crypto-assets money? *Economic Commentaries*, *5*, 14.

Tapscott, D., & Tapscott, A. (2016). *Blockchain revolution: how the technology behind bitcoin is changing money, business, and the world*. Penguin.

Tschorsch, F., & Scheuermann, B. (2016). Bitcoin and beyond: A technical survey on decentralized digital currencies. *IEEE Communications Surveys and Tutorials*, *18*(3), 2084–2123. doi:10.1109/COMST.2016.2535718

Vora, G. (2015). Cryptocurrencies: Are disruptive financial innovations here? *Modern Economy*, *6*(07), 816–832. doi:10.4236/me.2015.67077

Wang, H., He, D., & Ji, Y. (2020). Designated-verifier proof of assets for bitcoin exchange using elliptic curve cryptography. *Future Generation Computer Systems*, *107*, 854–862. doi:10.1016/j.future.2017.06.028

Wang, S., & Vergne, J.-P. (2017). Buzz factor or innovation potential: What explains cryptocurrencies' returns? *PLoS One*, *12*(1), e0169556. doi:10.1371/journal.pone.0169556 PMID:28085906

Yermack, D. (2013). Is Bitcoin a real currency? An economic appraisal (No. w19747). *National Bureau of Economic Research, 36*(2), 843-850.

Zhang, X., Lu, F., Tao, R., & Wang, S. (2021). The time-varying causal relationship between the Bitcoin market and internet attention. *Financial Innovation*, *7*(1), 1–19. doi:10.118640854-021-00275-9

Стойка, М. (2021). Cryptocurrency–Definition, functions, advantages and risks. *Підприємництво і торгівля,* (30), 5-10.

Compilation of References

Abbasi, K. (2021). P2P Lending FinTech's and SME's Access to Finance. *Economics Letters*, (204). https://www.sciencedirect.com/science/article/abs/pii/S0165176521001671?via%3Dihub

Abboushi, S. (2017). Global Virtual Currency–Brief Overview. *Journal of Applied Business & Economics*, *19*(6).

Abdullah, E. M. E., Rahman, A. A., & Rahim, R. A. (2018). Adoption of financial technology (FinTech) in mutual fund/unit trust investment among Malaysians: Unified Theory of Acceptance and Use of Technology (UTAUT). *Int. J. Eng. Technol, 7*(2), 110.

Abramova, S., & Böhme, R. (2016). *Perceived benefit and risk as multidimensional determinants of bitcoin use: A quantitative exploratory study*. Academic Press.

Abramson, J., Dawson, M., & Stevens, J. (2015). Examine the prior use of e-learning within an extended technology acceptance model and the factors that influence the behavioral intention of users to use m-learning. *SAGE Open*, *5*(4), 2158244015621114. doi:10.1177/2158244015621114

Abubakar, L., & Handayani, T. (2018). *Financial technology: Legal challenges for Indonesia financial sector*. Paper presented at the IOP Conference Series: Earth and Environmental Science. 10.1088/1755-1315/175/1/012204

Adams, D. A., Nelson, R. R., & Todd, P. A. (1992). Perceived usefulness, ease of use, and usage of information technology: A replication. *Management Information Systems Quarterly*, *16*(2), 227–247. doi:10.2307/249577

Adrián Risso, W., & Sánchez Carrera, E. J. (2019). On the impact of innovation and inequality in economic growth. *Economics of Innovation and New Technology*, *28*(1), 64–81. doi:10.108 0/10438599.2018.1429534

Afuah, A., & Tucci, C. (2000). Internet Business Models and Strategies: Text and Cases. Academic Press.

Agarwal, R., Thapliyal, T., & Shukla, S. (2022). Analyzing malicious activities and detecting adversarial behavior in cryptocurrency based permissionless blockchains: An Ethereum usecase. *Distributed Ledger Technologies: Research and Practice*.

Agarwal, R., & Karahanna, E. (2000). Time flies when you're having fun: Cognitive absorption and beliefs about information technology usage. *Management Information Systems Quarterly*, *24*(4), 665–694. doi:10.2307/3250951

Agarwal, S., Skiba, P. M., & Tobacman, J. (2009). Payday loans and credit cards: New liquidity and credit scoring puzzles? *The American Economic Review*, *99*(2), 412–417. doi:10.1257/aer.99.2.412

Aghion, P., & Tirole, J. (1997). Formal and real authority in organizations. *Journal of Political Economy*, *105*(1), 1–29. doi:10.1086/262063

Ahn, S., & Kim, J. (2019). The effect of managerial characteristics on the performance of technology-based start-ups in Korea. *International Journal of Global Business and Competitiveness*, *14*(1), 11–23. doi:10.100742943-019-00001-4

Ahorsu, D. K., Lin, C.-Y., Imani, V., Saffari, M., Griffiths, M. D., & Pakpour, A. H. (2020). The fear of COVID-19 scale: Development and initial validation. *International Journal of Mental Health and Addiction*, 1–9. PMID:32226353

Ajzen, I. (1991). The theory of planned behavior. *Organizational Behavior and Human Decision Processes*, *50*(2), 179–211. doi:10.1016/0749-5978(91)90020-T

Akhtar, T. (2021). Louis Vuitton, Cartier, Prada to Use Bespoke Blockchain to Tackle Counterfeit Goods. *CoinDesk*. https://www.coindesk.com/business/2021/04/20/louis-vuitton-cartier-prada-to-use-bespoke-blockchain-to-tackle-counterfeit-goods/

Akturan, U., & Tezcan, N. (2012). Mobile banking adoption of the youth market: Perceptions and intentions. *Marketing Intelligence & Planning*, *30*(4), 444–459. doi:10.1108/02634501211231928

Albayati, H., Kim, S. K., & Rho, J. J. (2020). Accepting financial transactions using blockchain technology and cryptocurrency: A customer perspective approach. *Technology in Society*, *62*, 101320. doi:10.1016/j.techsoc.2020.101320

Aldridge, J., & Decary-Hétu, D. (2016). Cryptomarkets and the future of illicit drug markets. *The Internet and Drug Markets*, 23-32.

Ali, R., Barrdear, J., Clews, R., & Southgate, J. (2014). The economics of digital currencies. *Bank of England Quarterly Bulletin*.

Ali, F., Hussain, K., & Raghavan, N. A. (2014). Memorable customer experience: Examining the effects of customers experience on memories and loyalty in Malaysian resort hotels. *Procedia: Social and Behavioral Sciences*, *144*, 273–279. doi:10.1016/j.sbspro.2014.07.296

Allam, A., & Dahlan, H. M. (2013). User experience: Challenges and opportunities. J. *Inform. Syst. Res. Innovat.*, *3*, 28–36.

Allayarov, S. A., & Ravshanova, M. (2021). Financial technology: Development of innovative FinTech start-ups and its application in banking system of Uzbekistan. *International Journal of Multicultural and Multireligious Understanding*, 8(9), 214–219. doi:10.18415/ijmmu.v8i9.3017

Allen, B., & Bryant, S. K. (2019). The market for cryptocurrency: How will it evolve? *Global Economy Journal*, 19(03), 1950019. doi:10.1142/S2194565919500192

Alon, N., Lokshtanov, D., & Saurabh, S. (2009). Fast fast. *Automata, Languages and Programming: 36th International Colloquium, ICALP 2009, Rhodes, Greece, July 5-12, 2009, Proceedings, Part I, 36.*

Alqahtani, F. (2018). An analysis of the determinants of Bitcoin adoption: How cultural and technological factors influence the decision to adopt cryptocurrencies. *Journal of Business Research*, 89, 187–195.

Alshamsi, A., & Azzam, A. (2019). The determinants of the adoption of cryptocurrency: A systematic review. *Journal of Risk and Financial Management*, 12(4), 175.

Amarasinghe, N., Boyen, X., & McKague, M. (2019). A survey of anonymity of cryptocurrencies. *Proceedings of the Australasian Computer Science Week Multiconference*. 10.1145/3290688.3290693

Amit, R., & Zott, C. (2010). Business Model Innovation: Creating Value In Times Of Change. SSRN *Electronic Journal, 23*. doi:10.2139/ssrn.1701660

Amit, R., & Zott, C. (2001). Value Creation in E-Business. *Strategic Management Journal*, 22(6-7), 493–520. doi:10.1002mj.187

Amsad, M. (2019). *ADBI Working Paper Series: Objectives of FinTech*. https://www.adb.org/sites/default/files/publication/533791/adbi-wp1016.pdf

Anamika, C. M., & Subramaniam, S. (2021). Does sentiment impact cryptocurrency? *Journal of Behavioral Finance*, 1–17.

Anderson, C., & Saleh, T. (2021). Investigating cyber attacks using domain and DNS data. *Network Security*, 2021(3), 6–8. doi:10.1016/S1353-4858(21)00028-3

Angerer, M., Hoffmann, C. H., Neitzert, F., & Kraus, S. (2021). Objective and subjective risks of investing into cryptocurrencies. *Finance Research Letters*, 40, 101737. doi:10.1016/j.frl.2020.101737

Anshari, M., Almunawar, M. N., & Masri, M. (2020). Financial technology and disruptive innovation in business: Concept and application. *International Journal of Asian Business and Information Management*, 11(4), 29–43. doi:10.4018/IJABIM.2020100103

Antonopoulos, A. M. (2014). *Mastering Bitcoin: unlocking digital cryptocurrencies*. O'Reilly Media, Inc.

Antonopoulos, A. M. (2014). *Mastering Bitcoin: Unlocking digital cryptocurrencies*. O'Reilly Media, Inc.

Anugerah, D. P., & Indriani, M. (2018). *Data Protection in financial technology services: Indonesian legal perspective*. Paper presented at the IOP Conference Series: Earth and Environmental Science.

Arias-Oliva, M., Pelegrín-Borondo, J., & Matías-Clavero, G. (2019). Variables influencing cryptocurrency use: A technology acceptance model in Spain. *Frontiers in Psychology*, *10*, 475. doi:10.3389/fpsyg.2019.00475 PMID:30949085

Arli, D., van Esch, P., Bakpayev, M., & Laurence, A. (2021). Do consumers really trust cryptocurrencies? *Marketing Intelligence & Planning*, *39*(1), 74–90. doi:10.1108/MIP-01-2020-0036

Armstrong, B. (2021). Coinbase: A comprehensive platform for cryptocurrency trading. *Journal of Cryptocurrency and Blockchain Technology*, *12*(3), 45–58.

Arner, Buckley, & Zetzsche. (2019). FinTech, Regtech and Systemic Risk: The Rise of Global Technology Risk. Systemic Risk in the Financial Sector: Ten Years after the Great Crash, 69.

Arner, D. W., Barberis, J. N., Walker, J., Buckley, R. P., Dahdal, A. M., & Zetzsche, D. A. (2020). *Digital finance & the COVID-19 crisis*. University of Hong Kong Faculty of Law Research Paper (2020/017).

Arner, D. W., Barberis, J. N., & Buckley, R. P. (2016). The Emergence of Regtech 2.0: From Know Your Customer to Know Your Data. *Journal of Financial Transformation*, *44*, 79. doi:10.2139srn.3044280

Arner, D. W., Barberis, J. N., & Buckley, R. P. (2016). The Evolution of FinTech: A New Post-Crisis Paradigm? *Geo. J. Int'l. L.*, *47*, 1271.

Arner, D. W., Zetzsche, D. A., Buckley, R. P., & Barberis, J. N. (2017). FinTech and RegTech: Enabling Innovation while Preserving Financial Stability. *Geo. J. Int'l. Aff.*, *18*, 47.

Arnold, S., & Auer, B. R. (2015). What do scientists know about inflation hedging? *The North American Journal of Economics and Finance*, *34*, 187–214. doi:10.1016/j.najef.2015.08.005

Arslanian, H., Fischer, F., Arslanian, H., & Fischer, F. (2019). The basics of cryptography and encryption. The Future of Finance: The Impact of FinTech, AI, and Crypto on Financial Services, 89-93.

Arslanian, H., Fischer, F., Arslanian, H., & Fischer, F. (2019). The rise of FinTech. The Future of Finance: The Impact of FinTech, AI, and Crypto on Financial Services, 25-56.

Ashta, A., & Biot-Paquerot, G. (2018). FinTech evolution: Strategic value management issues in a fast changing industry. *Strategic Change*, *27*(4), 301–311. doi:10.1002/jsc.2203

Asongu, S. A., & Le Roux, S. (2017). Enhancing ICT for inclusive human development in Sub-Saharan Africa. *Technological Forecasting and Social Change, 118*, 44–54. doi:10.1016/j. techfore.2017.01.026

Authority, E. B. (2014). *Eba opinion on virtual currencies.* Available on https://www. eba. europa. eu/documents/10180/657547/EBA-Op-2 014-08+ Opinion+ on+ Virtual+ Currencies. pdf

Autissier, D., Johnson, K. J., & Moutot, J. M. (2014, January 1). La conduite du changement pour et avec les technologies digitales. *Question(s) de Management, 3*(7), 79-89. doi:10.3917/ qdm.143.0079

Aysan, A. F., Demir, E., Gozgor, G., & Lau, C. K. M. (2019). Effects of the geopolitical risks on Bitcoin returns and volatility. *Research in International Business and Finance, 47*, 511–518. doi:10.1016/j.ribaf.2018.09.011

Aysan, A. F., & Ünal, İ. M. (2021). FinTech and blockchain in islamic finance: A bibliometric analysis. *Efil Journal, 4*(3), 21–37.

Aytekin, B. A., & Ulusoy, T. A. (2022). A netnography study examined consumer perception towards cryptocurrency investment during the COVID-19 pandemic. *Business & Management Studies: An International Journal, 11*(4), 1380–1396. doi:10.15295/bmij.v10i4.2151

Azarenkova, G., Shkodina, I., Samorodov, B., Babenko, M., & Onishchenko, I. (2018). The influence of financial technologies on the global financial system stability. *Investment Management & Financial Innovations, 15*(4), 229–238. doi:10.21511/imfi.15(4).2018.19

Baabdullah, A. M. (2018). Consumer adoption of Mobile Social Network Games (M-SNGs) in Saudi Arabia: The role of social influence, hedonic motivation and trust. *Technology in Society, 53*, 91–102. doi:10.1016/j.techsoc.2018.01.004

Baber, H. (2019). Relevance of e-SERVQUAL for determining the quality of FinTech services. *International Journal of Electronic Finance, 9*(4), 257–267. doi:10.1504/IJEF.2019.104070

Bai, J. J., Jin, W., McElheran, K., & Williams, R. (2018). *The effects of technology adoption on firms, supply chains, and rivals.* Academic Press.

Bains, P., & Singh, R. (2022). *Crypto's conservative coins.* IMF. https://www.imf.org/en/Publications/fandd/issues/2022/09/Bas ics-Crypto-conservative-coins-Bains-Singh

Bakar, N. A., Rosbi, S., & Uzaki, K. (2017). Cryptocurrency framework diagnostics from Islamic finance perspective: A new insight of Bitcoin system transaction. *International Journal of Management Science and Business Administration, 4*(1), 19–28. doi:10.18775/ ijmsba.1849-5664-5419.2014.41.1003

Bank for International Settlements. (2015). *Financial Inclusion Indicators.* https://www.bis.org/ ifc/publ/ifcb38.pdf

BankProv Annual Report. (2021). *Provident Bank.* https:// s29.q4cdn.com/115418717/files/2021-Annual-Report_Pro vident-Bancorp-Inc_Web.pdf

Barbu, C. M., Florea, D. L., Dabija, D.-C., & Barbu, M. C. (2021). Customer Experience in Fintech. *Journal of Theoretical and Applied Electronic Commerce Research, 16*(5), 1415–1433. doi:10.3390/jtaer16050080

Barroso, M., & Laborda, J. (2022). Digital transformation and the emergence of the FinTech sector: Systematic literature review. *Digital Business*, 100028.

Barry, J. J., & Street, O. L. (2020). *Re: Addressing the Regulatory.* Supervisory and Oversight Challenges Raised by Global Stablecoin Arrangements.

Barry, T. M. (2021). # NotFinancialAdvice: Empowering the Federal Trade Commission to Regulate Cryptocurrency Social Media Influencers. *Ohio St. Bus. LJ, 16*, 279.

Bartoletti, M., Lande, S., Loddo, A., Pompianu, L., & Serusi, S. (2021). Cryptocurrency scams: Analysis and perspectives. *IEEE Access: Practical Innovations, Open Solutions, 9*, 148353–148373. doi:10.1109/ACCESS.2021.3123894

Basole, R. C., & Patel, S. S. (2018). Transformation through unbundling: Visualizing the global FinTech ecosystem. *Service Science, 10*(4), 379–396. doi:10.1287erv.2018.0210

Bass, F. M. (1969). A new product growth for model consumer durables. *Journal of Management Science, 15*(5), 215–227.

Baur, A. W., Bühler, J., Bick, M., & Bonorden, C. S. (2015). Cryptocurrencies as a disruption? empirical findings on user adoption and future potential of bitcoin and co. *Open and Big Data Management and Innovation: 14th IFIP WG 6.11 Conference on e-Business, e-Services, and e-Society, I3E 2015, Delft, The Netherlands, October 13-15, 2015, Proceedings, 14.* 10.1007/978-3-319-25013-7_6

Bavassano, G., Ferrari, C., & Tei, A. (2020). Blockchain: How shipping industry is dealing with the ultimate technological leap. *Research in Transportation Business & Management, 34*, 100428. doi:10.1016/j.rtbm.2020.100428

BBC. (2022). The Kenyans lured to become unwitting 'love' fraudsters. *BBC.* https://www.bbc.com/news/world-africa-63654637

BCG (FinTech Control Tower). (2021). *Number of FinTech startups worldwide from 2018 to 2021, by region* [Graph]. Statista. Retrieved March 19, 2023, from https://www-statista-com.ezproxy.myucwest.ca/statistics/8939 54/number-FinTech-startups-by-region/

Beck, R., Müller-Bloch, C., & King, J. L. (2018). Governance in the blockchain economy: A framework and research agenda. *Journal of the Association for Information Systems, 19*(10), 1. doi:10.17705/1jais.00518

Bedjeti Baftijari, A., & Nakov, L. (2020). *An overview on managing changes for bank risks in times of fintech (r)evolution: A challenge or opportunity?* Academic Press. doi:10.1016/j.intfin.2021.101498

Belle, I. (2017). The architecture, engineering and construction industry and blockchain technology. *Digital Culture, 2017*, 279–284.

Benoit, D. (2022, November 10). Crypto Bank Silvergate Capital's stock falls further. *The Wall Street Journal.* https://www.wsj.com/livecoverage/stock-market-news-today-11-09-2022/card/crypto-bank-silvergate-s-stock-falls-further-rQ R1mdhX5s60V9Mzb5Iu#:~:text=Silvergate%20doesn't%20hold%20cryptocurrencies,cash%20 out%20at%20any%20time.

Berentsen, A., & Schär, F. (2018). A short introduction to the world of cryptocurrencies. *FRB of St. Louis Working Review.*

Białkowski, J. (2020). Cryptocurrencies in institutional investors' portfolios: Evidence from industry stop-loss rules. *Economics Letters, 191*, 108834. doi:10.1016/j.econlet.2019.108834

Bilan, A., Degryse, H., O'Flynn, K., Ongena, S., Bilan, A., Degryse, H., . . . Ongena, S. (2019). FinTech and the Future of Banking. *Banking and Financial Markets: How Banks and Financial Technology Are Reshaping Financial Markets*, 179-199.

Binance on Twitter. (n.d.). Retrieved from https://twitter.com/binance

Binance. (n.d.). *Binance Crypto Card.* https://www.binance.com/en/cards

Binance. (n.d.). *Products.* https://www.binance.com/en/products

Bistarelli, S., Fioravanti, F., & Nardelli, E. (2021). Cryptocurrencies and sustainability: A green approach. *Journal of Sustainable Finance, 7*(2), 124–139.

Bofondi, M., & Gobbi, G. (2017). The big promise of FinTech. *European Economy, 2*, 107–119.

Bohannon, J. (2016). *The bitcoin busts.* American Association for the Advancement of Science. doi:10.1126cience.351.6278.1144

Böhme, R., Christin, N., Edelman, B., & Moore, T. (2015). Bitcoin: Economics, technology, and governance. *The Journal of Economic Perspectives, 29*(2), 213–238. doi:10.1257/jep.29.2.213

Bohr, J., & Bashir, M. (2014). *Who uses bitcoin? an exploration of the bitcoin community.* Paper presented at the 2014 Twelfth Annual International Conference on Privacy, Security and Trust. 10.1109/PST.2014.6890928

Boot, A., Hoffmann, P., Laeven, L., & Ratnovski, L. (2021). FinTech: What's old, what's new? *Journal of Financial Stability, 53*, 100836. doi:10.1016/j.jfs.2020.100836

Bordo, M. D., & Levin, A. T. (2017). Central bank digital currency and the future of monetary policy (No. w23711). National Bureau of Economic Research.

Boret, N., Gawande, K., & Kobb, D. P. (2021). Can decentralization lower poverty? Cambodia's Commune and Sangkat Fund. *World Development*, *146*, 105548. doi:10.1016/j.worlddev.2021.105548

Bouri, E., Gupta, R., Hossein, S. M., & Roubaud, D. (2021). Mainstreaming cryptocurrencies: A new era of financial integration. *Financial Innovation*, *7*(1), 32–47.

Bouri, E., Molnár, P., Azzi, G., Roubaud, D., & Hagfors, L. I. (2017). On the hedge and safe haven properties of Bitcoin: Is it really more than a diversifier? *Finance Research Letters*, *20*, 192–198. doi:10.1016/j.frl.2016.09.025

Bouri, E., Shahzad, S. J. H., & Roubaud, D. (2019). Co-explosivity in the cryptocurrency market. *Finance Research Letters*, *29*, 178–183. doi:10.1016/j.frl.2018.07.005

Breidbach, C. F., Keating, B. W., & Lim, C. (2020). FinTech: Research directions to explore the digital transformation of financial service systems. *Journal of Service Theory and Practice*, *30*(1), 79–102. doi:10.1108/JSTP-08-2018-0185

Bridges, W. (2009). *Managing Transitions: Making the most of change* (3rd ed.). Nicholas Brealey Publishing.

Briere, M., Oosterlinck, K., & Szafarz, A. (2015). Virtual currency, tangible return: Portfolio diversification with bitcoin. *Journal of Asset Management*, *16*(6), 365–373. doi:10.1057/jam.2015.5

BrobyD. (2019). *Strategic Fintech*. Center for Financial Regulation and Innovation.

Brownsword, R. (2019). Regulatory fitness: FinTech, funny money, and smart contracts. *European Business Organization Law Review*, *20*(1), 5–27. doi:10.100740804-019-00134-2

Buchak, G., Matvos, G., Piskorski, T., & Seru, A. (2018). FinTech, regulatory arbitrage, and the rise of shadow banks. *Journal of Financial Economics*, *130*(3), 453–483. doi:10.1016/j.jfineco.2018.03.011

Budde, L., Benninghaus, C., Hänggi, R., & Friedli, T. (2022). Literature review on organizational change and digital transformation. *MDPI*, *2*, 463–483. doi:10.3390/digital2040025

Bunjaku, F., Gjorgieva-Trajkovska, O., & Miteva-Kacarski, E. (2017). Cryptocurrencies–advantages and disadvantages. *Journal of Economics*, *2*(1), 31–39.

Burnes, B. (2009). *Managing Change* (5th ed.). Pitman Imprint.

Buterin, V. (2021). The future of cryptocurrencies: A look at the market's potential. *Journal of Blockchain Research*, *6*(2), 112–126.

Caffyn, G. (2015). *What is the bitcoin block size debate and why does it matter*. http://www.coindesk.com/what-is-the-bitcoin-block-size-debate-and-why-does-it-matter/

Cai, C., Marrone, M., & Linnenluecke, M. (2022). Trends in FinTech research and practice: Examining the intersection with the information systems field. *Communications of the Association for Information Systems*, *50*(1), 40. doi:10.17705/1CAIS.05036

Cameron, E., & Green, M. (2020). *Making Sense of Change Management* (5th ed.). Kogan Page Limited.

Campbell, J. Y. (2006). Household finance. *The Journal of Finance*, *61*(4), 1553–1604. doi:10.1111/j.1540-6261.2006.00883.x

Capezza, M. (2023). Plan Distributions: Fiduciary Considerations for Cryptocurrency Investments in 401(k) Plans. *Journal of Pension Benefits: Issues in Administration*, *29*(4), 27–31.

Capgemini & EFMA. (2018). *Impact of non-traditional financial firms on selected banking products and services according to senior banking executives worldwide in 2018* [Graph]. Statista. Retrieved March 19, 2023, from https://www-statista-com.ezproxy.myucwest.ca/statistics/9468 86/impact-FinTech-banking-products-services-globally/

Carnall, C. A. (1986). Managing Strategic Change: An Integrated Approach. *Long Range Planning*, *19*(6), 105–115. doi:10.1016/0024-6301(86)90103-2

Carson, B., Romanelli, G., Walsh, P., & Zhumaev, A. (2018). Blockchain beyond the hype: What is the strategic business value. McKinsey & Company.

Casadesus-Masanell, R., & Ricart, J. (2010). From Strategy to Business Models and onto Tactics. *Long Range Planning*, *43*(2-3), 195–215. doi:10.1016/j.lrp.2010.01.004

Casey, M. J., & Vigna, P. (2015). Bitcoin and the digital-currency revolution. *The Wall Street Journal, 23*.

Casey, P. V. M. J. (2015). *The Age of Cryptocurrency: How Bitcoin and Digital Money Are Challenging the Global Economic Order Hardcover*. Academic Press.

Casey, M. J., & Vigna, P. (2018). *The truth machine: The blockchain and the future of everything*. St. Martin's Press.

Castro, J. G., Tito, E. A. H., Brandão, L. E. T., & Gomes, L. L. (2020). Crypto-assets portfolio optimization under the omega measure. *The Engineering Economist*, *65*(2), 114–134. doi:10.1 080/0013791X.2019.1668098

CBInsights. (2018). The Fintech 250: The top fintech startups of 2018. *Research Briefs*. https://www.cbinsights.com/research/fintech-250-startups-mos t-promising/

Central banks - summary of current interest rates. (2023). *Global-rates. com*. https://www.global-rates.com/en/interest-rates/central-banks /central-banks.aspx

Ceruleo, P. (2014). *Bitcoin: A rival to fiat money or a speculative financial asset?* Academic Press.

CFA Institute. (2023). *What is FinTech?* https://www. cfainstitute.org/en/research/foundation/2017/Fin Tech-and-regtech-in-a-nutshell-and-the-future-in-a-sandbox?s _cid=ppc_RF_Google_Search_FinTechandRegTech

Chaanoun, J., Rahmouni, A., & Alaoui, M. (2022). Literature review on organizational change and digital transformation. *International Journal on Optimization and Applications*, 2(3).

Chaikovskyi, Y., & Kovalchuk, Y. (2020). Modern FinTech directions in the banking sector. *Zeszyty Naukowe ZPSB Firma i Rynek*, (1 (57)), 71–79.

Chan, E. S. (2008). Barriers to EMS in the Hotel Industry. *International Journal of Hospitality Management*, 28(2), 187–196. doi:10.1016/j.ijhm.2007.07.011

Chang, Y., Wong, S. F., Lee, H., & Jeong, S. P. (2016). What motivates chinese consumers to adopt FinTech services: a regulatory focus theory. *Proceedings of the 18th annual international conference on electronic commerce: e-commerce in smart connected world*. 10.1145/2971603.2971643

Chang, H.-y., Liang, W., & Wang, Y. (2019). Do institutional investors still encourage patent-based innovation after the tech bubble period? *Journal of Empirical Finance*, 51, 149–164. doi:10.1016/j.jempfin.2019.02.003

Chang, S. E., Luo, H. L., & Chen, Y. (2019). Blockchain-enabled trade finance innovation: A potential paradigm shift on using letter of credit. *Sustainability*, 12(1), 188. doi:10.3390u12010188

Chaum, D. (1983). Blind signatures for untraceable payments. *Advances in Cryptology: Proceedings of Crypto, 82*.

Cheah, E.-T., & Fry, J. (2015). Speculative bubbles in Bitcoin markets? An empirical investigation into the fundamental value of Bitcoin. *Economics Letters*, 130, 32–36. doi:10.1016/j.econlet.2015.02.029

Chen, X., Miraz, M. H., Gazi, M. A. I., Rahaman, M. A., Habib, M. M., & Hossain, A. I. (2022). Factors affecting cryptocurrency adoption in digital business transactions: The mediating role of customer satisfaction. *Technology in Society*, 70, 102059. doi:10.1016/j.techsoc.2022.102059

Chen, X., Zheng, Z., & Wang, D. (2021). Designing user-friendly interfaces for cryptocurrency platforms. *International Journal of Human-Computer Interaction*, 14(4), 48–63.

Cheung, A., Roca, E., & Su, J.-J. (2015). Crypto-currency bubbles: An application of the Phillips–Shi–Yu (2013) methodology on Mt. Gox bitcoin prices. *Applied Economics*, 47(23), 2348–2358. doi:10.1080/00036846.2015.1005827

China Government Network. (2021). *Notice on Further Prevention and Handling of Risks of Hype in Virtual Currency Trading*. http://www.gov.cn/zhengce/zhengceku/2021-10/08/content_5641404.htm

Chiu, J., & Koeppl, T. (2021). Regulatory compliance in the age of cryptocurrencies. *Journal of Banking Regulation*, 22(3), 215–230.

Choi, J., Kim, J., Song, M., Kim, H., Park, N., Seo, M., & Shin, S. (2022). A Large-Scale Bitcoin Abuse Measurement and Clustering Analysis Utilizing Public Reports. *IEICE Transactions on Information and Systems*, *105*(7), 1296–1307. doi:10.1587/transinf.2021EDP7182

Chonsawat, N., & Sopadang, A. (2020). Defining SMEs' 4.0 readiness indicators. *Applied Sciences (Basel, Switzerland)*, *10*(24), 8998. doi:10.3390/app10248998

Choo, K. K. R. (2015). Cryptocurrency and virtual currency: Corruption and money laundering/terrorism financing risks? In *Handbook of digital currency* (pp. 283–307). Academic Press. doi:10.1016/B978-0-12-802117-0.00015-1

Christidis, K., & Devetsikiotis, M. (2016). Blockchains and smart contracts for the internet of things. *IEEE Access : Practical Innovations, Open Solutions*, *4*, 2292–2303. doi:10.1109/ACCESS.2016.2566339

Chuen, D., & Teo, E. (2017). *Emergence of FinTech and the LASIC Principles*. Academic Press.

Chuen, D. L. K., Guo, L., & Wang, Y. (2017). Cryptocurrency: A new investment opportunity? *Journal of Alternative Investments*, *20*(3), 16–40. doi:10.3905/jai.2018.20.3.016

Ciaian, P., Rajcaniova, M., & Kancs, D. (2016). The Economics of BitCoin Price Formation. *Applied Economics*, *48*(19), 1799–1815. doi:10.1080/00036846.2015.1109038

Claeys, G., Demertzis, M., & Efstathiou, K. (2018). *Cryptocurrencies and monetary policy*. EconStor. http://hdl.handle.net/10419/208013

Clark, T. (2021). Understanding non-fungible tokens (NFTs): A beginner's guide. *Journal of Digital Assets*, *5*(1), 21–36.

Clauson, K. A., Breeden, E. A., Davidson, C., & Mackey, T. K. (2018). Leveraging Blockchain Technology to Enhance Supply Chain Management in Healthcare: An exploration of challenges and opportunities in the health supply chain. *Blockchain in Healthcare Today*.

Coghlan, J. (2022). *350 new 'scam tokens' were created every day this year*. Solidus Labs.

Cohen, B. (2017). The rise of alternative currencies in post-capitalism. *Journal of Management Studies*, *54*(5), 739–746. doi:10.1111/joms.12245

Cohen, J. (2018). Q&A: George Church and company on genomic sequencing, blockchain, and better drugs. *Science*.

CoinA. T. M. Radar. (n.d.). Retrieved from https://coinatmradar.com/

Coinatmradar.com. (n.d.). *Bitcoin ATM geographical distribution*. https://coinatmradar.com/charts/geo-distribution/

Coinbase on Reddit. (n.d.). Retrieved from https://www.reddit.com/r/CoinBase/

Coinbase. (2021). *Coinbase Global, Inc. Direct listing.* Retrieved from https://investor.coinbase.com/news/news-details/2021/Coinbase-Global-Inc-Direct-Listing/

Coinbase. (n.d.). Retrieved from https://www.coinbase.com/

Coinbase. (n.d.a). *About us.* Retrieved from https://www.coinbase.com/about

Coinbase. (n.d.b). *Products.* Retrieved from https://www.coinbase.com/products

Coinmarketcap. (2023). *Binance.* https://coinmarketcap.com/exchanges/binance/

CoinMarketCap. (2023). *Top Cryptocurrency Spot Exchanges.* https://coinmarketcap.com/rankings/exchanges/

Colianni, S., Rosales, S., & Signorotti, M. (2015). Algorithmic trading of cryptocurrency based on Twitter sentiment analysis. *CS229 Project, 1*(5), 1-4.

Combe, C. (2006). *Introduction to E-Business: Management and Strategy.* Elsevier Ltd.

Conchar, M. P., Zinkhan, G. M., Peters, C., & Olavarrieta, S. (2004). An integrated framework for the conceptualization of consumers' perceived-risk processing. *Journal of the Academy of Marketing Science, 32*(4), 418–436. doi:10.1177/0092070304267551

Conlon, T., Corbet, S., & McGee, R. J. (2021). Inflation and cryptocurrencies revisited: A time-scale analysis. *Economics Letters, 206*, 109996. doi:10.1016/j.econlet.2021.109996

Consensus. (n.d.). Retrieved from https://www.coindesk.com/events/consensus

Conti, M., Kumar, E. S., Lal, C., & Ruj, S. (2018). A survey on security and privacy issues of bitcoin. *IEEE Communications Surveys and Tutorials, 20*(4), 3416–3452. doi:10.1109/COMST.2018.2842460

Cook, J. (2014). Paedophiles Have Created A Deep Web Version Of Kickstarter To Crowdfund Child Porn. *Business Insider.* https://www.businessinsider.com/pedophiles-have-created-a-deep-web-version-of-kickstarter-to-crowdfund-child-porn-2014-11

Corea, F., & Corea, F. (2019). The convergence of AI and blockchain. *Applied artificial intelligence: Where AI can be used in business*, 19-26.

Corelli, A. (2018). Cryptocurrencies and Exchange Rates: A Relationship and Causality Analysis. *Risks, 6*(4), 111. doi:10.3390/risks6040111

Corporate Finance Institute. (2022). *Inflation Hedge.* https://corporatefinanceinstitute.com/resources/wealth-management/inflation-hedge/#:~:text=Inflation%20hedge%20refers%20to%20investments,in%20value%20during%20inflationary%20cycles

Creasy, T. (n.d.). *An Introduction to Change Management: What it is and why it makes a difference in your organization.* Prosci, Inc.

Crypto.com. (2020a). *The history of money – from barter to currency.* https://crypto.com/university/history-of-money-barter-to-bit coin

Crypto.com. (2020b). *The history of money - From Fiat to Cryptocurrency.* https://crypto.com/university/history-of-money-fiat-to-crypt ocurrency?utm_source=crypto.com+university&utm_medium=referr al&utm_campaign=from+barter+to+currency&utm_content=evolutio n+from+fiat+to+cryptocurrency

Crypto.com. (n.d.). *Crypto.com Visa Card.* https://crypto.com/cards

D'Aveni, R. A. (1994). *Hypercompetition* (1st ed.). The Free Press.

da Gama Silva, P. V. J., Klotzle, M. C., Pinto, A. C. F., & Gomes, L. L. (2019). Herding behavior and contagion in the cryptocurrency market. *Journal of Behavioral and Experimental Finance, 22*, 41–50. doi:10.1016/j.jbef.2019.01.006

Dapp, T. (2017). Fintech: The Digital Transformation in the Financial Sector. Academic Press.

Dapp, T., & Slomka, L., AG, D. B., & Hoffmann, R. (2014). FinTech–The digital (r) evolution in the financial sector. *Deutsche Bank Research, 11*, 1–39.

Darlington III, J. K. (2014). *The future of Bitcoin: mapping the global adoption of world's largest cryptocurrency through benefit analysis.* Academic Press.

Davis, D. B. (2019). *Ransomware Activity Declines, But Remains Dangerous Threat.* Symantec Enterprise Blogs. Retrieved March 20, 2023, from https://symantec-enterprise-blogs.security.com/blogs/expert-perspectives/ransomware-activity-declines-remains-dangerous-threat

Davis, F. D. (1989). Perceived usefulness, perceived ease of use, and user acceptance of information technology. *Management Information Systems Quarterly, 13*(3), 319–339. doi:10.2307/249008

De Filippi, P. (2014). Bitcoin: a regulatory nightmare to a libertarian dream. *Internet Policy Review, 3*(2).

De Filippi, P., & Wright, A. (2018). Blockchain and the law: The rule of code. *Harvard Journal of Law & Technology, 28*(2), 614–638.

De Gregorio, J. (2018). *Productivity in Emerging-Market Economies: Slowdown or Stagnation?* Peterson Institute for International Economics Working Paper (18-12).

De-Best, R. (2023). Share of respondents who indicated they either owned or used cryptocurrencies in 56 countries and territories worldwide from 2019 to 2022. *Statista.* https://www.statista.com/statistics/1202468/global-cryptocur rency-ownership/

Decker, C., & Wattenhofer, R. (2013). Information propagation in the bitcoin network. *IEEE P2P 2013 Proceedings*. 10.1109/P2P.2013.6688704

Demir, A., Pesqué-Cela, V., Altunbas, Y., & Murinde, V. (2022). FinTech, financial inclusion and income inequality: A quantile regression approach. *European Journal of Finance*, *28*(1), 86–107. doi:10.1080/1351847X.2020.1772335

Demirguc-Kunt, A., Klapper, L., Singer, D., & Ansar, S. (2018). *The Global Findex Database 2017: Measuring financial inclusion and the fintech revolution*. World Bank Publications. doi:10.1596/978-1-4648-1259-0

Demirgüç-Kunt, A., Klapper, L., Singer, D., Ansar, S., & Hess, J. (2020). The Global Findex Database 2017: Measuring financial inclusion and opportunities to expand access to and use of financial services. *The World Bank Economic Review*, *34*(Supplement_1), S2–S8. doi:10.1093/wber/lhz013

Den Hartog, D. N., & Verburg, R. M. (2004). High performance work systems, organisational culture and firm effectiveness. *Human Resource Management Journal*, *14*(1), 55–78. doi:10.1111/j.1748-8583.2004.tb00112.x

Deng, H., Dong, C., Xiao, Y., & Liu, Z. (2020). FinTech Integration in E-Business: A Systematic Review. *International Journal of Information Management*. Advance online publication. doi:10.1016/j.ijinfomgt.2020.102180

Deshpandé, R., Farley, J. U., & Webster, F. E. Jr. (1993). Corporate culture, customer orientation, and innovativeness in Japanese firms: A quadrad analysis. *Journal of Marketing*, *57*(1), 23–37. doi:10.1177/002224299305700102

DeVries, P. D. (2016). An analysis of cryptocurrency, bitcoin, and the future. *International Journal of Business Management and Commerce*, *1*(2), 1–9.

Diaz, M. (2021). Digital assets beyond traditional cryptocurrencies: The rise of NFTs. *Journal of Digital Economy*, *10*(2), 87–104.

Dickens, S. (2021). Squid Game meme coin crashes by 99.9% after developers pull the plug. *Yahoo!* https://www.yahoo.com/now/squid-game-meme-coin-crashes-131908065.html

Diener, F., & Spacek, M. (2021, January 1). Digital Transformation in Banking: A Managerial Perspective on Barriers to Change. *Sustainability*, *13*(2032), 2032. Advance online publication. doi:10.3390u13042032

Dierksmeier, C., & Seele, P. (2018). Cryptocurrencies and business ethics. *Journal of Business Ethics*, *152*(1), 1–14. doi:10.100710551-016-3298-0

DiMaggio, P. (1997). Culture and cognition. *Annual Review of Sociology*, 23.

Dion-Schwarz, C., Manheim, D., & Johnston, P. B. (2019). *Terrorist use of cryptocurrencies: Technical and organizational barriers and future threats*. Rand Corporation. doi:10.7249/RR3026

Dodd, N. (2018). The social life of Bitcoin. *Theory, Culture & Society*, *35*(3), 35–56. doi:10.1177/0263276417746464

Đokić, K., Radman-Funarić, M., & Potnik Galić, K. (2015). The Relationship between the Cryptocurrency Value (Bitcoin) and Interest for it in the Region. *ENTRENOVA-ENTerprise REsearch InNOVAtion*, *1*(1), 419–426. doi:10.2139srn.3281915

Domingo, R.-S., Piñeiro-Chousa, J., & López-Cabarcos, M. Á. (2020). What factors drive returns on initial coin offerings? *Technological Forecasting and Social Change*, *153*, 119915. doi:10.1016/j.techfore.2020.119915

Domingos, P. (2012). A few useful things to know about machine learning. *Communications of the ACM*, *55*(10), 78–87. doi:10.1145/2347736.2347755

Doran, M. D. (2014). *A forensic look at bitcoin cryptocurrency*. Utica College.

Dorfleitner, G., & Hornuf, L. (2019). FinTech Business Models. In G. Dorfleitner & L. Hornuf (Eds.), *FinTech and Data Privacy in Germany: An Empirical Analysis with Policy Recommendations* (pp. 85–106). Springer International Publishing. doi:10.1007/978-3-030-31335-7_5

Dorfleitner, G., Hornuf, L., Schmitt, M., & Weber, M. (2017). *Definition of FinTech and Description of the FinTech Industry*. Springer. doi:10.1007/978-3-319-54666-7_2

Douglass, R. B. (1977). *Belief, attitude, intention, and behavior: An introduction to theory and research*. JSTOR.

Dumitrescu, G. C. (2017). Bitcoin–a brief analysis of the advantages and disadvantages. *Global Economic Observer*, *5*(2), 63–71.

Du, W. D., Pan, S. L., Leidner, D. E., & Ying, W. (2019). Affordances, experimentation and actualization of FinTech: A blockchain implementation study. *The Journal of Strategic Information Systems*, *28*(1), 50–65. doi:10.1016/j.jsis.2018.10.002

Dwyer, G. P. (2015). The economics of Bitcoin and similar private digital currencies. *Journal of Financial Stability*, *17*, 81–91.

Eickhoff, M., Muntermann, J., & Weinrich, T. (2017). *What do FinTechs actually do? A Taxonomy of FinTech Business Models*. Paper presented at the ICIS.

Einwiller, S. A., & Steilen, S. (2015). Handling complaints on social network sites–An analysis of complaints and complaint responses on Facebook and Twitter pages of large US companies. *Public Relations Review*, *41*(2), 195–204. doi:10.1016/j.pubrev.2014.11.012

El-Bannany, M., Sreedharan, M., & Khedr, A. M. (2020). A robust deep learning model for financial distress prediction. *International Journal of Advanced Computer Science and Applications*, *11*(2). Advance online publication. doi:10.14569/IJACSA.2020.0110222

Enoksen, F. A., & Landsnes, C. J. (2019). *What Can Predict Bubbles in Cryptocurrency Prices?* University of Stavanger.

Enserink, M. (2016). *Evidence on trial.* American Association for the Advancement of Science. doi:10.1126cience.351.6278.1128

Eom, C., & Kim, W. (2020). Predicting the adoption of cryptocurrency using system dynamics modeling. *Journal of Business Research, 112*, 98–109.

ErmakovaT.FabianB.BaumannA.IzmailovM.KrasnovaH. (2017). Bitcoin: drivers and impediments. *Available at* SSRN 3017190.

Ethereum.org. (2023). *Proof-of-Stake.* https://ethereum.org/en/developers/docs/consensus-mechanisms/pos/

Evans, P., Aré, L., Forth, P., Harlé, N., & Portincaso, M. (2016). *A Strategic Perspective on Blockchain and Digital Tokens.* Boston Consulting Group. Available at: https://www. bcg. com/en-gb/publications/2016/blockchain-thinking-outside-the-blocks.aspx

Falkner, B. (2019). Popular blockchain and cryptocurrency adoption models. An analysis of the applications and constraints. *Journal of Innovative Technology.*

Fanusie, Y., & Robinson, T. (2018). *Bitcoin laundering: An analysis of illicit flows into digital currency services.* Center on Sanctions and Illicit Finance Memorandum.

Faqih, K. M. (2016). An empirical analysis of factors predicting the behavioral intention to adopt Internet shopping technology among non-shoppers in a developing country context: Does gender matter? *Journal of Retailing and Consumer Services, 30*, 140–164. doi:10.1016/j.jretconser.2016.01.016

Farell, R. (2015). *An analysis of the cryptocurrency industry.* Academic Press.

Fermay, A. H., Santosa, B., Kertopati, A. Y., & Eprianto, I. M. (2018). The development of collaborative model between FinTech and bank in Indonesia. *Proceedings of the 2nd International Conference on E-commerce, E-Business and E-Government.* 10.1145/3234781.3234783

Fethi, M. D., & Pasiouras, F. (2010). Assessing bank efficiency and performance with operational research and artificial intelligence techniques: A survey. *European Journal of Operational Research, 204*(2), 189–198. doi:10.1016/j.ejor.2009.08.003

Feyen, E., Natarajan, H., & Saal, M. (2022). *FinTech and the Future of Finance Overview Paper.* The World Bank Group. https://documents.worldbank.org/curated/en/099450005162250110/P17300600228b70070914b0b5edf26e2f9f

Fichman, P., & Sanfillippo, M. R. (2020). The dark side of social media: Informing digital marketing with dark web analytics. *Journal of Business Research, 110*, 230–239.

FinTech Adoption Index. (2017). *The rapid emergence of FinTech.* Retrieved March 21, 2023, from https://assets.ey.com/content/dam/ey-sites/ey-com/en_gl/topics/megatrends/ey-megatrends-2020.pdf

Fitzgerald, M. (2016). General Motors relies on IoT to anticipate customers' needs. *MIT Sloan Management Review, 57*(4).

Flodmark, A., & Jakum, M. (2022). *Characterizing Bitcoin Spam Emails: An analysis of what makes certain Bitcoin spams generate millions of dollars.* Linköping University.

Flori, A. (2019). News and subjective beliefs: A Bayesian approach to Bitcoin investments. *Research in International Business and Finance, 50*, 336–356. doi:10.1016/j.ribaf.2019.05.007

Foley, S., Karlsen, J. R., & Putniņš, T. J. (2019). Sex, drugs, and bitcoin: How much illegal activity is financed through cryptocurrencies? *Review of Financial Studies, 32*(5), 1798–1853. doi:10.1093/rfs/hhz015

Folkinshteyn, D., & Lennon, M. (2016). Braving Bitcoin: A technology acceptance model (TAM) analysis. *Journal of Information Technology Case and Application Research, 18*(4), 220–249. doi:10.1080/15228053.2016.1275242

Forbes Magazine. (2022, September 20). *What really happened to Luna Crypto?* https://www.forbes.com/sites/qai/2022/09/20/what-really-happened-to-luna-crypto/?sh=1a7a684e4ff1

Forbes. (2021). *How To Prevent A Data Breach In Your Company.* https://www.forbes.com/sites/forbesbusinesscouncil/2021/07/30/how-to-prevent-a-data-breach-in-your-company/?sh=c14fde718da7

Forbes. (2023). *Uses of FinTech.* https://www.forbes.com/advisor/banking/what-is-FinTech/

Formica, P., & Curley, M. (2018). *Exploring the Culture of Open Innovation.* Emerald Bingley. doi:10.1108/9781787437890

Franceschi-Bicchierai. (2022). Meet the Blockchain Detectives Who Track Crypto's Hackers and Scammers. *Vice News.* https://www.vice.com/en/article/xgd9zw/meet-the-blockchain-detectives-who-track-cryptos-hackers-and-scammers

Franco, P. (2014). *Understanding Bitcoin: Cryptography, engineering and economics.* John Wiley & Sons. doi:10.1002/9781119019138

Frankenfield, J. (2023, January 3). *51% attack: Definition, who is at risk, example, and cost.* Investopedia. https://www.investopedia.com/terms/1/51-attack.asp#:~:text=for%20financial%20brands.-,What%20Is%20a%2051%25%20Attack%3F,power%20to%20alter%20the%20blockchain

Freberg, K., Graham, K., McGaughey, K., & Freberg, L. A. (2011). Who are the social media influencers? A study of public perceptions of personality. *Public Relations Review, 37*(1), 90–92. doi:10.1016/j.pubrev.2010.11.001

Frik, A., & Mittone, L. (2019). Factors influencing the perception of website privacy trustworthiness and users' purchasing intentions: The behavioral economics perspective. *Journal of Theoretical and Applied Electronic Commerce Research*, *14*(3), 89–125. doi:10.4067/S0718-18762019000300107

Frimpong, K., Shuridah, O., Wilson, A., & Sarpong, F. (2020). A cross-national investigation of trait antecedents of mobile-banking adoption. *Thunderbird International Business Review*, *62*(4), 411–424. doi:10.1002/tie.22132

Frost, J. (2020). *The economic forces driving FinTech adoption across countries*. Bank for International Settlements. https://www.bis.org/publ/work838.pdf

FSB. (2019). *Retrieved from Girling, P. X. (2022). Operational Risk Management: A Complete Guide for Banking and Fintech*. John Wiley & Sons.

Fu, J., & Mishra, M. (2020). *The global impact of COVID-19 on FinTech adoption*. Swiss Finance Institute Research Paper (20-38).

Fung, B. (2021). The world of non-fungible tokens: A revolution in digital asset ownership. *Digital Art and Culture*, *3*(2), 50–68.

Fung, B., & Halaburda, H. (2014). Understanding platform-based digital currencies. *Bank of Canada Review*, *2014*(Spring), 12–20.

Fuster, A., Plosser, M., Schnabl, P., & Vickery, J. (2019). The role of technology in mortgage lending. *Review of Financial Studies*, *32*(5), 1854–1899. doi:10.1093/rfs/hhz018

Gai, K., Qiu, M., & Sun, X. (2018). A survey on FinTech. *Journal of Network and Computer Applications*, *103*, 262–273. doi:10.1016/j.jnca.2017.10.011

Galbreath, J. (2010). Drivers of corporate social responsibility: The role of formal strategic planning and firm culture. *British Journal of Management*, *21*(2), 511–525.

Galen, D., Brand, N., Boucherle, L., Davis, R., Do, N., El-Baz, B., . . . Lee, J. (2018). *Blockchain for social impact: Moving beyond the hype*. Center for Social Innovation, RippleWorks.

Gandal, N., & Halaburda, H. (2016). Can we predict the winner in a market with network effects? Competition in cryptocurrency market. *Games*, *7*(3), 16. doi:10.3390/g7030016

Gao, Y., Zang, L., Roth, A., & Wang, P. (2017). Does democracy cause innovation? An empirical test of the popper hypothesis. *Research Policy*, *46*(7), 1272–1283. doi:10.1016/j.respol.2017.05.014

Garcia, D., & Schweitzer, F. (2015). Social signals and algorithmic trading of Bitcoin. *Royal Society Open Science*, *2*(9), 150288. doi:10.1098/rsos.150288 PMID:26473051

Gassmann, O., Enkel, E., & Chesbrough, H. (2010). The future of open innovation. *Research Management*, *40*(3), 213–221.

Gazel, M., & Schwienbacher, A. (2021). Entrepreneurial fintech clusters. *Small Business Economics*, *57*(2), 883–903. doi:10.100711187-020-00331-1

Gerken, T. (2023, January 6). *US Bank Silvergate hit with $8bn in crypto withdrawals.* BBC News. https://www.bbc.com/news/technology-64176446

Gerlach, J. M., & Lutz, J. K. (2019). Evidence on usage behavior and future adoption intention of FinTechs and digital finance solutions. *The International Journal of Business and Finance Research, 13*(2), 83–105.

Ghazinoory, S., Abdi, M., & Feizi, M. (2021). A systematic review of the blockchain technology adoption in supply chain management: Challenges and opportunities. *Journal of Cleaner Production, 312,* 127813.

Giglio, F. (2021). Fintech: A Literature Review. *European Research Studies Journal, 24*(2B), 600–627. doi:10.35808/ersj/2254

Gill, R. (2002). Change Management—Or change leadership? *Journal of Change Management, 3*(4), 307–318. doi:10.1080/714023845

Gimpel, H., Rau, D., & Röglinger, M. (2018). Understanding FinTech start-ups – a taxonomy of consumer-oriented service offerings. *Electronic Markets, 28*(3), 245–264. doi:10.100712525-017-0275-0

Giudici, P. (2018). Financial data science. *Statistics & Probability Letters, 136,* 160–164. doi:10.1016/j.spl.2018.02.024

Glaser, F. (2017). Pervasive decentralisation of digital infrastructures: A framework for blockchain enabled system and use case analysis. *Proceedings of the 50th Hawaii International Conference on System Sciences.* 10.24251/HICSS.2017.186

Glaser, F., Zimmermann, K., Haferkorn, M., Weber, M. C., & Siering, M. (2014). *Bitcoin-asset or currency? revealing users' hidden intentions. In Revealing Users' Hidden Intentions.* ECIS.

Gloor, P. (2012). *Making the e-Business Transformation.* Springer-Verlag. doi:10.1007/978-1-4471-0757-6

Goldfarb, A., & Tucker, C. (2019). Digital economics. *Journal of Economic Literature, 57*(1), 3–43. doi:10.1257/jel.20171452

Goldsmith, J. (2019). The IMF Must Develop Best Practices before Government-Backed Cryptocurrencies Destabilize the International Monetary System. *Emory Int'l L. Rev., 34,* 595.

Goldstein, I., Jiang, W., & Karolyi, G. A. (2019). To FinTech and beyond. *Review of Financial Studies, 32*(5), 1647–1661. doi:10.1093/rfs/hhz025

Gomber, P., Koch, J.-A., & Siering, M. (2017). Digital Finance and FinTech: Current research and future research directions. *Journal of Business Economics, 87*(5), 537–580. doi:10.100711573-017-0852-x

Gorbunov, E. (2021). *Changing Cryptocurrency Perceptions: An Experimental Study.* Academic Press.

Government of Canada. (2021). *Money laundering and terrorist financing indicators— Virtual currency transactions*. https://fintrac-canafe.canada.ca/guidance-directives/transac tion-operation/indicators-indicateurs/vc_mltf-eng

Gozman, D., Liebenau, J., & Mangan, J. (2018). The innovation mechanisms of FinTech start-ups: Insights from SWIFT's innotribe competition. *Journal of Management Information Systems*, *35*(1), 145–179. doi:10.1080/07421222.2018.1440768

Grant, A. M., & Mayer, D. M. (2009). Good soldiers and good actors: Prosocial and impression management motives as interactive predictors of affiliative citizenship behaviors. *The Journal of Applied Psychology*, *94*(4), 900–912. doi:10.1037/a0013770 PMID:19594233

Greenberg, J. (1990). Organizational justice: Yesterday, today, and tomorrow. *Journal of Management*, *16*(2), 399–432. doi:10.1177/014920639001600208

Grima, S., Özen, E., & Boz, H. (2020). *Contemporary Issues in Business, Economics and Finance* (Vol. 104). Emerald Publishing Bingley. doi:10.1108/9781839096051

Grohmann, A., Klühs, T., & Menkhoff, L. (2018). Does financial literacy improve financial inclusion? Cross country evidence. *World Development*, *111*, 84–96. doi:10.1016/j.worlddev.2018.06.020

Guadamuz, A. (2022). These are not the apes you are looking for. *Communications of the ACM*, *65*(9), 20–22. doi:10.1145/3548761

Guégan, D., & Renault, T. (2021). Does investor sentiment on social media provide robust information for Bitcoin returns predictability? *Finance Research Letters*, *38*, 101494. doi:10.1016/j.frl.2020.101494

Guo, Y., & Liang, C. (2016). Blockchain application and outlook in the banking industry. *Financial Innovation, 2*, 1-12.

Gupta, R., Mejia, C., Gianchandani, Y. B., & Kajikawa, Y. (2021). Ambidextrous firm strategy insights from internet of things linked interfirm deals. *IEEE Transactions on Engineering Management*, *70*(1), 112–127. doi:10.1109/TEM.2020.3041250

Gu, S., Ślusarczyk, B., Hajizada, S., Kovalyova, I., & Sakhbieva, A. (2021). Impact of the covid-19 pandemic on online consumer purchasing behavior. *Journal of Theoretical and Applied Electronic Commerce Research*, *16*(6), 2263–2281. doi:10.3390/jtaer16060125

Haddad, C., & Hornuf, L. (2019). The emergence of the global FinTech market: Economic and technological determinants. *Small Business Economics*, *53*(1), 81–105. doi:10.100711187-018-9991-x

Haddad, C., & Hornuf, L. (2022). How do fintech start-ups affect financial institutions' performance and default risk? *European Journal of Finance*, 1–32.

Haddad, H., Day, M., & Nelson, J. (2021). Cryptocurrency Adoption: A Literature Review. *Financial Counseling and Planning*, *32*(1), 52–65.

Halaburda, H. (2018). Blockchain revolution without the blockchain? *Communications of the ACM, 61*(7), 27–29. doi:10.1145/3225619

Han, W., Duong, V., Nguyen, L., & Mier, C. (2020, May). Darknet and bitcoin de-anonymization: Emerging development. In 2020 Zooming Innovation in Consumer Technologies Conference (ZINC) (pp. 222- 226). IEEE.

Han, H., Lee, K.-S., Radic, A., Ngah, A. H., & Kim, J. J. (2021). The extended self-identify-based electric product adoption model and airline business strategy: A new theoretical framework for green technology products. *Journal of Travel & Tourism Marketing, 38*(3), 247–262. doi:10.10 80/10548408.2021.1906386

Harrison, P. (2022). *The FinTech Times*. https://theFinTechtimes.com/88-of-cloud-breaches-are-due-to-human-error-heres-how-to-avoid-data-breaches/

Harvey, C., & Tymoigne, E. (2015). Do cryptocurrencies such as Bitcoin have a future. *Retrieved*, (July), 10.

Harwick, C. (2016). Cryptocurrency and the problem of intermediation. *The Independent Review, 20*(4), 569-588.

Hasan, R., Ashfaq, M., & Shao, L. (2021). Evaluating drivers of FinTech adoption in the Netherlands. *Global Business Review*. doi:10.1177/09721509211027402

Hassani, H., Huang, X., & Silva, E. (2018). Digitalisation and big data mining in banking. *Big Data and Cognitive Computing, 2*(3), 18. doi:10.3390/bdcc2030018

Hatammimi, J., & Krisnawati, A. (2018). Financial literacy for entrepreneur in the industry 4.0 era: A conceptual framework in Indonesia. *Proceedings of the 2018 10th International Conference on Information Management and Engineering*. 10.1145/3285957.3285985

Hayek, F. A. (1945). The use of knowledge in society. *American Economic Review*, 519-530.

Hayes, A. (2022). *Convertible Virtual Currency*. Investopedia. https://www.investopedia.com/terms/c/convertible-virtual-currency.asp#:~:text=Convertible%20virtual%20currency%20is%20an,as%20dollars%20via%20cryptocurrency%20exchanges

Hayes, A. (2016). *Decentralized banking: Monetary technocracy in the digital age*. Springer.

Hayes, A. (2021). PayPal and cryptocurrencies: Bridging the gap between traditional finance and digital assets. *Journal of FinTech, 9*(4), 190–203.

Hemantha, Y. (2022). Embracing block chain technology in supply chain to combat counterfeiting luxury and fashion brands. *Asian Journal of Management, 13*(2), 145–150.

Hendrikse, R. (2019). Can selfies spark the identity (r) evolution in financial services? *Biometric Technology Today, 2019*(4), 5–7. doi:10.1016/S0969-4765(19)30053-0

Hendriyani, C., & Raharja, S. u. J. (2019). Business agility strategy: Peer-to-peer lending of Fintech startup in the era of digital finance in Indonesia. *Review of Integrative Business and Economics Research, 8*, 239–246.

Hiatt, J. M. (2006). *ADKAR: A Model for Change in Business, Government, and Our Community* (1st ed.). Prosci Learning Center Publications.

Hileman, G., & Rauchs, M. (2017). *2017 global cryptocurrency benchmarking study.* Available at *SSRN* 2965436.

Hileman, G., & Rauchs, M. (2021). *Global cryptocurrency benchmarking study.* Cambridge Centre for Alternative Finance.

Hill, C., Hult, T., McKaig, T., & Cotae, F. (2021). *Global Business Today.* McGraw-Hill Ryerson Ltd.

Hippel, E., & Krogh, G. (2003). Open source software and the "private-collective" innovation model: Issues for organization science. *Organization Science, 14*(2), 209–223. doi:10.1287/orsc.14.2.209.14992

Hirst, T. (2015). *These are the top 9 countries for Islamic finance.* World Economic Forum. https://www.weforum.org/agenda/2015/07/top-9-countries-islamic-finance/

Hoepner, A. G., Kruger, T. H., & Scholz, H. (2020). Beyond Bitcoin – The blockchain revolution in financial services. *Journal of Business Research, 116*, 225–239.

Hoffman, J. (2020). Technology Adoption Life Cycle. *Journal of Technology Adoption, 3*(2), 145–156.

Hofstede, G. H., & Hofstede, G. (2001). *Culture's consequences: Comparing values, behaviors, institutions and organizations across nations.* Sage.

Hogg, R. (2022). Seth Green pays $260,000 ransom for a stolen Bored Ape Ethereum NFT meant to feature in his new TV show. *Business Insider.* https://www.businessinsider.com/seth-green-pays-260000-return-stolen-bored-ape-ethereum-nft-2022-6

Holt, T. J., Smirnova, O., Chua, Y. T., & Copes, H. (2015). Examining the risk reduction strategies of actors in online criminal markets. *Global Crime, 16*(2), 81–103. doi:10.1080/17440572.2015.1013211

Hooper, A., & Holtbrügge, D. (2020). Blockchain technology in international business: Changing the agenda for global governance. *Review of International Business and Strategy, 30*(2), 183–200. doi:10.1108/RIBS-06-2019-0078

Hope, O. K. (2003). Firm-level disclosures and the relative roles of culture and legal origin. *Journal of International Financial Management & Accounting, 14*(3), 218–248. doi:10.1111/1467-646X.00097

Horch, A., Schunck, C. H., & Ruff, C. (2022). Adversary Tactics and Techniques specific to Cryptocurrency Scams. *Open Identity Summit 2022.*

Hornuf, L., Klus, M. F., Lohwasser, T. S., & Schwienbacher, A. (2021). How do banks interact with fintech startups? *Small Business Economics, 57*(3), 1505–1526. doi:10.100711187-020-00359-3

Hoskins, P. (2023). *FTX: Collapsed crypto exchange says $415m was hacked.* BBC News. https://www.bbc.com/news/business-64313624

Houben, R., Snyers, A., & Van Kerckhove, K. (2021). Cryptocurrency exchanges and regulatory compliance. *Journal of Financial Regulation, 17*(1), 5–19.

Howard, L. (2013). Chinese Currency Manipulation: Are There Any Solutions? *Emory Int'l L. Rev., 27,* 1215.

Hsu, C.-L., & Lin, J. C.-C. (2015). What drives purchase intention for paid mobile apps?–An expectation confirmation model with perceived value. *Electronic Commerce Research and Applications, 14*(1), 46–57. doi:10.1016/j.elerap.2014.11.003

Huang, R. H. (2018). Online P2P lending and regulatory responses in China: Opportunities and challenges. *European Business Organization Law Review, 19*(1), 63–92. doi:10.100740804-018-0100-z

Huang, Y., Li, X., & Li, W. (2018). Factors affecting cryptocurrency prices: Evidence from Bitcoin, Ethereum, Dash, Bitcoin, and Monero. *Journal of Internet Banking and Commerce, 23*(1), 1–14.

Huang, Z., & Liu, Q. (2017). An empirical study on factors affecting the adoption of Bitcoin. *Applied Economics, 49*(11), 1111–1120.

Huerta, J. M., & Anand, A. (2018). Machine learning and artificial intelligence in consumer banking. *Journal of Digital Banking, 3*(1), 22–32.

Hughes, A., Park, A., Kietzmann, J., & Archer-Brown, C. (2019). Beyond Bitcoin: What blockchain and distributed ledger technologies mean for firms. *Business Horizons, 62*(3), 273–281. doi:10.1016/j.bushor.2019.01.002

Hutto, C., & Gilbert, E. (2014). Vader: A parsimonious rule-based model for sentiment analysis of social media text. *Proceedings of the international AAAI conference on web and social media.* 10.1609/icwsm.v8i1.14550

Hu, Z., Ding, S., Li, S., Chen, L., & Yang, S. (2019). Adoption intention of FinTech services for bank users: An empirical examination with an extended technology acceptance model. *Symmetry, 11*(3), 340. doi:10.3390ym11030340

Ibrahim, A. K., & Benabdelhadi, A. (2022). Organizational Change Management of Digital Administration. *International Journal of Human Resource Management, 3*(2), 339–356. doi:10.5281/zenodo.639041

Iman, N. (2018). Assessing the dynamics of FinTech in Indonesia. *Investment Management and Financial Innovations*, *15*(4), 296–303. doi:10.21511/imfi.15(4).2018.24

International Monetary Fund. (2017). *Islamic finance and the role of IMF*. https://www.imf.org/external/themes/islamicfinance/#1

International Monetary Fund. (2019). *FinTech: The Experience So Far*. https://www.imf.org/en/Publications/Policy-Papers/Issues/2019/06/27/FinTech-The-Experience-So-Far-47056

International Monetary Fund. (n.d.). *The end of the Bretton Woods System*. https://www.imf.org/external/about/histend.htm#:~:text=End%20of%20Bretton%20Woods%20system,-The%20system%20dissolved&text=In%20August%201971%2C%20U.S.%20President,the%20breakdown%20of%20the%20system

Irfan, E., Ali, Y., & Sabir, M. (2022). Analysing role of businesses' investment in digital literacy: A case of Pakistan. *Technological Forecasting and Social Change*, *176*, 121484. doi:10.1016/j.techfore.2022.121484

Irwin, A. S., & Milad, G. (2016). The use of crypto-currencies in funding violent jihad. *Journal of Money Laundering Control*, *19*(4), 407–425. doi:10.1108/JMLC-01-2016-0003

Ismanto, L., Ar, H. S., Fajar, A., & Bachtiar, S. (2019). *Blockchain as E-commerce platform in Indonesia*. Paper presented at the Journal of Physics: Conference Series.

Iwamura, M., Kitamura, Y., & Matsumoto, T. (2014). Is Bitcoin the Only Cryptocurrency in the Town? *Economics of Cryptocurrency*.

Jabotinsky, H. Y., & Sarel, R. (2022). How crisis affects crypto: Coronavirus as a test case. *The Hastings Law Journal*. Advance online publication. doi:10.2139srn.3557929

Jacobs, P., & Schain, L. (2011). The never ending attraction of the Ponzi Scheme. *Journal of Comprehensive Research*, *9*, 40–46.

Jeffries, I., Johnson, R., & Staples, M. (2022). *How inflation is flipping the economic script in seven charts*. McKinsey & Company. https://www.mckinsey.com/featured-insights/inflation/how-inflation-is-flipping-the-economic-script?cid=soc-web

Johar, S., Ahmad, N., Asher, W., Cruickshank, H., & Durrani, A. (2021). Research and applied perspective to blockchain technology: A comprehensive survey. *Applied Sciences (Basel, Switzerland)*, *11*(14), 6252. doi:10.3390/app11146252

Johnson, B., Laszka, A., Grossklags, J., Vasek, M., & Moore, T. (2014). *Game-theoretic analysis of DDoS attacks against Bitcoin mining pools*. Paper presented at the Financial Cryptography and Data Security: FC 2014 Workshops, BITCOIN and WAHC 2014, Christ Church, Barbados. 10.1007/978-3-662-44774-1_6

Jokić, S., Cvetković, A. S., Adamović, S., Ristić, N., & Spalević, P. (2019). Comparative analysis of cryptocurrency wallets vs traditional wallets. *Ekonomika, 65*(3), 65-75.

Jordan, M. I., & Mitchell, T. M. (2015). Machine learning: Trends, perspectives, and prospects. *Science, 349*(6245), 255–260. doi:10.1126cience.aaa8415 PMID:26185243

Jovarauskiene & Pilinkienė. (2009). E-Business or E-Technology? *Engineering Economics,* (1).

Joyce, W. F. (1999). *MegaChange* (1st ed.). The Free Press.

Juhász, P. L., Stéger, J., Kondor, D., & Vattay, G. (2018). A bayesian approach to identify bitcoin users. *PLoS One, 13*(12), e0207000. doi:10.1371/journal.pone.0207000 PMID:30543629

Kabulova, J., & Stankevičienė, J. (2020). Valuation of FinTech innovation based on patent applications. *Sustainability, 12*(23), 10158. doi:10.3390u122310158

Kaeble, D. (2018). *Time Served in State Prison, 2016 (NCJ 252205).* US Department of Justice, Bureau of Justice Statistics.

Kamal, M. A. (2019). The Technological–Organizational–Environmental (TOE) Framework: A Model for Understanding Cryptocurrency Adoption. *International Journal of Technological Learning, Innovation, and Development, 12*(3), 293–310.

Kamble, S., Gunasekaran, A., & Arha, H. (2019). Understanding the Blockchain technology adoption in supply chains-Indian context. *International Journal of Production Research, 57*(7), 2009–2033. doi:10.1080/00207543.2018.1518610

Kaminski, J. (2014). Nowcasting the Bitcoin market with Twitter signals. arXiv preprint arXiv:1406.7577.

Kapsis, I. (2020). Blockchain and cryptocurrencies: Essential tools in a two-tier financial system. *Capital Markets Law Journal, 15*(1), 18–47. doi:10.1093/cmlj/kmz025

Kavuri, A. S., & Milne, A. (2019). *FinTech and the future of financial services: What are the research gaps?* Academic Press.

Khan, I. U., Hameed, Z., & Khan, S. U. (2017). Understanding online banking adoption in a developing country: UTAUT2 with cultural moderators. *Journal of Global Information Management, 25*(1), 43–65. doi:10.4018/JGIM.2017010103

Kim & Kim. (2018). Consumer adoption of cryptocurrency: An examination of the technology acceptance model. *Journal of Electronic Commerce.*

Kim & Lee. (2019). Adoption of cryptocurrency: An analysis of consumer attitudes and behaviors. *Applied Economics, 49*(11), 11–1120.

Kim & Lee. (2020). *The Role of Trust in the Adoption of Cryptocurrency.* Academic Press.

Kim, J. (2019). A TOE Framework-Driven Model of Cryptocurrency Adoption. *International Journal of Technological Learning, Innovation, and Development.*

Kim, J., Song, H., & Lee, C.-K. (2016). Effects of corporate social responsibility and internal marketing on organizational commitment and turnover intentions. *International Journal of Hospitality Management, 55*, 25–32. doi:10.1016/j.ijhm.2016.02.007

Kim, T. (2015). The predecessors of bitcoin and their implications for the prospect of virtual currencies. *PLoS One, 10*(4), e0123071. doi:10.1371/journal.pone.0123071 PMID:25919027

Kim, T. (2017). On the transaction cost of Bitcoin. *Finance Research Letters, 23*, 300–305. doi:10.1016/j.frl.2017.07.014

Kim, Y. B., Kim, J. G., Kim, W., Im, J. H., Kim, T. H., Kang, S. J., & Kim, C. H. (2016). Predicting fluctuations in cryptocurrency transactions based on user comments and replies. *PLoS One, 11*(8), e0161197. doi:10.1371/journal.pone.0161197 PMID:27533113

Kirkpatrick, D. L. (2001). *Managing Change Effectively*. Butterworth-Heinemann.

Kishore, S. K., & Sequeira, A. H. (2016). An empirical investigation on mobile banking service adoption in rural Karnataka. *SAGE Open, 6*(1). doi:10.1177/2158244016633731

Kliber, A., Marszałek, P., Musiałkowska, I., & Świerczyńska, K. (2019). Bitcoin: Safe haven, hedge or diversifier? Perception of bitcoin in the context of a country's economic situation—A stochastic volatility approach. *Physica A, 524*, 246–257. doi:10.1016/j.physa.2019.04.145

Kondor, D., Pósfai, M., Csabai, I., & Vattay, G. (2014). Do the rich get richer? An empirical analysis of the Bitcoin transaction network. *PLoS One, 9*(2), e86197. doi:10.1371/journal.pone.0086197 PMID:24505257

Kostakis, V., & Giotitsas, C. (2014). The (A) political economy of bitcoin. *tripleC: Communication, Capitalism & Critique. Open Access Journal for a Global Sustainable Information Society, 12*(2), 431–440-431–440.

Kotler, P., Kartajaya, H., & Setiawan, I. (2021). *Marketing 4.0: Moving from traditional to digital*. John Wiley & Sons.

Kotler, P., Keller, K. L., & Burton, S. (2020). *Marketing management*. Pearson Australia.

Kotter, J. P. (1996). *Leading Change*. Harvard Business School Press.

Kotter, J. P. (2008). *Corporate culture and performance*. Simon and Schuster.

Kotter, J. P. (2012). Accelerate! *Harvard Business Review*. PMID:23155997

Kotter, J. P. (2014). *Accelerate: Building strategic agility for a faster-moving world*. Harvard Business Review Press.

Kotter, J. P., & Schlesinger, L. A. (2008, July-August). Choosing Strategies for Change. *Harvard Business Review*. PMID:10240501

Kou, G. (2019). Introduction to the special issue on FinTech. *Financial Innovation, 5*(1), 45.

Kramer, A. S., & Tiemann, B. J. (2022). When Are Cryptocurrencies Appropriate Investments for Retirement Plans and IRAs? US Labor Department Cautions 401(k) Plan Fiduciaries to Exercise Extreme Care. *Intellectual Property & Technology Law Journal, 34*(6), 3–6.

Kristoufek, L. (2013). BitCoin meets Google Trends and Wikipedia: Quantifying the relationship between phenomena of the Internet era. *Scientific Reports, 3*(1), 3415. doi:10.1038rep03415 PMID:24301322

Krombholz, K., Judmayer, A., Gusenbauer, M., & Weippl, E. (2017). The other side of the coin: User experiences with bitcoin security and privacy. *Financial Cryptography and Data Security: 20th International Conference, FC 2016, Christ Church, Barbados, February 22–26, 2016, Revised Selected Papers, 20.* 10.1007/978-3-662-54970-4_33

Kshetri, N. (2018). 1 The evolution of the internet of things industry and market in China: An interplay of institutions, demands and supply. *Telecommunications Policy, 42*(1), 3–16.

Kshetri, N. (2018). Blockchain's roles in meeting key supply chain management objectives. *International Journal of Information Management, 39*, 80–89. doi:10.1016/j.ijinfomgt.2017.12.005

Kshetri, N. (2021). The Economics of Central Bank Digital Currency. *Computer, 54*(6), 53–58. doi:10.1109/MC.2021.3070091

Lacity, M. C. (2018). *Enterprise blockchains: Eight sources of business value and the obstacles in their way.* https://walton. uark. edu/enterprise/downloads/blockchain/La cityBlockchainsExplained. pdf

Laidroo, L., Koroleva, E., Kliber, A., Rupeika-Apoga, R., & Grigaliuniene, Z. (2021). Business models of FinTechs–Difference in similarity? *Electronic Commerce Research and Applications, 46*, 101034. doi:10.1016/j.elerap.2021.101034

Lamon, C., Nielsen, E., & Redondo, E. (2017). Cryptocurrency price prediction using news and social media sentiment. *SMU Data Sci. Rev, 1*(3), 1–22.

Lam, S. Y., & Shankar, V. (2014). Asymmetries in the effects of drivers of brand loyalty between early and late adopters and across technology generations. *Journal of Interactive Marketing, 28*(1), 26–42. doi:10.1016/j.intmar.2013.06.004

Lansiti, M., & Lakhani, K. R. (2021). Marketing in the cryptocurrency industry: Challenges and opportunities. *Journal of Marketing Research, 58*(2), 319–334.

Lauer, T. (2021). *Change Management: Fundamentals and Success Factors.* Springer., doi:10.1007/978-3-662-62187-5

Lavorgna, A. (2014). Internet-mediated drug trafficking: Towards a better understanding of new criminal dynamics. *Trends in Organized Crime, 17*(4), 250–270. doi:10.100712117-014-9226-8

Lawal, I. M. I. M. (2019). The suitability of cryptocurrency in the structure of Islamic banking and finance. *Jurnal Perspektif Pembiayaan Dan Pembangunan Daerah, 6*(6), 639–648. doi:10.22437/ppd.v6i6.6603

Lee & Kim. (2019). *Cryptocurrency adoption: A study of consumer preferences and motivations.* Academic Press.

Lee, E.-Y., Lee, S.-B., & Jeon, Y. J. J. (2017). Factors influencing the behavioral intention to use food delivery apps. *Social Behavior and Personality*, *45*(9), 1461–1473. doi:10.2224bp.6185

Lee, I., & Shin, Y. J. (2018). FinTech: Ecosystem, business models, investment decisions, and challenges. *Business Horizons*, *61*(1), 35–46. doi:10.1016/j.bushor.2017.09.003

Lee, J. (2021). The diversification of cryptocurrency platforms: New products and services. *Journal of Cryptocurrency and Blockchain Technology*, *12*(1), 1–18.

Lee, K., Choi, Y., & Park, N. (2021). Mobile applications for cryptocurrency platforms: Usability and accessibility. *Journal of Mobile Applications*, *8*(3), 70–85.

Lee, M. R., Yen, D. C., & Hurlburt, G. F. (2018). Financial technologies and applications. *IT Professional*, *20*(2), 27–33. doi:10.1109/MITP.2018.021921648

Lee, M., Yun, J. J., Pyka, A., Won, D., Kodama, F., Schiuma, G., ... Jung, K. (2018). How to respond to the fourth industrial revolution, or the second information technology revolution? Dynamic new combinations between technology, market, and society through open innovation. *Journal of Open Innovation*, *4*(3), 21. doi:10.3390/joitmc4030021

Lele, S. (2023). *FinTech 2.0: A new era of financial inclusion.* https://www.pwc.in/industries/financial-services/FinTech/Fin Tech-insights/FinTech-2-0-a-new-era-of-financial-inclusion.h tml#:~:text=The%20wider%20objective%20of%20FinTech,larger%20 goal%20of%20financial%20inclusion

Leong, C., Tan, B., Xiao, X., Tan, F. T. C., & Sun, Y. (2017). Nurturing a FinTech ecosystem: The case of a youth microloan startup in China. *International Journal of Information Management*, *37*(2), 92–97. doi:10.1016/j.ijinfomgt.2016.11.006

Leuprecht, C., Jenkins, C., & Hamilton, R. (2022). Virtual money laundering: policy implications of the proliferation in the illicit use of cryptocurrency. *Journal of Financial Crime*.

Lewin, K. (1951). *Field Theory in Social Science.* Harper and Brothers Publishers NY.

Li & Rosenbloom. (2018). *Why Have Cryptocurrencies Not Been Widely Adopted? An Analysis of Consumer Attitudes.* Academic Press.

Li & Zhang. (2018). *The impact of perceived risk on cryptocurrency adoption: A study of consumer attitudes.* Academic Press.

Li & Zhang. (2019). *The role of trust in cryptocurrency adoption: An empirical study.* Academic Press.

Li, B. (2022, December 9). *Some key elements of crypto regulation*. International Monetary Fund. https://www.imf.org/en/News/Articles/2022/12/16/sp120922-some-key-elements-of-crypto-regulation

Liang, A. (2023, January 4). *US regulators warn banks over cryptocurrency risks*. BBC News. https://www.bbc.com/news/business-64159452

Liang, X., & Li, Y. (2018). Understanding individual adoption behavior of Bitcoin: An empirical study. *Journal of Business Research, 89*, 216–223.

Liberti, J. M., & Petersen, M. A. (2019). Information: Hard and soft. *Review of Corporate Finance Studies, 8*(1), 1–41. doi:10.1093/rcfs/cfy009

Li, R., Li, S., Yuan, D., & Zhu, H. (2021). Investor attention and cryptocurrency: Evidence from wavelet-based quantile Granger causality analysis. *Research in International Business and Finance, 56*, 101389. doi:10.1016/j.ribaf.2021.101389

Lischke, M., & Fabian, B. (2016). Analyzing the bitcoin network: The first four years. *Future Internet, 8*(1), 7.

Liu, Y., Liu, X., Zhang, L., Tang, C., & Kang, H. (2017). An efficient strategy to eliminate malleability of bitcoin transaction. In *2017 4th International Conference on Systems and Informatics (ICSAI)* (pp. 960-964). IEEE.

Liu, X., & Tsyvinski, A. (2020). Risks and returns of cryptocurrency. *Journal of Financial Economics, 135*(1), 1–19.

Li, Y., Liu, Y., & Xie, F. (2019). Technology directors and firm innovation. *Journal of Multinational Financial Management, 50*, 76–88. doi:10.1016/j.mulfin.2019.04.001

Li, Y., Urquhart, A., Wang, P., & Zhang, W. (2021). MAX momentum in cryptocurrency markets. *International Review of Financial Analysis, 77*, 101829. doi:10.1016/j.irfa.2021.101829

Li, Y., & Wang, J. (2021). The role of institutional investors in the cryptocurrency market: Evidence from Bitcoin. *Journal of Financial Economics, 141*(2), 431–452.

Lockton, D., Harrison, D., & Stanton, N. A. (2010). The Design with Intent Method: A design tool for influencing user behaviour. *Applied Ergonomics, 41*(3), 382–392. doi:10.1016/j.apergo.2009.09.001 PMID:19822311

Lu, H., Wu, Q., & Ye, J. (2020). *FinTech and the future of financial service: A literature review and research agenda*. Academic Press.

Luther, W. J. (2016). Cryptocurrencies, network effects, and switching costs. *Contemporary Economic Policy, 34*(3), 553–571. doi:10.1111/coep.12151

Luu Duc Huynh, T. (2019). Spillover risks on cryptocurrency markets: A look from VAR-SVAR granger causality and student's t copulas. *Journal of Risk and Financial Management, 12*(2), 52. doi:10.3390/jrfm12020052

Luu, L., Teutsch, J., Kulkarni, R., & Saxena, P. (2015). Demystifying incentives in the consensus computer. *Proceedings of the 22nd ACM SIGSAC conference on computer and communications security*. 10.1145/2810103.2813659

Luu, L., Chu, D.-H., Olickel, H., Saxena, P., & Hobor, A. (2016). Making smart contracts smarter. *Proceedings of the 2016 ACM SIGSAC conference on computer and communications security*. 10.1145/2976749.2978309

Lu, Y., & Cong, R. (2020). Cryptocurrency Adoption: An Empirical Study of Factors Affecting User Adoption of Bitcoin. *Journal of Business Research, 116*, 34–44.

Lwin, M., Wirtz, J., & Williams, J. D. (2007). Consumer online privacy concerns and responses: A power–responsibility equilibrium perspective. *Journal of the Academy of Marketing Science, 35*(4), 572–585. doi:10.100711747-006-0003-3

Lyons, B. (2012). *Canadian Macroeconomics: Problems & Policies* (10th ed.). Pearson Prentice Hall.

Macchiavello, E., & Siri, M. (2020). Sustainable finance and FinTech: Can technology contribute to achieving environmental goals. A Preliminary Assessment of 'Green FinTech'. SSRN *Electron. J.* doi:10.2139/ssrn.3672989

Mackenzie, S. (2022). Criminology towards the metaverse: Cryptocurrency scams, grey economy and the technosocial. *British Journal of Criminology, 62*(6), 1537–1552. doi:10.1093/bjc/azab118

Malik, S., Chadhar, M., Vatanasakdakul, S., & Chetty, M. (2021). Factors affecting the organizational adoption of blockchain technology: Extending the technology–organization–environment (TOE) framework in the Australian context. *Sustainability, 13*(16), 9404. doi:10.3390u13169404

Mann, M. (2021). Cryptocurrency security and the challenges faced by exchanges. *Journal of Cybersecurity, 7*(1), 10–24.

Manski, S. (2017). Building the blockchain world: Technological commonwealth or just more of the same? *Strategic Change, 26*(5), 511–522. doi:10.1002/jsc.2151

Mansoori, S. A., Saeidi, S. P., Azizi, R., & Rohani, V. A. (2019). Investigating the factors affecting cryptocurrency adoption in Iran. *Telematics and Informatics, 39*, 125–136.

Mărăcine, V., Voican, O., & Scarlat, E. (2020). The Digital Transformation and Disruption in Business Models of the Banks under the Impact of FinTech and BigTech. *Proceedings of the International Conference on Business Excellence, 14*(1), 294-305. 10.2478/picbe-2020-0028

Marquit, M. (2022). Proof of work vs. proof of stake: Why the difference matters | next advisor with time. *Time Magazine.* https://time.com/nextadvisor/investing/cryptocurrency/proof-of-work-vs-proof-of-stake/

Martínez-Jerez, F. A. (2019). Blockchain technology in business: A review of applications and challenges. *Journal of Business Economics and Management, 20*(2), 291–307.

Martin, J. (1992). *Cultures in organizations: Three perspectives.* Oxford University Press.

Martin, J. (2014). Lost on the Silk Road: Online drug distribution and the 'cryptomarket'. *Criminology & Criminal Justice, 14*(3), 351–367. doi:10.1177/1748895813505234

Martins, C., Oliveira, T., & Popovič, A. (2014). Understanding the Internet banking adoption: A unified theory of acceptance and use of technology and perceived risk application. *International Journal of Information Management, 34*(1), 1–13. doi:10.1016/j.ijinfomgt.2013.06.002

Maurer, B., Nelms, T. C., & Swartz, L. (2013). "When perhaps the real problem is money itself!": The practical materiality of Bitcoin. *Social Semiotics, 23*(2), 261–277. doi:10.1080/10350330 .2013.777594

McCarthy, J. (2007). *What is artificial intelligence.* Academic Press.

McGuire, M., & Dowling, S. (2013). Cyber crime: A review of the evidence. Research Report 75.

McLean, R. D., & Pontiff, J. (2016). Does academic research destroy stock return predictability? *The Journal of Finance, 71*(1), 5–32. doi:10.1111/jofi.12365

Mehrotra, A. (2019). *Financial inclusion through FinTech–a case of lost focus.* Paper presented at the 2019 International conference on automation, computational and technology management (ICACTM). 10.1109/ICACTM.2019.8776857

Melnychenko, S., Volosovych, S., & Baraniuk, Y. (2020). Dominant ideas of financial technologies in digital banking. *Baltic Journal of Economic Studies, 6*(1), 92-99.

Melnyk, N. (2019). *Cryptocurrency in international trade: accounting aspects.* Ternopil National Economic University. https://conf.ztu.edu.ua/wp-content/uploads/2019/06/156-1.pdf

Mendoza-Tello, J. C., Mora, H., Pujol-López, F. A., & Lytras, M. D. (2018). Social commerce as a driver to enhance trust and intention to use cryptocurrencies for electronic payments. *IEEE Access : Practical Innovations, Open Solutions, 6*, 50737–50751. doi:10.1109/ACCESS.2018.2869359

Mensah, I. K., & Mwakapesa, D. S. (2022). The drivers of the behavioral adoption intention of bitcoin payment from the perspective of Chinese citizens. *Security and Communication Networks, 2022*, 1–17. doi:10.1155/2022/7373658

Mention, A. L. (2019). The Future of FinTech. *Research Technology Management, 62*(4), 59–63. doi:10.1080/08956308.2019.1613123

Metzger, M. J., & Flanagin, A. J. (2013). Credibility and trust of information in online environments: The use of cognitive heuristics. *Journal of Pragmatics, 59*, 210–220. doi:10.1016/j. pragma.2013.07.012

Meunier, S. (2018). Blockchain 101: What is blockchain and how does this revolutionary technology work? In Transforming climate finance and green investment with Blockchains (pp. 23-34): Elsevier.

Miau, S., & Yang, J.-M. (2018). Bibliometrics-based evaluation of the Blockchain research trend: 2008–March 2017. *Technology Analysis and Strategic Management, 30*(9), 1029–1045. doi:10 .1080/09537325.2018.1434138

Min, H. (2019). Blockchain technology for enhancing supply chain resilience. *Business Horizons, 62*(1), 35–45. doi:10.1016/j.bushor.2018.08.012

Mizanur, R. M., & Sloan, T. R. (2017). User adoption of mobile commerce in Bangladesh: Integrating perceived risk, perceived cost and personal awareness with TAM. *International Technology Management Review*, 103-124.

Moggridge, E., & Montasari, R. (2022). A Critical Analysis of the Dark Web Challenges to Digital Policing. In *Artificial Intelligence and National Security* (pp. 157–167). Springer. doi:10.1007/978-3-031-06709-9_8

Momaya, K., Pandey, P., Vallaturu, V., Sonar, R., & Bodduri, A. (2020). FinTech platforms, and competitiveness: Exploring role of MoT as a differentiator for firms of Indian origin (FIOs). *Proceedings of the 29th International Conference on Management of Technology.*

Montecchi, M., Plangger, K., & Etter, M. (2019). It's real, trust me! Establishing supply chain provenance using blockchain. *Business Horizons, 62*(3), 283–293. doi:10.1016/j. bushor.2019.01.008

Moon, Y., & Hwang, J. (2018). Crowdfunding as an alternative means for funding sustainable appropriate technology: Acceptance determinants of backers. *Sustainability, 10*(5), 1456. doi:10.3390u10051456

Moore, T., & Christin, N. (2013). Beware the middleman: Empirical analysis of Bitcoin-exchange risk. In *International Conference on Financial Cryptography and Data Security* (pp. 25-33). Springer. 10.1007/978-3-642-39884-1_3

Moore, W., & Stephen, J. (2016). Should cryptocurrencies be included in the portfolio of international reserves held by central banks? *Cogent Economics & Finance, 4*(1), 1147119. do i:10.1080/23322039.2016.1147119

Mora, C., Rollins, R. L., Taladay, K., Kantarcioglu, M., & Kennedy, R. (2018). Bitcoin emissions alone could push global warming above 2°C. *Nature Climate Change, 8*(11), 931–933. doi:10.103841558-018-0321-8

Mora, C., Rollins, R. L., Taladay, K., & Kantar, M. (2021). Bitcoin's growing energy problem: A call for sustainability. *Joule, 5*(5), 1047–1062.

Moran, J. W., & Brightman, B. K. (2001). Leading Organizational Change. *Career Development International, 6*(2), 111–118.

Moreira-Santos, D., Au-Yong-Oliveira, M., & Palma-Moreira, A. (2022). FinTech Services and the Drivers of Their Implementation in Small and Medium Enterprises. *Information, 13*(9). https://doi-org.ezproxy.myucwest.ca/10.3390/info13090409

MoriniM. (2016). From'Blockchain hype'to a real business case for Financial Markets. *Available at* SSRN 2760184.

Morosan, C. (2012). Theoretical and empirical considerations of guests' perceptions of biometric systems in hotels: Extending the technology acceptance model. *Journal of Hospitality & Tourism Research (Washington, D.C.)*, *36*(1), 52–84. doi:10.1177/1096348010380601

Moro-Visconti, R., Cruz Rambaud, S., & López Pascual, J. (2020). Sustainability in FinTechs: An explanation through business model scalability and market valuation. *Sustainability*, *12*(24), 10316. doi:10.3390u122410316

Mougayar, W. (2016). *The business blockchain: Promise, practice, and application of the next internet technology*. John Wiley & Sons.

Murinde, V., Rizopoulos, E., & Zachariadis, M. (2022). The impact of the FinTech revolution on the future of banking: Opportunities and risks. *International Review of Financial Analysis*, *81*, 102103. doi:10.1016/j.irfa.2022.102103

Murphy,D.J.(2022).*FraudtargetingFISup41%in2021,mobiledevicesunderattack.*CNP20-sm-100. Retrieved March 20, 2023, from https://news.cardnotpresent.com/news/fraud-targeting-fis-up-41-in-2021-mobile-devices-under-attack

Musabegovic, I., Özer, M., Djukovic, S., & Jovanovic, S. (2019). Influence of financial technology (FinTech) on financial industry. *Ekonomika Poljoprivrede*, *66*(4), 1003–1021. doi:10.5937/ekoPolj1904003M

Musiala, R. A. Jr, Goody, T. M., Reynolds, V., Tenery, L., McGrath, M., Rowland, C., & Sekhri, S. (2020). *Cryptocurrencies: Forensic techniques to meet the challenge of new fraud and corruption risks | FVS eye on fraud*. AICP.

Nakamoto, S. (2008). Bitcoin: A peer-to-peer electronic cash system. *Decentralized Business Review*, 21260.

Nakamoto, S. (2008). *Bitcoin: A peer-to-peer electronic cash system.* https://bitcoin.org/bitcoin.pdf

Nakamoto, S. (2021). The evolution of the cryptocurrency industry: A decade in review. *Journal of Cryptocurrency and Blockchain Technology*, *12*(4), 60–76.

Narayanan, A., Bonneau, J., Felten, E., Miller, A., & Goldfeder, S. (2016). *Bitcoin and cryptocurrency technologies: a comprehensive introduction*. Princeton University Press.

Nasdaq. (2021). *Coinbase Global, Inc.* Retrieved from https://www.nasdaq.com/market-activity/stocks/coin

Nasir, A., Shaukat, K., Khan, K. I., Hameed, I. A., Alam, T. M., & Luo, S. (2020). What is core and what future holds for blockchain technologies and cryptocurrencies: A bibliometric analysis. *IEEE Access : Practical Innovations, Open Solutions*, *9*, 989–1004. doi:10.1109/ACCESS.2020.3046931

Nasir, M. A., Huynh, T. L. D., Nguyen, S. P., & Duong, D. (2019). Forecasting cryptocurrency returns and volume using search engines. *Financial Innovation*, 5(1), 1–13. doi:10.118640854-018-0119-8

National Services Scotland. (2020). *NHS counter fraud services rolling COVID-19*. Intelligence alert no. 14. Author.

Natsir, C. (2022). *The importance of accounting software for FinTech industry*. BusinessTech. Retrieved March 6, 2023, from https://www.hashmicro.com/blog/benefits-of-cloud-accounting-software-for-FinTech-industry/

Navaretti, G. B., Calzolari, G., Mansilla-Fernandez, J. M., & Pozzolo, A. F. (2018). *FinTech and banking. Friends or foes?* Friends or Foes. doi:10.2139srn.3099337

NeubertM. (2020). Pricing Decisions of FinTech Firms. SSRN 3634459.

Neykova, M., & Miltchev, R. (2019). Conceptual Approach To Introduce An Integrated Model Improving SMEs E-Business Technologies. *Management Theory and Studies for Rural Business and Infrastructure Development*, 41(3), 381–399. doi:10.15544/mts.2019.31

Nicoletti, B. (2017). *The Future of Fintech* (1st ed.). Palgrave Macmillan. doi:10.1007/978-3-319-51415-4

Niranjanamurthy, M., Nithya, B., & Jagannatha, S. (2019). Analysis of Blockchain technology: Pros, cons and SWOT. *Cluster Computing*, 22(S6), 14743–14757. doi:10.100710586-018-2387-5

Niu, B., Ren, J., Zhao, A., & Li, X. (2020). Lender trust on the P2P lending: Analysis based on sentiment analysis of comment text. *Sustainability*, 12(8), 3293. doi:10.3390u12083293

O'Dwyer, K. J., & Malone, D. (2014). *Bitcoin mining and its energy footprint*. Paper presented at the 25th IET Irish Signals & Systems Conference 2014 and 2014 China-Ireland International Conference on Information and Communications Technologies (ISSC 2014/CIICT 2014). 10.1049/cp.2014.0699

O'Halloran, S., & Nowaczyk, N. (2019). An artificial intelligence approach to regulating systemic risk. *Frontiers in Artificial Intelligence*, 2, 7. doi:10.3389/frai.2019.00007 PMID:33733096

Obu, O. C., & Ukpere, W. I. (2022). The Implications of the Incursion of Cryptocurrency on the Effectiveness of Fiscal Policy. *Review of Applied Socio-Economic Research*, 23(1), 134–150. doi:10.54609/reaser.v23i1.214

Odinet, C. K., & College, O. (2018). Consumer BitCredit and FinTech Lending. *Alabama Law Review*, 69, 781–858.

Oh, J. H., & Nguyen, K. (2018). The growing role of cryptocurrency: What does it mean for central banks and governments. *International Telecommunications Policy Review*, 251, 33–55.

OKEx. (2021, February 10). *OKEx partners with Polygon to bring greater liquidity to DeFi ecosystem.* Cision PR Newswire. https://www.prnewswire.com/news-releases/okex-partners-with-polygon-to-bring-greater-liquidity-to-defi-ecosystem-3012257 36.html

OKEx. (n.d.). *About OKEx.* https://www.okex.com/pages/products/about-okex.html

Okoye, M. C., & Clark, J. (2019). Toward cryptocurrency lending. In *International Conference on Financial Cryptography and Data Security* (pp. 367-380). Springer. 10.1007/978-3-662-58820-8_25

Oksman, O. (2018). The loyalty model: Cryptocurrency's killer app? An analysis of the applications and constraints. *Journal of Innovative Technology.*

Oliveira, T., & Martins, M. F. (2010). Understanding e-business adoption across industries in European countries. *Industrial Management & Data Systems, 110*(9), 1337–1354. doi:10.1108/02635571011087428

Olsen, T. L., & Tomlin, B. (2020). Industry 4.0: Opportunities and challenges for operations management. *Manufacturing & Service Operations Management, 22*(1), 113–122. doi:10.1287/msom.2019.0796

Orlikowski, W. J. (2007). Sociomaterial practices: Exploring technology at work. *Organization Studies, 28*(9), 1435–1448. doi:10.1177/0170840607081138

Osterwalder, A. (2004). *The Business Model Ontology – A Proposition in a Design Science Approach.* Academic Press.

Ouchi, W. G., & Wilkins, A. L. (1985). Organizational culture. *Annual Review of Sociology, 11*(1), 457–483. doi:10.1146/annurev.so.11.080185.002325

Pacolli, M. (2022). Importance of Change Management in Digital Transformation Sustainability. *Elsevier, 55*(39), 276-280.

Pakrou, M., & Amir, K. (2016). The relationship between perceived value and the intention of using bitcoin. *Journal of Internet Banking and Commerce, 21*(2).

Panchal, D., & Krishnamoorthy, B. (2019). Developing an instrument for business model dimensions: Exploring linkages with firm competitiveness. *International Journal of Global Business and Competitiveness, 14*(1), 24–41. doi:10.100742943-019-00004-1

Pandya, A.-D., & Bhogal. (2001). Management of Engineering and Technology. *Portland International Conference, (1).*

Pant, S. K. (2020). FinTech: Emerging Trends. *Telecom Business Review, 13*(1).

Pantielieieva, N., Krynytsia, S., Khutorna, M., & Potapenko, L. (2018). *FinTech, transformation of financial intermediation and financial stability.* Paper presented at the 2018 International Scientific-Practical Conference Problems of Infocommunications. Science and Technology (PIC S&T). 10.1109/INFOCOMMST.2018.8632068

Papadamou, S., Kyriazis, N. A., Tzeremes, P., & Corbet, S. (2021). Herding behaviour and price convergence clubs in cryptocurrencies during bull and bear markets. *Journal of Behavioral and Experimental Finance, 30,* 100469. doi:10.1016/j.jbef.2021.100469

Park, J. Y., Ryu, J. P., & Shin, H. J. (2016). Robo advisors for portfolio management. *Advanced Science and Technology Letters, 141*(1), 104–108. doi:10.14257/astl.2016.141.21

PayPal. (2020). *PayPal Launches New Service Enabling Users to Buy, Hold and Sell Cryptocurrency.* https://newsroom.paypal-corp.com/2020-10-21-PayPal-Launches-New-Service-Enabling-Users-to-Buy-Hold-and-Sell-Cryptocurren
cy

PayPal. (2021a). *PayPal and Cryptocurrencies.* https://www.paypal.com/us/webapps/mpp/cryptocurrency

PayPal. (2021b). *PayPal and Coinbase team up to enable cryptocurrency buying and selling.* https://www.paypal.com/us/webapps/mpp/cryptocurrency-news/pa
ypal-and-coinbase-team-up-to-enable-cryptocurrency-buying-an
d-selling

PayPal. (2021c). *Crypto Cashback.* https://www.paypal.com/us/webapps/mpp/crypto-cashback

PayPal. (2021d). *Uber & Lyft Cashback.* https://www.paypal.com/us/webapps/mpp/offers?view=offers&sho
wOverlay=true&overlay=10-50-off-uber-and-lyft-rides-paid-wit
h-paypal

Peters, G. W. (2021). Decentralized finance (DeFi): The future of finance? *Journal of Financial Innovation, 6*(3), 120–135.

Pham, T.-T. T., & Ho, J. C. (2015). The effects of product-related, personal-related factors and attractiveness of alternatives on consumer adoption of NFC-based mobile payments. *Technology in Society, 43,* 159–172. doi:10.1016/j.techsoc.2015.05.004

Philippon, T. (2016). *The FinTech Opportunity.* National Bureau of Economic Research. doi:10.3386/w22476

Phillips, R. C., & Gorse, D. (2018). Mutual-excitation of cryptocurrency market returns and social media topics. *Proceedings of the 4th international conference on frontiers of educational technologies.* 10.1145/3233347.3233370

Pilkington, M. (2018). Blockchain technology: Principles and applications. *Research Handbook on Digital Transformations,* 225-256.

Pilkington, M. (2016). Blockchain technology: principles and applications. In *Research handbook on digital transformations* (pp. 225–253). Edward Elgar Publishing. doi:10.4337/9781784717766.00019

Pilkington, M., & Pilkington, B. (2020). Cryptocurrency and Government: The Fight Against Money Laundering and Terrorism Financing. *Economic Affairs*, *40*(2), 280–295.

Polasik, M., Piotrowska, A. I., Wisniewski, T. P., Kotkowski, R., & Lightfoot, G. (2015). Price fluctuations and the use of bitcoin: An empirical inquiry. *International Journal of Electronic Commerce*, *20*(1), 9–49. doi:10.1080/10864415.2016.1061413

Prawirasasra, K. P. (2018). Financial technology in Indonesia: Disruptive or collaborative. *Reports on Economics and Finance*, *4*(2), 83–90. doi:10.12988/ref.2018.818

Presthus, W., & O'Malley, N. O. (2017). Motivations and barriers for end-user adoption of bitcoin as digital currency. *Procedia Computer Science*, *121*, 89–97. doi:10.1016/j.procs.2017.11.013

PricewaterhouseCoopers. (n.d.). *Making sense of bitcoin, cryptocurrency and Blockchain*. https://www.pwc.com/us/en/industries/financial-services/fintech/bitcoin-blockchain-cryptocurrency.html

Prosci, Inc. (n.d.a). *What is Change Management?* https://www.prosci.com/

Prosci, Inc. (n.d.b). *The Prosci ADKAR Model*. Prosci Learning Center Publications.

Proulx, S. (2001). Usages des technologies d'information et de communication: Reconsidering the field of study? *Proceedings of the National Congress of UNESCO CIS*.

Putri, G. A., Wijayanti, A. W., & Ariani, K. R. (2021). The application of technology acceptance model to assess the role of complexity toward customer acceptance on mobile banking. *Proceedings of International Conference on Smart Computing and Cyber Security: Strategic Foresight, Security Challenges and Innovation (SMARTCYBER 2020)*. 10.1007/978-981-15-7990-5_25

Queiroz, M. M., Telles, R., & Bonilla, S. H. (2020). Blockchain and supply chain management integration: A systematic review of the literature. *Supply Chain Management*, *25*(2), 241–254. doi:10.1108/SCM-03-2018-0143

Rajput, U., Abbas, F., Hussain, R., Eun, H., & Oh, H. (2014, August). A simple yet efficient approach to combat transaction malleability in bitcoin. In *International Workshop on Information Security Applications* (pp. 27-37). Springer.

Ramirez, D. (2023). *FTX Crash: Timeline, Fallout and What Investors Should Know*. Nerdwallet. https://www.nerdwallet.com/article/investing/ftx-crash#:~:text=FTX's%20crash%20has%20wide%2Dreaching,sinking%20prices%20and%20financial%20troubles

Raza, S. A., Ahmed, M., & Aloui, C. (2022). On the asymmetrical connectedness between cryptocurrencies and foreign exchange markets: Evidence from the nonparametric quantile on quantile approach. *Research in International Business and Finance, 61*, 101627. doi:10.1016/j.ribaf.2022.101627

Read, C. L. (2022). No More Duffel Bags Full of Cash. In *The Bitcoin Dilemma* (pp. 113–119). Palgrave Macmillan. doi:10.1007/978-3-031-09138-4_11

Rehman, M., Javed, I. T., Qureshi, K. N., Margaria, T., & Jeon, G. (2022). A Cyber Secure Medical Management System by Using Blockchain. *IEEE Transactions on Computational Social Systems*, 1–14. doi:10.1109/TCSS.2022.3215455

Revel, M. (2004). Un changement mesuré? *XV AGRH Convention, Montreal, Canada. AGRH.*

Ritchie, J. (2022). *The history of money: How our currency evolved from pelts to money.* MintLife Blog. https://mint.intuit.com/blog/investments/the-history-of-money/#:~:text=Before%20money%20was%20invented%2C%20people,were%20used%20to%20pay%20armies

Rogers, E. M. (2003). *Diffusion of innovations* (5th ed.). Free Press.

Rose, C. (2015). The evolution of digital currencies: Bitcoin, a cryptocurrency causing a monetary revolution. *International Business & Economics Research Journal, 14*(4), 617–622. doi:10.19030/iber.v14i4.9353

Rosengren, K. (2022). *Contribution of Open-Source Intelligence to Social Engineering Cyberattacks.* Turku University.

Roth, E. (2022). *Romance scammers collected $139 million in crypto last year.* The Verge.

Rupeika-Apoga, R., & Thalassinos, E. I. (2020). *Ideas for a regulatory definition of FinTech.* Academic Press.

Russell, S. J. (2010). *Artificial intelligence a modern approach.* Pearson Education, Inc.

Ryu, H.-S. (2018). What makes users willing or hesitant to use FinTech?: The moderating effect of user type. *Industrial Management & Data Systems, 118*(3), 541–569. doi:10.1108/IMDS-07-2017-0325

Saberi, S., Kouhizadeh, M., Sarkis, J., & Shen, L. (2019). Blockchain technology and its relationships to sustainable supply chain management. *International Journal of Production Research, 57*(7), 2117–2135. doi:10.1080/00207543.2018.1533261

Sai, A. R., Buckley, J., & Le Gear, A. (2021). Characterizing wealth inequality in cryptocurrencies. *Frontiers in Blockchain, 4*, 730122. doi:10.3389/fbloc.2021.730122

Saiedi, E., Mohammadi, A., Broström, A., & Shafi, K. (2022). Distrust in banks and fintech participation: The case of peer-to-peer lending. *Entrepreneurship Theory and Practice, 46*(5), 1170–1197. doi:10.1177/1042258720958020

Saksonova, S., & Kuzmina-Merlino, I. (2019). Cryptocurrency as an investment instrument in a modern financial market. *Economy Bulletin of St. Petersburg University*, *35*(2), 269–282. doi:10.21638pbu05.2019.205

Salloum, S. A., Alhamad, A. Q. M., Al-Emran, M., Monem, A. A., & Shaalan, K. (2019). Exploring students' acceptance of e-learning through the development of a comprehensive technology acceptance model. *IEEE Access : Practical Innovations, Open Solutions*, *7*, 128445–128462. doi:10.1109/ACCESS.2019.2939467

San Martín, S., & Camarero, C. (2009). How perceived risk affects online buying. *Online Information Review*, *33*(4), 629–654. doi:10.1108/14684520910985657

Santor, E. (2011). *The International Monetary System: An Assessment and Avenue for reform.* Bank of Canada Review.

Sartori, R., Costantini, A., Ceschi, A., & Tommasi, F. (2018). How Do You Manage Change in Organizations? Training, Development, Innovation, and Their Relationships. *Frontiers in Psychology*, *9*, 313. Advance online publication. doi:10.3389/fpsyg.2018.00313 PMID:29662463

Sartori, R., & Scalco, A. (2014). Managing organizational innovation through human resources, human capital and psychological capital. *European Journal of Business and Management*, *14*(2), 63–70. doi:10.18374/EJM-14-2.5

Sas, C., & Khairuddin, I. E. (2017). Design for trust: An exploration of the challenges and opportunities of bitcoin users. *Proceedings of the 2017 CHI Conference on Human Factors in Computing Systems.* 10.1145/3025453.3025886

Schaupp, L. C., & Festa, M. (2018). Cryptocurrency adoption and the road to regulation. *Proceedings of the 19th Annual International Conference on Digital Government Research: Governance in the Data Age.* 10.1145/3209281.3209336

Schindler, J. W. (2017). *FinTech and financial innovation: Drivers and depth.* Academic Press.

Schmandt-Besserat, D. (1977). An archaic recording system and the origin of writing. *Syro-Mesopotamian Studies, 1.*

Schueffel, P. (2016). Taming the Beast: A Scientific Definition of Fintech. *Journal of Innovation Management*, *4*(4), 32–54. doi:10.24840/2183-0606_004.004_0004

Schueffel, P. (2017). *The concise Fintech compendium.* Fribourg, Switzerland: School of Management Fribourg/Switzerland.

Schulman, D. (2021). PayPal's entry into the cryptocurrency market: A strategic move. *Journal of FinTech*, *9*(2), 120–137.

Schulte, P., & Liu, G. (2017). FinTech is merging with iot and AI to challenge banks: How entrenched interests can prepare. *Journal of Alternative Investments*, *20*(3), 41–57. doi:10.3905/jai.2018.20.3.041

Security, I. B. M. (2021). *Cost of a Data Breach Report 2021.* https://www.ibm.com/downloads/cas/OJDVQGRY

Shahzad, F., Xiu, G., Wang, J., & Shahbaz, M. (2018). An empirical investigation on the adoption of cryptocurrencies among the people of mainland China. *Technology in Society, 55*, 33–40. doi:10.1016/j.techsoc.2018.05.006

Shaikh, A. A., Glavee-Geo, R., & Karjaluoto, H. (2021). How relevant are risk perceptions, effort, and performance expectancy in mobile banking adoption? In *Research Anthology on Securing Mobile Technologies and Applications* (pp. 692–716). IGI Global. doi:10.4018/978-1-7998-8545-0.ch038

Shakhzodbek, E., Khurshidbek, T., & Shoxruxmirzo, A. (2022). From bank to fintech and the power of network effects. *Boshqaruv Va Etika Qoidalari Onlayn Ilmiy Jurnali*, 14-16.

Shams, S., & Park, J. (2022). Factors affecting the adoption of cryptocurrency for cross-border transactions. *Journal of Business Research, 141*, 64–75.

ShapeShift. (n.d.). https://info.shapeshift.io

Sharma, D., Verma, R., & Sam, S. (2021). Adoption of cryptocurrency: An international perspective. *International Journal of Technology Transfer and Commercialisation, 18*(3), 247–260. doi:10.1504/IJTTC.2021.118863

Shiller, R. J. (2020). *Narrative economics: How stories go viral and drive major economic events.* Princeton University Press.

Shin, Y. J., & Choi, Y. (2019). Feasibility of the FinTech industry as an innovation platform for sustainable economic growth in Korea. *Sustainability, 11*(19), 5351. doi:10.3390u11195351

Shrier, D., Wu, W., & Pentland, A. (2016). Blockchain & infrastructure (identity, data security). *Massachusetts Institute of Technology-Connection Science, 1*(3), 1–19.

Shukla, S. (2022). UN Says Crypto Use in Terror Financing Likely Soaring. *Bloomberg.* https://www.bloomberg.com/news/articles/2022-10-31/un-finding-more-cases-where-crypto-involved-in-terror-financing

Silinskyte, J. (2014). *Understanding Bitcoin adoption: Unified theory of acceptance and use of technology (UTAUT) application* [Unpublished master's dissertation]. University Leiden.

Simon, H. A. (1993). Altruism and economics. *The American Economic Review, 83*(2), 156–161.

Singh, S., Sahni, M. M., & Kovid, R. K. (2020). What drives FinTech adoption? A multi-method evaluation using an adapted technology acceptance model. *Management Decision, 58*(8), 1675–1697. doi:10.1108/MD-09-2019-1318

Sirkin, H., Keenan, P., & Jackson, A. (2005, November 1). The Hard Side of Change Management. *Harvard Business Review, 83*(10). Advance online publication. doi:10.1109/EMR.2014.6966953 PMID:16250629

Sjamsudin, S. H. (2019). The impact of the development of FinTech on the existing financial services in Indonesia. *International Journal of Advanced Research in Technology and Innovation*, *1*(1), 14–23.

SmalesL. A. (2022). *Cryptocurrency as an alternative inflation hedge?* https://ssrn.com/abstract=3883123

Smith & Smith. (2019). *Exploring consumer attitudes towards cryptocurrency adoption: A case study of Bitcoin.* Academic Press.

Smith, M. D., & Floro, M. S. (2021). The effects of domestic and international remittances on food insecurity in low-and middle-income countries. *The Journal of Development Studies*, *57*(7), 1198–1220. doi:10.1080/00220388.2020.1849619

Smuts, N. (2019). What drives cryptocurrency prices? An investigation of google trends and telegram sentiment. *Performance Evaluation Review*, *46*(3), 131–134. doi:10.1145/3308897.3308955

Söderberg, G. (2018). Are Bitcoin and other crypto-assets money? *Economic Commentaries*, *5*, 14.

Solodan, K. (2019). Legal regulation of cryptocurrency taxation in European countries. *European Journal of Law and Public Administration*, *6*(1), 64–74. doi:10.18662/eljpa/64

Solovykh, N. N., Koroleva, I. V., Stompeleva, E. S., Terskaya, G. A., & Aliev, V. M. (2019). Digital economy and socio-economic contradictions of information society. *Ubiquitous Computing and the Internet of Things: Prerequisites for the Development of ICT*, 655-662.

Song, K. (2015). Investigation of Business Model on FinTech Payment System. *The E-Business Studies, 16*(6), 65-94.

Song, D., & Li, Y. (2020). Cryptocurrency and Blockchain in China: Policies, Players, and Prospects. *Asia & the Pacific Policy Studies*, *7*(3), 382–397.

Sørensen, J. B. (2002). The strength of corporate culture and the reliability of firm performance. *Administrative Science Quarterly*, *47*(1), 70–91. doi:10.2307/3094891

Srinivasan, N., & Ratchford, B. T. (1991). An empirical test of a model of external search for automobiles. *The Journal of Consumer Research*, *18*(2), 233–242. doi:10.1086/209255

Srivastava, V., & Dashottar, S. (2020). Default probability assessment for project finance bank loans and Basel regulations: Searching for a new paradigm. *The Journal of Structured Finance*, *25*(4), 41–53. doi:10.3905/jsf.2019.1.088

Statista. (2022a). *Global consumer FinTech adoption rates 2015-2019, by category.* Statista Research Department. https://www.statista.com/statistics/1055356/FinTech-adoption-rates-globally-selected-countries-by-category/

Statista. (2022b). *Number of FinTech startups worldwide 2018-2021, by region.* Statista Research Department. https://www.statista.com/statistics/893954/number-FinTech-startups-by-region/

Statista. (2023). *Weekly market cap of all cryptocurrencies combined until January 2023* [Dataset]. https://www.statista.com/statistics/730876/cryptocurrency-market-value

Stern, C., Makinen, M., & Qian, Z. (2017). FinTechs in China–with a special focus on peer to peer lending. *Journal of Chinese Economic and Foreign Trade Studies.*

Stojanovic, S. D. (2006). Pricing and hedging of multi type contracts under multidimensional risks in incomplete markets modeled by general Itô SDE systems. *Asia-Pacific Financial Markets, 13*(4), 345–372. doi:10.100710690-007-9049-6

Stoll, C., Klaaßen, L., & Gallersdörfer, U. (2021). The carbon footprint of Bitcoin. *Joule, 5*(6), 1298–1312.

Stoltenberg, C., & Wagener, A. (2021). On the adoption and pricing of cryptocurrencies. *Journal of Financial Economics, 140*(1), 118–146.

Stolterman, E., & Fors, A. C. (2004). Information Technology and the Good Life. IFIP International Federation for Information Processing, 143, 687-692. doi:10.1007/1-4020-8095-6_45

Sun, J., Yan, J., & Zhang, K. Z. (2016). Blockchain-based sharing services: What blockchain technology can contribute to smart cities. *Financial Innovation, 2*(1), 1–9. doi:10.118640854-016-0040-y

Suryono, R. R., Marlina, E., Purwaningsih, M., Sensuse, D. I., & Sutoyo, M. A. H. (2019). *Challenges in P2P lending development: Collaboration with tourism commerce.* Paper presented at the 2019 International Conference on Computer Science, Information Technology, and Electrical Engineering (ICOMITEE).

Suryono, R. R., Budi, I., & Purwandari, B. (2020). Challenges and trends of financial technology (FinTech): A systematic literature review. *Information (Basel), 11*(12), 590. doi:10.3390/info11120590

Swan, M. (2015). Blockchain thinking: The brain as a decentralized autonomous corporation [commentary]. *IEEE Technology and Society Magazine, 34*(4), 41–52. doi:10.1109/MTS.2015.2494358

Swan, M. (2015). *Blockchain: Blueprint for a new economy.* O'Reilly Media, Inc.

Swidler, A. (1986). Culture in action: Symbols and strategies. *American Sociological Review, 51*(2), 273–286. doi:10.2307/2095521

Taherdoost, H. (2023). Fintech: Emerging Trends and the Future of Finance. *Financial Technologies and DeFi: A Revisit to the Digital Finance Revolution*, 29-39.

Taherdoost, H. (2023). FinTech: Emerging Trends and the Future of Finance. *Financial Technologies and DeFi: A Revisit to the Digital Finance Revolution*, 29-39.

Taherdoost, H., Madanchian, M., & Ebrahimi, M. (2021). Advancement of Cybersecurity and Information Security Awareness to Facilitate Digital Transformation: Opportunities and Challenges. Handbook of Research on Advancing Cybersecurity for Digital Transformation, 99-117.

Taherdoost, H. (2022). - Blockchain Technology and Artificial Intelligence Together: A Critical Review on Applications. *Applied Sciences (Basel, Switzerland)*, *12*(24), 12948. doi:10.3390/app122412948

Taherdoost, H. (2023). *The Role of Different Types of Management Information System Applications in Business Development: Concepts and Limitations.* Cloud Computing and Data Science.

Tapscott, D., & Tapscott, A. (2016). *Blockchain revolution: how the technology behind bitcoin is changing money, business, and the world.* Penguin.

Tapscott, D., & Tapscott, A. (2016). *Blockchain revolution: How the technology behind Bitcoin is changing money, business, and the world.* Penguin.

Tapscott, D., & Tapscott, A. (2021). Blockchain revolution: The changing landscape of the cryptocurrency industry. *Journal of Cryptocurrency and Blockchain Technology*, *12*(2), 20–34.

Taylor, J. W. (1974). The role of risk in consumer behavior: A comprehensive and operational theory of risk taking in consumer behavior. *Journal of Marketing*, *38*(2), 54–60.

Team, C. F. I. (2022, December 7). *FinTech (Financial Technology).* Corporate Finance Institute. https://corporatefinanceinstitute.com/resources/wealth-management/FinTech-financial-technology/

Temelkov, Z. (2018). *Fintech firms opportunity or threat for banks?* Academic Press.

Thakor, R. T., & Merton, R. C. (2018). Trust in lending. Academic Press. doi:10.3386/w24778

Thakor, A. V. (2020). FinTech and banking: What do we know? *Journal of Financial Intermediation*, *41*, 100833. doi:10.1016/j.jfi.2019.100833

Tharp, D. T. (2020). Potential Consumer Harm Due to Regulation on Financial Advisory Communication in the FinTech Age. *Financial Counseling and Planning*, *31*(1), 146–161. doi:10.1891/JFCP-18-00041

The Economist. (2022). *2022 has been a year of brutal inflation.* https://www.economist.com/finance-and-economics/2022/12/21/2022-has-been-a-year-of-brutal-inflation

The U.S. Commodity Future Trading Commission. (n.d.). *Bitcoin Basics.* https://www.cftc.gov/sites/default/files/2019-12/oceo_bitcoinbasics0218.pdf

The World Bank Group and International Monetary Fund. (2019). *FinTech: The Experience So Far.* The World Bank Group. https://documents1.worldbank.org/curated/en/130201561082549144/pdf/FinTech-The-Experience-so-Far-Executive-Summary.pdf

The World Bank Group. (2021). *Global FinTech-enabling regulations database*. https://www.worldbank.org/en/topic/FinTech/brief/global-FinTech-enabling-regulations-database

The World Bank. (n.d.). *Tax revenue (% of GDP)*. https://data.worldbank.org/indicator/GC.TAX.TOTL.GD.ZS

Theaud, B. (2022). *How to choose the right FinTech for your business*. Entrepreneur. Retrieved March 6, 2023, from https://www.entrepreneur.com/money-finance/how-to-choose-the-right-FinTech-for-your-business/422790

Theglobaleconomy.com. (2021). *Government spending, percent of GDP - Country rankings*. https://www.theglobaleconomy.com/rankings/government_size/G20/

Thomson, J. (2021). The role of marketing and branding in the cryptocurrency industry. *Journal of Marketing and Branding*, *15*(1), 40–54.

Tian, X., Han, R., Wang, L., Lu, G., & Zhan, J. (2015). Latency critical big data computing in finance. *The Journal of Finance and Data Science*, *1*(1), 33–41. doi:10.1016/j.jfds.2015.07.002

Tomić, N., Todorović, V., & Čakajac, B. (2020). The potential effects of cryptocurrencies on monetary policy. *The European Journal of Applied Economics*, *17*(1), 37–48. doi:10.5937/EJAE17-21873

Tomlinson, J. (1999). *Globalization and culture*. University of Chicago Press.

Trama, T. (2022). Brands are introducing new Blockchain Technologies to fight Counterfeit. *Lexology*. https://www.lexology.com/library/detail.aspx?g=a1559142-01a7-400e-97f9-31ef6a853640

Treiblmaier, H., & Sillaber, C. (2021). The impact of blockchain on e-commerce: A framework for salient research topics. *Electronic Commerce Research and Applications*, *48*, 101054. doi:10.1016/j.elerap.2021.101054

Trificana, J. (2022, October 3). *What is FinTech? 6 main types of FinTech and how they work*. Plaid. Retrieved April 1, 2023, from https://plaid.com/resources/FinTech/what-is-FinTech/

Trozze, A., Kamps, J., Akartuna, E. A., Hetzel, F. J., Kleinberg, B., Davies, T., & Johnson, S. D. (2022). Cryptocurrencies and future financial crime. *Crime Science*, *11*(1), 1–35. doi:10.118640163-021-00163-8 PMID:35013699

Truby, J., Brown, R., & Dahdal, A. (2020). Banking on AI: Mandating a proactive approach to AI regulation in the financial sector. *Law and Financial Markets Review*, *14*(2), 110–120. doi:10.1080/17521440.2020.1760454

Tschorsch, F., & Scheuermann, B. (2016). Bitcoin and beyond: A technical survey on decentralized digital currencies. *IEEE Communications Surveys and Tutorials*, *18*(3), 2084–2123. doi:10.1109/COMST.2016.2535718

Tschorsch, F., & Scheuermann, B. (2021). Driving mass adoption of cryptocurrencies: Technological advancements and user experience. *Journal of Digital Innovation*, 8(1), 5–18.

Tsvetkova, M., Yasseri, T., Meyer, E. T., Pickering, J. B., Engen, V., Walland, P., Lüders, M., Følstad, A., & Bravos, G. (2017). Understanding human-machine networks: A cross-disciplinary survey. *ACM Computing Surveys*, 50(1), 1–35. doi:10.1145/3039868

Uematsu, Y., & Tanaka, S. (2019). High-dimensional macroeconomic forecasting and variable selection via penalized regression. *The Econometrics Journal*, 22(1), 34–56. doi:10.1111/ectj.12117

US Department of the Treasury. (2021). *Anti-Money Laundering and Countering the Financing of Terrorism National Priorities* https://www.fincen.gov/sites/default/files/shared/AML_CFT%20 Priorities%20(June%2030%2C%202021).pdf

US Internal Revenue Service. (2021). *Notice 2014-21*. https://www.irs.gov/pub/irs-drop/n-14-21. pdf

US Law Library of Congress. (2021). *Regulation of Cryptocurrency Around the World*. https://tile.loc.gov/storage-services/service/ll/llglrd/2021 687419/2021687419.pdf

Van Hoek, R. (2019). Exploring blockchain implementation in the supply chain: Learning from pioneers and RFID research. *International Journal of Operations & Production Management*, 39(6/7/8), 829–859. doi:10.1108/IJOPM-01-2019-0022

Vandangeon-Derumez, I. (1998). *La dynamique des processus de changement*. Thèse de Doctorat en Sciences de Gestion.

Varga, D. (2017). FinTech, the new era of financial services. *Vezetéstudomány-Budapest Management Review*, 48(11), 22–32. doi:10.14267/VEZTUD.2017.11.03

Vasiljevic & Dealing. (2019). *Consumer Adoption of Cryptocurrency: A Review of the Literature*. Academic Press.

Vaz, J., & Brown, K. (2020). Sustainable development and cryptocurrencies as private money. *Economia e Politica Industriale*, 47(1), 163–184. doi:10.100740812-019-00139-5

Velasco, P. R. (2017). Computing ledgers and the political ontology of the blockchain. *Metaphilosophy*, 48(5), 712–726. doi:10.1111/meta.12274

Velazquez, P. V., Bobek, V., Vide, R. K., & Horvat, T. (2022). Lessons from Remarkable FinTech Companies for the Financial Inclusion in Peru. *Journal of Risk and Financial Management*, 15(2), 62. Advance online publication. doi:10.3390/jrfm15020062

Venkatesh, V., & Davis, F. D. (2000). A theoretical extension of the technology acceptance model: Four longitudinal field studies. *Management Science*, 46(2), 186–204. doi:10.1287/ mnsc.46.2.186.11926

Venkatesh, V., Morris, M. G., Davis, G. B., & Davis, F. D. (2003). User acceptance of information technology: Toward a unified view. *Management Information Systems Quarterly, 27*(3), 425–478. doi:10.2307/30036540

Venkatesh, V., Thong, J. Y., & Xu, X. (2012). Consumer acceptance and use of information technology: Extending the unified theory of acceptance and use of technology. *Management Information Systems Quarterly, 36*(1), 157–178. doi:10.2307/41410412

Venmo. (n.d.). *Venmo Credit Card.* https://venmo.com/about/creditcard/

Vigna, P., & Casey, M. J. (2016). *The age of cryptocurrency: how bitcoin and the blockchain are challenging the global economic order.* Macmillan.

Vijayasarathy, L. R., & Jones, J. M. (2000). Print and Internet catalog shopping: Assessing attitudes and intentions. *Internet Research, 10*(3), 191–202. doi:10.1108/10662240010331948

Viriyasitavat, W., & Hoonsopon, D. (2019). Blockchain characteristics and consensus in modern business processes. *Journal of Industrial Information Integration, 13*, 32–39. doi:10.1016/j.jii.2018.07.004

Vives, X. (2018). *The Impact of Fintech on Banking.* Academic Press.

Vo, N. N., & Xu, G. (2017). *The volatility of Bitcoin returns and its correlation to financial markets.* Paper presented at the 2017 International Conference on Behavioral, Economic, Socio-cultural Computing (BESC). 10.1109/BESC.2017.8256365

Von Der Linn, B. (2009, January 25). *Overview of GE's Change Acceleration Process (CAP).* Bob Von Der Linn's Change Management and Human Performance Technology Blog. Retrieved January 22, 2023, from https://bvonderlinn.wordpress.com/2009/01/25/overview-of-ges-change-acceleration-process-cap/

Voorhees, E. (2021). Shapeshift: A platform for seamless cryptocurrency trading and management. *Journal of Cryptocurrency and Blockchain Technology, 11*(4), 72–88.

Vora, G. (2015). Cryptocurrencies: Are disruptive financial innovations here? *Modern Economy, 6*(07), 816–832. doi:10.4236/me.2015.67077

Vučinić, M. (2020). FinTech and financial stability potential influence of FinTech on financial stability, risks and benefits. *Journal of Central Banking Theory and Practice, 9*(2), 43–66. doi:10.2478/jcbtp-2020-0013

Wang & Chen. (2019). *Cryptocurrency adoption in the digital age: A theoretical framework.* Academic Press.

Wang, H., Wang, Z., Zhang, B., & Zhou, J. (2019). *Information collection for fraud detection in P2P financial market.* arXiv preprint arXiv:1910.02009.10.2991/aebmr.k.210319.097

Wang, X., Xu, X., Feagan, L., Huang, S., Jiao, L., & Zhao, W. (2018). *Inter-bank payment system on enterprise blockchain platform.* Paper presented at the 2018 IEEE 11th international conference on cloud computing (CLOUD). 10.1109/CLOUD.2018.00085

Wang, H., He, D., & Ji, Y. (2020). Designated-verifier proof of assets for bitcoin exchange using elliptic curve cryptography. *Future Generation Computer Systems*, *107*, 854–862. doi:10.1016/j.future.2017.06.028

Wang, S., Liao, H., & Wang, L. (2015). Factors influencing the adoption of Bitcoin in China: A technology acceptance model approach. *Technology in Society*, *42*, 72–81.

Wang, S., & Vergne, J.-P. (2017). Buzz factor or innovation potential: What explains cryptocurrencies' returns? *PLoS One*, *12*(1), e0169556. doi:10.1371/journal.pone.0169556 PMID:28085906

Wang, Y., Singgih, M., Wang, J., & Rit, M. (2019). Making sense of blockchain technology: How will it transform supply chains? *International Journal of Production Economics*, *211*, 221–236. doi:10.1016/j.ijpe.2019.02.002

Wardley, P. (2011). Technological Innovation in Retail Finance: International Historical Perspectives. Routledge.

Wesselbaum, D., Wang, M., & Muhle-Karbe, J. (2019). Cryptocurrencies and the cross-section of stock returns. *Journal of Financial Economics*, *133*(1), 263–283.

Whyte, C. (2019). Cryptoterrorism: Assessing the utility of blockchain technologies for terrorist enterprise. *Studies in Conflict and Terrorism*, 1–24. doi:10.1080/1057610X.2018.1531565

Williamson, O. E. (1991). Comparative economic organization: The analysis of discrete structural alternatives. *Administrative Science Quarterly*, *36*(2), 269–296. doi:10.2307/2393356

Wilson, C. (2019). Cryptocurrencies: The future of finance? *Contemporary Issues in International Political Economy*, 359-394.

Wonglimpiyarat, J. (2017). FinTech banking industry: a systemic approach. *Foresight, 19*(6), 590-603.

Wonglimpiyarat, J. (2019). What is it about strategic implications of using financial models in the process of technology management? *The Journal of High Technology Management Research*, *30*(1), 82–90. doi:10.1016/j.hitech.2018.12.001

World Bank Group. (2022). *Fintech and the Digital Transformation of Financial Services: Implications for Market Structure and Public Policy.* International Bank for Reconstruction and Development.

Wu, M. (2019, April 26). *Paying with shells: Cowrie shell money is one of the oldest currencies still collected today.* Ancient Origins. https://www.ancient-origins.net/history-ancient-traditions/shell-money-0011793

Wu, J., & Tran, N. K. (2018). Application of blockchain technology in sustainable energy systems: An overview. *Sustainability*, *10*(9), 3067. doi:10.3390u10093067

Wunsche, A. (2016). *Technological disruption of capital markets and reporting? An introduction to blockchain. Chartered Professional Accountants Canada.* CPA.

Xu, J. (2022). Biometrics in FinTech: A Technological Review. *Future And FinTech, The: Abcdi and Beyond*, 361.

Xu, D. (2019). Free money, but not tax-free: A proposal for the tax treatment of cryptocurrency hard forks. *Fordham Law Review*, *87*(6), 2693–2723.

Yacoub, G. (2017). Collaborative Innovation and Appropriability in Start-ups: Evidence from the FinTech Sector. *Academy of Management Proceedings*. 10.5465/AMBPP.2017.13674abstract

Yang, H., Yu, J., Zo, H., & Choi, M. (2016). User acceptance of wearable devices: An extended perspective of perceived value. *Telematics and Informatics*, *33*(2), 256–269. doi:10.1016/j.tele.2015.08.007

Yermack, D. (2013). Is Bitcoin a real currency? An economic appraisal (No. w19747). *National Bureau of Economic Research*, *36*(2), 843-850.

Yermack, D. (2015). Corporate Governance and Blockchains. *Review of Finance*, *19*(3), 945–962.

Yli-Huumo, J., Ko, D., Choi, S., Park, S., & Smolander, K. (2016). Where is current research on blockchain technology? A systematic review. *PLoS One*, *11*(10), e0163477. doi:10.1371/journal.pone.0163477 PMID:27695049

Yuan, Y., & Wang, F.-Y. (2016). *Towards blockchain-based intelligent transportation systems.* Paper presented at the 2016 IEEE 19th international conference on intelligent transportation systems (ITSC).

Yun, J. J., & Liu, Z. (2019). *Micro-and macro-dynamics of open innovation with a quadruple-helix model* (Vol. 11). MDPI.

Zachariadis, M., & Ozcan, P. (2017). *The API economy and digital transformation in financial services: The case of open banking.* Academic Press.

Zachariadis, M., Ozcan, P., & Dinckol, D. (2018). The economics and strategy of platforms: Competing in the era of open banking. *The book on open banking: A series of essays on the next evolution of money*, 59-70.

Zak, P. J., & Knack, S. (2001). Trust and growth. *Economic Journal (London)*, *111*(470), 295–321. doi:10.1111/1468-0297.00609

Zavolokina, L., Dolata, M., & Schwabe, G. (2016). The FinTech phenomenon: Antecedents of financial innovation perceived by the popular press. *Financial Innovation*, *2*(1), 16. doi:10.118640854-016-0036-7

Zeithaml, V. A. (1988). Consumer perceptions of price, quality, and value: A means-end model and synthesis of evidence. *Journal of Marketing, 52*(3), 2–22. doi:10.1177/002224298805200302

Zhang, B. Z., Ashta, A., & Barton, M. E. (2021). Do FinTech and financial incumbents have different experiences and perspectives on the adoption of artificial intelligence? *Strategic Change, 30*(3), 223–234. doi:10.1002/jsc.2405

Zhang, J., van Gorp, D., & Kievit, H. (2022). Digital technology and national entrepreneurship: An ecosystem perspective. *The Journal of Technology Transfer.* Advance online publication. doi:10.100710961-022-09934-0 PMID:35602312

Zhang, X., Lu, F., Tao, R., & Wang, S. (2021). The time-varying causal relationship between the Bitcoin market and internet attention. *Financial Innovation, 7*(1), 1–19. doi:10.118640854-021-00275-9

Zhang, Y., & Boudreau, M. C. (2022). Can blockchain-enabled traceability increase the adoption of sustainable products? The role of informational and social influences. *Journal of Business Research, 143*, 424–437.

Zhang, Y., Wang, Y., & Zhang, J. (2021). Cryptocurrency adoption and integration into traditional financial systems: A global perspective. *Journal of Global Finance, 19*(1), 44–62.

Zhang, Z., Zhu, J., & Qin, Y. (2020). Empirical Analysis of Factors Affecting Cryptocurrency Adoption. *Journal of Financial Services Research, 58*, 81–99.

Zhao, J., Li, X., Yu, C.-H., Chen, S., & Lee, C.-C. (2022). Riding the FinTech innovation wave: FinTech, patents and bank performance. *Journal of International Money and Finance, 122*, 102552. doi:10.1016/j.jimonfin.2021.102552

Zohar, A. (2019). The changing faces of blockchain. *Computer, 52*(1), 14–17.

Zohar, A. (2021). The rise of decentralized finance: Opportunities and challenges. *Journal of Financial Innovation, 6*(1), 35–49.

Zott, C., Amit, R., & Massa, L. (2011). The Business Model: Recent Developments and Future Research. *Journal of Management, 37*(4), 1019–1042. Advance online publication. doi:10.1177/0149206311406265

Zyskind, G., & Nathan, O. (2015). *Decentralizing privacy: Using blockchain to protect personal data.* Paper presented at the 2015 IEEE Security and Privacy Workshops. 10.1109/SPW.2015.27

Стойка, М. (2021). Cryptocurrency–Definition, functions, advantages and risks. *Підприємництво і торгівля,* (30), 5-10.

About the Contributors

Hamed Taherdoost is an award-winning leader and R&D professional. He is founder of the Hamta Group | Hamta Business Corporation, and Associate Professor at University Canada West. He has over 20 years of experience in both industry and academia sectors. He has worked at international companies from Cyprus, the UK, Malta, Iran, Malaysia, and Canada and has been highly involved in development of several projects in different industries; healthcare, transportation, residential, oil and gas and IT. Apart from industry, he has been a university lecturer in three different parts of the world, Southeast Asia, the Middle East, and North America. Currently, he is an Adjunct Professor at Westcliff University, mentor at Futurpreneur Canada, Advisory Board of Cambridge Scholars Publishing, UK, Senior Technical Consultant at CI Solutions Ltd, Innotek Consulting Ltd & Quark Minded Technology Inc and Chair of Research and Scholarly Activities Committee at University Canada West. He is a certified cybersecurity technologist and a senior member of IEEE, IAEEEE, IASED, & IEDRC, Fellow Member of ISAC, WGM of IFIP TC11, member of CSIAC, ACT-IAC and AASHE. Hamed has been an active multidisciplinary researcher and R&D specialist involved in several academic and industrial research projects. Currently, he is involved in several multidisciplinary research projects, including studying innovation in information technology, blockchain, and cybersecurity, people's behavior, and technology acceptance.

* * *

Sakshi Bajaj is an MBA student at Lovely Professional University.

Angelo Brown received his master's at Arizona State University and his Ph.D. Criminal Justice and Criminology at Washington State University. His research and teaching in criminal justice and criminology are primarily on policy and policing from a comparative and intersectional perspective.

Rodrigo Alexander Cortez Solano is currently an international student in Vancouver, Canada. He is coursing a Bachelor of Commerce at the University of Canada West. Rodrigo is originally from El Salvador, where he has spent most of his life. He won first place at the Model of the United Nations (MUN) in El Salvador and was recognized for his leadership and diplomacy skills. He also graduated with honors at Colegio Augusto Walte, achieving CUM Laude, and after his graduation, he took the opportunity to continue his studies in Vancouver, Canada. During these previous years, he has also gained field experience in sales, marketing, management, video edition, content creation on social media platforms, and accounting. Rodrigo is an entrepreneur with an ongoing e-commerce business. He has also acquired certifications in commercial real estate, business strategy, and Microsoft Office.

Mona Ebrahimi is an accomplished finance and technology professional with years of industry experience and a background in business administration. They have a track record of success in both the private and public sectors, having worked for big and small businesses. In addition to their industry experience, Mona has also contributed to the field through their publications and studies in the areas of technology and finance. With an enthusiasm to excellence in financial models and a passion for technological innovations, Mona has provided this chapter.

Billy Grimaldi Milla is a Salvadorean artist born on August 23rd of 2001, who currently is completing a bachelor of commerce degree in Vancouver, Canada.

Manmeet Singh Juneja is an MBA student at Lovely Professional University.

Tavleen Kaur is pursuing MBA (Marketing and HR) from Lovely Professional University.

Dinesh Kumar is an accomplished professional with 16+ years of experience in the military, academia, business, and charity sectors. He is the founder of pomento. in and Mission Dost-E-Jahan. He is teaching in Lovely Professional University.

Nam Phuong Le is an Assistant Professor of Business Management at University Canada West (UCW). Dr. Le received his Doctor of Business Administration from Walden University (USA), Master of Business Administration from Vancouver Island University (Canada), and Master of Science in International Business from the University of Hertfordshire (UK). Dr. Le also holds the CITP®|FIBP® - a professional designation in international business. His research interest includes globalization, emerging economies, global migration, internationalization of SMEs, and doing business with East Asia.

Mitra Madanchian is a Ph.D. holder of Business Management from Universiti Teknologi MARA (Malaysia), a Master of Administrative Science: Human Resources from Fairleigh Dickinson University, and a Master and Bachelor holder of Applied Linguistics from University Putra Malaysia. She is passionate about business management and R&D and has done industrial practice in both SMEs and one of the Big Four (KPMG). With over 9 years of industry experience, she has established herself as an industry expert in the field of Business Management, and Research and Development. Mitra initiated her career in 2013 as an Assistant Marketing Manager at Asanware Sdn Bhd and held the role of visiting lecturer at IAU. She continued her professional career holding the roles of Researcher and Business Development Practitioner in different international companies with various fields of business activity such as IT, International Trade, Finance, and Education. Besides her industrial experiences, she has an enthusiastic experience in academic research, in areas of Business Management, Leadership, Human Resource Management, Marketing Management, FinTech, and IT Management. Her views in science have been published in reputable publishers such as Elsevier, IGI Global, and MDPI. She has authored over twenty-six scientific articles in authentic peer-reviewed international journals and conferences proceeding, seven book chapters as well as one book in the field of leadership.

Daniel Esteban Ortega Pinzon, known as Esteban Ortega, is an international student of Commerce at the University Canada West. Originally from Zipaquira, Colombia, where he spent most of his childhood. Outstanding student and scholarship holder from the San Viator school with a percentile of 99 in the ICFES tests at the national level. He participated in the departmental mathematics Olympics in his last year of school, in which he also participated in a robotics project. He took an economics and finance course at the Universidad del Rosario for six months before finishing school to have his first contact with the market. Then he took a year of exchange in the United States, where he completed his twelfth grade at Russellville High school, where he was part of the football and soccer teams where he was state champion with the latter. From an early age, he was introduced to the world of multilevel marketing, which led him to work a total of 3 years in two different companies between his graduation in Colombia and his studies in the United States. By the time he finished his studies, he had begun to gain experience in the world of customer service and financial markets working for different companies and studying independently. Certificate in cryptocurrency trading, which he has been practicing to date and led him to get involved in the world of trading in the stock market and strengthen his path and passion towards the world of economics, finance, and commerce, led him to get a scholarship at Canada West University causing him to move to Vancouver, Canada. Upon arriving in Canada, he developed his communication, leadership, and management skills in the culinary industry. Once involved in this new industry, he discovered a new passion that he could take hand in hand with his financial studies.

Kochar Sahibpreet Singh has more than five years of expertise in innovation research and works as a technology researcher. Working as a techie for a while before making the shift to research led me to pursue an MBA in Analytics' at Canada West. Kochar has spent his whole professional life investigating the ways in which modern technology impacts and is impacted by society. He has written extensively on subjects including online privacy, drone user interfaces, the Fourth Industrial Revolution, and the societal effects of new technologies. His research has been disseminated widely via scholarly publications and presented at conferences all around the globe. Kochar Sahibpreet is not only an academic researcher, but also a member of the Association for Computing Machinery and a Certified Technologist in Avixa. He has also represented both associations as a delegate to a number of scholarly publications and conferences.

Index

Ingram Content Group UK Ltd.
Milton Keynes UK
UKHW050918040623
422749UK00006BA/56

9 781668 483688